DIABETIC
COOKBOOK FOR BEGINNERS

600 EASY, AND SATIATING DIABETIC DIET RECIPES TO MANAGE PREDIABETES AND TYPE 2 DIABETES EATING THE FOODS YOU LOVE

(30 DAY MEAL PLAN INCLUDED)

ABIGAIL WHITE

Copyright - 2021 -

All rights reserved.

This document is geared towards providing exact and reliable information with regards to the topic and issue covered. The publication is sold with the idea that the publisher is not required to render accounting, officially permitted, or otherwise, qualified services. If advice is necessary, legal or professional, a practiced individual in the profession should be ordered.

- From a Declaration of Principles which was accepted and approved equally by a Committee of the American Bar Association and a Committee of Publishers and Associations.

In no way is it legal to reproduce, duplicate, or transmit any part of this document in either electronic means or in printed format. Recording of this publication is strictly prohibited and any storage of this document is not allowed unless with written permission from the publisher. All rights reserved.

The information provided herein is stated to be truthful and consistent, in that any liability, in terms of inattention or otherwise, by any usage or abuse of any policies, processes, or directions contained within is the solitary and utter responsibility of the recipient reader. Under no circumstances will any legal responsibility or blame be held against the publisher for any reparation, damages, or monetary loss due to the information herein, either directly or indirectly.

Respective authors own all copyrights not held by the publisher.

The information herein is offered for informational purposes solely, and is universal as so. The presentation of the information is without contract or any type of guarantee assurance.

The trademarks that are used are without any consent, and the publication of the trademark is without permission or backing by the trademark owner. All trademarks and brands within this book are for clarifying purposes only and are the owned by the owners themselves, not affiliated with this document.

Table of Contents

Introduction	17
Chapter 1: Type 1 and Type 2 Diabetes	21
Chapter 2: The Diabetic Diet	29
Chapter 3: 4-Week Meal Plan	37
Chapter 4: Breakfast	41
1. Berry-Oat Breakfast Bars	42
2. Whole-Grain Breakfast Cookies	42
3. Blueberry Breakfast Cake	43
4. Whole-Grain Pancakes	43
5. Buckwheat Grouts Breakfast Bowl	44
6. Peach Muesli Bake	44
7. Steel-Cut Oatmeal Bowl with Fruit and Nuts	45
8. Whole-Grain Dutch Baby Pancake	45
9. Mushroom, Zucchini, and Onion Frittata	46
10. Spinach and Cheese Quiche	46
11. Spicy Jalapeno Popper Deviled Eggs	47
12. Lovely Porridge	47
13. Salty Macadamia Chocolate Smoothie	48
14. Basil and Tomato Baked Eggs	48
15. Cinnamon and Coconut Porridge	49
16. An Omelet of Swiss Chard	49
17. Cheesy Low-Carb Omelet	50
18. Yogurt and Kale Smoothie	50
19. Bacon and Chicken Garlic Wrap	51
20. Grilled Chicken Platter	51
21. Parsley Chicken Breast	52
22. Mustard Chicken	52
23. Balsamic Chicken	53
24. Greek Chicken Breast	53
25. Chipotle Lettuce Chicken	54
26. Stylish Chicken-Bacon Wrap	54
27. Healthy Cottage Cheese Pancakes	55
28. Avocado Lemon Toast	55
29. Healthy Baked Eggs	56
30. Quick Low-Carb Oatmeal	56
31. Tofu and Vegetable Scramble	57

32. Breakfast Smoothie Bowl with Fresh Berries	57
33. Chia and Coconut Pudding	58
34. Tomato and Zucchini Saute'	58
35. Steamed Kale with Mediterranean Dressing	59
36. Healthy Carrot Muffins	59
37. Vegetable Noodles Stir-Fry	60

Chapter 5: Lunch — 61

38. Cauliflower Rice with Chicken	62
39. Turkey with Fried Eggs	63
40. Kale and White Bean Stew	64
41. Slow Cooker Two-Bean Sloppy Joes	64
42. Lighter Eggplant Parmesan	65
43. Coconut-Lentil Curry	65
44. Stuffed Portobello with Cheese	66
45. Lighter Shrimp Scampi	66
46. Maple-Mustard Salmon	67
47. Chicken Salad with Grapes and Pecans	67
48. Roasted Vegetables	68
49. Millet Pilaf	68
50. Sweet and Sour Onions	69
51. Sauteed Apples and Onions	69
52. Zucchini Noodles with Portobello Mushrooms	70
53. Grilled Tempeh with Pineapple	70
54. Courgettes in Cider Sauce	71
55. Baked Mixed Mushrooms	71
56. Spiced Okra	72
57. Lemony Salmon Burgers	72
58. Caprese Turkey Burgers	73
59. Pasta Salad	73
60. Chicken, Strawberry, and Avocado Salad	74
61. Lemon-Thyme Eggs	74
62. Spinach Salad with Bacon	75
63. Pea and Collards Soup	75
64. Spanish Stew	76
65. Creamy Taco Soup	76
66. Chicken with Caprese Salsa	77
67. Balsamic-Roasted Broccoli	77
68. Hearty Beef and Vegetable Soup	78
69. Cauliflower Muffin	78
70. Ham and Egg Cup	79

Chapter 6: Dinner — 81

71. Cauliflower Mac and Cheese	82
72. Easy Egg Salad	82
73. Baked Chicken Legs	83
74. Creamed Spinach	83

75. Stuffed Mushrooms	84
76. Vegetable Soup	84
77. Pork Chop Diane	85
78. Autumn Pork Chops with Red Cabbage and Apples	85
79. Chipotle Chili Pork Chops	86
80. Orange-Marinated Pork Tenderloin	86
81. Homestyle Herb Meatballs	87
82. Lime-Parsley Lamb Cutlets	87
83. Mediterranean Steak Sandwiches	88
84. Roasted Beef with Peppercorn Sauce	88
85. Coffee-and-Herb-Marinated Steak	89
86. Traditional Beef Stroganoff	89
87. Chicken and Roasted Vegetable Wraps	90
88. Spicy Chicken Cacciatore	90
89. Scallion Sandwich	91
90. Lean Lamb and Turkey Meatballs with Yogurt	91
91. Air Fried Section and Tomato	92
92. Cheesy Salmon Fillets	92
93. Salmon with Asparagus	93
94. Shrimp in Garlic Butter	93
95. Cobb Salad	94
96. Seared Tuna Steak	94
97. Beef Chili	95
98. Greek Broccoli Salad	95
99. Cheesy Cauliflower Gratin	96
100. Strawberry Spinach Salad	96
101. Misto Quente	97
102. Garlic Bread	97
103. Bruschetta	98
104. Cream Buns with Strawberries	98
105. Blueberry Buns	99
106. Cauliflower Mash	99
107. French Toast in Sticks	100
108. Muffins Sandwich	100
109. Bacon BBQ	101
110. Stuffed French Toast	101
111. Thai Quinoa Salad	104
112. Green Goddess Bowl and Avocado Cumin Dressing	104
113. 7 Sweet and Savory Salad	105
114. Kale Pesto's Pasta	105
115. Beet Salad with Basil Dressing	106
116. Basic Salad with Olive Oil Dressing	106
117. Spinach and Orange Salad with Oil Drizzle	107
118. Fruit Salad with Coconut-Lime Dressing	107
119. Cranberry and Brussels Sprouts with Dressing	108

120.	Parsnip, Carrot, and Kale Salad with Dressing	108
121.	Tomato Toasts	109
122.	Every Day Salad	109
123.	Super-Seedy Salad with Tahini Dressing	110
124.	Vegetable Salad	110
125.	Greek Salad	111
126.	Alkaline Spring Salad	111
127.	Fresh Tuna Salad	112
128.	Roasted Portobello Salad	112
129.	Shredded Chicken Salad	113
130.	Broccoli Salad	113
131.	Cherry Tomato Salad	114
132.	Ground Turkey Salad	114
133.	Asian Cucumber Salad	115
134.	Cauliflower Tofu Salad	115
135.	Scallop Caesar Salad	116
136.	Chicken Avocado Salad	116
137.	California Wraps	117
138.	Chicken Salad in Cucumber c.	117
139.	Sunflower Seeds and Arugula Garden Salad	118
140.	Supreme Caesar Salad	118
141.	Tabbouleh Arabian Salad	119

Chapter 8: Soup and Stew — 121

142.	Dill Celery Soup	122
143.	Creamy Avocado-Broccoli Soup	122
144.	Fresh Garden Vegetable Soup	123
145.	Raw Some Gazpacho Soup	123
146.	Alkaline Carrot Soup with Fresh Mushrooms	124
147.	Swiss Cauliflower-Omental-Soup	124
148.	Chilled Parsley-Gazpacho with Lime and Cucumber	125
149.	Chilled Avocado Tomato Soup	125
150.	Pumpkin and White Bean Soup with Sage	126
151.	Alkaline Pumpkin Tomato Soup	126
152.	Alkaline Pumpkin Coconut Soup	127
153.	Cold Cauliflower-Coconut Soup	127
154.	Raw Avocado-Broccoli Soup with Cashew Nuts	128
155.	White Bean Soup	128
156.	Kale Cauliflower Soup	129
157.	Healthy Broccoli Asparagus Soup	129
158.	Creamy Asparagus Soup	130
159.	Quick Broccoli Soup	130
160.	Green Lentil Soup	131
161.	Squash Soup	131
162.	Tomato Soup	132
163.	Basil Zucchini Soup	132

164. Summer Vegetable Soup	133
165. Almond-Red Bell Pepper Dip	133
166. Spicy Carrot Soup	134
167. Zucchini Soup	134
168. Kidney Bean Stew	135
169. Cabbage Soup	135
170. Pumpkin Spice Soup	136
171. Cream of Tomato Soup	136
172. Shiitake Soup	137
173. Spicy Pepper Soup	137
174. Zoodle Won-Ton Soup	138
175. Broccoli Stilton Soup	138
176. Lamb Stew	139
177. Irish Stew	139
178. Sweet and Sour Soup	140
179. Meatball Stew	140
180. Kebab Stew	141
181. French Onion Soup	141
182. Meatless Ball Soup	142
183. Fake-On Stew	142
184. Chickpea Soup	143
185. Chicken Zoodle Soup	143
186. Lemon-Tarragon Soup	144
187. Chilled Cucumber and Lime Soup	144
188. Coconut, Cilantro, and Jalapeño Soup	145
189. Spicy Watermelon Gazpacho	145
190. Roasted Carrot and Leek Soup	146
191. Creamy Lentil Stew	146
192. Roasted Garlic and Cauliflower Soup	147
193. Beefless "Beef" Stew	147
194. Creamy Mushroom Soup	148
195. Chilled Berry and Mint Soup	148
Chapter 9: Appetizer Recipes	149
196. Aromatic Toasted Pumpkin Seeds	150
197. Bacon-Wrapped Shrimps	150
198. Cheesy Broccoli Bites	151
199. Easy Caprese Skewers	151
200. Grilled Tofu with Sesame Seeds	152
201. Kale Chips	152
202. Simple Deviled Eggs	153
203. Sauteed Collard Greens and Cabbage	153
204. Roasted Delicata Squash with Thyme	154
205. Roasted Asparagus and Red Peppers	154
206. Tarragon Spring Peas	155
207. Butter-Orange Yams	155

208. Roasted Tomato Brussels Sprouts	156
209. Simple Sautéed Greens	156
210. Garlicky Mushrooms	157
211. Green Beans in the Oven	157
212. Parmesan Broiled Flounder	158
213. Fish with Fresh Tomato Basil Sauce	158
214. Baked Chicken	159
215. Seared Chicken with Roasted Vegetables	159
216. Fish Simmered in Tomato-Pepper Sauce	160
217. Cheese and Pea Casserole	160
218. Oven-Fried Tilapia	161
219. Chicken with Coconut Sauce	161
220. Fish with Fresh Herb Sauce	162
221. Skillet Turkey Patties	162
222. Turkey Loaf	163
223. Mushroom Pasta	163
224. Chicken Tikka Masala	164
225. Tomato and Roasted Cod	164
226. French Broccoli Salad	165
227. Tenderloin Grilled Salad	165
228. Barley Veggie Salad	166
229. Spinach Shrimp Salad	166
230. Roasted Beet Salad	167
231. Calico Salad	167
232. Mango and Jicama Salad	168
233. Asian Crispy Chicken Salad	168
234. Kale, Grape, and Bulgur Salad	169
235. Strawberry Salsa	169
236. Garden Wraps	170
237. Party Shrimp	170
238. Zucchini Mini Pizzas	171
239. Garlic-Sesame Pumpkin Seeds	171
Chapter 10: Seafood Recipes	173
240. Lemony Salmon	174
241. Shrimp with Green Beans	174
242. Crab Curry	175
243. Mixed Chowder	175
244. Mussels in Tomato Sauce	176
245. Citrus Salmon	176
246. Herbed Salmon	177
247. Salmon in Green Sauce	177
248. Braised Shrimp	178
249. Shrimp Coconut Curry	178
250. Trout Bake	179
251. Sardine Curry	179

252. Swordfish Steak	180
253. Lemon Sole	180
254. Tuna Sweet Corn Casserole	181
255. Lemon Pepper Salmon	181
256. Baked Salmon with Garlic Parmesan Topping	182
257. Blackened Shrimp	182
258. Cajun Catfish	183
259. Cajun Flounder and Tomatoes	183
260. Cajun Shrimp and Roasted Vegetables	184
261. Cilantro Lime Grilled Shrimp	184
262. Crab Frittata	185
263. Crunchy Lemon Shrimp	185
264. Grilled Tuna Steaks	186
265. Red Clam Sauce and Pasta	186
266. Salmon Milano	187
267. Shrimp and Artichoke Skillet	187
268. Tuna Carbonara	188
269. Mediterranean Fish Fillets	188
Chapter 11: Meat Recipes	189
270. Pork Chops with Grape Sauce	190
271. Roasted Pork and Apples	190
272. Pork with Cranberry Relish	191
273. Sesame Pork with Mustard Sauce	191
274. Steak with Mushroom Sauce	192
275. Steak with Tomato and Herbs	192
276. Barbecue Beef Brisket	193
277. Beef and Asparagus	193
278. Italian Beef	194
279. Lamb with Broccoli and Carrots	194
280. Rosemary Lamb	195
281. Mediterranean Lamb Meatballs	195
Chapter 12: Main	197
282. Blueberry and Chicken Salad	198
283. Beef and Red Bean Chili	198
284. Berry Apple Cider	199
285. Brunswick Stew	199
286. Buffalo Chicken Salads	200
287. Cacciatore Style Chicken	200
288. Carnitas Tacos	201
289. Chicken Chili	201
290. Chicken Vera Cruz	202
291. Chicken and Cornmeal Dumplings	202
292. Chicken and Pepperoni	203
293. Chicken and Sausage Gumbo	203
294. Chicken, Barley, and Leek Stew	204

295.	Cider Pork Stew	204
296.	Creamy Chicken Noodle Soup	205
297.	Cuban Pulled Pork Sandwich	205
298.	Gazpacho	206
299.	Tomato and Kale Soup	206
300.	Comforting Summer Squash Soup with Crispy Chickpeas	207
301.	Curried Carrot Soup	207
302.	Thai Peanut, Carrot, and Shrimp Soup	208
303.	Chicken Tortilla Soup	208
304.	Beef and Mushroom Barley Soup	209
305.	Cucumber, Tomato, and Avocado Salad	209
306.	Cabbage Slaw Salad	210
307.	Green Salad with Blackberries and Goat Cheese	210
308.	Three Bean and Basil Salad	211
309.	Rainbow Black Bean Salad	211
310.	Warm Barley and Squash Salad	212
311.	Winter Chicken and Citrus Salad	212

Chapter 13: Side — 213

312.	Brussels Sprouts	214
313.	Garlic and Herb Carrots	214
314.	Cilantro Lime Drumsticks	215
315.	Eggplant Spread	215
316.	Carrot Hummus	216
317.	Vegetable Rice Pilaf	216
318.	Curry Roasted Cauliflower Florets	217
319.	Mushroom Barley Risotto	217
320.	Braised Summer Squash	218
321.	Lemon Garlic Green Beans	218
322.	Brown Rice and Lentil Salad	219
323.	Mashed Butternut Squash	219
324.	Cilantro Lime Quinoa	220
325.	Oven-Roasted Veggies	220
326.	Parsley Tabbouleh	221
327.	Garlic Sautéd Spinach	221
328.	French Lentils	222
329.	Grain-Free Berry Cobbler	222
330.	Coffee-Steamed Carrots	223
331.	Dandelion Strawberry Salad	223
332.	Corn on the Cob	224
333.	Chili Lime Salmon	224
334.	Collard Greens	225
335.	Mashed Pumpkin	225
336.	Parmesan-Topped Acorn Squash	226
337.	Quinoa Tabbouleh	226
338.	Wild Rice Salad with Cranberries and Almonds	227

339. Basil Avocado Pasta Salad	227
340. Roasted Parsnips	228
341. Lower Carb Hummus	228
342. Sweet and Sour Red Cabbage	229
343. Pinto Beans	229
344. Parmesan Cauliflower Mash	230
345. Steamed Asparagus	230
346. Squash Medley	231
347. Eggplant Curry	231
348. Lentil and Eggplant Stew	232
349. Tofu Curry	232
350. Lentil and Chickpea Curry	233
351. Split Pea Stew	233
352. Fried Tofu Hotpot	234
353. Chili sin Carne	234
Chapter 14: Snacks and Bread	235
354. Chick Pea and Kale Dish	236
355. Zucchini Chips	236
356. Classic Blueberry Spelt Muffins	237
357. Genuine Healthy Crackers	237
358. Tortilla Chips	238
359. Pumpkin Spice Crackers	238
360. Spicy Roasted Nuts	239
361. Wheat Crackers	239
362. Veggie Fritters	240
363. Zucchini Pepper Chips	240
364. Apple Chips	241
365. Kale Crisps	241
366. Carrot Chips	242
367. Pita Chips	242
368. Awesome Lemon Bell Peppers	243
369. Spinach and Sesame Crackers	243
370. Mini Nacho Pizzas	244
371. Pizza Sticks	244
372. Raw Broccoli Poppers	245
373. Blueberry Cauliflower	245
374. Candied Ginger	246
375. Chia Crackers	246
376. Orange-Spiced Pumpkin Hummus	247
377. Crazy Mac and Cheese	247
378. Cheesy Kale Chips	248
379. Lemon Roasted Bell Pepper	248
380. Subtle Roasted Mushrooms	249
381. Fancy Spelt Bread	249
382. Crispy Crunchy Hummus	250

Chapter 15: Dessert — 251

- 383. Peanut Butter c. — 252
- 384. Fruit Pizza — 252
- 385. Choco Peppermint Cake — 253
- 386. Roasted Mango — 253
- 387. Roasted Plums — 254
- 388. Figs with Honey and Yogurt — 254
- 389. Lava Cake — 255
- 390. Cheese Cake — 255
- 391. Madeleine — 256
- 392. Waffles — 256
- 393. Pretzels — 257
- 394. Cheesy Taco Bites — 257
- 395. Nut Squares — 258
- 396. Pumpkin and Banana Ice Cream — 258
- 397. Brulee Oranges — 259
- 398. Frozen Lemon and Blueberry — 259
- 399. Peanut Butter Choco Chip Cookies — 260
- 400. Watermelon Sherbet — 260
- 401. Strawberry and Mango Ice Cream — 261
- 402. Sparkling Fruit Drink — 261
- 403. Tiramisu Shots — 262
- 404. Ice Cream Brownie Cake — 262
- 405. Berry Sorbet — 263
- 406. Quinoa Porridge — 263
- 407. Apple Quinoa — 264
- 408. Kamut Porridge — 264
- 409. Hot Kamut with Peaches, Walnuts, and Coconut — 265
- 410. Overnight "Oats" — 265
- 411. Blueberry Cupcakes — 266
- 412. Brazil Nut Cheese — 266
- 413. Slow Cooker Peaches — 267
- 414. Pumpkin Custard — 267
- 415. Blueberry Lemon Custard Cake — 268
- 416. Sugar Free Carrot Cake — 268
- 417. Sugar Free Chocolate Molten Lava Cake — 269
- 418. Chocolate Quinoa Brownies — 269
- 419. Blueberry Crisp — 270
- 420. Maple Custard — 270
- 421. Raspberry Cream Cheese Coffee Cake — 271
- 422. Pumpkin Pie Bars — 271
- 423. Dark Chocolate Cake — 272
- 424. Lemon Custard — 272
- 425. Baked Stuffed Pears — 273
- 426. Butternut Squash Pie — 273

427. Coconut Chia Cream Pot	274
428. Chocolate Avocado Mousse	274
429. Chia Vanilla Coconut Pudding	275
430. Sweet Tahini Dip with Ginger Cinnamon Fruit	275
431. Coconut Butter and Chopped Berries with Mint	276
432. Alkaline Raw Pumpkin Pie	276
433. Strawberry Sorbet	277
434. Blueberry Muffins	277
435. Banana Strawberry Ice Cream	278
436. Homemade Whipped Cream	278
437. Chocolate Crunch Bars	279
438. Homemade Protein Bar	279
439. Shortbread Cookies	280
440. Coconut Chip Cookies	280
441. Peanut Butter Bars	281
442. Zucchini Bread Pancakes	281
443. Flourless Chocolate Cake	282
444. Raspberry Cake with White Chocolate Sauce	283
445. Ketogenic Lava Cake	284
446. Ketogenic Cheese Cake	284
447. Cake with Whipped Cream Icing	285
448. Nut-Fruit Cake	286
449. Ginger Cake	287
450. Ketogenic Orange Cake	287
451. Lemon Cake	288
452. Cinnamon Cake	289
453. Banana Nut Muffins	290
454. Mango Nut Cheesecake	290
455. Blackberry Jam	291
456. Blackberry Bars	291
457. Detox Berry Smoothie	292
Chapter 16: Smoothies and Juice	293
458. Dandelion Avocado Smoothie	294
459. Amaranth Greens and Avocado Smoothie	294
460. Lettuce, Orange, and Banana Smoothie	295
461. Delicious Elderberry Smoothie	295
462. Peaches Zucchini Smoothie	296
463. Ginger Orange and Strawberry Smoothie	296
464. Kale Parsley and Chia Seeds Detox Smoothie	297
465. Watermelon Lemonade	297
466. Bubbly Orange Soda	298
467. Creamy Cashew Milk	298
468. Homemade Oat Milk	299
469. Lucky Mint Smoothie	299
470. Paradise Island Smoothie	300

471. Apple Pie Smoothie	300
472. Choco-Nut Milkshake	301
473. Pineapple and Strawberry Smoothie	301
474. Cantaloupe Smoothie	302
475. Berry Smoothie with Mint	302
476. Green Smoothie	303
477. Banana, Cauliflower, and Berry Smoothie	303
478. Berry and Spinach Smoothie	304
479. Peanut Butter Smoothie with Blueberries	304
480. Peach and Apricot Smoothie	305
481. Tropical Smoothie	305
482. Banana and Strawberry Smoothie	306
483. Cantaloupe and Papaya Smoothie	306
484. Watermelon and Cantaloupe Smoothie	307
485. Raspberry and Peanut Butter Smoothie	307
486. Strawberry, Kale, and Ginger Smoothie	308
487. Berry Mint Smoothie	308
488. Greenie Smoothie	309
489. Coconut Spinach Smoothie	309
490. Oats Coffee Smoothie	310
491. Veggie Smoothie	310
492. Avocado Smoothie	311
493. Orange Carrot Smoothie	311
494. Blackberry Smoothie	312
495. Key Lime Pie Smoothie	312
496. Cinnamon Roll Smoothie	313
497. Strawberry Cheesecake Smoothie	313
498. Peanut Butter Banana Smoothie	314
499. Avocado Turmeric Smoothie	314
500. Lemon Blueberry Smoothie	315
501. Matcha Green Smoothie	315
502. Blueberry Smoothie	316
503. Beet and Strawberry Smoothie	316
504. Kiwi Smoothie	317
505. Pineapple and Carrot Smoothie	317
506. Oats and Orange Smoothie	318
507. Pumpkin Smoothie	318
508. Red Veggie and Fruit Smoothie	319
509. Kale Smoothie	319
510. Green Tofu Smoothie	320
511. Grape and Swiss Chard Smoothie	320
512. Matcha Smoothie	321
513. Banana Smoothie	321
514. Strawberry Smoothie	322
515. Raspberry and Tofu Smoothie	322

516. Mango Smoothie	323
517. Pineapple Smoothie	323
518. Kale and Pineapple Smoothie	324
519. Green Veggies Smoothie	324
520. Avocado and Spinach Smoothie	325
521. Raisins-Plume Smoothie (RPS)	325
522. Nori Clove Smoothies (NCS)	326
523. Brazil Lettuce Smoothies (BLS)	326
524. Apple-Banana Smoothie (ABS)	327
525. Ginger-Pear Smoothie (GPS)	327
526. Cantaloupe-Amaranth Smoothie (CAS)	328
527. Garbanzo Squash Smoothie (GSS)	328
528. Strawberry-Orange Smoothies (SOS)	329
529. Tamarind-Pear Smoothie (TPS)	329
530. Currant Elderberry Smoothie (CES)	330
531. Sweet Dream Strawberry Smoothie	330
532. Alkaline Green Ginger, and Banana Cleansing Smoothie	331
533. Orange Mixed Detox Smoothie	331
534. Cucumber Toxin Flush Smoothie	332
535. Apple Blueberry Smoothie	332

Chapter 17: Herbal Tea Recipes — 333

536. Lemon Rooibos Iced Tea	334
537. Lemon Lavender Iced Tea	334
538. Cherry Vanilla Iced Tea	335
539. Elegant Blueberry Rose Water Iced Tea	335
540. Melba Iced Tea	336
541. Merry Raspberry Cherry Iced Tea	336
542. Vanilla Kissed Peach Iced Tea	337
543. Xtreme Berried Iced Tea	337
544. Refreshingly Peppermint Iced Tea	338
545. Lemongrass Mint Iced Tea	338
546. Spiced Tea	339
547. Infused Pumpkin Spice Latte	339
548. Infused Turmeric-Ginger Tea	340
549. Infused London Fog	340
550. Infused Cranberry-Apple Snug	341
551. Stomach Soother	341
552. Sarsaparilla Syrup	342
553. Dandelion "Coffee"	342
554. Chamomile Delight	343
555. Mucus Cleanse Tea	343
556. Immune Tea	344
557. Ginger Turmeric Tea	344
558. Tranquil Tea	345
559. Energizing Lemon Tea	345

560.	Respiratory Support Tea	346
561.	Thyme and Lemon Tea	346
562.	Sore Throat Tea	347
563.	Autumn Tonic Tea	347
564.	Adrenal and Stress Health	348
565.	Lavender Tea	348

Chapter 18: Other Diabetic Recipes — 349

566.	Chili Chicken Wings	350
567.	Garlic Chicken Wings	350
568.	Spinach Cheese Pie	351
569.	Tasty Harissa Chicken	351
570.	Roasted Balsamic Mushrooms	352
571.	Roasted Cumin Carrots	352
572.	Tasty and Tender Brussels Sprouts	353
573.	Sauteed Veggies	353
574.	Mustard Green Beans	354
575.	Zucchini Fries	354
576.	Broccoli Nuggets	355
577.	Zucchini Cauliflower Fritters	355
578.	Roasted Chickpeas	356
579.	Peanut Butter Mousse	356
580.	Coffee Mousse	357
581.	Wild Rice and Black Lentils Bowl	357
582.	Alkaline Spaghetti Squash Recipe	358
583.	Dairy-Free Fruit Tarts	358
584.	Spaghetti Squash with Peanut Sauce	359
585.	Cauliflower Alfredo Pasta	359
586.	Sloppy Joe	360
587.	Amaretti	360
588.	Green Fruit Juice	361
589.	Kale Chickpea Mash	361
590.	Quinoa and Apple	362
591.	Warm Avo and Quinoa Salad	362
592.	Tuna Salad	363
593.	Herring and Veggies Soup	363
594.	Salmon Soup	364
595.	Salmon and Shrimp Stew	364
596.	Salmon Curry	365
597.	Salmon with Bell Peppers	365
598.	Shrimp Salad	366
599.	Shrimp and Veggies Curry	366
600.	Shrimp with Zucchini	367
601.	Shrimp with Broccoli	367

CONCLUSION — 369

Introduction

Diabetes is a disease in which blood glucose, also called blood sugar, doesn't get properly regulated. Glucose is the form of sugar that's used by all cells for energy. In diabetes, the body either doesn't produce enough insulin or can't use the insulin that's produced. This a type of disease that occurs when the pancreas can't produce enough insulin, a hormone that is used to help cells use glucose (sugar) for energy. Diabetics must monitor their glucose levels regularly and take insulin to make sure the glucose stays within the normal range.

Diabetes symptoms include excessive thirst, frequent urination, hunger, blurred vision, unexplained weight loss, and sudden numbness or weakness of the arms or legs. Diabetics also experienced excessive sweating, itching, and a dry mouth.

Diabetes is also a disease associated with blood sugar i.e., the concentration of sugar in the blood that the body is unable to maintain within normal limits.

Hyperglycemia occurs when blood glucose exceeds 100 mg./dl fastings or 140 mg/dl two hours after a meal. This condition may depend on a defect in function or a deficit in the production of insulin, the hormone secreted by the pancreas, used for the metabolism of sugars and other components of food to be transformed into energy for the whole organism (such as petrol for the engine).

When blood glucose levels are twice equal to or greater than 126 mg./dl, diabetes is diagnosed. High blood glucose levels—if not treated—over time, lead to chronic complications with damage to the kidneys, retina, nerves peripheral, and cardiovascular system (heart and arteries).

Causes of Diabetes and Risk Factors

Although some of the causes are completely unclear, even trivial viral infections are recognized, which can affect insulin-producing cells in the pancreas, such as:

- Measles.
- Cytomegalovirus.
- Epstein-Barr.
- Coxsackievirus.

For type 2 diabetes, however, the main risk factors are:

- Overweight and obesity.
- Genetic factors: family history increases the risk of developing type 2 diabetes.
- Ethnicity: the highest number of cases is recorded in the populations of sub-Saharan Africa and the Middle East and North Africa.
- Environmental factors are especially related to incorrect lifestyles (sedentary lifestyle and obesity).
- Gestational diabetes, which is diabetes that happens during pregnancy.
- Age: type 2 diabetes increases with increasing age, especially above the age of 65.
- Diet high in fat promotes obesity.
- Alcohol consumption.
- Sedentary lifestyle.

Signs and Symptoms of Diabetes

Symptoms of the disease, which depend on blood sugar levels, are:

- Polyuria, i.e., the high amount of urine production even during the night (nocturia).
- Polydipsia (an intense feeling of thirst).
- Polyphagia (intense hunger).
- Dry mucous membranes (the body's need to replenish fluids and severe dehydration).
- Asthenia (feeling tired).
- Weight loss.

- Frequent infections.
- Blurred vision.

In type 1 diabetes they manifest rapidly and with great intensity. In type 2 diabetes, on the other hand, symptoms are less evident, develop much slower, and may go unnoticed for months or years. Diagnosis often occurs by chance, on the occasion of tests done for any reason: the finding of a glycemia greater than 126 mg/dl allows the diagnosis of type 2 diabetes, which must be confirmed with a second dosage of glycemia and HbA1c.

Chapter 1: Type 1 and Type 2 Diabetes

Diabetes is a common disease that leads to metabolic disorders of carbohydrates and water balance.

As a result, pancreatic functions are impaired. It is the pancreas that produces an important hormone called insulin.

Insulin regulates the level of blood sugar that is supplied with food. Without it, the body cannot convert sugar into glucose, and sugar starts accumulating in the body of a person with the disease.

Apart from the pancreas disorders, the water balance is impaired as well. As a result, the tissues do not retain water, and the kidneys excrete much fluid.

What Happens When a Person Has Diabetes?

When the condition develops, the body produces too little insulin. At the same time, the level of blood sugar increases, and the cells become starved for glucose, which is the primary source of energy.

Types of Diabetes

There are two types of diabetes.

Type 1 Diabetes

This condition is also known as insulin-dependent. It usually affects young people under 40. People with type 1 diabetes will need to take insulin injections for the rest of their lives because their body produces antibodies that destroy the beta-cells which produce the hormone.

Type 1 diabetes is hard to cure. However, it is possible to restore pancreatic functions by adhering to a healthy diet. Products with a high glycemic index such as soda, juice, and sweets should be excluded.

Type 2 Diabetes

This happens as a result of the lack of sensitivity of the pancreas cells towards insulin because of the excess of nutrients. People with excess weight are the most susceptible to the disease.

Difference

	Type 1	Type 2
Whom It Affects	Represent up to 5–10 % of all cases of diabetes. It was once called "juvenile-onset" diabetes because it was thought to develop most often in children and young adults. We now know it can occur in people of any age, including older adults.	Accounts for 90–95 % of all diagnosed cases of diabetes. It used to be called "adult-onset" diabetes, but it is now known that even children—mainly if they're overweight—can develop type 2 diabetes.
What Happens	The pancreas makes little if any insulin.	The pancreas doesn't produce enough insulin or the body doesn't respond properly to the insulin that is produced.
Risk Factors	Less well-defined, but autoimmune, genetic, and environmental factors are believed to be involved.	Older age, obesity, family history of diabetes, physical inactivity, and race/ethnicity.
Treatment	Individualized meal plans, insulin therapy (usually several injections a day), self-monitoring glucose testing several times a day, regular physical activity, and a healthy diet.	A healthy diet, weight loss (if overweight), regular exercise, and monitoring blood glucose levels. Some people are able to manage blood sugar through diet and exercise alone. However, diabetes tends to be a progressive disease, so oral medications and possibly insulin may be needed at some point.

Foods to Eat

Vegetables

Fresh vegetables never cause harm to anyone. So, adding a meal full of vegetables is the best shot for all diabetic patients. But not all vegetables contain the same number of macronutrients. Some vegetables contain a high amount of carbohydrates, so those are not suitable for a diabetic diet. We need to use vegetables which contain a low amount of carbohydrates.

1. Cauliflower
2. Spinach
3. Tomatoes
4. Broccoli
5. Lemons
6. Artichoke
7. Garlic
8. Asparagus
9. Spring onions
10. Onions
11. Ginger, etc.

Meat

Meat is not on the red list for the diabetic diet. It is fine to have some meat every now and then for diabetic patients. However certain meat types are better than others. For instance, red meat is not a preferable option for such patients. They should consume white meat more often whether it's seafood or poultry. Healthy options in meat are:

All fish, i.e., salmon, halibut, trout, cod, sardine, etc.

1. Scallops
2. Mussels
3. Shrimp
4. Oysters, etc.

Fruits

Not all fruits are good for diabetes. To know if the fruit is suitable for this diet, it is important to note its sugar content. Some fruits contain a high number of sugars in the form of sucrose and fructose, and those should be readily avoided. Here is the list of popularly used fruits that can be taken on the diabetic diet:

1. Peaches
2. Nectarines
3. Avocados
4. Apples
5. Berries
6. Grapefruit
7. Kiwi Fruit
8. Bananas
9. Cherries
10. Grapes
11. Orange
12. Pears
13. Plums
14. Strawberries

Nuts and Seeds

Nuts and seeds are perhaps the most enriched edibles, and they contain such a mix of macronutrients that can never harm anyone. So diabetic patients can take the nuts and seeds in their diet without any fear of a glucose spike.

1. Pistachios
2. Sunflower seeds
3. Walnuts
4. Peanuts
5. Pecans
6. Pumpkin seeds

7. Almonds

8. Sesame seeds, etc.

GRAINS

Diabetic patients should also be selective while choosing the right grains for their diet. The idea is to keep the amount of starch as minimum as possible. That is why you won't see any white rice in the list rather it is replaced with more fibrous brown rice.

1. Quinoa
2. Oats
3. Multigrain
4. Whole grains
5. Brown rice
6. Millet
7. Barley
8. Sorghum
9. Tapioca

FATS

Fat intake is the most debated topic as far as the diabetic diet is concerned. As there are diets like ketogenic, which are loaded with fats and still proved effective for diabetic patients. The key is the absence of carbohydrates. In any other situation, fats are as harmful to diabetics as any normal person. Switching to unsaturated fats is a better option.

1. Sesame oil
2. Olive oil
3. Canola oil
4. Grapeseed oil
5. Other vegetable oils
6. Fats extracted from plant sources

Diary

Any dairy product which directly or indirectly causes a glucose rise in the blood should not be taken on this diet. Other than those, all products are good to use. These items include:

1. Skimmed milk
2. Low-fat cheese
3. Eggs
4. Yogurt
5. Trans fat-free margarine or butter

Sugar Alternatives

Since ordinary sugars or sweeteners are strictly forbidden on a diabetic diet. There are artificial varieties that can add sweetness without raising the level of carbohydrates in the meal. These substitutes are:

1. Stevia
2. Xylitol
3. Natvia
4. Swerve
5. Monk fruit
6. Erythritol

Make sure to substitute them with extra care. The sweetness of each sweetener is entirely different from the table sugar, so add each in accordance with the intensity of their flavor. Stevia is the sweetest of them, and it should be used with more care. In place of 1 c of sugar, 1 tsp of stevia is enough. All other sweeteners are more or less similar to sugar in their intensity of sweetness.

Foods to Avoid

Knowing a general scheme of diet helps a lot, but it is equally important to be well familiar with the items which have to be avoided. With this list, you can make your diet 100 % sugar-free. There are many other food items that can cause some harm to a diabetic patient as the sugars do. So, let's discuss them in some detail here.

Sugars

Sugar is a big NO-GO for a diabetic diet. Once you are diabetic, you would need to say goodbye to all the natural sweeteners which are loaded with carbohydrates. They contain polysaccharides that readily break into glucose after getting into our body. And the list does not only include table sugars but other items like honey and molasses should also be avoided.

1. White sugar
2. Brown sugar
3. Confectionary sugar
4. Honey
5. Molasses
6. Granulated sugar

Your mind and your body, will not accept the abrupt change. It is recommended to go for a gradual change. It means start substituting it with low carb substitutes in a small amount, day by day.

High Fat Dairy Products

Once you are diabetic, you may get susceptible to a number of other fatal diseases including cardiovascular ones. That is why experts strictly recommend avoiding high-fat food products, especially dairy items. The high amount of fat can make your body insulin resistant. So even when you take insulin, it won't be of any use as the body will not work on it.

Saturated Animal Fats

Saturated animal fats are not good for anyone, whether diabetic or normal. So, better avoid using them in general. Whenever you are cooking meat, try to trim off all the excess fat. Cooking oils made out of these saturated fats should be avoided. Keep yourself away from any of the animal-origin fats.

High Carb Vegetables

As discussed above, vegetables with more starch are not suitable for diabetes. These veggies can increase the carbohydrate levels of food. So, omit these from the recipes and enjoy the rest of the less starchy vegetables. Some of the high carb vegetables are:

1. Potatoes
2. Sweet potatoes

3. Yams, etc.

Cholesterol Rich Ingredients

Bad cholesterol or high-density lipoprotein has the tendency to deposit in different parts of the body. That is why food items having high bad cholesterol are not good for diabetes. Such items should be replaced with the ones with low cholesterol.

High Sodium Products

Sodium is related to hypertension and blood pressure. Since diabetes is already the result of a hormonal imbalance in the body, in the presence of excess sodium—another imbalance—a fluid imbalance may occur which a diabetic body cannot tolerate. It adds up to already present complications of the disease. So, avoid using food items with a high amount of sodium. Mainly store packed items, processed foods, and salt all contain sodium, and one should avoid them all. Use only the unsalted variety of food products, whether it's butter, margarine, nuts, or other items.

Sugary Drinks

Cola drinks or other similar beverages are filled with sugars. If you had seen different video presentations showing the amount of the sugars present in a single bottle of soda, you would know how dangerous those are for diabetic patients. They can drastically increase the amount of blood glucose level within 30 minutes of drinking. Fortunately, there are many sugar-free varieties available in the drinks which are suitable for diabetic patients.

Sugar Syrups and Toppings

A number of syrups available in the markets are made out of nothing but sugar. Maple syrup is one good example. For a diabetic diet, the patient should avoid such sugary syrups and also stay away from the sugar-rich toppings available in the stores. If you want to use them at all, trust yourself and prepare them at home with a sugar-free recipe.

Sweet Chocolate and Candies

For diabetic patients, sugar-free chocolates or candies are the best way out. Other processed chocolate bars and candies are extremely damaging to their health, and all of these should be avoided. You can try and prepare healthy bars and candies at home with sugar-free recipes.

Alcohol

Alcohol has the tendency to reduce the rate of our metabolism and take away our appetite, which can render a diabetic patient into a very life-threatening condition. Alcohol in a very small amount cannot harm the patient, but the regular or constant intake of alcohol is bad for health and glucose levels.

Chapter 2: The Diabetic Diet

Many nutritionists believe the diet followed by diabetics is a good diet for everyone. Anyone who follows it lowers their risk of developing diabetes and other health conditions.

Characteristics of a Diabetic Diet

Experts say that the ideal diabetic diet has the following characteristics:

It is low in calories. Diabetics should eat a low-calorie diet, as opposed to a low carbohydrate diet. Lowering calories means you lower the actual amount of carbohydrate and fat you need to burn.

Low-carbohydrate and low-fat diets may not work for diabetics, as they may then increase proteins in the digestive tract and the bloodstream to a dangerous level. Diabetic people should not consume a large amount of protein, as it may increase their risk of neuropathy and other complications. If the amount of fat and carbs, in the diet, is significantly decreased, while the amount of protein remains at a proportionate level, the diabetic may suffer from malnutrition. Thus, the solution is to lower the overall calorie intake.

The number of carbohydrates should not be less than 45 %, but no more than 60 % of the total calorie intake each day.

For pregnant and breastfeeding women, the amount should not be less than 50 %.

The amount of protein should not exceed 1 g., for every 0.45 kg of their ideal weight, and no lower than 0.4 g.

The amount of fat in a diabetic's diet should not be more than 25 % of the amount of the ideal total calorie allowance for the day.

Their diet should have less fried and processed food.

Fried and processed foods are high in unhealthy fat and refined carbohydrates. They increase the level of glucose in the blood, blocking insulin receptors and increasing cravings for sweet and greasy food.

Foods that retain their natural flavor are usually high in fiber and low in sugar. Fiber aids digestion and helps "choose" which nutrients are absorbed, or not, by the body.

Carbohydrate Counting

Carbohydrates are the primary macronutrient responsible for raising blood sugars. All of the carbohydrates you eat get digested within one to two hours. Quick-acting sugars, like juice, may act in five minutes, whereas more complex starches, such as bread, raise blood sugars more slowly. Whichever carbohydrate you choose, it's important to understand that the total carbohydrate intake at each meal should be coordinated with insulin action.

The first step to counting carbs requires understanding which foods contain carbohydrates and what equals a serving size. Measuring cups and/or a digital food scale will prove handy tools in your kitchen. All nutrition labels list the serving in ounces or weight in grams, so you'll want a scale that has both ounces and grams. The following chart provides general information about carbohydrate values in different food groups.

Protein and fats do not contain significant amounts of carbohydrates and are not traditionally accounted for when carbohydrate counting. If you eat large quantities of fat or protein, you may need to consider this when calculating your insulin dose.

Carbohydrate Content in Food Groups

Food Group	Carbohydrate Grams	Example
Starch	15	1-oz. slice whole-wheat bread
		1/3 c. rice or pasta
		1/2 c. beans
		1/2 English muffin
		3/4 c. cold cereal
		1/2 c. peas or corn
		1 c. butternut squash

Fruit	15	1 small apple or 4 oz of juice
		1/2 banana, mango, or pear
		15–17 grapes
		1 1/4 c. strawberries
		12 cherries
Milk	15	8 oz. milk
		8 oz. yogurt
		8 oz. soy milk
Meat and Protein	0	1-oz. chicken, fish, or turkey
		1-oz. beef or pork
		1 egg
		3 egg whites
		4 oz. tofu
Fats	0	1 tsp. butter or oil
		1 tbsp. cream cheese
		1/8 avocado
		1 slice bacon
Vegetables	5	1/2 c. cooked vegetables
		1/2 c. corn or peas
		1 c. raw vegetables

What About Low-Carb Diets?

Low-carbohydrate diets, such as Atkins, Protein Power, or the ketogenic diet, are making headline news and are extremely controversial. There is evidence that low-carb diets may help with weight reduction, and there are long-standing studies that show limiting carbohydrates can prevent seizures in individuals with epilepsy. However, there is not sufficient evidence to warrant low-carbohydrate diets for all patients with type 1 diabetes. Low-carb diets may translate to lower insulin dosing, but this does not necessarily mean that such diets are beneficial to overall health. Before recommending or advocating any extreme diets, I look at the entire medical history, check kidney function, cholesterol levels, and blood sugars, and then discuss how much carbohydrate intake is indicated for that individual. The Academy of Nutrition and Dietetics does not have any specific guidelines for carbohydrate intake; however, according to the National Academy of Medicine, the minimum requirement is 130 g. daily. Recommendations by many health organizations indicate carbohydrates at each meal. A typical distribution looks like this: 30–45 g. carbohydrates at breakfast; 5–25 g. at snacks; 30–60 g. at lunch, and 30–60 g. at dinner. Athletes may need a much higher carbohydrate intake. Keep an open mind and look at new evidence-based publications to understand how low-carb diets with less than 50 g of carbs daily fit into the world of type 1 diabetes and the ever-changing science of nutrition.

The average American consumes 22 tsps of sugar a day, for a whopping 355 kcal. People with diabetes often ask me if sugar substitutes are a better choice than real sugar. Sugar substitutes, also known as nonnutritive sweeteners or artificial sweeteners, contain few or no carbohydrates and have little effect on blood sugar. Examples include aspartame, acesulfame-K, Neotame, saccharin, and sucralose. Another sugar substitute is stevia, which comes from a plant.

Sugar substitutes can be found in many foods and beverages, including diet soda and other dietetic products. Compare a 12-oz. diet soda, which has 0 kcal. and 0 g of carbohydrate, to a regular soda with 155 kcal. and 40 g of carbohydrate.

People have debated the safety of sugar for years. The FDA has approved them as safe, and people with diabetes and those trying to lose weight have used them for years. The FDA also considers stevia as generally recognized as safe (GRAS).

To date, there has been no clear evidence these sweeteners cause cancer or other serious health problems in humans. However, some research suggests that artificial sweeteners can affect the microbes in our gut that digest food, which in turn can impair some people's ability to process glucose. Other studies suggest the intensely sweet taste of artificial sweeteners may lead to a preference for sweet foods, which may lead to overeating. It is also possible that artificial sweeteners lead to an increased intake of calories later in the day, beyond what would have been consumed in the absence of the use of these sweeteners. But more studies need to be done to conclusively prove any of these possibilities.

The decision is yours. Your best bet is to choose moderation—whether it be a real sugar or a nonnutritive sweetener. If you do choose real sugar, just keep in mind that 1 tbsp. contains 15 g of carbohydrate. If you are testing your own blood sugar, pay attention to how sugar affects you.

How to Break Free of Your Sugar Habit

So, maybe you're at risk of diabetes, or maybe you already have it but don't know what you can do to lessen your sugar consumption habits. The good news is it isn't that bad to break these habits. It can take a while, and you need willpower, but if you have that, you should be able to fight off the habits as well. All you have to do is be willing to make some significant changes to your diet. Ultimately, people are hardwired to desire sugar—when we didn't have easy access to sugar, we needed to want as many carbs as possible to keep ourselves healthy and alive; the carbs would help us to create fats. They would also help to keep us full. However, nowadays, because we don't have to forage or hunt and gather for food, we have our own problems. Nowadays, the problem is that food is too easy to find. Because it is so readily available, you run into the problem of potentially storing up too much fat as a direct result. However, you can learn to prevent this from being a problem.

We are hardwired to want to go for those sugary choices. Most animals are—studies have shown that animals will go out of their way to choose sugar over cocaine in lab tests. However, sugar is not good for us in excess, as we have established thus far. This means that you will need to be mindful of what you are doing to prevent yourself from getting ill. You will need to figure out how you can make sure that you do not unintentionally poison yourself with too much sugar. Now, let's look at what goes into breaking that habit—or even that addiction in some cases.

A Brief Guide to Eliminating Sugar

First, before we begin, consider the fact that sugar comes in all sorts of forms. It comes in the form of sucrose and fructose. Lactose and maltose are two others. Sucrose can be found, as well. As you can see, they all end in "-ose." That is the sign that you are looking at a sugar if you don't see the actual word written in front of you. Because sugars come in so many different forms, it can be difficult to truly eliminate them. It can be impossible for you to figure out what you will need to do to prevent yourself from getting ill from these effects—you will need to make sure that you are working hard to ensure that your diet is well-managed. Ultimately, if you are able to recognize these different forms of sugar, you will be able to prevent yourself from eating things that aren't going to help you.

As an additional note before we begin, consider the fact that you don't need to cut out all forms of sugar—you just want to cut it out when it is added to your diet. This means that it is okay to eat whole food that breaks down into carbs—but you don't want to eat something that is laden with high fructose corn syrup. Eating foods that are loaded up with sugars can be a big problem, and most people don't even realize that they are doing it—they just do so because they think that since the word sugar isn't on the ingredient list, they are safe to eat it without a concern.

If you are ready to cut out sugar from your diet, there are a few steps that you should follow to help yourself do so. These aren't necessarily difficult to do, but many people find that it is hard to stick to it. They get caught up in the cravings, or they give into the withdrawals that they feel when they do cut them out. Your body gets used to those higher levels of sugar in your diet and comes to rely on them; when you cut them out, you are likely to run into some symptoms as your body has to develop and adjust to its new normal.

Cutting Sugar by Tossing Out Added Sugar Sources

The first step to making sure that you can eliminate sugar is to take the time to genuinely cut it out in the first place. If you have added sugar options in your home, such as white and brown sugars, or also eliminating the honey. If you are going to make yourself coffee or tea, you want to make sure that you aren't adding these. At first, make sure that you do so gradually. You want to start out by cutting the amounts of sugar in half and slowly weaning down over the period of a couple of weeks. This is what is best for you.

Cut Out Liquid Sugars

All too often, people drink sugars that they don't even realize. Soda is one of the biggest sources of sugar that we get. Additionally, you can see that adding honey or sugar to coffees and teas is another common source, as is drinking juice. None of these are very healthy options; you need to make sure that you are cutting out those sugars over time. Coffee and tea are fine, so long as you are mindful of the sugars that you put into them.

Choose Fresh Fruits

If you want something sweet, go for fruit, but still, be mindful. Fresh fruit is usually the best for you, but you can also go for unsweetened frozen fruit or even canned fruit if it is in water or natural juices. Make sure that you avoid the fruit that is canned in heavy syrups; this is a common source of sugars that people don't realize that they are using. You can also use fruit as a natural sweetener. If you are going to use a sweetener of some sort for yogurt, cereals, or oatmeal, this is a great option for you. Fruits are a great option to flavor your teas or water as well if you are someone that's used to sweetened and flavored drinks.

Always Compare Food Labels

When you look at your food labels, make sure that you choose those that have the lowest amounts of added sugars. Many foods are naturally going to have carbohydrates in them—and that's okay in moderation. You must make sure that you are cutting out those high added sugar foods to keep yourself healthy. This means that if you have a food with 22 g of sugar and 18 are added, and you can also choose a food that has 25 g of sugar with just 4 or 5 added, the second food is going to be the healthier choice because it doesn't involve adding any natural sugars.

Extracts for Flavor

Instead of relying on sweeteners like sugar, you can use extracts like vanilla or lemon to add some richness and flavor without the calories.

Non-Nutritive Sweeteners

If you just can't cut the sugar entirely, you can make it a point to limit the sugar that you do consume, switching it out with non-nutritive sweeteners. However, treat this as a crutch rather than a permanent option. It is better for you to just keep things natural and avoid adding any sweeteners entirely.

Substitute or Replace It

If you are cooking something, there are several options that you can use as a way of avoiding the sugar entirely. You could use spices to enhance the foods instead of using sweeteners. You can also use ingredients such as applesauce to replace sugar and fats in many baking dishes as a nice way to cut out the added sugars.

Chapter 3: 4-Week Meal Plan

Day	Breakfast	Lunch	Dinner	Dessert
1	Berry-oat breakfast bars	Kale, and white bean stew	Salmon with asparagus	Tuna salad
2	Whole-grain breakfast cookies	Slow cooker two-bean sloppy joes	Shrimp in garlic butter	Roasted portobello salad
3	Blueberry breakfast cake	Lighter eggplant parmesan	Cobb salad	Shredded chicken salad
4	Whole-grain pancakes	Coconut-lentil curry	Seared tuna steak	Mango and jicama salad
5	Buckwheat grouts breakfast bowl	Stuffed portobello with cheese	Beef chili	Roasted beet salad
6	Peach muesli bake	Lighter shrimp scampi	Greek broccoli salad	Calico salad
7	Steel-cut oatmeal bowl with fruit and nuts	Maple-mustard salmon	Cheesy cauliflower gratin	Spinach shrimp salad
8	Whole-grain Dutch baby pancake	Chicken salad with grapes and pecans	Strawberry spinach salad	Barley veggie salad

9	Mushroom, zucchini, and onion frittata	Lemony salmon burgers	Cauliflower mac and cheese	Tenderloin grilled salad
10	Spinach and cheese quiche	Caprese turkey burgers	Easy egg salad	Broccoli salad
11	Spicy jalapeno popper deviled eggs	Pasta salad	Baked chicken legs	Broccoli salad Cherry tomato salad
12	Lovely porridge	Chicken, strawberry, and avocado salad	Creamed spinach	Tabbouleh—Arabian salad
13	Salty macadamia chocolate smoothie	Lemon-thyme eggs	Stuffed mushrooms	Arugula garden salad
14	Basil and tomato baked eggs	Spinach salad with bacon	Vegetable soup	Supreme Caesar salad
15	Cinnamon and coconut porridge	Pea and collards soup	Misto quente	Sunflower seeds and
16	An omelet of Swiss chard	Spanish stew	Garlic bread	Chicken salad in cucumber cups
17	Cheesy low-carb omelet	Creamy taco soup	Bruschetta	California wraps
18	Yogurt and kale smoothie	Chicken with Caprese salsa	Cream buns with strawberries	Chicken avocado salad
19	Bacon and chicken garlic wrap	Balsamic-roasted broccoli	Blueberry buns	Ground turkey salad
20	Grilled chicken platter	Hearty beef and vegetable soup	Cauliflower mash	Scallop Caesar salad
21	Parsley chicken breast	Cauliflower muffin	French toast in sticks	Asian cucumber salad

22	Mustard chicken	Cauliflower rice with chicken	Muffins sandwich	Cauliflower tofu salad
23	Balsamic chicken	Ham and egg cups	Bacon BBQ	Tuna salad
24	Greek chicken breast	Turkey with fried eggs	Stuffed French toast	Roasted portobello salad
25	Chipotle lettuce chicken	Kale, and white bean stew	Scallion sandwich	Shredded chicken salad
26	Stylish chicken-bacon wrap	Slow cooker two-bean sloppy joes	Lean lamb and turkey meatballs with yogurt	Mango and jicama salad
27	Healthy cottage cheese pancakes	Lighter eggplant parmesan	Air fried section and tomato	Roasted beet salad
28	Avocado lemon toast	Coconut-lentil curry	Cheesy salmon fillets	Calico salad

Chapter 4: Breakfast

1. Berry-Oat Breakfast Bars

Preparation time: 10'

Cooking time: 25'

Servings: 12

Ingredients

- 2 c. fresh raspberries or blueberries
- 2 tbsps sugar
- 2 tbsps freshly squeezed lemon juice
- 1 tbsp. cornstarch
- 1 1/2 c. rolled oats
- 1/2 c. whole-wheat flour
- 1/2 c. walnuts
- 1/4 c. chia seeds
- 1/4 c. extra-virgin olive oil
- 1/4 c. honey
- 1 large egg

Directions

1. Preheat the oven to 350 °F.
2. In a small saucepan over medium heat, stir together the berries, sugar, lemon juice, and cornstarch. Bring to a simmer. Reduce the heat and simmer for 2–3 minutes, until the mixture thickens.
3. In a food processor or high-speed blender, combine the oats, flour, walnuts, and chia seeds. Process until powdered. Add the olive oil, honey, and egg. Pulse a few more times, until well combined. Press half of the mixture into a 9-in. square baking dish.
4. Spread the berry filling over the oat mixture. Add the remaining oat mixture on top of the berries. Bake for 25 minutes, until browned.
5. Let cool completely, cut into 12 pieces, and serve. Store in a covered container for up to 5 days.

Nutrition

- Calories 201
- Total fat 10 g.
- Saturated fat 1 g.
- Protein 5 g.
- Carbohydrates 26 g.
- Sugar 9 g.
- Fiber 5 g.
- Cholesterol 16 mg.
- Sodium 8 mg.

2. Whole-Grain Breakfast Cookies

Preparation time: 20'

Cooking time: 10'

Servings: 18 cookies

Ingredients

- 2 c. rolled oats
- 1/2 c. whole-wheat flour
- 1/4 c. ground flaxseed
- 1 tsp. baking powder
- 1 c. unsweetened applesauce
- 2 large eggs
- 2 tbsps vegetable oil
- 2 tsps. vanilla extract
- 1 tsp. ground cinnamon
- 1/2 c. dried cherries
- 1/4 c. unsweetened shredded coconut
- 2 oz. dark chocolate, chopped

Directions

1. Preheat the oven to 350 °F.
2. In a large bowl, combine the oats, flour, flaxseed, and baking powder. Stir well to mix.
3. In a medium bowl, whisk the applesauce, eggs, vegetable oil, vanilla, and cinnamon. Pour the wet mixture into the dry mixture, and stir until combined.
4. Fold in the cherries, coconut, and chocolate. Drop tablespoon-size balls of dough onto a baking sheet. Bake for 10–12 minutes, until browned and cooked through.
5. Let cool for about 3 minutes, remove from the baking sheet, and cool completely before serving. Store in an airtight container for up to 1 week.

Nutrition

- Calories 136
- Total fat 7 g.
- Saturated fat 3 g.
- Protein 4 g.
- Carbohydrates 14 g.
- Sugar 4 g.
- Fiber 3 g.
- Cholesterol 21 mg.
- Sodium 11 mg.

3. Blueberry Breakfast Cake

PREPARATION TIME: **15'**

COOKING TIME: **45'**

SERVINGS: **12**

Ingredients

For the Topping
- 1/4 c. finely chopped walnuts
- 1/2 tsp. ground cinnamon
- 2 tbsps butter, chopped into small pieces
- 2 tbsps sugar

For the Cake
- Nonstick cooking spray
- 1 c. whole-wheat pastry flour
- 1 c. oat flour
- 1/4 c. sugar
- 2 tsps. baking powder
- 1 large egg, beaten
- 1/2 c. skim milk
- 2 tbsps butter, melted
- 1 tsp. grated lemon peel
- 2 c. fresh or frozen blueberries

Directions

To Make the Topping
1. In a small bowl, stir together the walnuts, cinnamon, butter, and sugar. Set aside.
2. To Make the Cake
3. Preheat the oven to 350 °F. Spray a 9-in. square pan with cooking spray. Set aside.
4. In a large bowl, stir together the pastry flour, oat flour, sugar, and baking powder.
5. Add the egg, milk, butter, and lemon peel, and stir until there are no dry spots.
6. Stir in the blueberries, and gently mix until incorporated. Press the batter into the prepared pan, using a spoon to flatten it into the dish.
7. Sprinkle the topping over the cake.
8. Bake for 40-45 minutes until a toothpick inserted into the cake comes out clean and serve.

Nutrition

- Calories 177
- Total fat 7 g.
- Saturated fat 3 g.
- Protein 4 g.
- Carbohydrates 26 g.
- Sugar 9 g.
- Fiber 3 g.
- Cholesterol 26 mg.
- Sodium 39 mg.

4. Whole-Grain Pancakes

PREPARATION TIME: **10'**

COOKING TIME: **15'**

SERVINGS: **4-6**

Ingredients

- 2 c. whole-wheat pastry flour
- 4 tsps. baking powder
- 2 tsps. ground cinnamon
- 1/2 tsp. salt
- 2 c. skim milk, plus more as needed
- 2 large eggs
- 1 tbsp. honey
- Nonstick cooking spray
- Maple syrup, for serving
- Fresh fruit, for serving

Directions

1. In a large bowl, stir together the flour, baking powder, cinnamon, and salt.
2. Add the milk, eggs, and honey, and stir well to combine. If needed, add more milk, 1 tbsp. at a time, until there are no dry spots and you have a pourable batter.
3. Heat a large skillet over medium-high heat, and spray it with cooking spray.
4. Using a 1/4-cup measuring cup, scoop 2 or 3 pancakes into the skillet at a time. Cook for a couple of minutes, until bubbles form on the surface of the pancakes, flip, and cook for 1-2 minutes more, until golden brown and cooked through. Repeat with the remaining batter.
5. Serve topped with maple syrup or fresh fruit.

Nutrition

- Calories 392
- Total fat 4 g.
- Saturated fat 1 g.
- Protein 15 g.
- Carbohydrates 71 g.
- Sugar 11 g.
- Fiber 9 g.
- Cholesterol 95 mg.
- Sodium 396 mg.

5. Buckwheat Grouts Breakfast Bowl

PREPARATION TIME: 5' + OVERNIGHT TO SOAK
COOKING TIME: 10-12'
SERVINGS: 4

Ingredients

- 3 c. skim milk
- 1 c. buckwheat grouts
- 1/4 c. chia seeds
- 2 tsps. vanilla extract
- 1/2 tsp. ground cinnamon
- Pinch salt
- 1 c. water
- 1/2 c. unsalted pistachios
- 2 c. sliced fresh strawberries
- 1/4 c. cacao nibs (optional)

Directions

1. In a large bowl, stir together the milk, groats, chia seeds, vanilla, cinnamon, and salt. Cover and refrigerate overnight.
2. The next morning, transfer the soaked mixture to a medium pot and add the water. Bring to a boil over medium-high heat, reduce the heat to maintain a simmer, and cook for 10-12 minutes, until the buckwheat is tender and thickened.
3. Transfer to bowls and serve, topped with the pistachios, strawberries, and cacao nibs (if using).

Nutrition

- Calories 340
- Total fat 8 g.
- Saturated fat 1 g.
- Protein 15 g.
- Carbohydrates 52 g.
- Sugar 14 g.
- Fiber 10 g.
- Cholesterol 4 mg.
- Sodium 140 mg.

6. Peach Muesli Bake

PREPARATION TIME: 10'
COOKING TIME: 40'
SERVINGS: 8

Ingredients

- Nonstick cooking spray
- 2 c. skim milk
- 1 1/2 c. rolled oats
- 1/2 c. chopped walnuts
- 1 large egg
- 2 tbsps maple syrup
- 1 tsp. ground cinnamon
- 1 tsp. baking powder
- 1/2 tsp. salt
- 2-3 peaches, sliced

Directions

1. Preheat the oven to 375 °F. Spray a 9-in. square baking dish with cooking spray. Set aside.
2. In a large bowl, stir together the milk, oats, walnuts, egg, maple syrup, cinnamon, baking powder, and salt. Spread half the mixture in the prepared baking dish.
3. Place half the peaches in a single layer across the oat mixture.
4. Spread the remaining oat mixture over the top. Add the remaining peaches in a thin layer over the oats. Bake for 35-40 minutes, uncovered until thickened and browned.
5. Cut into 8 squares and serve warm.

Nutrition

- Calories 138
- Total fat 3 g.
- Saturated fat 1 g.
- Protein 6 g.
- Carbohydrates 22 g.
- Sugar 10 g.
- Fiber 3 g.
- Cholesterol 24 mg.
- Sodium 191 mg.

7. Steel-Cut Oatmeal Bowl with Fruit and Nuts

PREPARATION TIME: **5'**

COOKING TIME: **20'**

SERVINGS: **4**

Ingredients

- 1 c. steel-cut oats
- 2 c. almond milk
- 3/4 c. water
- 1 tsp. ground cinnamon
- 1/4 tsp. salt
- 2 c. chopped fresh fruit, such as blueberries, strawberries, raspberries, or peaches
- 1/2 c. chopped walnuts
- 1/4 c. chia seeds

Directions

1. In a medium saucepan over medium-high heat, combine the oats, almond milk, water, cinnamon, and salt. Bring to a boil, reduce the heat to low, and simmer for 15-20 minutes, until the oats are softened and thickened.
2. Top each bowl with 1/2 c of fresh fruit, 2 tbsps of walnuts, and 1 tbsp of chia seeds before serving.

Nutrition

- Calories 288
- Total fat 11 g.
- Saturated fat 1 g.
- Protein 10 g.
- Carbohydrates 38 g.
- Sugar 7 g.
- Fiber 10 g.
- Cholesterol 0 mg.
- Sodium 329 mg.

8. Whole-Grain Dutch Baby Pancake

PREPARATION TIME: **5'**

COOKING TIME: **25'**

SERVINGS: **4**

Ingredients

- 2 tbsps coconut oil
- 1/2 c. whole-wheat flour
- 1/4 c. skim milk
- 3 large eggs
- 1 tsp. vanilla extract
- 1/2 tsp. baking powder
- 1/4 tsp. salt
- 1/4 tsp. ground cinnamon
- Powdered sugar, for dusting

Directions

1. Preheat the oven to 400 °F.
2. Put the coconut oil in a medium oven-safe skillet, and place the skillet in the oven to melt the oil while it preheats.
3. In a blender, combine the flour, milk, eggs, vanilla, baking powder, salt, and cinnamon. Process until smooth.
4. Carefully remove the skillet from the oven and tilt to spread the oil around evenly.
5. Pour the batter into the skillet and return it to the oven for 23-25 minutes, until the pancake puffs and lightly browns.
6. Remove, dust lightly with powdered sugar, cut into 4 wedges, and serve.

Nutrition

- Calories 195
- Total fat 11 g.
- Saturated fat 7 g.
- Protein 8 g.
- Carbohydrates 16 g.
- Sugar 1 g.
- Fiber 2 g.
- Cholesterol 140 mg.
- Sodium 209 mg.

9. Mushroom, Zucchini, and Onion Frittata

Preparation time: 10'
Cooking time: 20'
Servings: 4

Ingredients

- 1 tbsp. extra-virgin olive oil
- 1/2 onion, chopped
- 1 medium zucchini, chopped
- 1 1/2 c. sliced mushrooms
- 6 large eggs, beaten
- 2 tbsps skim milk
- Salt
- Freshly ground black pepper
- 1-oz. feta cheese, crumbled

Directions

1. Preheat the oven to 400 °F.
2. In a medium oven-safe skillet over medium-high heat, heat the olive oil.
3. Add the onion and sauté for 3-5 minutes, until translucent.
4. Add the zucchini and mushrooms, and cook for 3-5 more minutes, until the vegetables are tender.
5. Meanwhile, in a small bowl, whisk the eggs, milk, salt, and pepper. Pour the mixture into the skillet, stirring to combine, and transfer the skillet to the oven. Cook for 7-9 minutes, until set.
6. Sprinkle with the feta cheese, and cook for 1-2 minutes more, until heated through.
7. Remove, cut into 4 wedges, and serve.

Nutrition

- Calories 178
- Total fat 13 g.
- Saturated fat 4 g.
- Protein 12 g.
- Carbohydrates 5 g.
- Sugar 3 g.
- Fiber 1 g.
- Cholesterol 285 mg.
- Sodium 234 mg.

10. Spinach and Cheese Quiche

Preparation time: 10' + 10' to rest
Cooking time: 50'
Servings: 4-6

Ingredients

- Nonstick cooking spray
- 1 tbsp. + 2 tsps. extra-virgin olive oil, divided
- 1/2 tsp. salt
- Freshly ground black pepper
- 1 onion, finely chopped
- 1 (10-oz.) bag fresh spinach
- 4 large eggs
- 1/2 c. skim milk
- 1-oz. Gruyere cheese, shredded

Directions

1. Preheat the oven to 350 °F. Spray a 9-in. pie dish with cooking spray. Set aside.
2. In a large skillet over medium-high heat, heat olive oil.
3. Add the onion and sauté for 3-5 minutes, until softened.
4. By handfuls, add the spinach, stirring between each addition, until it just starts to wilt before adding more. Cook for about 1 minute, until it cooks down.
5. In a medium bowl, whisk the eggs and milk. Add the gruyere, and season with salt and some pepper. Fold the eggs into the spinach. Pour the mixture into the pie dish and bake for 25 minutes, until the eggs are set.
6. Let rest for 10 minutes before serving.

Nutrition

- Calories 445
- Total fat 14 g.
- Saturated fat 4 g.
- Protein 19 g.
- Carbohydrates 68 g.
- Sugar 6 g.
- Fiber 7 g.
- Cholesterol 193 mg.
- Sodium 773 mg.

11. Spicy Jalapeno Popper Deviled Eggs

PREPARATION TIME: 5'

COOKING TIME: 5'

SERVINGS: 4

Ingredients

- 4 large whole eggs, hardboiled
- 2 tbsps keto-friendly mayonnaise
- 1/4 c. cheddar cheese, grated
- 2 slices bacon, cooked and crumbled
- 1 jalapeno, sliced

Directions

1. Cut eggs in half, remove the yolk, and put them in a bowl.
2. Lay egg whites on a platter.
3. Mix in the remaining ingredients and mash them with the egg yolks.
4. Transfer the yolk mixture back to the egg whites.
5. Serve and enjoy!

Nutrition

- Calories 176
- Fat 14 g.
- Carbohydrates 0.7 g.
- Protein 10 g.

12. Lovely Porridge

PREPARATION TIME: 15'

COOKING TIME: NIL

SERVINGS: 2

Ingredients

- 2 tbsps coconut flour
- 2 tbsps vanilla protein powder
- 3 tbsps Golden Flaxseed meal
- 1 1/2 c. almond milk, unsweetened
- Powdered erythritol

Directions

1. Take a bowl and mix with flaxseed meal, protein powder, coconut flour, and mix well.
2. Add the mix to the saucepan (placed over medium heat).
3. Add almond milk and stir, let the mixture thicken.
4. Add your desired amount of sweetener and serve.
5. Enjoy!

Nutrition

- Calories 259
- Fat 13 g.
- Carbohydrates 5 g.
- Protein 16 g.

13. Salty Macadamia Chocolate Smoothie

Preparation time: 5'

Cooking time: NIL

Servings: 1

Ingredients

- 2 tbsps macadamia nuts, salted
- 1/3 c. chocolate whey protein powder, low carb
- 1 c. almond milk, unsweetened

Directions

1. Add the listed ingredients to your blender and blend until you have a smooth mixture.
2. Chill and enjoy it!

Nutrition

- Calories 165
- Fat 2 g.
- Carbohydrates 1 g.
- Protein 12 g.

14. Basil and Tomato Baked Eggs

Preparation time: 10'

Cooking time: 15'

Servings: 2

Ingredients

- 1 garlic clove, minced
- 1 c. canned tomatoes
- 1/4 c. fresh basil leaves, roughly chopped
- 1/2 tsp. chili powder
- 1 tbsp. olive oil
- 4 whole eggs
- Salt and pepper to taste

Directions

1. Preheat your oven to 375 °F.
2. Take a small baking dish and grease it with olive oil.
3. Add garlic, basil, tomatoes, chili, olive oil into a dish and stir.
4. Crackdown eggs into a dish, keeping space between the two.
5. Sprinkle the whole dish with salt and pepper.
6. Place in oven and cook for 12 minutes until eggs are set and tomatoes are bubbling.
7. Serve with basil on top.
8. Enjoy!

Nutrition

- Calories 235
- Fat 16 g.
- Carbohydrates 7 g.
- Protein 14 g.

15. Cinnamon and Coconut Porridge

PREPARATION TIME: 5'

COOKING TIME: 5'

SERVINGS: 4

Ingredients

- 2 c of water
- 1 c. 36 % heavy cream
- 1/2 c. unsweetened dried coconut, shredded
- 2 tbsps flaxseed meal
- 1 tbsp. butter
- 1 and 1/2 tsp. stevia
- 1 tsp. cinnamon
- Salt to taste
- Toppings as blueberries

Directions

1. Add the listed ingredients to a small pot, mix well.
2. Transfer the pot to a stove and place it over medium-low heat.
3. Bring the mix to a slow boil.
4. Stir well and remove the heat.
5. Divide the mix into equal servings and let them sit for 10 minutes.
6. Top with your desired toppings and enjoy!

Nutrition

- Calories 1/1
- Fat 16 g.
- Carbohydrates 6 g.
- Protein 2 g.

16. An Omelet of Swiss Chard

PREPARATION TIME: 5'

COOKING TIME: 5'

SERVINGS: 4

Ingredients

- 4 eggs, lightly beaten
- 4 c. Swiss chard, sliced
- 2 tbsps butter
- 1/2 tsp. garlic salt
- Fresh pepper

Directions

1. Take a non-stick frying pan and place it over medium-low heat.
2. Once the butter melts, add Swiss chard and stir cook for 2 minutes.
3. Pour egg into the pan and gently stir them into the Swiss chard.
4. Season with garlic salt and pepper.
5. Cook for 2 minutes.
6. Serve and enjoy!

Nutrition

- Calories 260
- Fat 21 g.
- Carbohydrates 4 g.
- Protein 14 g.

17. Cheesy Low-Carb Omelet

Preparation Time: 5'
Cooking Time: 5'
Servings: 5

Ingredients

- 2 whole eggs
- 1 tbsp. water
- 1 tbsp. butter
- 3 thin slices of salami
- 5 fresh basil leaves
- 5 thin slices, fresh ripe tomatoes
- 2 oz. fresh mozzarella cheese
- Salt and pepper as needed

Directions

1. Take a small bowl and whisk in eggs and water.
2. Take a non-stick pan and place it over medium heat, add the butter and let it melt.
3. Pour egg mixture and cook for 30 seconds.
4. Spread salami slices on half of the egg mix and top with cheese, tomatoes, basil slices.
5. Season with salt and pepper according to your taste.
6. Cook for 2 minutes and fold the egg with the empty half.
7. Cover and cook on low for 1 minute.
8. Serve and enjoy!

Nutrition

- Calories 451
- Fat 36 g.
- Carbohydrates 3 g.
- Protein: 33 g.

18. Yogurt and Kale Smoothie

Preparation Time: 10'
Cooking Time: 0'
Servings: 1

Ingredients

- 1 c. whole milk yogurt
- 1 c. baby green kale
- 1 pack stevia
- 1 tbsp. MCT oil
- 1 tbsp. sunflower seeds
- 1 c of water

Directions

1. Add listed ingredients to the blender.
2. Blend until you have a smooth and creamy texture.
3. Serve chilled and enjoy!

Nutrition

- Calories 329
- Fat 26 g.
- Carbohydrates 15 g.
- Protein 11 g.

19. Bacon and Chicken Garlic Wrap

Preparation time: 15'
Cooking time: 10'
Servings: 4

Ingredients

- 1 chicken fillet, cut into small cubes
- 8-9 thin slices of bacon, cut into small cubes
- 6 garlic cloves, minced

Directions

1. Preheat your oven to 400 °F.
2. Line a baking tray with aluminum foil.
3. Add minced garlic to a bowl and rub each chicken piece with it.
4. Wrap bacon piece around each garlic chicken bite.
5. Secure with a toothpick.
6. Transfer bites to the baking sheet, keeping a little bit of space between them.
7. Bake for about 15-20 minutes until crispy.
8. Serve and enjoy!

Nutrition

- Calories 260
- Fat 19 g.
- Carbohydrates 5 g.
- Protein 22 g.

20. Grilled Chicken Platter

Preparation time: 5'
Cooking time: 10'
Servings: 6

Ingredients

- 3 large chicken breasts, sliced half lengthwise
- 10-oz. spinach, frozen and drained
- 3-oz. mozzarella cheese, part-skim
- 1/2 a cup of roasted red peppers, cut in long strips
- 1 tsp of olive oil
- 2 garlic cloves, minced
- Salt and pepper as needed

Directions

1. Preheat your oven to 400 °F.
2. Slice 3 chicken breast lengthwise.
3. Take a non-stick pan and grease with cooking spray.
4. Bake for 2-3 minutes on each side.
5. Take another skillet and cook spinach and garlic in oil for 3 minutes.
6. Place chicken on an oven pan and top with spinach, roasted peppers, and mozzarella.
7. Bake until the cheese melted.
8. Enjoy!

Nutrition

- Calories 195
- Fat 7 g.
- Net carbohydrates 3 g.
- Protein 30 g.

21. Parsley Chicken Breast

Preparation time: 10'
Cooking time: 40'
Servings: 4

Ingredients

- 1 tbsp. dry parsley
- 1 tbsp. dry basil
- 4 chicken breast halves, boneless and skinless
- 1/2 tsp. salt
- 1/2 tsp. red pepper flakes, crushed
- 2 tomatoes, sliced

Directions

1. Preheat your oven to 350 °F.
2. Take a 9x13 in. baking dish and grease it up with cooking spray.
3. Sprinkle 1 tbsp of parsley, 1 tsp of basil, and spread the mixture over your baking dish.
4. Arrange the chicken breast halves over the dish and sprinkle garlic slices on top.
5. Take a small bowl and add 1 tsp. parsley, 1 tsp of basil, salt, basil, red pepper and mix well. Pour the mixture over the chicken breast.
6. Top with tomato slices and cover; bake for 25 minutes.
7. Remove the cover and bake for 15 more minutes.
8. Serve and enjoy!

Nutrition

- Calories 150
- Fat 4 g.
- Carbohydrates 4 g.
- Protein 25 g.

22. Mustard Chicken

Preparation time: 10'
Cooking time: 40'
Servings: 4

Ingredients

- 4 chicken breasts
- 1/2 c. chicken broth
- 3-4 tbsps mustard
- 3 tbsps olive oil
- 1 tsp. paprika
- 1 tsp. chili powder
- 1 tsp. garlic powder

Directions

1. Take a small bowl and mix mustard, olive oil, paprika, garlic powder, chicken broth, and chili.
2. Add chicken breast and marinate for 30 minutes.
3. Take a lined baking sheet and arrange the chicken.
4. Bake for 35 minutes at 375 °F.
5. Serve and enjoy!

Nutrition

- Calories 531
- Fat 23 g.
- Carbohydrates 10 g.
- Protein 64 g.

23. Balsamic Chicken

PREPARATION TIME: 10'

COOKING TIME: 25'

SERVINGS: 6

Ingredients

- 6 chicken breast halves, skinless and boneless
- 1 tsp. garlic salt
- Ground black pepper
- 2 tbsps olive oil
- 1 onion, thinly sliced
- 14- and 1/2-oz. tomatoes, diced
- 1/2 c. balsamic vinegar
- 1 tsp. dried basil
- 1 tsp. dried oregano
- 1 tsp. dried rosemary
- 1/2 tsp. dried thyme

Directions

1. Season both sides of your chicken breasts thoroughly with pepper and garlic salt.
2. Take a skillet and place it over medium heat.
3. Add some oil and cook your seasoned chicken for 3-4 minutes per side until the breasts are nicely browned.
4. Add the onion and cook for another 3-4 minutes until the onion is browned.
5. Pour the diced-up tomatoes and balsamic vinegar over your chicken and season with some rosemary, basil, thyme, and oregano.
6. Simmer the chicken for about 15 minutes until they are no longer pink.
7. Take an instant-read thermometer and check if the internal temperature gives a reading of 165 °F.
8. If yes, then you are good to go!

Nutrition

- Calories 196
- Fat 7 g.
- Carbohydrates 7 g.
- Protein 23 g.

53

24. Greek Chicken Breast

PREPARATION TIME: 10'

COOKING TIME: 25'

SERVINGS: 4

Ingredients

- 4 chicken breast halves, skinless, and boneless
- 1 c. extra-virgin olive oil
- 1 lemon, juiced
- 2 tsps. garlic, crushed
- 1 1/2 tsps. black pepper
- 1/3 tsp. paprika
- Salt, to taste

Directions

1. Cut 3 slits in the chicken breast.
2. Take a small bowl and whisk in olive oil, salt, lemon juice, garlic, paprika, pepper, and whisk for 30 seconds
3. Place chicken in a large bowl and pour the marinade
4. Rub the marinade all over using your hands
5. Refrigerate overnight
6. Pre-heat grill to medium heat and oil the grate
7. Cook chicken in the grill until the center is no longer pink
8. Serve and enjoy!

Nutrition

- Calories 644
- Fat 57 g.
- Carbohydrates 2 g.
- Protein 27 g.

25. Chipotle Lettuce Chicken

Preparation time: 10'
Cooking time: 25'
Servings: 6

Ingredients

- 1 lb. chicken breast, cut into strips
- Splash of olive oil
- 1 red onion, finely sliced
- 14 oz. tomatoes
- 1 tsp. chipotle, chopped
- 1/2 tsp. cumin
- Pinch of sugar
- Lettuce as needed
- Fresh coriander leaves
- Jalapeno chilies, sliced
- Fresh tomato slices for garnish
- Lemon wedges

Directions

1. Take a non-stick frying pan and place it over medium heat.
2. Add oil and heat it up.
3. Add chicken and cook until brown.
4. Keep the chicken on the side.
5. Add tomatoes, sugar, chipotle, cumin to the same pan and simmer for 25 minutes until you have a nice sauce.
6. Add the chicken into the sauce and cook for 5 minutes.
7. Transfer the mix to another place.
8. Use the lettuce wraps to take a portion of the mixture and serve with lemon wedges, tomato slices, coriander, and jalapeno.
9. Enjoy!

Nutrition

- Calories 332
- Fat 15 g.
- Carbohydrates 13 g.
- Protein 34 g.

26. Stylish Chicken-Bacon Wrap

Preparation time: 5'
Cooking time: 50'
Servings: 3

Ingredients

- 8 oz. lean chicken breast
- 6 bacon slices
- 3 oz. shredded cheese
- 4 slices ham

Directions

1. Cut the chicken breast into bite-sized portions.
2. Transfer the shredded cheese onto the ham slices.
3. Roll up the chicken breast and ham slices in bacon slices.
4. Take a skillet and place it over medium heat.
5. Add olive oil and brown bacon.
6. Remove rolls and transfer them to your oven.
7. Bake for 45 minutes at 325 °F.
8. Serve and enjoy!

Nutrition

- Calories 275
- Fat 11 g.
- Carbohydrates 0.5 g.
- Protein 40 g.

27. Healthy Cottage Cheese Pancakes

PREPARATION TIME: **10'**

COOKING TIME: **15'**

SERVINGS: **1**

Ingredients

- 1/2 c of cottage cheese (low-fat)
- 1/3 c. (approx. 2 egg whites) egg whites
- 1/4 c of oats
- 1 tsp of vanilla extract
- Olive oil cooking spray
- 1 tbsp of stevia (raw)
- Berries or sugar-free jam (optional)

Directions

1. Begin by taking a food blender and adding in the egg whites and cottage cheese. Also add in the vanilla extract, a pinch of stevia, and oats. Pulse until the consistency is well smooth.
2. Get a nonstick pan and oil it nicely with the cooking spray. Position the pan on low heat.
3. After it has been heated, scoop out half of the batter and pour it on the pan. Cook for about 2 1/2 minutes on each side.
4. Position the cooked pancakes on a serving plate and cover them with sugar-free jam or berries.

Nutrition

- Calories 205
- Fat 1.5 g.
- Protein 24.5 g.
- Carbohydrates 19 g.

28. Avocado Lemon Toast

PREPARATION TIME: **10'**

COOKING TIME: **13'**

SERVINGS: **2**

Ingredients

- 2 slices whole-grain bread
- 2 tbsps fresh cilantro, chopped
- 1/4 tsp. lemon zest
- 1 pinch of fine sea salt
- 1/2 avocado
- 1 tsp. fresh lemon juice
- 1 pinch of cayenne pepper
- 1/4 tsp. chia seeds

Directions

1. Begin by getting a medium-sized mixing bowl and adding in the avocado. Make use of a fork to crush it properly.
2. Then, add in the cilantro, lemon zest, lemon juice, sea salt, and cayenne pepper. Mix well until combined.
3. Toast the bread slices in a toaster until golden brown. It should take about 3 minutes.
4. Top the toasted bread slices with the avocado mixture and finalize by drizzling with chia seeds.

Nutrition

- Calories 72
- Protein 3.6 g.
- Fat 1.2 g.
- Carbohydrates 11.6 g.

29. Healthy Baked Eggs

Preparation Time: 10'
Cooking Time: 1 hour
Servings: 6

Ingredients

- 1 tbsp. olive oil
- 2 cloves garlic
- 8 large eggs
- 1/2 tsp. sea salt
- 3 c. shredded mozzarella cheese (medium-fat)
- Olive oil spray
- 1 medium onion, chopped
- 8 oz. spinach leaves
- 1 c. half-and-half
- 1 tsp. black pepper
- 1/2 c. feta cheese

Directions

1. Begin by heating the oven to 375 °F.
2. Get a glass baking dish and grease it with olive oil spray. Set aside.
3. Now take a nonstick pan and pour in olive oil. Heat the pan.
4. Then toss in the garlic, spinach, and onion. Prepare for about 5 minutes. Set aside.
5. Get a large mixing bowl and add in the half-n-half, eggs, pepper, and salt. Whisk thoroughly to combine.
6. Put in the feta cheese and chopped mozzarella cheese (reserve 1/2 c of mozzarella cheese for later).
7. Put the egg mixture and prepared spinach into the prepared glass baking dish. Blend well to combine. Drizzle the reserved cheese over the top.
8. Bake the egg mix for about 45 minutes.
9. Extract the baking dish from the oven and allow it to stand for 10 minutes.
10. Serve!

Nutrition

- Calories 323
- Fat 22.3 g.
- Protein 22.6 g.
- Carbohydrates 7.9 g.

30. Quick Low-Carb Oatmeal

Preparation Time: 10'
Cooking Time: 15'
Servings: 2

Ingredients

- 1/2 c. almond flour
- 2 tbsps flax meal
- 1 tsp. cinnamon, ground
- 1 1/2 c. almond milk, unsweetened
- Salt, to taste
- 2 tbsps chia seeds
- 10-15 drops liquid stevia
- 1 tsp. vanilla extract

Directions

1. Begin by taking a large mixing bowl and adding in the almond flour, ground cinnamon, flax seed powder, and chia seeds. Mix properly to combine.
2. Position a stockpot on low heat and add in the dry ingredients. Also add in the liquid stevia, vanilla extract, and almond milk. Mix well to combine.
3. Combine the flour and almond milk for about 4 minutes. Add salt if needed.
4. Move the oatmeal to a serving bowl and top with nuts, seeds, and berries.

Nutrition

- Protein 11.7 g.
- Fat 24.3 g.
- Carbohydrates 16.7 g.

31. Tofu and Vegetable Scramble

PREPARATION TIME: 10'

COOKING TIME: 15'

SERVINGS: 2

Ingredients

- 16 oz. firm tofu, drained
- 1/2 tsp. sea salt
- 1 tsp. garlic powder
- Fresh coriander, for garnishing
- 1/2 medium red onion
- 1 tsp. cumin powder
- 1 tsp. turmeric
- 1 tsp. chili powder
- Water
- Lemon juice, for topping
- 1/2 tsp. chili flakes
- 1 medium green bell pepper
- 1 tomato

Directions

1. Begin by preparing the ingredients. For this, extract the seeds of the tomato and green bell pepper. Shred the onion, bell pepper, and tomato into small cubes.
2. Get a small mixing bowl and position the tofu inside it. Make use of your hands to break the tofu. Set aside.
3. Get a nonstick pan and add in the onion, tomato, and bell pepper. Mix and cook for about 3 minutes.
4. Put the crumbled tofu into the pan and combine well.
5. Get a small bowl and put in water, turmeric, garlic powder, cumin powder, and chili powder. Combine well and stream it over the tofu and vegetable mixture.
6. Allow the tofu and vegetable crumble cook with seasoning for 5 minutes. Continuously stir so that the pan is not holding the ingredients.
7. Drizzle the tofu scramble with chili flakes and salt. Combine well.
8. Transfer the prepared scramble to a serving bowl and give it a proper spray of lemon juice.
9. Finalize by garnishing with fresh coriander. Serve while hot!

Nutrition

- Calories 238
- Carbohydrates 16.6 g.
- Fat 11 g.

32. Breakfast Smoothie Bowl with Fresh Berries

PREPARATION TIME: 10'

COOKING TIME: 5'

SERVINGS: 2

Ingredients

- 1/2 c. almond milk, unsweetened
- 1/2 tsp. psyllium husk powder
- 2 oz. strawberries, chopped
- 1 tbsp. coconut oil
- 3 c. crushed ice
- 5-10 drops liquid stevia
- 1/3 c. pea protein powder
- Coconut flakes
- Strawberries

Directions

1. Begin by taking a blender and adding in the mashed ice cubes. Allow them to rest for about 30 seconds.
2. Then put in the almond milk, shredded strawberries, pea protein powder, psyllium husk powder, coconut oil, and liquid stevia. Blend well until it turns into a smooth and creamy puree.
3. Pour the prepared smoothie into 2 glasses.
4. Cover with coconut flakes and strawberries.

Nutrition

- Calories 166
- Fat 9.2 g.
- Carbohydrates 4.1 g.
- Protein 17.6 g.

33. Chia and Coconut Pudding

Preparation Time: 10'
Cooking Time: 5'
Servings: 2

Ingredients

- 7 oz. light coconut milk
- 3–4 drops of liquid stevia
- 1 kiwi
- 1/4 c. chia seeds
- 1 clementine
- Shredded coconut, unsweetened

Directions

1. Begin by getting a mixing bowl and putting in the light coconut milk. Set in the liquid stevia to sweeten the milk. Combine well.
2. Put the chia seeds into the milk and whisk until well-combined. Set aside.
3. Scrape the clementine and carefully extract the skin from the wedges. Leave aside.
4. Also, scrape the kiwi and dice it into small pieces.
5. Get a glass jar and gather the pudding. For this, position the fruits at the bottom of the jar; then put a dollop of chia pudding. Then spray the fruits and then put another layer of chia pudding.
6. Finalize by garnishing with the rest of the fruits and chopped coconut.

Nutrition

- Calories
- Protein 5.4 g.
- Fat 10 g.
- Carbohydrates 22.8 g.

34. Tomato and Zucchini Saute'

Preparation Time: 10'
Cooking Time: 43'
Servings: 6

Ingredients

- 1 tbsp. vegetable oil
- 2 tomatoes, chopped
- 1 green bell pepper, chopped
- Black pepper, freshly ground, to taste
- 1 onion, sliced
- 2 lbs. zucchini, peeled and cut into 1-in.-thick slices
- Salt, to taste
- 1/4 c. uncooked white rice

Directions

1. Begin by getting a nonstick pan and putting it over low heat. Stream in the oil and allow it to heat through.
2. Put in the onion and sauté for about 3 minutes.
3. Then pour in the zucchini and green peppers. Mix well and spice with black pepper and salt.
4. Reduce the heat and cover the pan with a lid. Allow the veggies to cook on low for 5 minutes.
5. While you're done, put in the water and rice. Place the lid back on and cook on low for 20 minutes.

Nutrition

- Calories 94
- Fat 2.8 g.
- Protein 3.2 g.
- Carbohydrates 16.1 g.

35. Steamed Kale with Mediterranean Dressing

Preparation Time: 10'
Cooking Time: 25'
Servings: 6

Ingredients

- 12 c. kale, chopped
- 1 tbsp. olive oil
- 1 tsp. soy sauce
- Pepper, freshly ground, to taste
- 2 tbsps lemon juice
- 1 tbsp. garlic, minced
- Salt, to taste

Directions

1. Get a gas steamer or an electric steamer and fill the bottom pan with water. If you're making use of a gas steamer, position it on high heat. If you're making use of an electric steamer, place it in the highest setting.
2. Immediately the water comes to a boil, put in the shredded kale, and cover with a lid. Boil for about 8 minutes. The kale should be tender by now.
3. While the kale is boiling, take a big mixing bowl and put in the olive oil, lemon juice, soy sauce, garlic, pepper, and salt. Whisk well to mix.
4. Now toss in the steamed kale and carefully enclose it into the dressing. Be assured the kale is well-coated.
5. Serve while it's hot!

Nutrition

- Calories 91
- Fat 3.5 g.
- Protein 4.6 g.
- Carbohydrates 14.5 g.

36. Healthy Carrot Muffins

Preparation Time: 10'
Cooking Time: 40'
Servings: 8

Ingredients

Dry Ingredients:
- 1/4 c. tapioca starch
- 1 tsp. baking soda
- 1 tbsp. cinnamon
- 1/4 tsp. cloves

Wet Ingredients:
- 1 tsp. vanilla extract
- 1 1/2 c. water
- 1 1/2 c. carrots, shredded
- 1 3/4 c. almond flour
- 1/2 c. granulated sweetener of choice
- 1 tsp. baking powder
- 1 tsp. nutmeg
- 1 tsp. salt
- 1/3 c. coconut oil
- 4 tbsps flax meal
- 1 medium banana, mashed

Directions

1. Begin by heating the oven to 350 °F.
2. Get a muffin tray and position paper cups in all the molds. Set aside.
3. Get a small glass bowl and put half a cup of water and a flax meal. Allow this to rest for about 5 minutes. Your flax egg is ready.
4. Get a large mixing bowl and put in the almond flour, tapioca starch, granulated sugar, baking soda, baking powder, cinnamon, nutmeg, cloves, and salt. Mix well to combine.
5. Form a well in the middle of the flour mixture and pour in the coconut oil, vanilla extract, and flax egg. Mix well to make a mushy dough.
6. Then put in the chopped carrots and mashed banana. Mix until well-combined.
7. Make use of a spoon to scoop out an equal amount of mixture into 8 muffin cups.
8. Position the muffin tray in the oven and allow it to bake for about 40 minutes.
9. Extract the tray from the oven and allow the muffins to set for about 10 minutes.
10. Extract the muffin cups from the tray and allow them to chill until they reach room temperature.
11. Serve and enjoy!

Nutrition

- Calories 189
- Fat 13.9 g.
- Protein 3.8 g.
- Carbohydrates 17.3 g.

37. Vegetable Noodles Stir-Fry

Preparation time: 10'

Cooking time: 40'

Servings: 4

Ingredients

- 8 oz. zucchini
- 2 large garlic cloves, finely chopped
- 2 tbsps vegetable broth
- Salt, to taste
- 8 oz. carrots
- 1 shallot, finely chopped
- 1 red chili, finely chopped
- 1 tbsp. olive oil
- Pepper, to taste

Directions

1. Begin by scrapping the carrots. Make use of a spiralizer to make noodles out of the carrots.
2. Rinse the zucchini thoroughly and spiralize it as well.
3. Get a large skillet and position it on a high flame. Stream in the vegetable broth and allow it to come to a boil.
4. Toss in the spiralized carrots. Then put in the chili, garlic, and shallots. Stir everything using tongs and cook for some minutes.
5. Transfer the vegetable noodles into a serving platter and generously spice with pepper and salt.
6. Finalize by sprinkling olive oil over the noodles. Serve while hot!

Nutrition

- Calories 169
- Fat 3.7 g.
- Protein 3.6 g.
- Carbohydrates 31.2 g.

Chapter 5: Lunch

38. Cauliflower Rice with Chicken

Preparation time: 15'
Cooking time: 15'
Servings: 4

Ingredients

- 1/2 large cauliflower
- 3/4 c. cooked meat
- 1/2 bell pepper
- 1 carrot
- 2 ribs celery
- 1 tbsp. stir fry sauce (low carb)
- 1 tbsp. extra-virgin olive oil
- Salt and pepper to taste

Directions

1. Chop cauliflower in a processor to "rice." Place in a bowl.
2. Properly chop all vegetables in a food processor into thin slices.
3. Add cauliflower and other plants to a wok with heated oil. Fry until all veggies are tender.
4. Add chopped meat and sauce to the wok and fry for 10 minutes.
5. Serve.

This dish is very mouth-watering!

Nutrition

- Calories 200
- Protein 10 g.
- Fat 12 g.
- Carbohydrates 10 g.

39. Turkey with Fried Eggs

PREPARATION TIME: **10'**

COOKING TIME: **20'**

SERVINGS: **4**

Ingredients

- 1 cooked turkey thigh
- 1 large onion (about 2 c. diced)
- Butter
- Chile flakes
- 4 eggs
- Salt to taste
- Pepper to taste

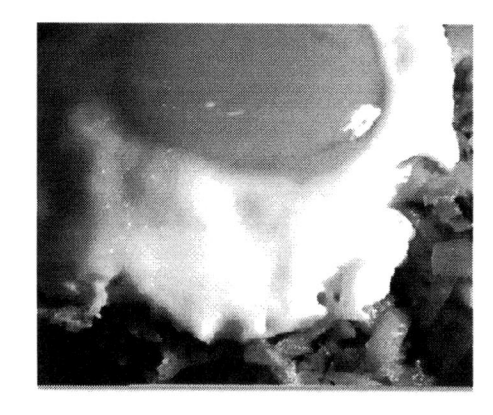

Directions

1. Dice the turkey.
2. Cook the onion in as much unsalted butter as you feel comfortable with until it's fragrant and translucent.
3. Add 1 c of diced cooked turkey, salt, and pepper to taste, and cook for 20 minutes.
4. Top each with a fried egg. Yummy!

Nutrition

- Calories 170
- Protein 19 g.
- Fat 7 g.
- Carbohydrates 6 g.

40. Kale and White Bean Stew

Preparation time: 15'
Cooking time: 25'
Servings: 4

Ingredients

- 1 (15-oz.) can low-sodium cannellini beans, rinsed and drained, divided
- 1 tbsp. olive oil
- 1 medium onion, chopped
- 2 garlic cloves, minced
- 2 celery stalks, chopped
- 3 medium carrots, chopped
- 2 c. low-sodium vegetable broth
- 1 tsp. apple cider vinegar
- 2 c. chopped kale
- 1 c. shelled edamame
- 1/4 c. quinoa
- 1 tsp. dried thyme
- 1/2 tsp. cayenne pepper
- 1/2 tsp. salt
- 1/4 tsp. freshly ground black pepper

Directions

1. Put half the beans into a blender and blend until smooth. Set aside.
2. In a large soup pot over medium heat, heat the oil. When the oil is shining, include the onion and garlic, and cook until the onion softens and the garlic is sweet, for about 3 minutes. Add the celery and carrots, and continue cooking until the vegetables soften, for about 5 minutes.
3. Add the broth, vinegar, unblended beans, kale, edamame, and quinoa, and bring the mixture to a boil. Reduce the heat and simmer until the vegetables soften, for about 10 minutes.
4. Add the blended beans, thyme, cayenne, salt, and black pepper, increase the heat to medium-high, and bring the mixture to a boil. Reduce the heat and simmer, uncovered, until the flavors combine, for about 5 minutes.
5. Into each of 4 containers, scoop 1 3/4 cups of stew.

Nutrition

- Calories 373
- Total fat 7 g.
- Saturated fat 1 g.
- Protein 15 g.
- Total carbs 65 g.
- Fiber 15 g.
- Sugar 13 g.
- Sodium 540 mg.

41. Slow Cooker Two-Bean Sloppy Joes

Preparation time: 10'
Cooking time: 6 hours
Servings: 4

Ingredients

- 1 (15-oz.) can of low-sodium black beans
- 1 (15-oz.) can of low-sodium pinto beans
- 1 (15-oz.) can of no-salt-added diced tomatoes
- 1 medium green bell pepper, cored, seeded, and chopped
- 1 medium yellow onion, chopped
- 1/4 c. low-sodium vegetable broth
- 2 garlic cloves, minced
- 2 servings (1/4 c.) meal prep barbecue sauce or bottled barbecue sauce
- 1/4 tsp. salt
- 1/4 tsp. freshly ground black pepper
- 4 whole-wheat buns

Directions

1. In a slow cooker, combine the black beans, pinto beans, diced tomatoes, bell pepper, onion, broth, garlic, meal prep barbecue sauce, salt, and black pepper. Stir the ingredients, then cover and cook on low for 6 hours.
2. Into each of 4 containers, spoon 1 1/4 c of sloppy joe mix. Serve with 1 whole-wheat bun.
3. Storage: place airtight containers in the refrigerator for up to 1 week. To freeze, place freezer-safe containers in the freezer for up to 2 months. To defrost, refrigerate overnight.

To reheat individual portions, microwave uncovered on high for 2–2 1/2 minutes. Alternatively, reheat the entire dish in a saucepan on the stovetop. Bring the sloppy joes to a boil, then reduce the heat and simmer until heated through, for 10–15 minutes. Serve with a whole-wheat bun.

Nutrition

- Calories 392
- Total fat 3 g.
- Saturated fat 0 g.
- Protein 17 g.
- Total carbs 79 g.
- Fiber 19 g.
- Sugar 15 g.
- Sodium 759 mg.

42. Lighter Eggplant Parmesan

Preparation time: 15'
Cooking time: 35'
Servings: 4

Ingredients

- Nonstick cooking spray
- 3 eggs, beaten
- 1 tbsp. dried parsley
- 2 tsps. ground oregano
- 1/8 tsp. freshly ground black pepper
- 1 c. panko bread crumbs, preferably whole-wheat
- 1 large eggplant (about 2 lbs.)
- 5 servings (2 1/2 c.) chunky tomato sauce or jarred low-sodium tomato sauce
- 1 c. part-skim mozzarella cheese
- 1/4 c. grated parmesan cheese

Directions

1. Preheat the oven to 450 °F. Coat a baking sheet with cooking spray.
2. In a medium bowl, whisk together the eggs, parsley, oregano, and pepper.
3. Pour the panko into a separate medium bowl.
4. Slice the eggplant into 1/4-in.-thick slices. Dip each slice of eggplant into the egg mixture, shaking off the excess. Then dredge both sides of the eggplant in the panko bread crumbs. Place the coated eggplant on the prepared baking sheet, leaving a 1/2-in. space between each slice.
5. Bake for about 15 minutes until soft and golden brown. Remove from the oven and set aside to slightly cool.
6. Pour 1/2 c of chunky tomato sauce on the bottom of an 8-by-15-in. baking dish. Using a spatula or the back of a spoon spread the tomato sauce evenly. Place half the slices of the cooked eggplant, slightly overlapping, in the dish, and top with 1 c of chunky tomato sauce, 1/2 c of mozzarella, and 2 tbsps of grated parmesan. Repeat the layer, ending with the cheese.
7. Bake uncovered for 20 minutes until the cheese is bubbling and slightly browned.
8. Remove from the oven and allow cooling for 15 minutes before dividing the eggplant equally into 4 separate containers.

Nutrition

- Calories 333
- Total fat 14 g.
- Saturated fat 6 g.
- Protein 20 g.
- Total carbs 35 g.
- Fiber 11 g.
- Sugar 15 g.
- Sodium 994 mg.

43. Coconut-Lentil Curry

Preparation time: 15'
Cooking time: 35'
Servings: 4

Ingredients

- 1 tbsp. olive oil
- 1 medium yellow onion, chopped
- 1 garlic clove, minced
- 1 medium red bell pepper, diced
- 1 (15-oz.) can green or brown lentils, rinsed and drained
- 1 (15-oz.) can no-salt-added diced tomatoes
- 2 tbsps tomato paste
- 4 tsps. curry powder
- 1/8 tsp. ground cloves
- 1 (15-oz.) can light coconut milk
- 1/4 tsp. salt
- 2 pieces' whole-wheat naan bread, halved, or 4 slices crusty bread

Directions

1. In a large saucepan over medium heat, heat the olive oil. When the oil is shimmering, add both the onion and garlic and cook until the onion softens and the garlic is sweet, for about 3 minutes.
2. Add the bell pepper and continue cooking until it softens, about 5 minutes more. Add the lentils, tomatoes, tomato paste, curry powder, and cloves, and bring the mixture to a boil. Reduce the heat to medium-low, cover, and simmer
3. Add the coconut milk and salt, and return to a boil. Reduce the heat and simmer until the flavors combine, for about 5 minutes.
4. Into each of 4 containers, spoon 2 c of curry.
5. Enjoy each serving with half of a piece of naan bread or 1 slice of crusty bread.

Nutrition

- Calories 559
- Total fat 16 g.
- Saturated fat 7 g.
- Protein 16 g.
- Total carbs 86 g.
- Fiber 16 g.
- Sugar 18 g.
- Sodium 819 mg.

44. Stuffed Portobello with Cheese

Preparation time: 15'
Cooking time: 25'
Servings: 4

Ingredients

- 4 portobello mushroom caps
- 1 tbsp. olive oil
- 1/2 tsp. salt, divided
- 1/4 tsp. freshly ground black pepper, divided
- 1 c. baby spinach, chopped
- 1 1/2 c. part-skim ricotta cheese
- 1/2 c. part-skim shredded mozzarella cheese
- 1/4 c. grated parmesan cheese
- 1 garlic clove, minced
- 1 tbsp. dried parsley
- 2 tsps. dried oregano
- 4 tsps. unseasoned bread crumbs, divided
- 4 servings (4 c.) roasted broccoli with shallots

Directions

1. Preheat the oven to 375 °F. Line a baking sheet with aluminum foil.
2. Brush the mushroom caps with olive oil, and sprinkle with 1/4 tsp. salt and 1/8 tsp. pepper. Put the mushroom caps on the prepared baking sheet and bake until soft, about 12 minutes.
3. In a medium bowl, mix together the spinach, ricotta, mozzarella, parmesan, garlic, parsley, oregano, and the remaining 1/4 tsp of salt and 1/8 tsp of pepper.
4. Spoon 1/2 c of cheese mixture into each mushroom cap, and sprinkle each with 1 tsp of bread crumbs. Return the mushrooms to the oven for an additional 8-10 minutes until warmed through.
5. Remove from the oven and allow the mushrooms to cool for about 10 minutes before placing each in an individual container. Add 1 c of roasted broccoli with shallots to each container.

Nutrition

- Calories 419
- Total fat 30 g.
- Saturated fat 10 g.
- Protein 23 g.
- Total carbs 19 g.
- Fiber 2 g.
- Sugar 3 g.
- Sodium 790 mg.

45. Lighter Shrimp Scampi

Preparation time: 15'
Cooking time: 15'
Servings: 4

Ingredients

- 1 1/2 lbs. large peeled and deveined shrimp
- 1/4 tsp. salt
- 1/8 tsp. freshly ground black pepper
- 2 tbsps olive oil
- 1 shallot, chopped
- 2 garlic cloves, minced
- 1/4 c. cooking white wine
- Juice of 1/2 lemon (1 tbsp.)
- 1/2 tsp. sriracha
- 2 tbsps unsalted butter, at room temperature
- 1/4 c. chopped fresh parsley
- 4 servings (6 c.) zucchini noodles with lemon vinaigrette

Directions

1. Season the shrimp with salt and pepper.
2. In a medium saucepan over medium heat, heat the oil. Add the shallot and garlic, and cook until the shallot softens and the garlic is fragrant, for about 3 minutes. Add the shrimp, cover, and cook until opaque, 2–3 minutes on each side. Using a slotted spoon, transfer the shrimp to a large plate.
3. Add the wine, lemon juice, and sriracha to the saucepan, and stir to combine. Bring the mixture to a boil, then reduce the heat and simmer until the liquid is reduced by about half, 3 minutes. Add the butter and stir until melted, about 3 minutes. Return the shrimp to the saucepan and toss to coat. Add the parsley and stir to combine.
4. Into each of 4 containers, place 1 1/2 c of zucchini noodles with lemon vinaigrette, and top with 3/4 c of scampi.

Nutrition

- Calories 364
- Total fat 21 g.
- Saturated fat 6 g.
- Protein 37 g.
- Total carbs 10 g.
- Fiber 2 g.
- Sugar 6 g.
- Sodium 557 mg.

46. Maple-Mustard Salmon

PREPARATION TIME: 10' + 30' MARINATING TIME

COOKING TIME: 20'

SERVINGS: 4

Ingredients

- Nonstick cooking spray
- 1/2 c. 100 % maple syrup
- 2 tbsps Dijon mustard
- 1/4 tsp. salt
- 4 (5-oz.) salmon fillets
- 4 servings (4 c.) roasted broccoli with shallots
- 4 servings (2 c.) parleyed whole-wheat couscous

Directions

1. Preheat the oven to 400 °F. Line a baking sheet with aluminum foil and coat with cooking spray.
2. In a medium bowl, whisk together the maple syrup, mustard, and salt until smooth.
3. Put the salmon fillets into the bowl and toss to coat. Cover and place in the refrigerator to marinate for at least 30 minutes and up to overnight.
4. Shake off excess marinade from the salmon fillets and place them on the prepared baking sheet, leaving a 1-in. space between each fillet. Discard the extra marinade.
5. Bake for about 20 minutes until the salmon is opaque and a thermometer inserted in the thickest part of a fillet reads 145 °F.
6. Into each of 4 resealable containers, place 1 salmon fillet, 1 c of roasted broccoli with shallots, and 1/2 c of parleyed whole-wheat couscous.

Nutrition

- Calories 601
- Total fat 29 g.
- Saturated fat 4 g.
- Protein 36 g.
- Total carbs 51 g.
- Fiber 3 g.
- Sugar 23 g.
- Sodium 610 mg.

47. Chicken Salad with Grapes and Pecans

PREPARATION TIME: 15'

COOKING TIME: 5'

SERVINGS: 4

Ingredients

- 1/3 c. unsalted pecans, chopped
- 10 oz. cooked skinless, boneless chicken breast or rotisserie chicken, finely chopped
- 1/2 medium yellow onion, finely chopped
- 1 celery stalk, finely chopped
- 3/4 c. red or green seedless grapes, halved
- 1/4 c. light mayonnaise
- 1/4 c. nonfat plain Greek yogurt
- 1 tbsp. Dijon mustard
- 1 tbsp. dried parsley
- 1/4 tsp. salt
- 1/8 tsp. freshly ground black pepper
- 1 c. shredded romaine lettuce
- 4 (8-in.) whole-wheat pitas

Directions

1. Heat a small skillet over medium-low heat to toast the pecans. Cook the pecans until fragrant, about 3 minutes. Remove from the heat and set aside to cool.
2. In a medium bowl, mix the chicken, onion, celery, pecans, and grapes.
3. In a small bowl, whisk together the mayonnaise, yogurt, mustard, parsley, salt, and pepper. Spoon the sauce over the chicken mixture and stir until well combined.
4. Into each of 4 containers, place 1/4 c of lettuce and top with 1 c of chicken salad. Store the pitas separately until ready to serve.
5. When ready to eat, stuff the serving of salad and lettuce into 1 pita.

Nutrition

- Calories 418
- Total fat 14 g.
- Saturated fat 2 g.
- Protein 31 g.
- Total carbs 43 g.
- Fiber 6 g.

48. Roasted Vegetables

PREPARATION TIME: 14'

COOKING TIME: 17'

SERVINGS: 3

Ingredients

- 4 tbsp. olive oil, reserve some for greasing
- 2 heads, large garlic, tops sliced off
- 2 large eggplants/aubergines, tops removed, cubed
- 2 large shallots, peeled, quartered
- 1 large carrot, peeled, cubed
- 1 large parsnip, peeled, cubed
- 1/2 tsp. rosemary leaves
- 1 small green bell pepper, deseeded, ribbed, cubed
- 1 small red bell pepper, deseeded, ribbed, cubed
- 1/2 lb. Brussels sprouts, halved, do not remove cores
- 1 sprig, large thyme, leaves picked
- Sea salt, coarse-grained

For garnish
- 1 large lemon, halved, 1/2 squeezed, 1/2 sliced into smaller wedges
- 1/8 c. fennel bulb, minced

Directions

1. From 425 °F or 220°C preheat the oven for at least 5 minutes before using.
2. Line deep roasting pan with aluminum foil; lightly grease with oil. Tumble in bell peppers, Brussels sprouts, carrots, eggplants, garlic, parsnips, rosemary leaves, shallots, and thyme. Add a pinch of sea salt; drizzle in remaining oil and lemon juice. Toss well to combine.
3. Cover roasting pan with a sheet of aluminum foil. Place this on the middle rack of the oven. Bake for 20–30 minutes. Remove aluminum foil. Roast, for another 5–10 minutes, or until the vegetables are brown at the edges. Remove roasting pan from oven. Cool slightly before ladling equal portions into plates.
4. Garnish with fennel and a wedge of lemon. Squeeze lemon juice on top of the dish before eating.

Nutrition

- Calories 163
- Total fat 4.2 g.
- Saturated fat 0.8 g.
- Cholesterol 0 mg.
- Sodium 861 mg.
- Total carbs 22.5 g.
- Fiber 6.3 g.
- Sugar 2.3 g.
- Protein 9.2 g.

49. Millet Pilaf

PREPARATION TIME: 10'

COOKING TIME: 15'

SERVINGS: 4

Ingredients

- 1 c. millet
- 2 tomatoes, rinsed, seeded, and chopped
- 1 3/4 cups filtered water
- 2 tbsps extra-virgin olive oil
- 1/4 c. chopped dried apricot
- Zest of 1 lemon
- Juice of 1 lemon
- 1/2 c. fresh parsley, rinsed and chopped
- Himalayan pink salt
- Freshly ground black pepper

Directions

1. In an electric pressure cooker, combine the millet, tomatoes, and water. Lock the lid into place, select Manual and High Pressure, and cook for 7 minutes.
2. When the beep sounds, quick release the pressure by pressing Cancel and twisting the steam valve to the Venting position. Carefully remove the lid.
3. Stir in olive oil, apricot, lemon zest, lemon juice, and parsley. Taste, season with salt and pepper and serve.

Nutrition

- Calories 270
- Total fat 8 g.
- Total carbohydrates 42 g.
- Fiber 5 g.
- Sugar 3 g.
- Protein 6 g.

50. Sweet and Sour Onions

PREPARATION TIME: **10'**

COOKING TIME: **11'**

SERVINGS: **4**

Ingredients

- 4 large onions, halved
- 2 garlic cloves, crushed
- 3 c. vegetable stock
- 1 1/2 tbsp. balsamic vinegar
- 1/2 teaspoon Dijon mustard
- 1 tbsp. sugar

Directions

1. Combine onions and garlic in a pan. Fry for 3 minutes, or till softened.
2. Pour stock, vinegar, Dijon mustard, and sugar. Bring to a boil.
3. Reduce heat. Cover and let the mixture simmer for 10 minutes.
4. Remove from the heat. Continue stirring until the liquid is reduced and the onions are brown. Serve.

Nutrition

- Calories 203
- Total Fat 41.2 g.
- Saturated Fat 0.8 g.
- Cholesterol 0 mg.
- Sodium 861 mg.
- Total Carbohydrates 29.5 g.
- Fiber 16.3 g.
- Sugar 29.3 g.
- Protein 19.2 g.

51. Sauteed Apples and Onions

PREPARATION TIME: **14'**

COOKING TIME: **16'**

SERVINGS: **3**

Ingredients

- 2 c. dry cider
- 1 large onion, halved
- 2 c. vegetable stock
- 4 apples, sliced into wedges
- Pinch of salt
- Pinch of pepper

Directions

1. Combine cider and onion in a saucepan. Bring to a boil until the onions are cooked and the liquid is almost gone.
2. Pour the stock and the apples. Season with salt and pepper. Stir occasionally. Cook for about 10 minutes or until the apples are tender but not mushy. Serve.

Nutrition

- Calories 343
- Total Fat 51.2 g.
- Saturated Fat 0.8 g.
- Cholesterol 0 mg.
- Sodium 861 mg.
- Total Carbohydrates 22.5 g.
- Fiber 6.3 g.
- Sugar 2.3 g.
- Protein 9.2 g.

52. Zucchini Noodles with Portobello Mushrooms

Preparation time: 14'
Cooking time: 16'
Servings: 3

Ingredients

- 1 zucchini, processed into spaghetti-like noodles
- 3 garlic cloves, minced
- 2 white onions, thinly sliced
- 1 thumb-sized ginger, julienned
- 1 lb. chicken thighs
- 1 lb. portobello mushrooms, sliced into thick slivers
- 2 c. chicken stock
- 3 c. water
- Pinch of sea salt, add more if needed
- Pinch of black pepper, add more if needed
- 2 tsp. sesame oil
- 4 tbsp. coconut oil, divided
- 1/4 c. fresh chives, minced, for garnish

Directions

1. Pour 2 tbsps of coconut oil into a large saucepan. Fry mushroom slivers in batches for 5 minutes or until seared brown. Set aside. Transfer these to a plate.
2. Sauté the onion, garlic, and ginger for 3 minutes or until tender. Add in chicken thighs, cooked mushrooms, chicken stock, water, salt, and pepper, and stir well. Bring to a boil.
3. Decrease gradually the heat and allow simmering for 20 minutes or until the chicken is forking tender. Add sesame oil.
4. Serve by placing an equal amount of zucchini noodles into bowls. Ladle soup and garnish with chives.

Nutrition

- Calories 163
- Total fat 4.2 g.
- Saturated fat 0.8 g.
- Cholesterol 0 mg.
- Sodium 861 mg.
- Total carbs 22.5 g.
- Fiber 6.3 g.
- Sugar 2.3 g.
- Protein 9.2 g

53. Grilled Tempeh with Pineapple

Preparation time: 12'
Cooking time: 16'
Servings: 3

Ingredients

- 10 oz. tempeh, sliced
- 1 red bell pepper, quartered
- 1/4 pineapple, sliced into rings
- 6 oz. green beans
- 1 tbsp. coconut aminos
- 2 1/2 tbsp. orange juice, freshly squeeze
- 1 1/2 tbsp. lemon juice, freshly squeezed
- 1 tbsp. extra-virgin olive oil
- 1/4 c. hoisin sauce

Directions

1. Blend together the olive oil, orange and lemon juices, coconut aminos or soy sauce, and hoisin sauce in a bowl. Add the diced tempeh and set aside.
2. Heat up the grill or place a grill pan over a medium-high flame. Once hot, lift the marinated tempeh from the bowl with a pair of tongs and transfer them to the grill or pan.
3. Grille for 2–3 minutes, or until browned all over.
4. Grill the sliced pineapples alongside the tempeh, then transfer them directly onto the serving platter.
5. Place the grilled tempeh beside the grilled pineapple and cover with aluminum foil to keep warm.
6. Meanwhile, place the green beans and bell peppers in a bowl and add just enough of the marinade to coat.
7. Prepare the grill pan and add the vegetables. Grill until fork tender and slightly charred.
8. Transfer the grilled vegetables to the serving platter and arrange artfully with the tempeh and pineapple. Serve at once.

Nutrition

- Calories 163
- Total fat 4.2 g.
- Saturated fat 0.8 g.
- Cholesterol 0 mg.
- Sodium 861 mg.
- Total carbs 22.5 g.
- Fiber 6.3 g.
- Sugar 2.3 g.
- Protein 9.2 g.

54. Courgettes in Cider Sauce

PREPARATION TIME: **13'**

COOKING TIME: **17'**

SERVINGS: **3**

Ingredients

- 2 c. baby courgettes
- 3 tbsps vegetable stock
- 2 tbsps apple cider vinegar
- 1 tbsp. light brown sugar
- 4 spring onions, finely sliced
- 1-piece fresh ginger root, grated
- The rind of 1 lemon
- Juice of 1 lemon
- The rind of 1 orange
- Juice of 1 orange
- 1 tsp. cornflour
- 2 tsps. water

Directions

1. Bring a pan with salted water to a boil. Add courgettes. Bring to a boil for 5 minutes.
2. Meanwhile, in a pan, combine vegetable stock, apple cider vinegar, brown sugar, onions, ginger root, lemon juice and rind, and orange juice and rind. Take to a boil. Lower the heat and allow simmering for 3 minutes.
3. Mix the cornflour with water. Stir well. Pour into the sauce. Continue stirring until the sauce thickens.
4. Drain courgettes. Transfer to the serving dish. Spoon over the sauce. Toss to coat courgettes. Serve.

Nutrition

- Calories 173
- Total fat 9.2 g.
- Saturated fat 0.8 g.
- Cholesterol 0 mg.
- Sodium 861 mg.
- Total carbs 22.5 g.
- Fiber 6.3 g.
- Sugar 2.3 g.
- Protein 9.2 g.

55. Baked Mixed Mushrooms

71

PREPARATION TIME: **8'**

COOKING TIME: **20'**

SERVINGS: **3**

Ingredients

- 2 c. mixed wild mushrooms
- 1 c. chestnut mushrooms
- 2 c. dried porcini
- 2 shallots
- 4 garlic cloves
- 3 c. raw pecans
- 1/2 bunch fresh thyme
- 1 bunch flat-leaf parsley
- 2 tbsps olive oil
- 2 fresh bay leaves
- 1 1/2 c. stale bread
- Pinch of black pepper and sea salt

Directions

1. Remove skin and finely chop garlic and shallots. Roughly chop the wild mushrooms and chestnut mushrooms. Pick the leaves of the thyme and tear the bread into small pieces. Put inside the pressure cooker.
2. Place the pecans and roughly chop the nuts. Pick the parsley leaves and roughly chop.
3. Place the porcini in a bowl then add 300 ml of boiling water. Set aside until needed.
4. Heat oil in the pressure cooker. Add the garlic and shallots. Cook for 3 minutes while stirring occasionally.
5. Drain porcini and reserve the liquid. Add the porcini into the pressure cooker together with the wild mushrooms and chestnut mushrooms. Add the bay leaves and thyme.
6. Position the lid and lock it in place. Put to high heat and bring to high pressure. Adjust heat to stabilize. Cook for 10 minutes. Adjust taste if necessary.
7. Transfer the mushroom mixture into a bowl and set aside to cool completely.
8. Once the mushrooms are completely cool, add the bread, pecans, a pinch of black pepper and sea salt, and half of the reserved liquid into the bowl. Mix well. Add more reserved liquid if the mixture seems dry.
9. Add more than half of the parsley into the bowl and stir. Transfer the mixture into a 20x25 cm. lightly greased baking dish and cover with tin foil.
10. Bake in the oven for 35 minutes. Then, get rid of the foil and cook for another 10 minutes. Once done, sprinkle the remaining parsley on top and serve with bread or crackers.

Nutrition

- Calories 343
- Total fat 4.2 g.
- Saturated fat 0.8 g.
- Cholesterol 0 mg.
- Sodium 861 mg.
- Total carbs 22.5 g.
- Fiber 6.3 g.
- Sugar 2.3 g.
- Protein 9.2 g.

56. Spiced Okra

Preparation time: 14'

Cooking time: 16'

Servings: 3

Ingredients

- 2 c. okra
- 1/4 tsp. stevia
- 1 tsp. chili powder
- 1/2 teaspoon ground turmeric
- 1 tbsp. ground coriander
- 2 tbsps fresh coriander, chopped
- 1 tbsp. ground cumin
- 1/4 tsp. salt
- 1 tbsp. desiccated coconut
- 3 tbsps vegetable oil
- 1/2 teaspoon black mustard seeds
- 1/2 teaspoon cumin seeds
- Fresh tomatoes, to garnish

Directions

1. Trim the okra. Wash and dry.
2. Combine stevia, chili powder, turmeric, ground coriander, fresh coriander, cumin, salt, and desiccated coconut in a bowl.
3. Heat the oil in a pan. Cook mustard and cumin seeds for 3 minutes. Stir continuously. Add okra. Tip in the spice mixture. Cook on low heat for 8 minutes.
4. Transfer to a serving dish. Garnish with fresh tomatoes.

Nutrition

- Calories 163
- Total fat 4.2 g.
- Saturated fat 0.8 g.
- Cholesterol 0 mg.
- Sodium 861 mg.
- Total carbs 22.5 g.
- Fiber 6.3 g.
- Sugar 2.3 g.
- Protein 9.2 g.

57. Lemony Salmon Burgers

Preparation time: 10'

Cooking time: 10'

Servings: 4

Ingredients

- 2 (3-oz) cans boneless, skinless pink salmon
- 1/4 c. panko breadcrumbs
- 4 tsp. lemon juice
- 1/4 c. red bell pepper
- 1/4 c. sugar-free yogurt
- 1 egg
- 2 (1.5-oz) whole wheat hamburger

Directions

1. Mix drained and flaked salmon, finely-chopped bell pepper, panko breadcrumbs.
2. Combine 2 tbsp. sugar-free yogurt, 3 tsp. fresh lemon juice, and egg in a bowl. Shape mixture into 2 (3-in.) patties, bake on the skillet over medium heat for 4–5 minutes per side.
3. Stir together 2 tbsp. sugar-free yogurt and 1 tsp. lemon juice; spread over bottom halves of buns.
4. Top each with 1 patty, and cover with bun tops.
5. This dish is very mouth-watering!

Nutrition

- Calories 131
- Protein 12 g.
- Fat 1 g.
- Carbohydrates 19 g.

58. Caprese Turkey Burgers

Preparation Time: 10'
Cooking Time: 10'
Servings: 4

Ingredients

- 1/2 lb. 93 % lean ground turkey
- 2 (1.5-oz) whole-wheat hamburger buns (toasted)
- 1/4 c. shredded mozzarella cheese (part-skim)
- 1 egg
- 1 big tomato
- 1 small clove garlic
- 4 large basil leaves
- 1/8 tsp. salt
- 1/8 tsp. pepper

Directions

1. Mix turkey, white egg, minced garlic, salt, and pepper until combined.
2. Shape into 2 cutlets. Put the cutlets into a skillet; cook for 5 / minutes per side.
3. Top cutlets properly with cheese and sliced tomato at the end of cooking.
4. Put 1 cutlet on the bottom of each bun.
5. Top each patty with 2 basil leaves. Cover with bun tops.
6. My guests enjoy this dish every time they visit my home.

Nutrition

- Calories 180
- Protein / g.
- Fat 4 g.
- Carbohydrates 20 g.

59. Pasta Salad

Preparation Time: 15'
Cooking Time: 15'
Servings: 4

Ingredients

- 8 oz. whole-wheat pasta
- 2 tomatoes
- 1 (5-oz) pkg. spring mix
- 9 slices bacon
- 1/3 c. mayonnaise (reduced-fat)
- 1 tbsp. Dijon mustard
- 3 tbsp. apple cider vinegar
- 1/4 tsp. salt
- 1/2 tsp. pepper

Directions

1. Cook pasta.
2. Chilled pasta, chopped tomatoes, and spring mix in a bowl.
3. Crumble cooked bacon over pasta.
4. Combine mayonnaise, mustard, vinegar, salt, and pepper in a small bowl.
5. Pour dressing over pasta, stirring to coat.
6. Understanding diabetes is the first step in curing.

Nutrition

- Calories 200
- Protein 15 g.
- Fat 3 g.
- Carbohydrates 6 g.

60. Chicken, Strawberry, and Avocado Salad

Preparation time: 10'

Cooking time: 5'

Servings: 4

Ingredients

- 1.5 c. chicken (skin removed)
- 1/4 c. almonds
- 2 (5-oz) pkg. salad greens
- 1 (16-oz) pkg. strawberries
- 1 avocado
- 1/4 c. green onion
- 1/4 c. lime juice
- 3 tbsp. extra-virgin olive oil
- 2 tbsp. honey
- 1/4 tsp. salt
- 1/4 tsp. pepper

Directions

1. Toast almonds until golden and fragrant.
2. Mix lime juice, oil, honey, salt, and pepper.
3. Mix greens, sliced strawberries, chicken, diced avocado, and sliced green onion, and sliced almonds; drizzle with dressing. Toss to coat.
4. Yummy!

Nutrition

- Calories 150
- Protein 15 g.
- Fat 10 g.
- Carbohydrates 5 g.

61. Lemon-Thyme Eggs

Preparation time: 10'

Cooking time: 5'

Servings: 4

Ingredients

- 7 large eggs
- 1/4 c. mayonnaise (reduced-fat)
- 2 tsp. lemon juice
- 1 tsp. Dijon mustard
- 1 tsp. chopped fresh thyme
- 1/8 tsp. cayenne pepper

Directions

1. Bring eggs to a boil.
2. Peel and cut each egg in half lengthwise.
3. Remove the yolks to a bowl. Add mayonnaise, lemon juice, mustard, thyme, and cayenne to the egg yolks; mash to blend. Fill the egg white halves with the yolk mixture.
4. Chill until ready to serve.
5. Please your family with a delicious meal.

Nutrition

- Calories 40
- Protein 10 g.
- Fat 6 g.
- Carbohydrates 2 g.

62. Spinach Salad with Bacon

PREPARATION TIME: **15'**

COOKING TIME: **0'**

SERVINGS: **4**

Ingredients

- 8 slices center-cut bacon
- 3 tbsp. extra-virgin olive oil
- 1 (5-oz) pkg. baby spinach
- 1 tbsp. apple cider vinegar
- 1 tsp. Dijon mustard
- 1/2 tsp. honey
- 1/4 tsp. salt
- 1/2 tsp. pepper

Directions

1. Mix vinegar, mustard, honey, salt, and pepper in a bowl.
2. Whisk in oil. Place spinach in a serving bowl; drizzle with dressing, and toss to coat.
3. Sprinkle with cooked and crumbled bacon.

Nutrition

- Calories 110
- Protein 6 g.
- Fat 2 g.
- Carbohydrates 1 g.

63. Pea and Collards Soup

PREPARATION TIME: **10'**

COOKING TIME: **50'**

SERVINGS: **4**

Ingredients

- 1/2 (16-oz) pkg. black-eyed peas
- 1 onion
- 2 carrots
- 1.5 c. ham (low-sodium)
- 1 (1-lb) bunch collard greens (trimmed)
- 1 tbsp. extra-virgin olive oil
- 2 cloves garlic
- 1/2 tsp. black pepper
- Hot sauce

Directions

1. Sauté chopped onion and carrots for 10 minutes.
2. Add peas, diced ham, collards, and minced garlic. Cook for 5 minutes.
3. Add broth, 3 c. water, and pepper. Bring to a boil; simmer for 35 minutes, adding water if needed.
4. Serve with favorite sauce.

Nutrition

- Calories 86
- Protein 15 g.
- Fat 2 g.
- Carbohydrates 9 g.

64. Spanish Stew

PREPARATION TIME: 10'

COOKING TIME: 25'

SERVINGS: 4

Ingredients

- 1.1/2 (12-oz) pkg. smoked chicken sausage links
- 1 (5-oz) pkg. baby spinach
- 1 (15-oz) can chickpeas
- 1 (14.5-oz) can tomatoes with basil, garlic, and oregano
- 1/2 tsp. smoked paprika
- 1/2 tsp. cumin
- 3/4 c. onions
- 1 tbsp. extra-virgin olive oil

Directions

1. Cook sliced sausage in hot oil until browned. Remove from the pot.
2. Add chopped onions; cook until tender.
3. Add sausage, drained and rinsed chickpeas, diced tomatoes, paprika, and ground cumin. Cook for 15 minutes.
4. Add in spinach; cook for 1-2 minutes.
5. This dish is ideal for every day and for a festive table.

Nutrition

- Calories 200
- Protein 10 g.
- Fat 20 g.
- Carbohydrates 1 g.

76

65. Creamy Taco Soup

PREPARATION TIME: 10'

COOKING TIME: 20'

SERVINGS: 4

Ingredients

- 3/4 lb. ground sirloin
- 1/2 (8-oz) cream cheese
- 1/2 onion
- 1 clove garlic
- 1 (10-oz) can tomatoes and green chilies
- 1 (14.5-oz) can beef broth
- 1/4 c. heavy cream
- 1.5 tsp. cumin
- 1/2 tsp. chili powder
- Pepper and salt to taste

Directions

1. Cook beef, chopped onion, and minced garlic until the meat is browned and crumbly; drain and return to pot.
2. Add ground cumin, chili powder, and cream cheese cut into small pieces and softened, stirring until cheese is melted.
3. Add diced tomatoes, broth, and cream; bring to a boil, and simmer for 10 minutes. Season with pepper and salt to taste.
4. You've got to give someone the recipe for this soup dish!

Nutrition

- Calories 60
- Protein 3 g.
- Fat 1 g.
- Carbohydrates 8 g.

66. Chicken with Caprese Salsa

PREPARATION TIME: **15'**

COOKING TIME: **5'**

SERVINGS: **4**

Ingredients

- 3/4 lb. boneless, skinless chicken breasts
- 2 big tomatoes
- 1/2 (8-oz) ball fresh mozzarella cheese
- 1/4 c. red onion
- 2 tbsp. fresh basil
- 1 tbsp. balsamic vinegar
- 2 tbsp. extra-virgin olive oil (divided)
- 1/2 tsp. salt (divided)
- 1/4 tsp. pepper (divided)

Directions

1. Sprinkle cut in half lengthwise chicken with 1/4 tsp. salt and 1/8 tsp. pepper.
2. Heat 1 tbsp. olive oil and cook the chicken for 5 minutes.
3. Meanwhile, mix chopped tomatoes, diced cheese, finely chopped onion, chopped basil, vinegar, 1 tbsp. oil, and 1/4 tsp. salt and 1/8 tsp. pepper.
4. Spoon salsa over the chicken.
5. Chicken with Caprese Salsa is a nutritious, simple, and very tasty dish that can be prepared in a few minutes.

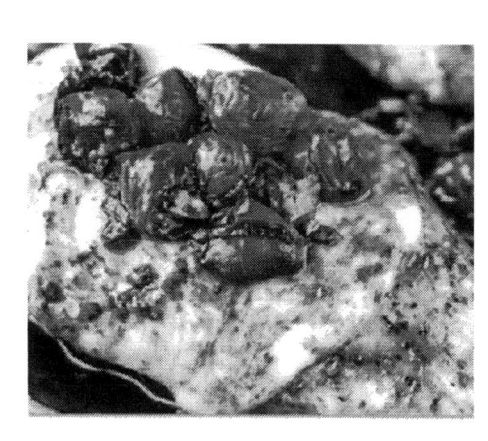

Nutrition

- Calories 210
- Protein 28 g.
- Fat 17 g.
- Carbohydrates 0,1 g.

67. Balsamic-Roasted Broccoli

PREPARATION TIME: **10'**

COOKING TIME: **15'**

SERVINGS: **4**

Ingredients

- 1 lb. broccoli
- 1 tbsp. extra-virgin olive oil
- 1 tbsp. balsamic vinegar
- 1 clove garlic
- 1/8 tsp. salt
- Pepper to taste

Directions

1. Preheat the oven to 450 °F.
2. Combine broccoli, olive oil, vinegar, minced garlic, salt, and pepper; toss.
3. Spread the broccoli on a baking sheet.
4. Bake for 12-15 minutes.
5. Really good!

Nutrition

- Calories 27
- Protein 3 g.
- Fat 0,3 g.
- Carbohydrates 4 g.

68. Hearty Beef and Vegetable Soup

Preparation time: 10'
Cooking time: 30'
Servings: 4

Ingredients

- 1/2 lb. lean ground beef
- 2 c. beef broth
- 1.5 tbsp. vegetable oil (divided)
- 1 c. green bell pepper
- 1/2 c. red onion
- 1 c. green cabbage
- 1 c. frozen mixed vegetables
- 1/2 can tomatoes
- 1.5 tsp. Worcestershire sauce
- 1 small bay leaf
- 1.8 tsp. pepper
- 2 tbsp. ketchup

Directions

1. Cook beef in 1/2 tbsp. hot oil for 2 minutes.
2. Stir in chopped bell pepper and chopped onion; cook for 4 minutes.
3. Add chopped cabbage, mixed vegetables, stewed tomatoes, broth, Worcestershire sauce, bay leaf, and pepper; bring to a boil.
4. Reduce heat to medium; cover, and cook for 15 minutes.
5. Stir in ketchup and 1 tbsp. oil, and remove from heat. Let stand for 10 minutes.
6. The right diet is an excellent diabetes remedy.

Nutrition

- Calories 170
- Protein 17 g.
- Fat 8 g.
- Carbohydrates 3 g.

69. Cauliflower Muffin

Preparation time: 15'
Cooking time: 30'
Servings: 4

Ingredients

- 2.5 c. cauliflower
- 2/3 c. ham
- 2.5 c of cheese
- 2/3 c. champignon
- 1.5 tbsp. flaxseed
- 3 eggs
- 1/4 tsp. salt
- 1/8 tsp. pepper

Directions

1. Preheat the oven to 375 °F.
2. Put muffin liners in a 12-muffin tin.
3. Combine diced cauliflower, ground flaxseed, beaten eggs, cup diced ham, grated cheese, and diced mushrooms, salt, pepper.
4. Divide mixture rightly between muffin liners.
5. Bake 30 minutes.
6. This is a great lunch for the whole family.

Nutrition

- Calories 116
- Protein 10 g.
- Fat 7 g.
- Carbohydrates 3 g.

70. Ham and Egg Cup

PREPARATION TIME: **10'**

COOKING TIME: **15'**

SERVINGS: **4**

Ingredients

- 5 slices ham
- 4 tbsp. cheese
- 1.5 tbsp. cream
- 3 egg whites
- 1.5 tbsp. pepper (green)
- 1 tsp. salt
- Pepper to taste

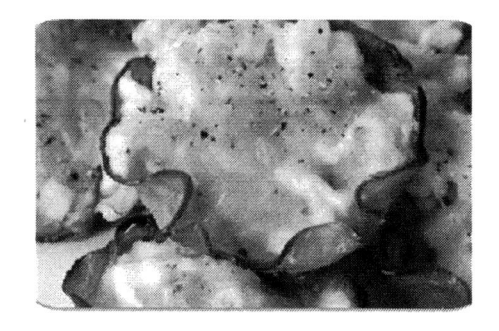

Directions

1. Preheat the oven to 350 °F.
2. Arrange each slice of thinly sliced ham into 4 muffin tin.
3. Put 1/4 of grated cheese into a ham cup.
4. Mix eggs, cream, salt, and pepper and divide it into 2 tins.
5. Bake in the oven for 15 minutes; after baking, sprinkle with green onions.
6. If you want to keep your current shape, also pay attention to this dish.

Nutrition

- Calories 180
- Protein 13 g.
- Fat 13 g.
- Carbohydrates 2 g.

Chapter 6: Dinner

71. Cauliflower Mac and Cheese

PREPARATION TIME: 5'

COOKING TIME: 25'

SERVINGS: 4

Ingredients

- 1 cauliflower head, torn into florets
- Salt and black pepper, as needed
- 1/4 c. almond milk, unsweetened
- 1/4 c. heavy cream
- 3 tbsp. butter, preferably grass-fed
- 1 c. cheddar cheese, shredded

Directions

1. Preheat the oven to 450 °F.
2. Melt the butter in a small microwave-safe bowl and heat it for 30 seconds.
3. Pour the melted butter over the cauliflower florets along with salt and pepper. Toss them well.
4. Place the cauliflower florets in a parchment paper-covered large baking sheet.
5. Bake them for 15 minutes or until the cauliflower is crisp-tender.
6. Once baked, mix the heavy cream, cheddar cheese, almond milk, and the remaining butter in a large microwave-safe bowl and heat it on high heat for 2 minutes or until the cheese mixture is smooth. Repeat the procedure until the cheese has melted.
7. Finally, stir in the cauliflower to the sauce mixture and coat well.

Nutrition

- Calories 294
- Fat 23 g.
- Carbohydrates 7 g.
- Proteins 11 g.

72. Easy Egg Salad

PREPARATION TIME: 5'

COOKING TIME: 15-20'

SERVINGS: 4

Ingredients

- 6 eggs, preferably free-range
- 1/4 tsp. salt
- 2 tbsp. mayonnaise
- 1 tsp. lemon juice
- 1 tsp. Dijon mustard
- Pepper, to taste
- Lettuce leaves, to serve

Directions

1. Keep the eggs in a saucepan of water and pour cold water until it covers the egg by another 1 in.
2. Bring to a boil and then remove the eggs from heat.
3. Peel the eggs under cold running water.
4. Transfer the cooked eggs into a food processor and pulse them until chopped.
5. Stir in the mayonnaise, lemon juice, salt, Dijon mustard, pepper and mix them well.
6. Taste for seasoning and add more if required.
7. Serve in the lettuce leaves.

Nutrition

- Calories 166
- Fat 14 g.
- Carbohydrates - 0.85 g.
- Proteins 10 g.
- Sodium 132 mg.

73. Baked Chicken Legs

Preparation Time: 10'
Cooking Time: 40'
Servings: 6

Ingredients

- 6 chicken legs
- 1/4 tsp. black pepper
- 1/4 c. butter
- 1/2 tsp. sea salt
- 1/2 tsp. smoked paprika
- 1/2 tsp. garlic powder

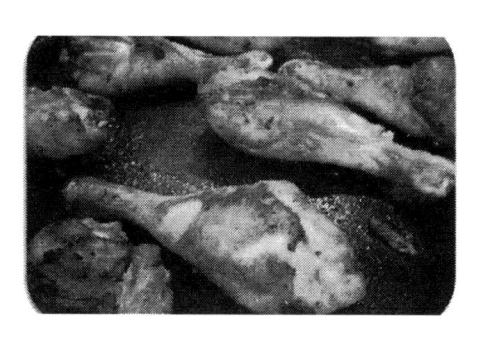

Directions

1. Preheat the oven to 425 °F.
2. Pat the chicken legs with a paper towel to absorb any excess moisture.
3. Marinate the chicken pieces by first applying the butter over them and then with the seasoning. Set it aside for a few minutes.
4. Bake them for 25 minutes. Turnover and bake for further 10 minutes or until the internal temperature reaches 165 °F.
5. Serve them hot.

Nutrition

- Calories 236
- Fat 16 g.
- Carbohydrates 0 g.
- Protein 22 g.
- Sodium 314 mg.

74. Creamed Spinach

Preparation Time: 5'
Cooking Time: 10'
Servings: 4

Ingredients

- 3 tbsp. butter
- 1/4 tsp. black pepper
- 4 cloves of garlic, minced
- 1/4 tsp. sea salt
- 10 oz. baby spinach, chopped
- 1 tsp. Italian seasoning
- 1/2 c. heavy cream
- 3 oz. cream cheese

Directions

1. Melt butter in a large sauté pan over medium heat.
2. Once the butter has melted, spoon in the garlic and sauté for 30 seconds or until aromatic.
3. Spoon in the spinach and cook for 3-4 minutes or until wilted.
4. Add all the remaining ingredients to it and continuously stir until the cream cheese melts and the mixture gets thickened.
5. Serve hot.

Nutrition

- Calories 274
- Fat 27 g.
- Carbohydrates 4 g.
- Protein 4 g.
- Sodium 114 mg.

75. Stuffed Mushrooms

Preparation time: 10'

Cooking time: 20'

Servings: 4

Ingredients

- 4 portobello mushrooms, large
- 1/2 c. mozzarella cheese, shredded
- 1/2 c. marinara, low-sugar
- Olive oil spray

Directions

1. Preheat the oven to 375 °F.
2. Take out the dark gills from the mushrooms with the help of a spoon.
3. Keep the mushroom stem upside down and spoon it with 2 tbsps of marinara sauce and mozzarella cheese.
4. Bake for 18 minutes or until the cheese is bubbly.

Nutrition

- Calories 113
- Fat 6 g.
- Carbohydrates 4 g.
- Protein 7 g.
- Sodium 14 mg.

76. Vegetable Soup

Preparation time: 10'

Cooking time: 30'

Servings: 5

Ingredients

- 8 c. vegetable broth
- 2 tbsp. olive oil
- 1 tbsp. Italian seasoning
- 1 onion, large and diced
- 2 bay leaves, dried
- 2 bell pepper, large and diced
- Sea salt and black pepper, as needed
- 4 cloves of garlic, minced
- 28 oz. tomatoes, diced
- 1 cauliflower head, medium and torn into florets
- 2 c. green beans, trimmed and chopped

Directions

1. Heat oil in a Dutch oven over medium heat.
2. Once the oil becomes hot, stir in the onions and pepper.
3. Cook for 10 minutes or until the onion is softened and browned.
4. Spoon in the garlic and sauté for a minute or until fragrant.
5. Add all the remaining ingredients to it. Mix until everything comes together.
6. Bring the mixture to a boil. Lower the heat and cook for further 20 minutes or until the vegetables have softened.
7. Serve hot.

Nutrition

- Calories 79
- Fat 2 g.
- Carbohydrates 8 g.
- Protein 2 g.
- Sodium 187 mg.

77. Pork Chop Diane

PREPARATION TIME: **10'**

COOKING TIME: **20'**

SERVINGS: **4**

Ingredients

- 1/4 c. low-sodium chicken broth
- 1 tbsp. freshly squeezed lemon juice
- 2 tsps. Worcestershire sauce
- 2 tsps. Dijon mustard
- 4 (5-oz.) boneless pork top loin chops
- 1 tsp. extra-virgin olive oil
- 1 tsp. lemon zest
- 1 tsp. butter
- 2 tsps. chopped fresh chives

Directions

1. Blend together the chicken broth, lemon juice, Worcestershire sauce, and Dijon mustard and set it aside.
2. Season the pork chops lightly.
3. Situate a large skillet over medium-high heat and add the olive oil.
4. Cook the pork chops, turning once, until they are no longer pink, about 8 minutes per side.
5. Put aside the chops.
6. Pour the broth mixture into the skillet and cook until warmed through and thickened, about 2 minutes.
7. Blend lemon zest, butter, and chives.
8. Garnish with a generous spoonful of sauce.

Nutrition

- Calories 200
- Fat 8 g.
- Carbohydrates 1 g.

78. Autumn Pork Chops with Red Cabbage and Apples

PREPARATION TIME: **15'**

COOKING TIME: **30'**

SERVINGS: **4**

Ingredients

- 1/4 c. apple cider vinegar
- 2 tbsps granulated sweetener
- 4 (4-oz.) pork chops, about 1 in. thick
- 1 tbsp. extra-virgin olive oil
- 1/2 red cabbage, finely shredded
- 1 sweet onion, thinly sliced
- 1 apple, peeled, cored, and sliced
- 1 tsp. chopped fresh thyme
- Salt and pepper, to taste

Directions

1. Mix vinegar and sweetener. Set it aside.
2. Season the pork with salt and pepper.
3. Position a big skillet over medium-high heat and add the olive oil.
4. Cook the pork chops until no longer pink, turning once, about 8 minutes per side.
5. Put chops aside.
6. Add the cabbage and onion to the skillet and sauté until the vegetables have softened, for about 5 minutes.
7. Add the vinegar mixture and the apple slices to the skillet and bring the mixture to a boil.
8. Adjust heat to low and simmer, covered, for 5 additional minutes.
9. Return the pork chops to the skillet, along with any accumulated juices and thyme, cover, and cook for 5 more minutes.

Nutrition

- Calories 223
- Carbohydrates 12 g.
- Fiber 3 g.

79. Chipotle Chili Pork Chops

PREPARATION TIME: 4 HOURS

COOKING TIME: 20'

SERVINGS: 4

Ingredients

- Juice and zest of 1 lime
- 1 tbsp. extra-virgin olive oil
- 1 tbsp. chipotle chili powder
- 2 tsps. minced garlic
- 1 tsp. ground cinnamon
- Pinch sea salt
- 4 (5-oz.) pork chops
- Lime wedges

Directions

1. Combine the lime juice and zest, oil, chipotle chili powder, garlic, cinnamon, and salt in a resealable plastic bag. Add the pork chops. Remove as much air as possible and seal the bag.
2. Marinate the chops in the refrigerator for at least 4 hours, and up to 24 hours, turning them several times.
3. Ready the oven to 400 °F and set a rack on a baking sheet. Let the chops rest at room temperature for 15 minutes, then arrange them on the rack and discard the remaining marinade.
4. Roast the chops until cooked through, turning once, about 10 minutes per side.
5. Serve with lime wedges.

Nutrition

- Calories 204
- Carbohydrates 1 g.
- Sugar 1 g.

80. Orange-Marinated Pork Tenderloin

PREPARATION TIME: 2H 30'

COOKING TIME: 30'

SERVINGS: 4

Ingredients

- 1/4 c. freshly squeezed orange juice
- 2 tsps. orange zest
- 2 tsps. minced garlic
- 1 tsp. low-sodium soy sauce
- 1 tsp. grated fresh ginger
- 1 tsp. honey
- 1 1/2 lbs. pork tenderloin roast
- 1 tbsp. extra-virgin olive oil

Directions

1. Blend together the orange juice, zest, garlic, soy sauce, ginger, and honey.
2. Pour the marinade into a resealable plastic bag and add the pork tenderloin.
3. Remove as much air as possible and seal the bag. Marinate the pork in the refrigerator, turning the bag a few times, for 2 hours.
4. Preheat the oven to 400 °F.
5. Pull out tenderloin from the marinade and discard the marinade.
6. Position big ovenproof skillet over medium-high heat and add the oil.
7. Sear the pork tenderloin on all sides, about 5 minutes in total.
8. Position skillet to the oven and roast for 25 minutes.
9. Put aside for 10 minutes before serving.

Nutrition

- Calories 228
- Carbohydrates 4 g.
- Sugar 3 g.

81. Homestyle Herb Meatballs

PREPARATION TIME: 10'

COOKING TIME: 15'

SERVINGS: 4

Ingredients

- 1/2-lb. lean ground pork
- 1/2-lb. lean ground beef
- 1 sweet onion, finely chopped
- 1/4 c. bread crumbs
- 2 tbsps chopped fresh basil
- 2 tsps. minced garlic
- 1 egg
- Salt and pepper, to taste

Directions

1. Preheat the oven to 350 °F.
2. Prepare a baking tray with parchment paper and set it aside.
3. In a large bowl, mix together the pork, beef, onion, bread crumbs, basil, garlic, egg, salt, and pepper until very well mixed.
4. Roll the meat mixture into 2-in. meatballs.
5. Transfer the meatballs to the baking sheet and bake until they are browned and cooked through, about 15 minutes.
6. Serve the meatballs with your favorite marinara sauce and some steamed green beans.

Nutrition

- Calories 332
- Carbohydrates 13 g.
- Sugar 3 g.

82. Lime-Parsley Lamb Cutlets

PREPARATION TIME: 4 HOURS

COOKING TIME: 10'

SERVINGS: 4

Ingredients

- 1/4 c. extra-virgin olive oil
- 1/4 c. freshly squeezed lime juice
- 2 tbsps lime zest
- 2 tbsps chopped fresh parsley
- 12 lamb cutlets (about 1 1/2 lbs. total)
- Salt and pepper, to taste

Directions

1. Scourge the oil, lime juice, zest, parsley, salt, and pepper.
2. Pour the marinade into a resealable plastic bag.
3. Add the cutlets to the bag and remove as much air as possible before sealing.
4. Marinate the lamb in the refrigerator for about 4 hours, turning the bag several times.
5. Preheat the oven to broil.
6. Remove the chops from the bag and arrange them on an aluminum foil-lined baking sheet. Discard the marinade.
7. Broil the chops for 4 minutes per side for medium doneness.
8. Let the chops rest for 5 minutes before serving.

Nutrition

- Calories 413
- Carbohydrates 1 g.
- Protein 31 g.

83. Mediterranean Steak Sandwiches

PREPARATION TIME: 1 HOUR

COOKING TIME: 10'

SERVINGS: 4

Ingredients

- 2 tbsps extra-virgin olive oil
- 2 tbsps balsamic vinegar
- 2 tsps. garlic
- 2 tsps. lemon juice
- 2 tsps. fresh oregano
- 1 tsp. fresh parsley
- 1-pound flank steak
- 4 whole-wheat pitas
- 2 c. shredded lettuce
- 1 red onion, thinly sliced
- 1 tomato, chopped
- 1 oz. low-sodium feta cheese

Directions

1. Scourge olive oil, balsamic vinegar, garlic, lemon juice, oregano, and parsley.
2. Add the steak to the bowl, turning to coat it completely.
3. Marinate the steak for 1 hour in the refrigerator, turning it over several times.
4. Preheat the broiler. Line a baking sheet with aluminum foil.
5. Put the steak out of the bowl and discard the marinade.
6. Situate the steak on the baking sheet and broil for 5 minutes per side for medium.
7. Set aside for 10 minutes before slicing.
8. Stuff the pitas with the sliced steak, lettuce, onion, tomato, and feta.

Nutrition

- Calories 344
- Carbohydrates 22 g.
- Fiber 3 g.

84. Roasted Beef with Peppercorn Sauce

PREPARATION TIME: 10'

COOKING TIME: 90'

SERVINGS: 4

Ingredients

- 1 1/2 lbs. top rump beef roast
- 3 tsps. extra-virgin olive oil
- 3 shallots, minced
- 2 tsps. minced garlic
- 1 tbsp. green peppercorns
- 2 tbsps dry sherry
- 2 tbsps all-purpose flour
- 1 c. sodium-free beef broth
- Salt and pepper, to taste

Directions

1. Heat the oven to 300 °F.
2. Season the roast with salt and pepper.
3. Position a big skillet over medium-high heat and add 2 tsps of olive oil.
4. Brown the beef on all sides, about 10 minutes in total, and transfer the roast to a baking dish.
5. Roast until desired doneness, about 1 1/2 hours for medium. When the roast has been in the oven for 1 hour, start the sauce.
6. In a medium saucepan over medium-high heat, sauté the shallots in the remaining 1 tsp of olive oil until translucent, about 4 minutes.
7. Stir in the garlic and peppercorns, and cook for another minute. Whisk in the sherry to deglaze the pan.
8. Whisk in the flour to form a thick paste, cooking for 1 minute and stirring constantly.
9. Fill in the beef broth and whisk for 4 minutes. Season the sauce.
10. Serve the beef with a generous spoonful of sauce.

Nutrition

- Calories 330
- Carbohydrates 4 g.
- Protein 36 g.

85. Coffee-and-Herb-Marinated Steak

Preparation time: 2 hours
Cooking time: 10'
Servings: 3

Ingredients

- 1/4 c. whole coffee beans
- 2 tsps. garlic
- 2 tsps. rosemary
- 2 tsps. thyme
- 1 tsp. black pepper
- 2 tbsps apple cider vinegar
- 2 tbsps extra-virgin olive oil
- 1-pound flank steak, trimmed of visible fat

Directions

1. Place the coffee beans, garlic, rosemary, thyme, and black pepper in a coffee grinder or food processor and pulse until coarsely ground.
2. Transfer the coffee mixture to a resealable plastic bag and add the vinegar and oil. Shake to combine.
3. Add the flank steak and squeeze the excess air out of the bag. Seal it. Marinate the steak in the refrigerator for at least 2 hours, occasionally turning the bag over.
4. Preheat the broiler. Line a baking sheet with aluminum foil.
5. Pull the steak out and discard the marinade.
6. Position steak on the baking sheet and broil until it is done to your liking.
7. Put aside for 10 minutes before cutting it.
8. Serve with your favorite side dish.

Nutrition

- Calories 313
- Fat 20 g.
- Protein 31 g.

86. Traditional Beef Stroganoff

Preparation time: 10'
Cooking time: 30'
Servings: 4

Ingredients

- 1 tsp. extra-virgin olive oil
- 1-lb. top sirloin, cut into thin strips
- 1 c. sliced button mushrooms
- 1/2 sweet onion, finely chopped
- 1 tsp. minced garlic
- 1 tbsp. whole-wheat flour
- 1/2 c. low-sodium beef broth
- 1/4 c. dry sherry
- 1/2 c. fat-free sour cream
- 1 tbsp. chopped fresh parsley
- Salt and pepper, to taste

Directions

1. Position the skillet over medium-high heat and add the oil.
2. Sauté the beef until browned, about 10 minutes, then remove the beef with a slotted spoon to a plate and set it aside.
3. Add the mushrooms, onion, and garlic to the skillet and sauté until lightly browned, for about 5 minutes.
4. Whisk in the flour and then whisk in the beef broth and sherry.
5. Return the sirloin to the skillet and bring the mixture to a boil.
6. Reduce the heat to low and simmer until the beef is tender, about 10 minutes.
7. Stir in the sour cream and parsley. Season with salt and pepper.

Nutrition

- Calories 257
- Carbohydrates 6 g.
- Fiber 1 g.

87. Chicken and Roasted Vegetable Wraps

PREPARATION TIME: 10'

COOKING TIME: 20'

SERVINGS: 4

Ingredients

- 1/2 small eggplant
- 1 red bell pepper
- 1 medium zucchini
- 1/2 small red onion, sliced
- 1 tbsp. extra-virgin olive oil
- 2 (8-oz.) cooked chicken breasts, sliced
- 4 whole-wheat tortilla wraps
- Salt and pepper, to taste

Directions

1. Preheat the oven to 400 °F.
2. Wrap a baking sheet with foil and set it aside.
3. In a large bowl, toss the eggplant, bell pepper, zucchini, and red onion with olive oil.
4. Transfer the vegetables to the baking sheet and lightly season with salt and pepper.
5. Roast the vegetables until soft and slightly charred, about 20 minutes.
6. Divide the vegetables and chicken into four portions.
7. Wrap 1 tortilla around each portion of chicken and grilled vegetables, and serve.

Nutrition

- Calories 483
- Carbohydrates 45 g.
- Fiber 3 g.

88. Spicy Chicken Cacciatore

PREPARATION TIME: 20'

COOKING TIME: 1 HOUR

SERVINGS: 6

Ingredients

- 1 (2-lb.) chicken
- 1/4 c. all-purpose flour
- 2 tbsps extra-virgin olive oil
- 3 slices bacon
- 1 sweet onion
- 2 tsps. minced garlic
- 4 oz. button mushrooms, halved
- 1 (28-oz.) can of low-sodium stewed tomatoes
- 1/2 c. red wine
- 2 tsps. chopped fresh oregano
- 2 tsps. red pepper flakes
- Salt and pepper, to taste

Directions

1. Cut the chicken into pieces 2 drumsticks, 2 thighs, 2 wings, and 4 breast pieces.
2. Dredge the chicken pieces in the flour and season each piece with salt and pepper.
3. Place a large skillet over medium-high heat and add the olive oil.
4. Brown the chicken pieces on all sides, about 20 minutes in total. Transfer the chicken to a plate.
5. Cook the chopped bacon in the skillet for 5 minutes. With a slotted spoon, transfer the cooked bacon to the same plate as the chicken.
6. Pour off most of the oil from the skillet, leaving just a light coating. Sauté the onion, garlic, and mushrooms in the skillet until tender, about 4 minutes.
7. Stir in the tomatoes, wine, oregano, and red pepper flakes.
8. Bring the sauce to a boil. Return the chicken and bacon, plus any accumulated juices from the plate, to the skillet.
9. Reduce the heat to low and simmer until the chicken is tender, about 30 minutes.

Nutrition

- Calories 230
- Carbohydrates 14 g.
- Fiber 2 g.

89. Scallion Sandwich

Preparation time: 10'
Cooking time: 10'
Servings: 1

Ingredients

- 2 slices wheat bread
- 2 tsps. butter, low-fat
- 2 scallions, sliced thinly
- 1 tbsp of parmesan cheese, grated
- 3/4 c of cheddar cheese, reduced-fat, grated

Directions

1. Preheat the Air fryer to 356 °F.
2. Spread butter on a slice of bread. Place inside the cooking basket with the butter side facing down.
3. Place cheese and scallions on top. Spread the rest of the butter on the other slice of bread. Put it on top of the sandwich and sprinkle it with parmesan cheese.
4. Cook for 10 minutes.

Nutrition

- Calorie 154
- Carbohydrate 9 g.
- Fat 2.5 g.
- Protein 8.6 g.
- Fiber 2.4 g.

90. Lean Lamb and Turkey Meatballs with Yogurt

Preparation time: 10'
Cooking time: 4'
Servings: 8

Ingredients

For the Meatballs
- 1 egg white
- 4 oz. ground lean turkey
- 1 lb of ground lean lamb
- 1 tsp. each of cayenne pepper, ground coriander, red chili pastes, salt, and ground cumin
- 2 garlic cloves, minced
- 1 1/2 tbsps parsley, chopped
- 1 tbsp. mint, chopped
- 1/4 c of olive oil

For the Yogurt
- 2 tbsps of buttermilk
- 1 garlic clove, minced
- 1/4 c. mint, chopped
- 1/2 c of Greek yogurt, non-fat
- Salt to taste

Directions

1. Set the air fryer to 390 °F.
2. Mix all the ingredients for the meatballs in a bowl. Roll and mold them into golf-size round pieces. Arrange in the cooking basket. Cook for 8 minutes.
3. While waiting, combine all the ingredients for the mint yogurt in a bowl. Mix well.
4. Serve the meatballs with mint yogurt. Top with olives and fresh mint.

Nutrition

- Calorie 154
- Carbohydrate 9 g.
- Fat 2.5 g.
- Protein 8.6 g.
- Fiber 2.4 g.

91. Air Fried Section and Tomato

Preparation time: 10'
Cooking time: 5'
Servings: 2

Ingredients

- 1 aubergine, sliced thickly into 4 disks
- 1 tomato, sliced into 2 thick disks
- 2 tsp. feta cheese, reduced-fat
- 2 fresh basil leaves, minced
- 2 balls, small buffalo mozzarella, reduced-fat, roughly torn
- Pinch of salt
- Pinch of black pepper

Directions

1. Preheat air fryer to 330 °F.
2. Spray a small amount of oil into the air fryer basket. Fry the aubergine slices for 5 minutes or until golden brown on both sides. Transfer to a plate.
3. Fry tomato slices in batches for 5 minutes or until seared on both sides.
4. To serve, stack salad starting with an aborigine base, buffalo mozzarella, basil leaves, tomato slice, and 1/2-teaspoon feta cheese.
5. Top of with another slice of aborigine and 1/2 tsp. feta cheese. Serve.

Nutrition

- Calorie 140.3
- Carbohydrate 26.6
- Fat 3.4 g.
- Protein 4.2 g.
- Fiber 7.3 g.

92. Cheesy Salmon Fillets

Preparation time: 15'
Cooking time: 20'
Servings: 2-3

Ingredients

For the Salmon Fillets
- 2 pieces, 4 oz. each salmon fillets, choose even cuts
- 1/2 c. sour cream, reduced-fat
- 1/4 c. cottage cheese, reduced-fat
- 1/4 c. Parmigiano-Reggiano cheese, freshly grated

For the Garnish
- Spanish paprika
- 1/2-piece lemon, cut into wedges

Directions

1. Preheat the air fryer to 330 °F.
2. To make the salmon fillets, mix sour cream, cottage cheese, and Parmigiano-Reggiano cheese in a bowl.
3. Layer salmon fillets in the Air fryer basket. Fry for 20 minutes or until cheese turns golden brown.
4. To assemble, place a salmon fillet and sprinkle paprika. Garnish with lemon wedges and squeeze lemon juice on top. Serve.

Nutrition

- Calorie 274
- Carbohydrate 1 g.
- Fat 19 g.
- Protein 24 g.
- Fiber 0.5 g.

93. Salmon with Asparagus

Preparation time: 5'

Cooking time: 10'

Servings: 3

Ingredients

- 1 lb. salmon, sliced into fillets
- 1 tbsp. olive oil
- Salt and pepper, as needed
- 2 cloves of garlic, minced
- Zest and juice of 1/2 lemon
- 1 tbsp. butter, salted

Directions

1. Spoon in the butter and olive oil into a large pan and heat it over medium-high heat.
2. Once it becomes hot, place the salmon and season it with salt and pepper.
3. Cook for 4 minutes per side and then cook the other side.
4. Stir in the garlic and lemon zest to it.
5. Cook for further 2 minutes or until slightly browned.
6. Off the heat and squeeze the lemon juice over it.
7. Serve it hot.

Nutrition

- Calories 409
- Carbohydrates 2.7 g.
- Proteins 32.8 g.
- Fat 28.8 g.
- Sodium 497 mg.

94. Shrimp in Garlic Butter

Preparation time: 5'

Cooking time: 20'

Servings: 4

Ingredients

- 1 lb. shrimp, peeled and deveined
- 1/4 tsp. red pepper flakes
- 6 tbsp. butter, divided
- 1/2 c. chicken stock
- Salt and pepper, as needed
- 2 tbsp. parsley, minced
- 5 cloves of garlic, minced
- 2 tbsp. lemon juice

Directions

1. Heat a large bottomed skillet over medium-high heat.
2. Spoon in 2 tbsps of the butter and melt it. Add the shrimp.
3. Season it with salt and pepper. Sear for 4 minutes or until shrimp gets cooked.
4. Transfer the shrimp to a plate and stir in the garlic.
5. Sauté for 30 seconds or until aromatic.
6. Pour the chicken stock and whisk it well. Allow it to simmer for 5-10 minutes or until it has reduced to half.
7. Spoon the remaining butter, red pepper, and lemon juice into the sauce. Mix.
8. Continue cooking for another 2 minutes.
9. Take off the pan from the heat and add the cooked shrimp to it.
10. Garnish with parsley and transfer to the serving bowl.
11. Enjoy.

Nutrition

- Calories 307
- Carbohydrates 3 g.
- Proteins 27 g.
- Fat 20 g.
- Sodium 522 mg.

95. Cobb Salad

Preparation time: 5'
Cooking time: 5'
Servings: 1

Ingredients

- 4 cherry tomatoes, chopped
- 1/4 c. bacon, cooked and crumbled
- 1/2 of 1 avocado, chopped
- 2 oz. chicken breast, shredded
- 1 egg, hardboiled
- 2 c. mixed green salad
- 1 oz. feta cheese, crumbled

Directions

1. Toss all the ingredients for the cobb salad in a large mixing bowl and toss well.
2. Serve and enjoy it.

Nutrition

- Calories 307
- Carbohydrates 3 g.
- Proteins 27 g.
- Fat 20 g.
- Sodium 522 mg.

96. Seared Tuna Steak

Preparation time: 10'
Cooking time: 10'
Servings: 2

Ingredients

- 1 tsp. sesame seeds
- 1 tbsp. sesame oil
- 2 tbsp. soya sauce
- Salt and pepper, to taste
- 2 (6 oz.) ahi tuna steaks

Directions

1. Seasoning the tuna steaks with salt and pepper. Keep it aside on a shallow bowl.
2. In another bowl, mix soya sauce and sesame oil.
3. Pour the sauce over the salmon and coat them generously with the sauce.
4. Keep it aside for 10-15 minutes and then heat a large skillet over medium heat.
5. Once hot, keep the tuna steaks and cook them for 3 minutes or until seared underneath.
6. Flip the fillets and cook them for a further 3 minutes.
7. Transfer the seared tuna steaks to the serving plate and slice them into 1/2-in. slices. Top with sesame seeds.

Nutrition

- Calories 255
- Fat 9 g.
- Carbohydrates 1 g.
- Proteins 40.5 g.
- Sodium 293 mg.

97. Beef Chili

Preparation time: 10'
Cooking time: 20'
Servings: 4

Ingredients

- 1/2 tsp. garlic powder
- 1 tsp. coriander, grounded
- 1 lb. beef, grounded
- 1/2 tsp. sea salt
- 1/2 tsp. cayenne pepper
- 1 tsp. cumin, grounded
- 1/2 tsp. pepper, grounded
- 1/2 c. salsa, low-carb and no-sugar

Directions

1. Heat a large-sized pan over medium-high heat and cook the beef in it until browned.
2. Stir in all the spices and cook them for 7 minutes or until everything is combined.
3. When the beef gets cooked, spoon in the salsa.
4. Bring the mixture to a simmer and cook for another 8 minutes or until everything comes together.
5. Take it from heat and transfer it to a serving bowl.

Nutrition

- Calories 229
- Fat 10 g.
- Carbohydrates 2 g.
- Proteins 33 g.
- Sodium 675 mg.

98. Greek Broccoli Salad

Preparation time: 10'
Cooking time: 15'
Servings: 4

Ingredients

- 1 1/4 lb. broccoli, sliced into small bites
- 1/4 c. almonds, sliced
- 1/3 c. sun-dried tomatoes
- 1/4 c. feta cheese, crumbled
- 1/4 c. red onion, sliced

For the Dressing
- 1/4 c. olive oil
- Dash of red pepper flakes
- 1 garlic clove, minced
- 1/4 tsp. salt
- 2 tbsp. lemon juice
- 1/2 tsp. Dijon mustard
- 1 tsp. low carb sweetener syrup
- 1/2 tsp. oregano, dried

Directions

1. Mix broccoli, onion, cheese, almonds, and sun-dried tomatoes in a large mixing bowl.
2. In another small-sized bowl, combine all the dressing ingredients until emulsified.
3. Spoon the dressing over the broccoli salad.
4. Allow the salad to rest for half an hour before serving.

Nutrition

- Calories 272
- Carbohydrates 11.9 g.
- Proteins 8 g.
- Fat 21.6 g.
- Sodium 321 mg.

99. Cheesy Cauliflower Gratin

Preparation time: 5'
Cooking time: 25'
Servings: 6

Ingredients

- 6 deli slices pepper jack cheese
- 4 c. cauliflower florets
- Salt and pepper, as needed
- 4 tbsp. butter
- 1/3 c. heavy whipping cream

Directions

1. Mix the cauliflower, cream, butter, salt, and pepper in a safe microwave bowl and combine well.
2. Microwave the cauliflower mixture for 25 minutes on high until it becomes soft and tender.
3. Remove the ingredients from the bowl and mash with the help of a fork.
4. Taste for seasonings and spoon in salt and pepper as required.
5. Arrange the slices of Pepper Jack cheese on top of the cauliflower mixture and microwave for 3 minutes until the cheese starts melting.
6. Serve warm.

Nutrition

- Calories 421
- Carbohydrates 3 g.
- Proteins 19 g.
- Fat 37 g.
- Sodium 111 mg.

100. Strawberry Spinach Salad

Preparation time: 5'
Cooking time: 10'
Servings: 4

Ingredients

- 4 oz. feta cheese, crumbled
- 8 strawberries, sliced
- 2 oz. almonds
- 6 slices bacon, thick-cut, crispy, and crumbled
- 10 oz. spinach leaves, fresh
- 2 Roma tomatoes, diced
- 2 oz. red onion, sliced thinly

Directions

1. For making this healthy salad, mix all the ingredients needed to make the salad in a large-sized bowl and toss them well.

Nutrition

- Calories 255
- Fat 16 g.
- Carbohydrates 8 g.
- Proteins 14 g.
- Sodium 27 mg.

101. Misto Quente

PREPARATION TIME: 5'

COOKING TIME: 10'

SERVINGS: 4

Ingredients

- 4 slices of bread without shell
- 4 slices of turkey breast
- 4 slices of cheese
- 2 tbsp. cream cheese
- 2 spoons of butter

Directions

1. Preheat the air fryer. Set the timer of 5 minutes and the temperature to 200 °C.
2. Pass the butter on one side of the slice of bread, and on the other side of the slice, the cream cheese.
3. Mount the sandwiches placing 2 slices of turkey breast and 2 slices of cheese between the bread, with the cream cheese inside and the side with butter.
4. Place the sandwiches in the basket of the air fryer. Set the timer of the air fryer for 5 minutes and press the power button.

Nutrition

- Calories 340
- Fat 15 g.
- Carbohydrates 32 g.
- Protein 15 g.
- Sugar 0 g.
- Cholesterol 0 mg

102. Garlic Bread

PREPARATION TIME: 10'

COOKING TIME: 15'

SERVINGS: 4-5

Ingredients

- 2 stale French rolls
- 4 tbsp. crushed or crumpled garlic
- 1 c of mayonnaise
- Powdered grated Parmesan
- 1 tbsp. olive oil

Directions

1. Preheat the air fryer. Set the time of 5 minutes and the temperature to 200 °C.
2. Mix mayonnaise with garlic and set aside.
3. Cut the French rolls into slices, but without separating them completely.
4. Fill the cavities of equals. Brush with olive oil and sprinkle with grated cheese.
5. Place in the basket of the air fryer. Set the timer to 10 minutes, adjust the temperature to 180 °C, and press the power button.

Nutrition

- Calories 340
- Fat 15 g.
- Carbohydrates 32 g.
- Protein 15 g.
- Sugar 0 g.
- Cholesterol 0 mg.

103. Bruschetta

PREPARATION TIME: **5'**

COOKING TIME: **10'**

SERVINGS: **2**

Ingredients

- 4 slices of Italian bread
- 1 c. chopped tomato tea
- 1 c. grated mozzarella tea
- Olive oil
- Oregano, salt, and pepper
- 4 fresh basil leaves

Directions

1. Preheat the air fryer. Set the timer of 5 minutes and the temperature to 200 °C.
2. Sprinkle the slices of Italian bread with olive oil. Divide the chopped tomatoes and mozzarella between the slices. Season with salt, pepper, and oregano.
3. Put oil in the filling. Place a basil leaf on top of each slice.
4. Put the bruschetta in the basket of the air fryer being careful not to spill the filling. Set the timer of 5 minutes, set the temperature to 180 °C, and press the power button.
5. Transfer the bruschetta to a plate and serve.

Nutrition

- Calories 434
- Fat 14 g.
- Carbohydrates 63 g.
- Protein 11 g.
- Sugar 8 g.
- Cholesterol 0 mg.

104. Cream Buns with Strawberries

PREPARATION TIME: **10'**

COOKING TIME: **12'**

SERVINGS: **6**

Ingredients

- 240 g. all-purpose flour
- 50 g. granulated sugar
- 8 g. baking powder
- 1 g of salt
- 85 g. chopped cold butter
- 84 g. chopped fresh strawberries
- 120 ml whipping cream
- 2 large eggs
- 10 ml vanilla extract
- 5 ml of water

Directions

1. Sift flour, sugar, baking powder, and salt in a large bowl. Put the butter with the flour with the use of a blender or your hands until the mixture resembles thick crumbs.
2. Mix the strawberries in the flour mixture. Set aside for the mixture to stand. Beat the whipping cream, 1 egg, and the vanilla extract in a separate bowl.
3. Put the cream mixture in the flour mixture until they are homogeneous, and then spread the mixture to a thickness of 38 mm.
4. Use a round cookie cutter to cut the buns. Spread the buns with a combination of egg and water. Set aside.
5. Preheat the air fryer, set it to 180 °C.
6. Place baking paper in the preheated inner basket.
7. Place the buns on top of the baking paper and cook for 12 minutes at 180 °C, until golden brown.

Nutrition

- Calories 150
- Fat 14 g.
- Carbohydrates 3 g.
- Protein 11 g.
- Sugar 8 g.
- Cholesterol 0 mg.

105. Blueberry Buns

Preparation time: 10'

Cooking time: 12'

Servings: 6

Ingredients

- 240 g. all-purpose flour
- 50 g. granulated sugar
- 8 g. baking powder
- 2 g. of salt
- 85 g. chopped cold butter
- 85 g. of fresh blueberries
- 3 g. grated fresh ginger
- 113 ml whipping cream
- 2 large eggs
- 4 ml vanilla extract
- 5 ml of water

Directions

1. Put sugar, flour, baking powder, and salt in a large bowl.
2. Put the butter with the flour using a blender or your hands until the mixture resembles thick crumbs.
3. Mix the blueberries and ginger in the flour mixture and set aside
4. Mix the whipping cream, 1 egg, and the vanilla extract in a different container.
5. Put the cream mixture with the flour mixture until combined.
6. Shape the dough until it reaches a thickness of approximately 38 mm and cut it into eighths.
7. Spread the buns with a combination of egg and water. Set aside.
8. Preheat the air fryer to 180 °C.
9. Place baking paper in the preheated inner basket and place the buns on top of the paper. Cook for 12 minutes at 180 °C, until golden brown

Nutrition

- Calories 105
- Fat 1.64 g.
- Carbohydrates 20.09 g.
- Protein 2.43 g.
- Sugar 2.1 g.
- Cholesterol 0 mg.

106. Cauliflower Mash

Preparation time: 30'

Cooking time: 4'

Servings: 5

Ingredients

- 2 tbsp. butter
- 1/4 c. milk
- 10 oz. cauliflower florets
- 3/4 tsp. salt

Directions

1. Add water to the saucepan and bring to boil.
2. Reduce the heat and simmer for 10 minutes.
3. Drain the vegetables well. Transfer vegetables, butter, milk, and salt to a blender and blend until smooth.
4. Serve and enjoy.

Nutrition

- Calories 128
- Fat 6.2 g.
- Sugar 3.3 g.
- Protein 3.2 g.
- Cholesterol 17 mg.

107. French Toast in Sticks

Preparation time: 5'
Cooking time: 10'
Servings: 4

Ingredients

- 4 slices of white bread, 38 mm. thick, preferably hard
- 2 eggs
- 60 ml of milk
- 15 ml maple sauce
- 2 ml vanilla extract
- Nonstick spray oil
- 38 g of sugar
- 3 g. ground cinnamon
- Maple syrup, to serve
- Powdered sugar to sprinkle

Directions

1. Cut each slice of bread into thirds making 12 pieces. Place sideways
2. Beat the eggs, milk, maple syrup, and vanilla.
3. Preheat the air fryer, set it to 175 °C.
4. Dip the sliced bread into the egg mixture and place it in the preheated air fryer. Sprinkle French toast generously with oil spray.
5. Cook French toast for 10 minutes at 175 °C. Turn the toast halfway through cooking.
6. Mix the sugar and cinnamon in a bowl.
7. Cover the French toast with the sugar and cinnamon mixture when you have finished cooking.
8. Serve with maple syrup and sprinkle with powdered sugar

Nutrition

- Calories 128
- Fat 6.2 g.
- Carbohydrates 16.3 g.
- Sugar 3.3 g.
- Protein 3.2 g.
- Cholesterol 17 mg.

108. Muffins Sandwich

Preparation time: 2'
Cooking time: 10'
Servings: 1

Ingredients

- Nonstick spray oil
- 1 slice of white cheddar cheese
- 1 slice of Canadian bacon
- 1 English muffin, divided
- 15 ml. hot water
- 1 large egg
- Salt and pepper to taste

Directions

1. Spray the inside of an 85 g. mold with oil spray and place it in the air fryer.
2. Preheat the air fryer, set it to 160 °C.
3. Add the cheese and Canadian bacon to the preheated air fryer.
4. Pour the hot water and the egg into the hot pan and season with salt and pepper.
5. Select Bread, set to 10 minutes.
6. Take out the English muffins after 7 minutes, leaving the egg for the full time.
7. Build your sandwich by placing the cooked egg on top of the English muffing and serve

Nutrition

- Calories 400
- Fat 26 g.
- Carbohydrates 26 g.
- Sugar 15 g.
- Protein 3 g.
- Cholesterol 155 mg.

109. Bacon BBQ

PREPARATION TIME: 2'

COOKING TIME: 8'

SERVINGS: 2

Ingredients

- 13 g. dark brown sugar
- 5 g. chili powder
- 1 g. ground cumin
- 1 g. cayenne pepper
- 4 slices of bacon, cut in half

Directions

1. Mix seasonings until well combined.
2. Dip the bacon in the dressing until it is completely covered. Leave aside.
3. Preheat the air fryer, set it to 160 °C.
4. Place the bacon in the preheated air fryer
5. Select Bacon and press Start/Pause.

Nutrition

- Calories 1,124
- Fat 72 g.
- Carbohydrates 59 g.
- Protein 49 g.
- Sugar 11 g.
- Cholesterol 77 mg.

110. Stuffed French Toast

PREPARATION TIME: 4'

COOKING TIME: 10'

SERVINGS: 1

Ingredients

- 1 slice of brioche bread, 64 mm. thick, preferably rancid
- 113 g. cream cheese
- 2 eggs
- 15 ml of milk
- 30 ml whipping cream
- 38 g of sugar
- 3 g. cinnamon
- 2 ml vanilla extract
- Nonstick spray oil
- Pistachios chopped to cover
- Maple syrup, to serve

Directions

1. Preheat the air fryer, set it to 175 °C.
2. Cut a slit in the middle of the bread.
3. Fill the inside of the slit with cream cheese. Leave aside.
4. Mix the eggs, milk, whipping cream, sugar, cinnamon, and vanilla extract.
5. Moisten the stuffed bread in the egg mixture for 10 seconds on each side.
6. Sprinkle each side of the bread with oil spray.
7. Place the French toast in the preheated air fryer and cook for 10 minutes at 175 °C
8. Stir the French toast carefully with a spatula when you finish cooking.
9. Serve topped with chopped pistachios and maple syrup.

Nutrition

- Calories 159
- Fat 7.5 g.
- Carbohydrates 25.2 g.
- Protein 14 g.
- Sugar 0 g.
- Cholesterol 90 mg.

Chapter 7: Salad

111. Thai Quinoa Salad

Preparation time: 10'
Cooking time: 0'
Servings: 1-2

Ingredients

For the Dressing
- 1 tbsp. sesame seed
- 1 tsp. chopped garlic
- 1 tsp. lemon, fresh juice
- 3 tsp. apple cider vinegar
- 2 tsp. tamari, gluten-free.
- 1/4 c of tahini (sesame butter)
- 1 pitted date
- 1/2 tsp. salt
- 1/2 tsp. toasted sesame oil

For the Salad
- 1 c of quinoa, steamed
- 1 big handful of arugulas
- 1 tomato cut into pieces
- 1/4 of the red onion, diced

Directions

1. Add filtered water and all the ingredients for the dressing into a small blender. Mix.
2. Steam the quinoa in a steamer or a rice pan, then set aside.
3. Combine the quinoa, the arugula, the tomatoes sliced, the red onion diced on a serving plate or bowl, add the Thai dressing and serve with a spoon.

Nutrition

- Calories 100
- Carbohydrates 12 g.

112. Green Goddess Bowl and Avocado Cumin Dressing

Preparation time: 10'
Cooking time: 0'
Servings: 1-2

Ingredients

For the Avocado Cumin Dressing
- 1 avocado
- 1 tbsp. cumin powder
- 2 limes, freshly squeezed
- 1 c of filtered water
- 1/4 seconds. sea salt
- 1 tbsp. olive extra-virgin olive oil
- Cayenne pepper dash
- Optional: 1/4 tsp. smoked pepper

For the Lemon Tahini Dressing
- 1/4 c of tahini (sesame butter)
- 1/2 c of filtered water (more if you want it thinner; less if you want it thicker)
- 1/2 lemon, freshly squeezed
- 1 clove of minced garlic
- 3/4 tsp. sea salt (Celtic Gray, Himalayan, Redmond Real Salt)
- 1 tbsp. olive extra-virgin olive oil
- Black pepper taste

For the Salad
- 3 c of kale, chopped
- 1/2 c of broccoli flowers, chopped
- 1/2 zucchini (make spiral noodles)
- 1/2 c of kelp noodles, soaked and drained
- 1/3 c of cherry tomatoes, halved.
- 2 tsp. hemp seeds

Directions

1. Gently steam the kale and the broccoli (set the steam for 4 minutes), set aside.
2. Mix the zucchini noodles and kelp noodles and toss with a generous portion of the smoked avocado cumin dressing. Add the cherry tomatoes and stir again.
3. Place the steamed kale and broccoli and drizzle with the lemon tahini dressing. Top the kale and the broccoli with the noodles and tomatoes and sprinkle the whole dish with the hemp seeds.

Nutrition

- Calories 89
- Carbohydrates 11 g.
- Fat 1.2 g.
- Protein 4 g.

113. 7 Sweet and Savory Salad

PREPARATION TIME: **10'**

COOKING TIME: **0'**

SERVINGS: **1-2**

Ingredients
- 1 big head of butter lettuce
- 1/2 of cucumber, sliced
- 1 pomegranate, seed, or 1/3 c of seed
- 1 avocado, 1 cubed
- 1/4 c of shelled pistachio, chopped

For the Dressing
- 1/4 c of apple cider vinegar
- 1/2 c of olive oil
- 1 clove of garlic, minced

Directions
1. Put the butter lettuce in a salad bowl.
2. Add the remaining ingredients and toss with the salad dressing.

Nutrition
- Calories 68
- Carbohydrates 8 g.
- Fat 1.2 g.
- Protein 2 g.

114. Kale Pesto's Pasta

PREPARATION TIME: **10'**

COOKING TIME: **0'**

SERVINGS: **1-2**

Ingredients
- 1 bunch of kale
- 2 c of fresh basil
- 1/4 c of extra-virgin olive oil
- 1/2 c of walnuts
- 2 limes, freshly squeezed
- Sea salt and chili pepper
- 1 zucchini, noodle (spiralizer)
- Optional: garnish with chopped asparagus, spinach leaves, and tomato.

Directions
1. The night before, soak the walnuts in order to improve absorption.
2. Put all the kale pesto ingredients in a blender and blend until the consistency of the cream is reached.
3. Add the zucchini noodles and enjoy.

Nutrition
- Calories 55
- Carbohydrates 9 g
- Fat 1.2 g.

115. Beet Salad with Basil Dressing

Preparation Time: 10'
Cooking Time: 0'
Servings: 4

Ingredients

For the Dressing
- 1/4 c. blackberries
- 1/4 c. extra-virgin olive oil
- Juice of 1 lemon
- 2 tbsps minced fresh basil
- 1 tsp. poppy seeds
- A pinch of sea salt

For the Salad
- 2 celery stalks, chopped
- 4 cooked beets, peeled and chopped
- 1 c. blackberries
- 4 c. spring mix

Directions

1. To make the dressing, mash the blackberries in a bowl. Whisk in the oil, lemon juice, basil, poppy seeds, and sea salt.
2. To make the salad: Add the celery, beets, blackberries, and spring mix to the bowl with the dressing.
3. Combine and serve.

Nutrition

- Calories 192
- Fat 15 g.
- Carbohydrates 15 g.
- Protein 2 g.

116. Basic Salad with Olive Oil Dressing

Preparation Time: 10'
Cooking Time: 0'
Servings: 4

Ingredients

- 1 c. coarsely chopped iceberg lettuce
- 1 c. coarsely chopped romaine lettuce
- 1 c. fresh baby spinach
- 1 large tomato, hulled and coarsely chopped
- 1 c. diced cucumber
- 2 tbsps extra-virgin olive oil
- 1/4 tsp of sea salt

Directions

1. In a bowl, combine the spinach and lettuces. Add the tomato and cucumber.
2. Drizzle with oil and sprinkle with sea salt.
3. Mix and serve.

Nutrition

- Calories 77
- Fat 4 g.
- Carbohydrates 3 g.
- Protein 1 g.

117. Spinach and Orange Salad with Oil Drizzle

Preparation time: 10'

Cooking time: 0'

Servings: 4

Ingredients

- 4 c. fresh baby spinach
- 1 blood orange, coarsely chopped
- 1/2 red onion, thinly sliced
- 1/2 shallot, finely chopped
- 2 tbsp. minced fennel fronds
- Juice of 1 lemon
- 1 tbsp. extra-virgin olive oil
- Pinch sea salt

Directions

1. In a bowl, toss together the spinach, orange, red onion, shallot, and fennel fronds.
2. Add the lemon juice, oil, and sea salt.
3. Mix and serve.

Nutrition

- Calories 79
- Fat 2 g.
- Carbohydrates 8 g.
- Protein 1 g.

118. Fruit Salad with Coconut-Lime Dressing

Preparation time: 5'

Cooking time: 0'

Servings: 4

Ingredients

For the Dressing
- 1/4 c. full-fat canned coconut milk
- 1 tbsp. raw honey
- Juice of 1/2 lime
- Pinch sea salt

For the salad
- 2 bananas, thinly sliced
- 2 mandarin oranges, segmented
- 1/2 c. strawberries, thinly sliced
- 1/2 c. raspberries
- 1/2 c. blueberries

Directions

1. To make the dressing: Whisk all the dressing ingredients in a bowl.
2. To make the salad: Add the salad ingredients to a bowl and mix.
3. Drizzle with the dressing and serve.

Nutrition

- Calories 141
- Fat 3 g.
- Carbohydrates 30 g.
- Protein 2 g.

119. Cranberry and Brussels Sprouts with Dressing

Preparation time: **10'**

Cooking time: **0'**

Servings: **4**

Ingredients

For the Dressing
- 1/3 c. extra-virgin olive oil
- 2 tbsp. apple cider vinegar
- 1 tbsp. pure maple syrup
- Juice of 1 orange
- 1/2 tbsp. dried rosemary
- 1 tbsp. scallion, whites only
- Pinch sea salt

For the Salad
- 1 bunch scallions, greens only, finely chopped
- 1 c. Brussels sprouts, stemmed, halved, and thinly sliced
- 1/2 c. fresh cranberries
- 4 c. fresh baby spinach

Directions

1. To make the dressing: In a bowl, whisk the dressing ingredients.
2. To make the salad: Add the scallions, Brussels sprouts, cranberries, and spinach to the bowl with the dressing.
3. Combine and serve.

Nutrition

- Calories 267
- Fat 18 g.
- Carbohydrates 26 g.
- Protein 2 g.

120. Parsnip, Carrot, and Kale Salad with Dressing

Preparation time: **10'**

Cooking time: **0'**

Servings: **4**

Ingredients

For the Dressing
- 1/3 c. extra-virgin olive oil
- Juice of 1 lime
- 2 tbsp. minced fresh mint leaves
- 1 tsp. pure maple syrup
- Pinch sea salt

For the Salad
- 1 bunch kale, chopped
- 1/2 parsnip, grated
- 1/2 carrot, grated
- 2 tbsp. sesame seeds

Directions

1. To make the dressing, mix all the dressing ingredients in a bowl.
2. To make the salad, add the kale to the dressing and massage the dressing into the kale for 1 minute.
3. Add the parsnip, carrot, and sesame seeds.
4. Combine and serve.

Nutrition

- Calories 214
- Fat 2 g.
- Carbohydrates 12 g.
- Protein 2 g.

121. Tomato Toasts

PREPARATION TIME: 5'

COOKING TIME: 5'

SERVINGS: 4

Ingredients

- 4 slices of sprouted bread toasts
- 2 tomatoes, sliced
- 1 avocado, mashed
- 1 tsp. olive oil
- 1 pinch of salt
- 3/4 teaspoon ground black pepper

Directions

1. Blend together the olive oil, mashed avocado, salt, and ground black pepper.
2. When the mixture is homogenous, spread it over the sprouted bread.
3. Then place the sliced tomatoes over the toasts.
4. Enjoy!

Nutrition

- Calories 125
- Fat 11.1 g.
- Carbohydrates 7.0 g.
- Protein 1.5 g.

122. Every Day Salad

PREPARATION TIME: 10'

COOKING TIME: 40'

SERVINGS: 6

Ingredients

- 5 halved mushrooms
- 6 halved cherry (plum) tomatoes
- 6 rinsed lettuce leaves
- 10 olives
- 1/2 chopped cucumber
- Juice from 1/2 key lime
- 1 tsp. olive oil
- Pure sea salt

Directions

1. Tear rinsed lettuce leaves into medium pieces and put them in a medium salad bowl.
2. Add mushrooms halves, chopped cucumber, olives, and cherry tomato halves into the bowl. Mix well. Pour olive and key lime juice over the salad.
3. Add pure sea salt to taste. Mix it all till it is well combined.

Nutrition

- Calories 88
- Carbohydrates 11 g.
- Fat: .5 g.
- Protein: .8 g.

123. Super-Seedy Salad with Tahini Dressing

Preparation Time: 10'
Cooking Time: 0'
Servings: 1-2

Ingredients

- 1 slice stale sourdough, torn into chunks
- 50 g. mixed seeds
- 1 tsp. cumin seeds
- 1 tsp. coriander seeds
- 50 g. baby kale
- 75 g. long-stemmed broccoli, blanched for a few minutes then roughly chopped
- 1/2 red onion, thinly sliced
- 100 g. cherry tomatoes, halved
- 1/2 a small bunch-flat-leaf parsley, torn

For the Dressing
- 100 ml. natural yogurt
- 1 tbsp. tahini
- 1 lemon, juiced

Directions

1. Heat the oven to 200 °C/fan 180 °C/gas 6. Put the bread into a food processor and pulse into very rough breadcrumbs. Put into a bowl with the mixed seeds and spices, season, and spray well with oil. Tip onto a non-stick baking tray and roast for 15-20 minutes, stirring and tossing regularly, until golden brown.
2. Whisk together the dressing ingredients, some seasoning, and a splash of water in a large bowl. Tip the baby kale, broccoli, red onion, cherry tomatoes, and flat-leaf parsley into the dressing, and mix well. Divide between 2 plates and top with the crispy breadcrumbs and seeds.

Nutrition

- Calories 78
- Carbohydrates 6 g
- Fat 2 g.
- Protein 1.5 g.

124. Vegetable Salad

Preparation Time: 10'
Cooking Time: 0'
Servings: 1-2

Ingredients

- 4 c. each of raw spinach and romaine lettuce
- 2 c. each of cherry tomatoes, sliced cucumber, chopped baby carrots, chopped red, orange, and yellow bell pepper
- 1 c. each of chopped broccoli, sliced yellow squash, zucchini, and cauliflower.

Directions

1. Wash all these vegetables.
2. Mix in a large mixing bowl and top off with a non-fat or low-fat dressing of your choice.

Nutrition

- Calories 48
- Carbohydrates 11 g.
- Protein 3 g.

125. Greek Salad

PREPARATION TIME: **10'**

COOKING TIME: **0'**

SERVINGS: **1-2**

Ingredients

- 1 Romaine head, torn in bits
- 1 cucumber sliced
- 1-pint cherry tomatoes, halved
- 1 green pepper, thinly sliced
- 1 onion sliced into rings
- 1 c. kalamata olives
- 1 1/2 c. feta cheese, crumbled

For dressing combine:
- 1 c. olive oil
- 1/4 c. lemon juice
- 2 tsp. oregano
- Salt and pepper

Directions

1. Put the ingredients on a plate.
2. Drizzle the dressing over the salad.

Nutrition

- Calories 107
- Carbohydrates 18 g.
- Fat 1.2 g
- Protein 1 g.

126. Alkaline Spring Salad

PREPARATION TIME: **10'**

COOKING TIME: **0'**

SERVINGS: **1-2**

Ingredients

Eating seasonal fruits and vegetables is a fabulous way of taking care of yourself and the environment at the same time. This alkaline-electric salad is delicious and nutritious.

- 4 c. seasonal approved greens of your choice
- 1 c. cherry tomatoes
- 1/4 c. walnuts
- 1/4 c. approved herbs of your choice

For the Dressing
- 3-4 key limes
- 1 tbsp of homemade raw sesame "tahini" butter
- Sea salt and cayenne pepper

Directions

1. First, get the juice of the key limes. In a small bowl, whisk together the key lime juice with the homemade raw sesame "tahini" butter. Add sea salt and cayenne pepper, to taste.
2. Cut the cherry tomatoes in half.
3. In a large bowl, combine the greens, cherry tomatoes, walnuts, and herbs. Pour the dressing on top and "massage" with your hands.
4. Let the greens soak up the dressing. Add more sea salt, cayenne pepper, and herbs on top if you wish. Enjoy!

Nutrition

- Calories 77
- Carbohydrates 11 g.

127. Fresh Tuna Salad

PREPARATION TIME: 10'

COOKING TIME: NONE

SERVINGS: 3

Ingredients

- 1 can tuna (6 oz.)
- 1/3 c. fresh cucumber, chopped
- 1/3 c. fresh tomato, chopped
- 1/3 c. avocado, chopped
- 1/3 c. celery, chopped
- 2 garlic cloves, minced
- 4 tsp. olive oil
- 2 tbsp. lime juice
- Pinch of black pepper

Directions

1. Prepare the dressing by combining olive oil, lime juice, minced garlic, and black pepper.
2. Mix the remaining ingredients in a salad bowl and drizzle with the dressing.

Nutrition

- Carbohydrates 4.8 g.
- Protein 14.3 g.
- Total sugars 1.1 g.
- Calories 212 g.

128. Roasted Portobello Salad

PREPARATION TIME: 10'

COOKING TIME: NONE

SERVINGS: 4

Ingredients

- 1 1/2 lb. portobello mushrooms, stems trimmed
- 3 heads Belgian endive, sliced
- 1 small red onion, sliced
- 4 oz. blue cheese
- 8 oz. mixed salad greens
- For the Dressing
- 3 tbsp. red wine vinegar
- 1 tbsp. Dijon mustard
- 2/3 c. olive oil
- Salt and pepper to taste

Directions

1. Preheat the oven to 450 °F.
2. Prepare the dressing by whisking together vinegar, mustard, salt, and pepper. Slowly add olive oil while whisking.
3. Cut the mushrooms and arrange them on a baking sheet, stem-side up. Coat the mushrooms with some dressing and bake for 15 minutes.
4. In a salad bowl toss the salad greens with onion, endive, and cheese. Sprinkle with the dressing.
5. Add mushrooms to the salad bowl.

Nutrition

- Calories 501
- Carbohydrates 22.3 g.
- Protein 14.9 g.
- Total sugars 2.1 g.

129. Shredded Chicken Salad

PREPARATION TIME: 5'

COOKING TIME: 10'

SERVINGS: 6

Ingredients

- 2 chicken breasts, boneless, skinless
- 1 head iceberg lettuce, cut into strips
- 2 bell peppers, cut into strips
- 1 fresh cucumber, quartered, sliced
- 3 scallions, sliced
- 2 tbsp. chopped peanuts
- 1 tbsp. peanut vinaigrette
- Salt to taste
- 1 c of water

Directions

1. In a skillet simmer one cup of salted water.
2. Add the chicken breasts, cover, and cook on low for 5 minutes. Remove the cover. Then remove the chicken from the skillet and shred with a fork.
3. In a salad bowl mix the vegetables with the cooled chicken, season with salt and sprinkle with peanut vinaigrette and chopped peanuts.

Nutrition

- Carbohydrates 9 g.
- Protein 11.6 g.
- Total sugars 4.2 g.
- Calories 117

130. Broccoli Salad

PREPARATION TIME: 10'

COOKING TIME: NONE

SERVINGS: 6

Ingredients

- 1 medium head broccoli, raw, florets only
- 1/2 c. red onion, chopped
- 12 oz. turkey bacon, chopped, fried until crisp
- 1/2 c. cherry tomatoes, halved
- 1/4 c. sunflower kernels
- 3/4 c. raisins
- 3/4 c. mayonnaise
- 2 tbsp. white vinegar

Directions

1. In a salad bowl combine the broccoli, tomatoes, and onion.
2. Mix mayo with vinegar and sprinkle over the broccoli.
3. Add the sunflower kernels, raisins, and bacon and toss well.

Nutrition

- Calories 220
- Carbohydrates 17.3 g.
- Protein 11 g.
- Total sugars 10 g.

131. Cherry Tomato Salad

PREPARATION TIME: **10'**

COOKING TIME: **NONE**

SERVINGS: **6**

Ingredients

- 40 cherry tomatoes, halved
- 1 c. mozzarella balls, halved
- 1 c. green olives, sliced
- 1 can (6 oz.) black olives, sliced
- 2 green onions, chopped
- 3 oz. roasted pine nuts

- For the Dressing
- 1/2 c. olive oil
- 2 tbsp. red wine vinegar
- 1 tsp. dried oregano
- Salt and pepper to taste

Directions

1. In a salad bowl, combine the tomatoes, olives, and onions.
2. Prepare the dressing by combining olive oil with red wine vinegar, dried oregano, salt, and pepper.
3. Sprinkle with the dressing and add the nuts.
4. Let marinate in the fridge for 1 hour.

Nutrition

- Carbohydrates 10.7 g.
- Protein 2.4 g.
- Total sugars 3.6 g.

132. Ground Turkey Salad

PREPARATION TIME: **10'**

COOKING TIME: **35'**

SERVINGS: **6**

Ingredients

- 1 lb. lean ground turkey
- 1/2-in. ginger, minced
- 2 garlic cloves, minced
- 1 onion, chopped
- 1 tbsp. olive oil
- 1 bag lettuce leaves (for serving)
- 1/4 c. fresh cilantro, chopped
- 2 tsp. coriander powder
- 1 tsp. red chili powder
- 1 tsp. turmeric powder
- Salt to taste

- 4 c. water
- For the Dressing:
- 2 tbsp. fat-free yogurt
- 1 tbsp. sour cream, non-fat
- 1 tbsp. low-fat mayonnaise
- 1 lemon, juiced
- 1 tsp. red chili flakes
- Salt and pepper to taste

Directions

1. In a skillet, sauté the garlic and ginger in olive oil for 1 minute. Add onion and season with salt. Cook for 10 minutes over medium heat.
2. Add the ground turkey and sauté for 3 more minutes. Add the spices (turmeric, red chili powder, and coriander powder).
3. Add 4 c of water and cook for 30 minutes, covered.
4. Prepare the dressing by combining yogurt, sour cream, mayo, lemon juice, chili flakes, salt, and pepper.
5. To serve arrange the salad leaves on serving plates and place the cooked ground turkey on them. Top with the dressing.

Nutrition

- Carbohydrates 9.1 g.
- Protein 17.8 g.
- Total sugars 2.5 g.
- Calories 176

133. Asian Cucumber Salad

PREPARATION TIME: 10'

COOKING TIME: NONE

SERVINGS: 6

Ingredients

- 1 lb. cucumbers, sliced
- 2 scallions, sliced
- 2 tbsp. sliced pickled ginger, chopped
- 1/4 c. cilantro
- 1/2 red jalapeño, chopped
- 3 tbsp. rice wine vinegar
- 1 tbsp. sesame oil
- 1 tbsp. sesame seeds

Directions

1. In a salad bowl combine all ingredients and toss them together.

Nutrition

- Carbohydrates 5.7 g.
- Protein 1 g.
- Total sugars 3.1 g.
- Calories 52

134. Cauliflower Tofu Salad

PREPARATION TIME: 10'

COOKING TIME: 15'

SERVINGS: 4

Ingredients

- 2 c. cauliflower florets, blended
- 1 fresh cucumber, diced
- 1/2 c. green olives, diced
- 1/3 c. red onion, diced
- 2 tbsp. toasted pine nuts
- 2 tbsp. raisins
- 1/3 c. feta, crumbled
- 1/2 c. pomegranate seeds
- 2 lemons (juiced, zest grated)
- 8 oz. tofu
- 2 tsp. oregano
- 2 garlic cloves, minced
- 1/2 tsp. red chili flakes
- 3 tbsp. olive oil
- Salt and pepper to taste

Directions

1. Season the blended cauliflower with salt and transfer to a strainer to drain.
2. Prepare the marinade for the tofu by combining 2 tbsp. lemon juice, 1.5 tbsp. olive oil, minced garlic, chili flakes, oregano, salt, and pepper. Coat the tofu in the marinade and set it aside.
3. Preheat the oven to 450 °F.
4. Bake the tofu on a baking sheet for 12 minutes.
5. In a salad bowl mix the remaining marinade with onions, cucumber, cauliflower, olives, and raisins. Add in the remaining olive oil and grated lemon zest.
6. Top with tofu, pine nuts, feta, and pomegranate seeds.

Nutrition

- Carbohydrates 34.1 g.
- Protein 11.1 g.
- Total sugars 11.5 g.
- Calories 328

135. Scallop Caesar Salad

PREPARATION TIME: 5'
COOKING TIME: 2'
SERVINGS: 2

Ingredients

- 8 sea scallops
- 4 c. romaine lettuce
- 2 tsp. olive oil
- 3 tbsp. Caesar salad dressing
- 1 tsp. lemon juice
- Salt and pepper to taste

Directions

1. In a frying pan heat olive oil and cook the scallops in one layer no longer than 2 minutes on both sides. Season with salt and pepper to taste.
2. Arrange the lettuce on plates and place scallops on top.
3. Pour over the Caesar dressing and lemon juice.

Nutrition

- Carbohydrates 14 g.
- Protein 30.7 g.
- Total sugars 2.2 g.
- Calories 340 g.

136. Chicken Avocado Salad

PREPARATION TIME: 30'
COOKING TIME: 15'
SERVINGS: 4

Ingredients

- 1 lb. chicken breast, cooked, shredded
- 1 avocado, pitted, peeled, sliced
- 2 tomatoes, diced
- 1 cucumber, peeled, sliced
- 1 head lettuce, chopped
- 3 tbsp. olive oil
- 2 tbsp. lime juice
- 1 tbsp. cilantro, chopped
- Salt and pepper to taste

Directions

1. In a bowl, whisk together oil, lime juice, cilantro, salt, and a pinch of pepper.
2. Combine lettuce, tomatoes, cucumber in a salad bowl and toss with half of the dressing.
3. Toss chicken with the remaining dressing and combine with vegetable mixture.
4. Top with avocado.

Nutrition

- Carbohydrates 10 g.
- Protein 38 g.
- Total sugars 11.5 g.
- Calories 380

137. CALIFORNIA WRAPS

PREPARATION TIME: 5'
COOKING TIME: 15'
SERVINGS: 4

INGREDIENTS

- 4 slices turkey breast, cooked
- 4 slices ham, cooked
- 4 lettuce leaves
- 4 slices tomato
- 4 slices avocado
- 1 tsp. lime juice
- A handful of watercress leaves
- 4 tbsp. Ranch dressing, sugar-free

DIRECTIONS

1. Top a lettuce leaf with turkey slice, ham slice, and tomato.
2. In a bowl combine avocado and lime juice and place on top of tomatoes. Top with watercress and dressing.
3. Repeat with the remaining ingredients for 4. Topping each lettuce leaf with a turkey slice, ham slice, tomato, and dressing.

NUTRITION

- Carbohydrates 4 g.
- Protein 9 g.
- Total sugars 0.5 g.
- Calories 140

138. CHICKEN SALAD IN CUCUMBER C.

PREPARATION TIME: 5'
COOKING TIME: 15'
SERVINGS: 4

INGREDIENTS

- 1/2 chicken breast, skinless, boiled, and shredded
- 2 long cucumbers, cut into 8 thick rounds each, scooped out
- 1 tsp. ginger, minced
- 1 tsp. lime zest, grated
- 4 tsp. olive oil
- 1 tsp. sesame oil
- 1 tsp. lime juice
- Salt and pepper to taste

DIRECTIONS

1. In a bowl combine lime zest, juice, olive and sesame oils, ginger, and season with salt.
2. Toss the chicken with the dressing and fill the cucumber cups with the salad.

NUTRITION

- Carbohydrates 4 g.
- Protein 12 g.
- Total sugars 0.5 g.
- Calories 116 g

139. Sunflower Seeds and Arugula Garden Salad

Preparation time: 5'
Cooking time: 10'
Servings: 6

Ingredients

- 1/4 tsp. black pepper
- 1/4 tsp. salt
- 1 tsp. fresh thyme, chopped
- 2 tbsp. sunflower seeds, toasted
- 2 c. red grapes, halved
- 7 c. baby arugula, loosely packed
- 1 tbsp. coconut oil
- 2 tsp. honey
- 3 tbsp. red wine vinegar
- 1/2 tsp. stone-ground mustard

Directions

1. In a small bowl, whisk together mustard, honey, and vinegar. Slowly pour oil as you whisk.
2. In a large salad bowl, mix thyme, seeds, grapes, salt, pepper, and arugula.
3. Drizzle with the dressing and serve.

Nutrition

- Calories 86.7 g.
- Protein 1.6 g.
- Carbohydrates 13.1 g.
- Fat 3.1 g.

140. Supreme Caesar Salad

Preparation time: 5'
Cooking time: 10'
Servings: 4

Ingredients

- 1/4 c. olive oil
- 3/4 c. mayonnaise
- 1 head romaine lettuce, torn into bite-sized pieces
- 1 tbsp. lemon juice
- 1 tsp. Dijon mustard
- 1 tsp. Worcestershire sauce
- 3 cloves garlic, peeled and minced
- 3 cloves garlic, peeled and quartered
- 4 c. day-old bread, cubed
- 5 anchovy filets, minced
- 6 tbsp. grated parmesan cheese, divided
- Ground black pepper to taste
- Salt to taste

Directions

1. In a small bowl, whisk well lemon juice, mustard, Worcestershire sauce, 2 tbsp. parmesan cheese, anchovies, mayonnaise, and minced garlic. Season with pepper and salt to taste. Set aside in the ref.
2. On medium fire, place a large nonstick saucepan and heat oil.
3. Sauté quartered garlic until browned around 1-2 minute. Remove and discard.
4. Add bread cubes in the same pan, sauté until lightly browned. Season with pepper and salt. Transfer to a plate.
5. In a large bowl, place lettuce and pour in the dressing. Toss well to coat. Top with remaining parmesan cheese.
6. Garnish with bread cubes, serve, and enjoy.

Nutrition

- Calories 443.3 g.
- Fat 32.1 g.
- Protein 11.6 g.
- Carbohydrates 27 g.

141. Tabbouleh Arabian Salad

Preparation time: 5'

Cooking time: 10'

Servings: 6

Ingredients

- 1/4 c. chopped fresh mint
- 1 2/3 c. boiling water
- 1 cucumber, peeled, seeded, and chopped
- 1 c. bulgur
- 1 c. chopped fresh parsley
- 1 c. chopped green onions
- 1 tsp. salt
- 1/3 c. lemon juice
- 1/3 c. olive oil
- 3 tomatoes, chopped
- Ground black pepper to taste

Directions

1. In a large bowl, mix together boiling water and bulgur. Let soak and set aside for 1 hour while covered.
2. After 1 hour, toss in cucumber, tomatoes, mint, parsley, onions, lemon juice, and oil. Then season with black pepper and salt to taste. Toss well and refrigerate for another hour while covered before serving.

Nutrition

- Calories 185.5 g.
- Fat 13.1 g.
- Protein 4.1 g.
- Carbohydrates 12.8 g.

Chapter 8: Soup and Stew

142. Dill Celery Soup

Preparation time: 10'
Cooking time: 30'
Servings: 4

Ingredients

- 6 c. celery stalk, chopped
- 2 c. filtered alkaline water
- 1 medium onion, chopped
- 1/2 tsp. dill
- 1 c of coconut milk
- 1/4 tsp. sea salt

Directions

1. Combine all elements into the instant pot and mix fine.
2. Cover the pot with a lid and select the soup mode that takes 30 minutes.
3. Release pressure using the quick release setting then open the lid carefully.
4. Blend the soup utilizing a submersion blender until smooth.
5. Stir well and serve.

Nutrition

- Calories 193
- Fat 15.3 g.
- Carbohydrates 10.9 g.
- Protein 5.2 g.
- Sugar 5.6 g.
- Cholesterol 0 mg.

143. Creamy Avocado-Broccoli Soup

Preparation time: 10'
Cooking time: 15'
Servings: 1-2

Ingredients

- 2-3 flowers broccoli
- 1 small avocado
- 1 yellow onion
- 1 green or red pepper
- 1 celery stalk
- 2 c. vegetable broth (yeast-free)
- Celtic sea salt to taste

Directions

1. Warmth vegetable stock (don't bubble). Include hacked onion and broccoli, and warm for a few minutes. At that point, put in a blender, including the avocado, pepper, and celery, and blend until the soup is smooth (include some more water whenever wanted). Season and serve warm. Delicious!!

Nutrition

- Calories 60 g.
- Carbohydrates 11 g.
- Fat 2 g
- Protein 2 g.

144. Fresh Garden Vegetable Soup

PREPARATION TIME: **7'**

COOKING TIME: **20'**

SERVINGS: **1-2**

Ingredients
- 2 big carrots
- 1 small zucchini
- 1 celery stem
- 1 c of broccoli
- 3 stalks of asparagus
- 1 yellow onion
- 1 quart of (alkaline) water
- 4-5 tsps. yeast vegetable stock
- 1 tsp. fresh basil
- 2 tsps. sea salt to taste

Directions
1. Put water in the pot, including the vegetable stock just as the onion, and bring to boil.
2. In the meantime, mix the zucchini, the broccoli, the asparagus, the carrots, and the celery in a food processor.
3. When the water is bubbling, it would be ideal if you turn off the oven as we would prefer not to heat up the vegetables. Simply put them all in the high temp water and hold up until the vegetables arrive at wanted delicacy.
4. Permit to cool somewhat, at that point put all fixings into a blender and blend until you get a thick, smooth consistency.

Nutrition
- Calories 43
- Carbohydrates 7 g.
- Fat 1 g.

145. Raw Some Gazpacho Soup

PREPARATION TIME: **7'**

COOKING TIME: **3 HOURS**

SERVINGS: **3-4**

Ingredients
- 500 g. tomatoes
- 1 small cucumber
- 1 red pepper
- 1 onion
- 2 cloves of garlic
- 1 small chili
- 1 quart of water (preferably alkaline water)
- 4 tbsp. cold-pressed olive oil
- Juice of one fresh lemon
- 1 dash of cayenne pepper
- Sea salt to taste

Directions
1. Remove the skin of the cucumber and cut all vegetables into large pieces.
2. Put all the ingredients except the olive oil in a blender and mix until smooth.
3. Add the olive oil and mix again until the oil is emulsified.
4. Put the soup in the fridge and chill for at least 2 hours (soup should be served ice cold).
5. Add some salt and pepper to taste, mix, place the soup in bowls, garnish with chopped scallions, cucumbers, tomatoes, and peppers and enjoy!

Nutrition
- Calories 39
- Carbohydrates 8 g.
- Fat 0.5 g.
- Protein 0.2 g.

146. Alkaline Carrot Soup with Fresh Mushrooms

Preparation time: 10'

Cooking time: 20'

Servings: 1-2

Ingredients

- 4 mid-sized carrots
- 10 big mushrooms (champignons or chanterelles)
- 1/2 white onion
- 2 tbsp. olive oil (cold-pressed, extra-virgin)
- 3 c. vegetable stock
- 2 tbsp. parsley, fresh and cleaved
- Salt and fresh black pepper

Directions

1. Wash and strip carrots and dice them.
2. Warm-up the vegetable stock in a pot on medium heat. Cook carrots for around 15 minutes. Meanwhile, finely cut the onion and sauté in a skillet with olive oil for around 3 minutes.
3. Wash the mushrooms, slice them to the wanted size, and add to the skillet, cooking approx. an additional 5 minutes, blending at times. Blend carrots, vegetable stock, and put the mixture of the skillet into a pot.
4. When nearly done, season with parsley, salt, and pepper and serve hot. Enjoy this alkalizing soup!

Nutrition

- Calories 75
- Carbohydrates 13 g.
- Fat 1.8 g.
- Protein 1 g.

147. Swiss Cauliflower-Omental-Soup

Preparation time: 10'

Cooking time: 15'

Servings: 3-4

Ingredients

- 2 c. cauliflower pieces
- 2 c. vegetable stock (without yeast)
- 3 tbsp. Swiss Emmental cheddar, cubed
- 2 tbsp. fresh chives
- 1 tbsp. pumpkin seeds
- 1 touch of nutmeg and cayenne pepper

Directions

1. Cook cauliflower in vegetable stock until soft and mix with a blender.
2. Season the soup with nutmeg and cayenne, and a pinch of salt and pepper.
3. Include Emmental cheddar and chives and mix a couple of minutes until the soup is smooth and prepared to serve. Enhance it with pumpkin seeds.

Nutrition

- Calories 65
- Carbohydrates 13 g.
- Fat 2 g.
- Protein 1 g.

148. Chilled Parsley-Gazpacho with Lime and Cucumber

PREPARATION TIME: **10'**

COOKING TIME: **2 HOURS**

SERVINGS: **1**

Ingredients

- 4-5 middle-sized tomatoes
- 2 tbsp. olive oil, extra-virgin and cold-pressed
- 2 c. fresh parsley
- 2 ripe avocados
- 2 cloves garlic, diced
- 2 limes, juiced
- 4 c. vegetable broth
- 1 middle-sized cucumber
- 2 small red onions, diced
- 1 tsp. dried oregano
- 1 1/2 tsp. paprika powder
- 1/2 tsp. cayenne pepper
- Sea salt and freshly ground pepper to taste

Directions

1. In a pan, heat up olive oil and sauté onions and garlic until translucent. Set aside to cool down.
2. Use a large blender and blend parsley, avocado, tomatoes, cucumber, vegetable broth, lime juice, and onion-garlic mix until smooth. Add some water if desired, and season with cayenne pepper, paprika powder, oregano, salt, and pepper. Blend again and put in the fridge for at least 1/2 hours.
3. Tip: Add chives or dill to the gazpacho. Enjoy this great alkaline (cold) soup!

Nutrition

- Calories 48
- Carbohydrates 12 g.
- Fat 0.8 g.

149. Chilled Avocado Tomato Soup

PREPARATION TIME: **7'**

COOKING TIME: **20'**

SERVINGS: **1-2**

Ingredients

- 2 small avocados
- 2 large tomatoes
- 1 stalk of celery
- 1 small onion
- 1 clove of garlic
- Juice of 1 fresh lemon
- 1 c of water (best: alkaline water)
- A handful of fresh lavages
- Parsley and sea salt to taste

Directions

1. Scoop the avocados and cut all veggies into little pieces.
2. Spot all fixings in a blender and blend until smooth.
3. Serve chilled and enjoy this nutritious soup!

Nutrition

- Calories 68
- Carbohydrates 15 g.
- Fat 2 g.
- Protein: .8 g.

150. Pumpkin and White Bean Soup with Sage

Preparation Time: 10'
Cooking Time: 40'
Servings: 3-4

Ingredients

- 1 1/2 lbs. pumpkin
- 1/2 lb. yams
- 1/2 lb. white beans
- 1 onion
- 2 cloves of garlic
- 1 tbsp of cold-pressed, extra-virgin olive oil
- 1 tbsp of spices (your top picks)
- 1 tbsp of sage
- 1½-qt. water (best: alkaline water)
- A spot of sea salt and pepper

Directions

1. Cut the pumpkin in shapes, cut the onion, and the garlic, the spices, and the sage into fine pieces.
2. Sauté the onion and also the garlic in olive oil for around 2-3 minutes.
3. Include the pumpkin, spices, and sage and fry for an additional 5 minutes.
4. At that point, include the water and cook for around 30 minutes until vegetables are soft.
5. At long last include the beans and some salt and pepper.

Cook for an additional 5 minutes and serve right away. Enjoy this alkaline soup. Alkalizing tasty!

Nutrition

- Calories 78
- Carbohydrates 12 g.

151. Alkaline Pumpkin Tomato Soup

Preparation Time: 15'
Cooking Time: 30'
Servings: 3-4

Ingredients

- 1 qt of water (if accessible: soluble water)
- 400 g. fresh tomatoes, stripped and diced
- 1 medium-sized sweet pumpkin
- 5 yellow onions
- 1 tbsp. cold-pressed, extra-virgin olive oil
- 2 tsp. sea salt or regular salt
- Touch of cayenne pepper
- Your preferred spices
- Bunch of fresh parsley

Directions

1. Cut onions into little pieces and sauté with oil in a big pot.
2. Cut the pumpkin down the middle, at that point remove the stem and scoop out the seeds. Put it in the pot.
3. Include the tomatoes and the water and cook for around 20 minutes.
4. At that point, empty the soup into a food processor and blend well for a couple of minutes. Sprinkle with salt, pepper, and other spices.
5. Fill the bowls and trimming with fresh parsley. Make the most of your alkalizing soup!

Nutrition

- Calories 78
- Carbohydrates 20
- Fat 0.5 g.
- Protein 1.5 g.

152. Alkaline Pumpkin Coconut Soup

PREPARATION TIME: **10'**

COOKING TIME: **15'**

SERVINGS: **3-4**

Ingredients

- 2 lb. pumpkin
- 6 c. water (best: soluble water delivered with a water ionizer)
- 1 c. low-fat coconut milk
- 2 big onions
- 3 oz. leek
- 1 bunch of fresh parsley
- 1 touch of nutmeg
- 1 touch of cayenne pepper
- 1 tsp. sea salt or natural salt
- 4 tbsp. cold-pressed, extra-virgin olive oil

Directions

1. Cut the onions, the pumpkin, just as they leek into little pieces.
2. At that point, heat the olive oil in a big pot and sauté the onions for a couple of minutes.
3. At that point, include the water and heat up the pumpkin and the leek until soft.
4. Include coconut milk.
5. Use a hand blender and puree for around 1 minute. The soup should turn out very soft.
6. Season with salt, pepper, and nutmeg; lastly, include parsley.
7. Enjoy this alkalizing pumpkin soup hot or cold!

Nutrition

- Calories 88
- Carbohydrates 23 g.
- Fat 2.5 g.
- Protein 1.8 g.

153. Cold Cauliflower-Coconut Soup

PREPARATION TIME: **7'**

COOKING TIME: **20'**

SERVINGS: **3-4**

Ingredients

- 1 lb. (450 g.) fresh cauliflower
- 1 1/4 c. (300 ml.) unsweetened coconut milk
- 1 c. water (best: alkaline water)
- 2 tbsp. fresh lime juice
- 1/3 c. cold-pressed, extra-virgin olive oil
- 1 c. fresh coriander leaves, chopped
- Pinch of salt and cayenne pepper
- 1 bunch of unsweetened coconut chips

Directions

1. Steam the cauliflower for around 10 minutes.
2. At that point, set up the cauliflower with coconut milk and water in a food processor and blend until extremely smooth.
3. Include lime squeeze, salt and pepper, a large portion of the coriander, and oil and blend for an additional couple of minutes.
4. Pour in soup bowls and embellishment with coriander and coconut chips. Enjoy!

Nutrition

- Calories 65
- Carbohydrates 11 g.
- Fat 0.3 g.
- Protein 1.5 g.

154. Raw Avocado-Broccoli Soup with Cashew Nuts

PREPARATION TIME: **10'**

COOKING TIME: **30'**

SERVINGS: **1-2**

Ingredients

- 1/2 c. water (if available: alkaline water)
- 1/2 avocado
- 1 c. chopped broccoli
- 1/2 c. cashew nuts
- 1/2 c. alfalfa sprouts
- 1 clove of garlic
- 1 tbsp. cold-pressed, extra-virgin olive oil
- 1 pinch of sea salt and pepper
- Some parsley to garnish

Directions

1. Put the cashew nuts in a blender or food processor, include some water and puree for a couple of minutes.
2. Include the various fixings (with the exception of the avocado) individually and puree each for a couple of minutes.
3. Dispense the soup in a container and warm it up to the normal room temperature. Enhance with salt and pepper. Dice the avocado and cut the parsley.
4. Dispense the soup in a container or plate; include the avocado dices and embellishment with parsley.
5. That's it! Enjoy this excellent healthy soup!

Nutrition

- Calories 48
- Carbohydrates 18 g.
- Fat 3 g.
- Protein 1.4 g.

155. White Bean Soup

PREPARATION TIME: **10'**

COOKING TIME: **40'**

SERVINGS: **6**

Ingredients

- 2 c. white beans, rinsed
- 1/4 tsp. cayenne pepper
- 1 tsp. dried oregano
- 1/2 tsp. fresh rosemary, chopped
- 3 c. filtered alkaline water
- 3 c. unsweetened almond milk
- 3 garlic cloves, minced
- 2 carrots
- 2 celery stalks, diced
- 1 onion, chopped
- 1 tbsp. olive oil
- 1/2 tsp. sea salt

Directions

1. Add oil into the instant pot and set the pot on sauté mode.
2. Add carrots, celery, and onion in oil and sauté until softened, about 5 minutes.
3. Add garlic and sauté for a minute.
4. Add beans, seasonings, water, and almond milk and stir to combine.
5. Cover the pot with a lid and cook on high pressure for 35 minutes.
6. When finished, allow releasing pressure naturally then open the lid.
7. Stir well and serve.

Nutrition

- Calories 276
- Fat 4.8 g.
- Carbohydrates 44.2 g.
- Sugar 2.3 g.
- Protein 16.6 g.
- Cholesterol 0 mg.

156. Kale Cauliflower Soup

PREPARATION TIME: 10'

COOKING TIME: 25'

SERVINGS: 4

Ingredients

- 2 c. baby kale
- 1/2 c. unsweetened coconut milk
- 4 c of water
- 1 large cauliflower head, chopped
- 3 garlic cloves, peeled
- 2 carrots, peeled and chopped
- 2 onions, chopped
- 3 tbsp. olive oil
- Pepper
- Salt

Directions

1. Add oil into the instant pot and set the pot on sauté mode.
2. Add carrot, garlic, and onion to the pot and sauté for 5 7 minutes.
3. Add water and cauliflower and stir well.
4. Cover the pot with a lid and cook on high pressure for 20 minutes.
5. When finished, release the pressure using the quick release setting then open the lid.
6. Add kale and coconut milk and stir well.
7. Blend the soup utilizing a submersion blender until smooth.
8. Season with pepper and salt.

Nutrition

- Calories 261
- Fat 18.1 g.
- Carbohydrates 23.9 g.
- Sugar 9.9 g.
- Protein 6.6 g.
- Cholesterol 0 mg.

157. Healthy Broccoli Asparagus Soup

PREPARATION TIME: 10'

COOKING TIME: 20'

SERVINGS: 6

Ingredients

- 2 c. broccoli florets, chopped
- 15 asparagus spears, ends trimmed and chopped
- 1 tsp. dried oregano
- 1 tbsp. fresh thyme leaves
- 1/2 c. unsweetened almond milk
- 3 1/2 c. filtered alkaline water
- 2 c. cauliflower florets, chopped
- 2 tsp. garlic, chopped
- 1 c. onion, chopped
- 2 tbsp. olive oil
- Pepper
- Salt

Directions

1. Add oil in the instant pot and set the pot on sauté mode.
2. Add onion to the olive oil and sauté until onion is softened.
3. Add garlic and sauté for 30 seconds.
4. Add all vegetables and water and stir well.
5. Cover the pot with a lid and cook on manual mode for 3 minutes.
6. When finished, allow releasing pressure naturally then open the lid.
7. Blend the soup utilizing a submersion blender until smooth.
8. Stir in almond milk, herbs, pepper, and salt.
9. Serve and enjoy.

Nutrition

- Calories 85
- Fat 5.2 g.
- Carbohydrates 8.8 g.
- Sugar 3.3 g.
- Protein 3.3 g.
- Cholesterol 0 mg.

158. Creamy Asparagus Soup

Preparation time: 10'
Cooking time: 30'
Servings: 6

Ingredients

- 2 lbs. fresh asparagus cut off woody stems
- 1/4 tsp. lime zest
- 2 tbsp. lime juice
- 14 oz. coconut milk
- 1 tsp. dried thyme
- 1/2 tsp. oregano
- 1/2 tsp. sage
- 1 1/2 c. filtered alkaline water
- 1 cauliflower head, cut into florets
- 1 tbsp. garlic, minced
- 1 leek, sliced
- 3 tbsp. coconut oil
- Pinch of Himalayan salt

Directions

1. Preheat the oven to 400 F/ 200 C.
2. Line a baking tray with parchment paper and set it aside.
3. Arrange asparagus spears on a baking tray. Drizzle with 2 tbsps of coconut oil and sprinkle with salt, thyme, oregano, and sage.
4. Bake in preheated oven for 20-25 minutes.
5. Add remaining oil in the instant pot and set the pot on sauté mode.
6. Put some garlic and leek to the pot and sauté for 2-3 minutes.
7. Add cauliflower florets and water in the pot and stir well.
8. Cover the pot with a lid, select the steam mode, and set the timer for 4 minutes.
9. When finished, release pressure using the quick release setting.
10. Add roasted asparagus, lime zest, lime juice, and coconut milk and stir well.
11. Blend the soup utilizing a submersion blender until smooth.
12. Serve and enjoy.

Nutrition

- Calories 265
- Fat 22.9 g.
- Carbohydrates 14.7 g.
- Sugar 6.7 g.
- Protein 6.1 g.
- Cholesterol 0 mg.

159. Quick Broccoli Soup

Preparation time: 5'
Cooking time: 10'
Servings: 6

Ingredients

- 1 lb. broccoli, chopped
- 6 c. filtered alkaline water
- 1 onion, diced
- 2 tbsp. olive oil
- Pepper
- Salt

Directions

1. Add oil into the instant pot and set the pot on sauté mode.
2. Add the onion in olive oil and sauté until softened.
3. Add broccoli and water and stir well.
4. Cover the pot with a lid and cook on manual high pressure for 3 minutes.
5. When finished, release pressure using the quick release setting then open the lid.
6. Blend the soup utilizing a submersion blender until smooth.
7. Season soup with pepper and salt.
8. Serve and enjoy.

Nutrition

- Calories 73
- Fat 4.9 g.
- Carbohydrates 6.7 g.
- Protein 2.3 g.
- Sugar 2.1 g.
- Cholesterol 0 mg.

160. Green Lentil Soup

Preparation time: 10'

Cooking time: 30'

Servings: 4

Ingredients

- 1 1/2 c. green lentils, rinsed
- 4 c. baby spinach
- 4 c. filtered alkaline water
- 1 tsp. Italian seasoning
- 2 tsp. fresh thyme
- 14 oz. tomatoes, diced
- 3 garlic cloves, minced
- 2 celery stalks, chopped
- 1 carrot, chopped
- 1 onion, chopped
- Pepper
- Sea salt

Directions

1. Add all the ingredients except spinach into the instant pot and mix fine.
2. Cover pot with top and cook on manual high pressure for 18 minutes.
3. When finished, release pressure using the quick release setting then open the lid.
4. Add spinach and stir well.
5. Serve and enjoy.

Nutrition

- Calories 306
- Fat 1.5 g.
- Carbohydrates 53.7 g.
- Sugar 6.4 g.
- Protein 21 g.
- Cholesterol 1 mg.

161. Squash Soup

Preparation time: 10'

Cooking time: 40'

Servings: 4

Ingredients

- 3 lbs. butternut squash, peeled and cubed
- 1 tbsp. curry powder
- 1/2 c. unsweetened coconut milk
- 3 c. filtered alkaline water
- 2 garlic cloves, minced
- 1 large onion, minced
- 1 tsp. olive oil
- Salt, to taste

Directions

1. Add olive oil in the instant pot and set the pot on sauté mode.
2. Add the onion and cook until tender, about 8 minutes.
3. Add curry powder and garlic and sauté for a minute.
4. Add butternut squash, water, and salt and stir well.
5. Cover the pot with a lid and cook in soup mode for 30 minutes.
6. When finished, allow releasing pressure naturally for 10 minutes then release using the quick-release setting then open the lid.
7. Blend the soup utilizing a submersion blender until smooth.
8. Add coconut milk and stir well.
9. Serve warm and enjoy.

Nutrition

- Calories 254
- Fat 8.9 g.
- Carbohydrates 46.4 g.
- Sugar 10.1 g.
- Protein 4.8 g.
- Cholesterol 0 mg.

162. Tomato Soup

PREPARATION TIME: 5'

COOKING TIME: 20'

SERVINGS: 4

Ingredients

- 6 tomatoes, chopped
- 1 onion, diced
- 14 oz. coconut milk
- 1 tsp. turmeric
- 1 tsp. garlic, minced
- 1/4 c. cilantro, chopped
- 1/2 tsp. cayenne pepper
- 1 tsp. ginger, minced
- 1/2 tsp. sea salt

Directions

1. Add all the ingredients into the instant pot and mix well.
2. Cover the instant pot with a lid and cook on manual high pressure for 5 minutes.
3. When finished, allow releasing pressure naturally for 10 minutes then release using the quick release mode.
4. Blend the soup utilizing a submersion blender until smooth.
5. Stir well and serve.

Nutrition

- Calories 81
- Fat 3.5 g.
- Carbohydrates 11.6 g.
- Sugar 6.1 g.
- Protein 2.5 g.
- Cholesterol 0 mg.

163. Basil Zucchini Soup

PREPARATION TIME: 10'

COOKING TIME: 20'

SERVINGS: 4

Ingredients

- 3 medium zucchinis, peeled and chopped
- 1/4 c. basil, chopped
- 1 large leek, chopped
- 3 c. filtered alkaline water
- 1 tbsp. lemon juice
- 3 tbsp. olive oil
- 2 tsp. sea salt

Directions

1. Add 2 tbsp. oil into the pot and set the pot on sauté mode.
2. Add zucchini and sauté for 5 minutes.
3. Add basil and leeks and sauté for 2-3 minutes.
4. Add lemon juice, water, and salt. Stir well.
5. Cover the pot with a lid and cook on high pressure for 8 minutes.
6. When finished, allow releasing pressure naturally then open the lid.
7. Blend the soup utilizing a submersion blender until smooth.
8. Top with remaining olive oil and serve.

Nutrition

- Calories 157
- Fat 11.9 g.
- Carbohydrates 8.9 g.
- Protein 5.8 g.
- Sugar 4 g.
- Cholesterol 0 mg.

164. Summer Vegetable Soup

PREPARATION TIME: 5'

COOKING TIME: 20'

SERVINGS: 10

Ingredients

- 1/2 c. basil, chopped
- 2 bell peppers, seeded and sliced
- 1/ cup green beans, trimmed and cut into pieces
- 8 c. filtered alkaline water
- 1 medium summer squash, sliced
- 1 medium zucchini, sliced
- 2 large tomatoes, sliced
- 1 small eggplant, sliced
- 6 garlic cloves, smashed
- 1 medium onion, diced
- Pepper
- Salt

Directions

1. Combine all the ingredients into the instant pot and mix well.
2. Cover the pot with a lid and cook in soup mode for 10 minutes.
3. Release pressure using the quick-release setting then open the lid.
4. Blend the soup utilizing a submersion blender until smooth.
5. Serve and enjoy.

Nutrition

- Calories 84
- Fat 1.6 g.
- Carbohydrates 12.8 g.
- Protein 6.1 g.
- Sugar 6.1 g.
- Cholesterol 0 mg.

165. Almond-Red Bell Pepper Dip

PREPARATION TIME: 14'

COOKING TIME: 16'

SERVINGS: 3

Ingredients

- 2-3 garlic cloves
- 1 pinch of sea salt
- 1 pinch of cayenne pepper,
- 1 tbsp. extra-virgin olive oil (cold-pressed),
- 60 g. almonds
- 280 g. red bell pepper

Directions

1. First of all, cook garlic and pepper until they are soft.
2. Add all the ingredients to a mixer and blend until the mix becomes smooth and creamy.
3. Finally, add pepper and salt to taste.
4. Serve.

Nutrition

- Calories 51
- Carbohydrates 10 g.
- Fat 1 g.
- Protein 2 g.

166. Spicy Carrot Soup

Preparation time: 10'

Cooking time: 20'

Servings: 6

Ingredients

- 8 large carrots, peeled and chopped
- 1 1/2 c. filtered alkaline water
- 14 oz. coconut milk
- 3 garlic cloves, peeled
- 1 tbsp. red curry paste
- 1/4 c. olive oil
- 1 onion, chopped
- Salt

Directions

1. Combine all the ingredients into the instant pot and mix well.
2. Cover the pot with a lid, select manual, and set the timer for 15 minutes.
3. Allow releasing pressure naturally then open the lid.
4. Blend the soup utilizing a submersion blender until smooth.
5. Serve and enjoy.

Nutrition

- Calories 267
- Fat 22 g.
- Carbohydrates 13 g.
- Protein 4 g.
- Sugar 5 g.
- Cholesterol 20 mg.

167. Zucchini Soup

Preparation time: 10'

Cooking time: 30'

Servings: 6

Ingredients

- 10 c. zucchini, chopped
- 32 oz. filtered alkaline water
- 13.5 oz. coconut milk
- 1 tbsp. Thai curry paste

Directions

1. Combine all elements into the instant pot and mix fine.
2. Cover the pot with a lid and cook on manual high pressure for 10 minutes.
3. Release pressure using the quick-release mode then open the lid.
4. Using a blender, blend the soup until smooth.
5. Serve and enjoy.

Nutrition

- Calories 122
- Fat 9.8 g.
- Carbohydrates 6.6 g.
- Protein 4.1 g.
- Sugar 3.6 g.
- Cholesterol 0 mg.

168. Kidney Bean Stew

PREPARATION TIME: **15'**

COOKING TIME: **15'**

SERVINGS: **2**

Ingredients

- 1 lb. cooked kidney beans
- 1 c. tomato passata
- 1 c. low sodium beef broth
- 3 tbsp. Italian herbs

Directions

1. Mix all the ingredients in your instant pot.
2. Cook on Stew for 15 minutes.
3. Release the pressure naturally.

Nutrition

- Calories 270
- Carbohydrates 16 g.
- Sugar 3 g.
- Fat 10 g.
- Protein 23 g.
- GI : 8 g.

169. Cabbage Soup

PREPARATION TIME: **10'**

COOKING TIME: **35'**

SERVINGS: **2**

Ingredients

- 1 lb. shredded cabbage
- 1 c. low sodium vegetable broth
- 1 shredded onion
- 2 tbsp. mixed herbs
- 1 tbsp. black pepper

Directions

1. Mix all the ingredients in your instant pot.
2. Cook on Stew for 35 minutes.
3. Release the pressure naturally.

Nutrition

- Calories 60
- Carbohydrates 2 g.
- Sugar 0 g.
- Fat 2 g.
- Protein 4 g.
- GI: 1 g.

170. Pumpkin Spice Soup

PREPARATION TIME: **10'**

COOKING TIME: **35'**

SERVINGS: **2**

Ingredients

- 1 lb. cubed pumpkin
- 1 c. low sodium vegetable broth
- 2 tbsp. mixed spice

Directions

1. Mix all the ingredients in your instant pot.
2. Cook on Stew for 35 minutes.
3. Release the pressure naturally.
4. Blend the soup.

Nutrition

- Calories 100
- Carbohydrates 7 g.
- Sugar 1 g.
- Fat 2 g.
- Protein 3 g.
- GL: 1 g.

171. Cream of Tomato Soup

PREPARATION TIME: **15'**

COOKING TIME: **15'**

SERVINGS: **2**

Ingredients

- 1 lb. fresh tomatoes, chopped
- 1.5 c. low sodium tomato puree
- 1 tbsp. black pepper

Directions

1. Mix all the ingredients in your instant pot.
2. Cook on Stew for 15 minutes.
3. Release the pressure naturally.
4. Blend.

Nutrition

- Calories 20
- Carbohydrates 2 g.
- Sugar 1 g.
- Fat 0 g.
- Protein 3 g.
- GL: 1 g.

172. Shiitake Soup

PREPARATION TIME: **15'**

COOKING TIME: **35'**

SERVINGS: **2**

Ingredients

- 1 c. shiitake mushrooms
- 1 c. diced vegetables
- 1 c. low sodium vegetable broth
- 2 tbsp. 5 spice seasoning

Directions

1. Mix all the ingredients in your instant pot.
2. Cook on Stew for 35 minutes.
3. Release the pressure naturally.

Nutrition

- Calories 70
- Carbohydrates 5 g.
- Sugar 1 g.
- Fat 2 g.
- Protein 2 g.
- GL: 1 g.

173. Spicy Pepper Soup

PREPARATION TIME: **15'**

COOKING TIME: **15'**

SERVINGS: **2**

Ingredients

- 1 lb. chopped mixed sweet peppers
- 1 c. low sodium vegetable broth
- 3 tbsp. chopped chili peppers
- 1 tbsp. black pepper

Directions

1. Mix all the ingredients in your instant pot.
2. Cook on Stew for 15 minutes.
3. Release the pressure naturally. Blend.

Nutrition

- Calories 100
- Carbohydrates 11 g.
- Sugar 4 g.
- Fat 2 g.
- Protein 3 g.
- GL: 6 g.

174. Zoodle Won-Ton Soup

Preparation time: 15'
Cooking time: 5'
Servings: 2

Ingredients

- 1 lb. spiralized zucchini
- 1 pack unfried wontons
- 1 c. low sodium beef broth
- 2 tbsp. soy sauce

Directions

1. Mix all the ingredients in your instant pot.
2. Cook on Stew for 5 minutes.
3. Release the pressure naturally.

Nutrition

- Calories 300
- Carbohydrates 6 g.
- Sugar 1 g.
- Fat 9 g.
- Protein 43 g.
- GL: 2 g.

175. Broccoli Stilton Soup

Preparation time: 15'
Cooking time: 35'
Servings: 2

Ingredients

- 1 lb. chopped broccoli
- 0.5 lb. chopped vegetables
- 1 c. low sodium vegetable broth
- 1 c. Stilton

Directions

1. Mix all the ingredients in your instant pot.
2. Cook on Stew for 35 minutes.
3. Release the pressure naturally.
4. Blend the soup.

Nutrition

- Calories 280
- Carbohydrates 9 g.
- Sugar 2 g.
- Fat 22 g.
- Protein 13 g.
- GL: 4 g.

176. Lamb Stew

PREPARATION TIME: **15'**

COOKING TIME: **35'**

SERVINGS: **2**

Ingredients

- 1 lb. diced lamb shoulder
- 1 lb. chopped winter vegetables
- 1 c. low sodium vegetable broth
- 1 tbsp. yeast extract
- 1 tbsp. star anise spice mix

Directions

1. Mix all the ingredients in your instant pot.
2. Cook on Stew for 35 minutes.
3. Release the pressure naturally.

Nutrition

- Calories 320
- Carbohydrates 10 g.
- Sugar 2 g.
- Fat 8 g.
- Protein 42 g.
- GL : 3 g.

177. Irish Stew

PREPARATION TIME: **15'**

COOKING TIME: **35'**

SERVINGS: **2**

Ingredients

- 1.5 lb. diced lamb shoulder
- 1 lb. chopped vegetables
- 1 c. low sodium beef broth
- 3 minced onions
- 1 tbsp. ghee

Directions

1. Mix all the ingredients in your instant pot.
2. Cook on Stew for 35 minutes.
3. Release the pressure naturally.

Nutrition

- Calories 330
- Carbohydrates 9 g.
- Sugar 2 g.
- Fat 12 g.
- Protein 49 g.
- GL : 3 g.

178. Sweet and Sour Soup

Preparation time: 15'

Cooking time: 25'

Servings: 2

Ingredients

- 1 lb. cubed chicken breast
- 1 lb. chopped vegetables
- 1 c. low carb sweet and sour sauce
- 0.5 c. diabetic marmalade

Directions

1. Mix all the ingredients in your instant pot.
2. Cook on Stew for 35 minutes.
3. Release the pressure naturally.

Nutrition

- Calories 120
- Carbohydrates 9 g.
- Sugar 1 g.
- Fat 23g.
- Protein 21 g.
- GL: 1 g.

179. Meatball Stew

Preparation time: 15'

Cooking time: 25'

Servings: 2

Ingredients

- 1 lb. sausage meat
- 2 c. chopped tomato
- 1 c. chopped vegetables
- 2 tbsp. Italian seasonings
- 1 tbsp. vegetable oil

Directions

1. Roll the sausage into meatballs.
2. Put the instant pot on Sauté and fry the meatballs in the oil until brown.
3. Mix all the ingredients in your instant pot.
4. Cook on Stew for 25 minutes.
5. Release the pressure naturally.

Nutrition

- Calories 300
- Carbohydrates 4 g.
- Sugar 1 g.
- Fat 12 g.
- Protein 40 g.
- GL: 2 g.

180. Kebab Stew

Preparation time: 15'

Cooking time: 35'

Servings: 2

Ingredients

- 1 lb. cubed, seasoned kebab meat
- 1 lb. cooked chickpeas
- 1 c. low sodium vegetable broth
- 1 tbsp. black pepper

Directions

1. Mix all the ingredients in your instant pot.
2. Cook on Stew for 35 minutes.
3. Release the pressure naturally.

Nutrition

- Calories 290
- Carbohydrates 22 g.
- Sugar 4 g.
- Fat 10 g.
- Protein 34 g.
- GL: 6 g.

181. French Onion Soup

Preparation time: 35'

Cooking time: 35'

Servings: 2

Ingredients

- 6 onions, chopped finely
- 2 c. vegetable broth
- 2 tbsp. oil
- 2 tbsp. Gruyere

Directions

1. Place the oil in your instant pot and cook the onions on Sauté until soft and brown.
2. Mix all the ingredients in your instant pot.
3. Cook on Stew for 35 minutes.
4. Release the pressure naturally.

Nutrition

- Calories 110
- Carbohydrates 8 g.
- Sugar 3 g.
- Fat 10 g.
- Protein 3 g.
- GL: 4 g.

182. Meatless Ball Soup

Preparation time: 15'
Cooking time: 15'
Servings: 2

Ingredients

- 1 lb. minced tofu
- 0.5 lb. chopped vegetables
- 2 c. low sodium vegetable broth
- 1 tbsp. almond flour
- Salt and pepper

Directions

1. Mix the tofu, flour, salt, and pepper.
2. Form the meatballs.
3. Place all the ingredients in your instant pot.
4. Cook on Stew for 15 minutes.
5. Release the pressure naturally.

Nutrition

- Calories 240
- Carbohydrates 9 g.
- Sugar 3 g.
- Fat 10 g.
- Protein 35 g.
- GL: 5 g.

183. Fake-On Stew

Preparation time: 15'
Cooking time: 25'
Servings: 2

Ingredients

- 0.5 lb. soy bacon
- 1 lb. chopped vegetables
- 1 c. low sodium vegetable broth
- 1 tbsp. nutritional yeast

Directions

1. Mix all the ingredients in your instant pot.
2. Cook on Stew for 25 minutes.
3. Release the pressure naturally.

Nutrition

- Calories 200
- Carbohydrates 12 g.
- Sugar 3 g.
- Fat 7 g.
- Protein 41 g.
- GL: 5 g.

184. Chickpea Soup

PREPARATION TIME: **15'**

COOKING TIME: **35'**

SERVINGS: **2**

Ingredients

- 1 lb. cooked chickpeas
- 1 lb. chopped vegetables
- 1 c. low sodium vegetable broth
- 2 tbsp. mixed herbs

Directions

1. Mix all the ingredients in your instant pot.
2. Cook on Stew for 35 minutes.
3. Release the pressure naturally.

Nutrition

- Calories 310
- Carbohydrates 20 g.
- Sugar 3 g.
- Fat 5 g.
- Protein 27 g.
- GL : 5 g.

185. Chicken Zoodle Soup

PREPARATION TIME: **15'**

COOKING TIME: **35'**

SERVINGS: **2**

Ingredients

- 1 lb. chopped cooked chicken
- 1 lb. spiralized zucchini
- 1 c. low sodium chicken soup
- 1 c. diced vegetables

Directions

1. Mix all the ingredients except the zucchini in your instant pot.
2. Cook on Stew for 35 minutes.
3. Release the pressure naturally.
4. Stir in the zucchini and allow to heat thoroughly.

Nutrition

- Calories 250
- Carbohydrates 5 g.
- Sugar 0 g.
- Fat 10 g.
- Protein 40 g.
- GL: 1 g.

186. Lemon-Tarragon Soup

PREPARATION TIME: **10'**

COOKING TIME: **10'**

SERVINGS: **1-2**

Ingredients

- 1 tbsp. avocado oil
- 1/2 c. diced onion
- 3 garlic cloves, crushed
- 1/4 plus 1/8 tsp. sea salt
- 1/4 plus 1/8 tsp. freshly ground black pepper
- 1 (13.5-oz.) can full-fat coconut milk
- 1 tbsp. freshly-squeezed lemon juice
- 1/2 c. raw cashews
- 1 celery stalk
- 2 tbsps chopped fresh tarragon

Directions

1. In a medium skillet over medium-high warmth, heat the avocado oil. Add the onion, garlic, salt, and pepper, and sauté for 3-5 minutes or until the onion is soft.
2. In a high-speed blender, blend together the coconut milk, lemon juice, cashews, celery, and tarragon with the onion mixture until smooth. Adjust seasonings, if necessary.
3. Fill 1 big or 2 small dishes and enjoy immediately, or transfer to a medium saucepan and warm on low heat for 3-5 minutes before serving.

Nutrition

- Calories 60
- Carbohydrates 13 g.
- Protein 0.8 g.

187. Chilled Cucumber and Lime Soup

PREPARATION TIME: **5'**

COOKING TIME: **20'**

SERVINGS: **1-2**

Ingredients

- 1 cucumber, peeled
- 1/2 zucchini, peeled
- 1 tbsp. freshly squeezed lime juice
- 1 tbsp. fresh cilantro leaves
- 1 garlic clove, crushed
- 1/4 tsp. sea salt

Directions

1. In a blender, blend together the cucumber, zucchini, lime juice, cilantro, garlic, and salt until well combined. Add more salt, if necessary.
2. Fill 1 big or 2 small dishes and enjoy immediately, or refrigerate for 15-20 minutes to chill before serving.

Nutrition

- Calories 48
- Carbohydrates 8 g.
- Fat 1 g.
- Protein: .5 g.

188. Coconut, Cilantro, and Jalapeño Soup

PREPARATION TIME: 5'

COOKING TIME: 5'

SERVINGS: 1-2

Ingredients

- 2 tbsps avocado oil
- 1/2 c. diced onions
- 3 garlic cloves, crushed
- 1/4 tsp. sea salt
- 1/4 tsp. pepper
- 1 (13.5-oz.) can full-fat coconut milk
- 1 tbsp. freshly squeezed lime juice
- 1/2 to 1 jalapeño
- 2 tbsps fresh cilantro leaves

Directions

1. In a medium skillet over medium-high warmth, heat the avocado oil. Include the garlic, onion, salt, and pepper, and sauté for 3-5 minutes, or until the onions are soft.
2. In a blender, blend together the coconut milk, lime juice, jalapeño, and cilantro with the onion mixture until creamy.
3. Fill in 1 big or 2 small dishes and enjoy.

Nutrition

- Calories 75
- Carbohydrates 13 g.
- Fat 2 g.
- Protein 4 g.

189. Spicy Watermelon Gazpacho

PREPARATION TIME: 5'

COOKING TIME: 5'

SERVINGS: 1-2

Ingredients

- 2 c. cubed watermelon
- 1/4 c. diced onion
- 1/4 c. packed cilantro leaves
- 1/2 to 1 jalapeño
- 2 tbsps freshly squeezed lime juice

Directions

1. In a blender or food processor, pulse to combine the watermelon, onion, cilantro, jalapeño, and lime juice only long enough to break down the ingredients, leaving them very finely diced and taking care to not over process.
2. Pour into 1 large or 2 small bowls and enjoy.

Nutrition

- Calories 35
- Carbohydrates 12 g.
- Fat: .4 g.

190. Roasted Carrot and Leek Soup

Preparation Time: 4'

Cooking Time: 30'

Servings: 3-4

Ingredients

- 6 carrots
- 1 c. chopped onion
- 1 fennel bulb, cubed
- 2 garlic cloves, crushed
- 2 tbsps avocado oil
- 1 tsp. sea salt
- 1 tsp. freshly ground black pepper
- 2 c. almond milk, plus more if desired

Directions

1. Preheat the oven to 400 °F. Line a baking sheet with parchment paper.
2. Cut the carrots into thirds, and then cut each third in half. Transfer to a medium bowl.
3. Add the onion, fennel, garlic, and avocado oil, and toss to coat. Season with salt and pepper, and toss again.
4. Transfer the vegetables to the prepared baking sheet, and roast for 30 minutes.
5. Remove from the oven and allow the vegetables to cool.
6. In a high-speed blender, blend together the almond milk and roasted vegetables until creamy and smooth. Adjust the seasonings, if necessary, and add additional milk if you prefer a thinner consistency.
7. Pour into 2 large or 4 small bowls and enjoy.

Nutrition

- Calories 55
- Carbohydrates 12 g.
- Fat 1.5 g.
- Protein 1.8 g.

191. Creamy Lentil Stew

Preparation Time: 10'

Cooking Time: 30'

Servings: 4

Ingredients

- 2 tbsps avocado oil
- 1/2 c. diced onion
- 2 garlic cloves, crushed
- 1-1 1/2 tsps. sea salt
- 1 tsp. freshly ground black pepper
- 1 c. dry lentils
- 2 carrots, sliced
- 1 celery stalk, diced
- 2 fresh oregano sprigs, chopped
- 2 fresh tarragon sprigs, chopped
- 5 c. vegetable broth, divided
- 1 (13.5-oz.) can full-fat coconut milk

Directions

1. In a great soup pot over medium-high heat, heat the avocado oil. Include the garlic, onion, salt, and pepper, and sauté for 3–5 minutes, or until the onion is soft.
2. Add the lentils, carrots, celery, oregano, tarragon, and 2 1/2 c of vegetable broth, and stir.
3. Get to a boil, decrease the heat to medium-low, and cook, stirring frequently and adding additional vegetable broth a half cup at a time to make sure there is enough liquid for the lentils to cook, for 20–25 minutes, or until the lentils are soft.
4. Take away from the heat, and stir in the coconut milk. Pour into 4 soup bowls and enjoy.

Nutrition

- Calories 85
- Carbohydrates 20 g.
- Fat 3 g.
- Protein 3 g.

192. Roasted Garlic and Cauliflower Soup

Preparation Time: 10'
Cooking Time: 35'
Servings: 1-2

Ingredients

- 4 c. bite-size cauliflower florets
- 5 garlic cloves
- 1 1/2 tbsps avocado oil
- 3/4 teaspoon sea salt
- 1/2 teaspoon freshly ground black pepper
- 1 c. almond milk
- 1 c. vegetable broth, plus more if desired

Directions

1. Preheat the oven to 450 °F. Line a baking sheet with parchment paper.
2. In a medium bowl, toss the cauliflower and garlic with the avocado oil to coat. Season with salt and pepper, and toss again.
3. Transfer to the prepared baking sheet and roast for 30 minutes. Cool before adding to the blender.
4. In a high-speed blender, blend together the cooled vegetables, almond milk, and vegetable broth until creamy and smooth. Adjust the salt and pepper, if necessary, and add additional vegetable broth if you prefer a thinner consistency.
5. Transfer to a medium saucepan and lightly warm on medium-low heat for 3-5 minutes.
6. Ladle into 1 large or 2 small bowls and enjoy.

Nutrition

- Calories 48
- Carbohydrates 11 g.
- Protein 1.5 g.

193. Beefless "Beef" Stew

Preparation Time: 10'
Cooking Time: 0'
Servings: 4

Ingredients

- 1 tbsp. avocado oil
- 1 c. onion, diced
- 2 garlic cloves, crushed
- 1 tsp. sea salt
- 1 tsp. freshly ground black pepper
- 3 c. vegetable broth, plus more if desired
- 2 c. water, plus more if desired
- 3 c. sliced carrot
- 2 celery stalks, diced
- 1 tsp. dried oregano
- 1 dried bay leaf

Directions

1. In a medium soup pot over medium heat, heat the avocado oil. Include the onion, garlic, salt, and pepper, and sauté for 2-3 minutes, or until the onion is soft.
2. Add the vegetable broth, water, carrot, celery, oregano, and bay leaf, and stir. Get to a boil, decrease the heat to medium-low, and cook for 30-45 minutes, or until the carrots are soft.
3. Adjust the seasonings, if necessary, and add additional water or vegetable broth, if a soupier consistency is preferred, in half-cup increments.
4. Ladle into 4 soup bowls and enjoy.

Nutrition

- Calories 59
- Carbohydrates 12 g.

194. Creamy Mushroom Soup

Preparation time: 5'
Cooking time: 20'
Servings: 4

Ingredients

- 1 tbsp. avocado oil
- 1 c. sliced shiitake mushrooms
- 1 c. sliced cremini mushrooms
- 1 c. diced onion
- 1 garlic clove, crushed
- 3/4 teaspoon sea salt
- 1/2 teaspoon freshly ground black pepper
- 1 c. vegetable broth
- 1 (13.5-oz.) can full-fat coconut milk
- 1/2 teaspoon dried thyme
- 1 tbsp. coconut aminos

Directions

1. In a great soup pot over medium-high heat, heat the avocado oil. Add the mushrooms, onion, garlic, salt, and pepper, and sauté for 2–3 minutes, or until the onion is soft.
2. Add the vegetable broth, coconut milk, thyme, and coconut aminos. Reduce the heat to medium-low, and simmer for about 15 minutes, stirring occasionally.
3. Adjust seasonings, if necessary, ladle into 2 large or 4 small bowls, and enjoy.

Nutrition

- Calories 65
- Carbohydrates 12 g.
- Fat 2 g.
- Protein 2 g.

195. Chilled Berry and Mint Soup

Preparation time: 5'
Cooking time: 20'
Servings: 1-2

Ingredients

For the Sweetener
- 1/4 c. unrefined whole cane sugar, such as Sucanat
- 1/4 c. water, plus more if desired

For the Soup
- 1 c. mixed berries (raspberries, blackberries, blueberries)
- 1/2 c. water
- 1 tsp. freshly squeezed lemon juice
- 8 fresh mint leaves

Directions

1. To prepare the sweetener: In a small saucepan over medium-low, heat the sugar and water, stirring continuously for 1–2 minutes, until the sugar is dissolved. Cool.
2. To prepare the soup: In a blender, blend together the cooled sugar water with the berries, water, lemon juice, and mint leaves until well combined.
3. Transfer the mixture to the refrigerator and allow chilling completely, about 20 minutes.
4. Ladle into 1 large or 2 small bowls and enjoy.

Nutrition

- Calories 89
- Carbohydrates 12 g.
- Fat 6 g.
- Protein 2.2 g.

Chapter 9: Appetizer Recipes

196. Aromatic Toasted Pumpkin Seeds

PREPARATION TIME: **5'**

COOKING TIME: **45'**

SERVINGS: **4**

Ingredients

- 1 c. pumpkin seeds
- 1 tsp. cinnamon
- 2 packets stevia
- 1 tbsp. canola oil
- 1/4 tsp. sea salt

Directions

1. Prep the oven to 300 °F (150°C).
2. Combine the pumpkin seeds with cinnamon, stevia, canola oil, and salt in a bowl. Stir to mix well.
3. Pour the seeds in a single layer on a baking sheet, then arrange the sheet in the preheated oven.
4. Bake for 45 minutes or until well toasted and fragrant. Shake the sheet twice to bake the seeds evenly.
5. Serve immediately.

Nutrition

- Calories 202
- Carbohydrates 5.1 g.
- Fiber 2.3 g.

197. Bacon-Wrapped Shrimps

PREPARATION TIME: **10'**

COOKING TIME: **6'**

SERVINGS: **10**

Ingredients

- 20 shrimps, peeled and deveined
- 7 slices bacon
- 4 leaves romaine lettuce

Directions

1. Set the oven to 205 °C.
2. Wrap each shrimp with each bacon strip, then arrange the wrapped shrimps in a single layer on a baking sheet, seam side down.
3. Broil for 6 minutes. Flip the shrimps halfway through the cooking time.
4. Take out from the oven and serve on lettuce leaves.

Nutrition

- Calories 70
- Fat 4.5 g.
- Protein 7 g.

198. Cheesy Broccoli Bites

PREPARATION TIME: 10'

COOKING TIME: 25'

SERVINGS: 6

Ingredients

- 2 tbsps olive oil
- 2 heads broccoli, trimmed
- 1 egg
- 1/3 c. reduced-fat shredded Cheddar cheese
- 1 egg white
- 1/2 c. onion, chopped
- 1/3 c. bread crumbs
- 1/4 tsp. salt
- 1/4 tsp. black pepper

Directions

1. Ready the oven at 400 °F (205 °C). Coat a large baking sheet with olive oil.
2. Arrange a colander in a saucepan, then place the broccoli in the colander. Pour the water into the saucepan to cover the bottom. Boil, then reduce the heat to low. Close and simmer for 6 minutes. Allow cooling for 10 minutes.
3. Blend the broccoli and the remaining ingredients in a food processor. Let sit for 10 minutes.
4. Make the bites: Drop 1 tbsp of the mixture on the baking sheet. Repeat with the remaining mixture.
5. Bake in the preheated oven for 25 minutes. Flip the bites halfway through the cooking time.
6. Serve immediately.

Nutrition

- Calories 100
- Carbohydrates 13 g.
- Fiber 3 g.

151

199. Easy Caprese Skewers

PREPARATION TIME: 5'

COOKING TIME: 0'

SERVINGS: 2

Ingredients

- 12 cherry tomatoes
- 8 (1-in.) pieces Mozzarella cheese
- 12 basil leaves
- 1/4 c. Italian Vinaigrette, for serving

Directions

1. Thread the tomatoes, cheese, and bay leaf alternatively through the skewers.
2. Place the skewers on a big plate and baste with the Italian vinaigrette. Serve immediately.

Nutrition

- Calories 230
- Carbohydrates 8.5 g.
- Fiber 1.9 g.

200. Grilled Tofu with Sesame Seeds

PREPARATION TIME: 45'

COOKING TIME: 20'

SERVINGS: 6

Ingredients

- 1 1/2 tbsps brown rice vinegar
- 1 scallion
- 1 tbsp. ginger root
- 1 tbsp. no-sugar-added applesauce
- 2 tbsps naturally brewed soy sauce
- 1/4 tsp. dried red pepper flakes
- 2 tsps. sesame oil, toasted
- 1 (14-oz./397 g.) package extra-firm tofu
- 2 tbsps fresh cilantro
- 1 tsp. sesame seeds

Directions

1. 1 1/2 tbsps brown rice vinegar
2. 1 scallion
3. 1 tbsp. ginger root
4. 1 tbsp. no-sugar-added applesauce
5. 2 tbsps naturally brewed soy sauce
6. 1/4 tsp. dried red pepper flakes
7. 2 tsps. sesame oil, toasted
8. 1 (14-oz./397 g.) package extra-firm tofu
9. 2 tbsps fresh cilantro
10. 1 tsp. sesame seeds

Nutrition

- Calories 90
- Carbohydrates 3 g.
- Fiber 1 g.

201. Kale Chips

PREPARATION TIME: 5'

COOKING TIME: 15'

SERVINGS: 1

Ingredients

- 1/4 tsp. garlic powder
- Pinch cayenne to taste
- 1 tbsp. extra-virgin olive oil
- 1/2 teaspoon sea salt, or to taste
- 1 (8-oz.) bunch kale

Directions

1. Prepare the oven at 180 ☒C. Line 2 baking sheets with parchment paper.
2. Toss the garlic powder, cayenne pepper, olive oil, and salt in a large bowl, then dunk the kale in the bowl.
3. Situate the kale in a single layer on one of the baking sheets.
4. Arrange the sheet in the preheated oven and bake for 7 minutes. Remove the sheet from the oven and pour the kale into the single layer of the other baking sheet.
5. Move the sheet of kale back to the oven and bake for another 7 minutes.
6. Serve immediately.

Nutrition

- Calories 136
- Carbohydrates 3 g.
- Fiber 1.1 g.

202. Simple Deviled Eggs

PREPARATION TIME: **5'**

COOKING TIME: **8'**

SERVINGS: **12**

Ingredients

- 6 large eggs
- 1/8 tsp. mustard powder
- 2 tbsps light mayonnaise
- Salt and pepper, to taste

Directions

1. Sit the eggs in a saucepan, then pour in enough water to cover the egg. Bring to a boil, then boil the eggs for another 8 minutes. Turn off the heat and cover, then let sit for 15 minutes.
2. Transfer the boiled eggs to a pot of cold water and peel under the water.
3. Transfer the eggs to a large plate, then cut in half. Remove the egg yolks and place them in a bowl, then mash with a fork.
4. Add the mustard powder, mayo, salt, and pepper to the bowl of yolks, then stir to mix well.
5. Spoon the yolk mixture in the egg white on the plate. Serve immediately.

Nutrition

- Calories 45
- Carbohydrates 1 g.
- Fiber 0.9 g.

203. Sauteed Collard Greens and Cabbage

PREPARATION TIME: **10'**

COOKING TIME: **10'**

SERVINGS: **2**

Ingredients

- 2 tbsps extra-virgin olive oil
- 1 collard greens bunch
- 1/2 small green cabbage
- 6 garlic cloves
- 1 tbsp. low-sodium soy sauce

Directions

1. Cook olive oil in a large skillet over medium-high heat.
2. Sauté the collard greens in the oil for about 2 minutes, or until the greens start to wilt.
3. Toss in the cabbage and mix well. Set to medium-low, cover, and cook for 5-7 minutes, stirring occasionally, or until the greens are softened.
4. Fold in the garlic and soy sauce and stir to combine. Cook for about 30 seconds more until fragrant.
5. Remove from the heat to a plate and serve.

Nutrition

- Calories 73
- Carbohydrates 5.9 g.
- Fiber 2.9 g.

204. Roasted Delicata Squash with Thyme

Preparation Time: 10'
Cooking Time: 20'
Servings: 4

Ingredients

- 1 (1 1/2-pound) Delicata squash
- 1 tbsp. extra-virgin olive oil
- 1/2 teaspoon dried thyme
- 1/4 tsp. salt
- 1/4 tsp. freshly ground black pepper

Directions

1. Prep the oven to 400 °F (205 °C). Prepare a baking sheet with parchment paper and set it aside.
2. Add the squash strips, olive oil, thyme, salt, and pepper in a large bowl, and toss until the squash strips are fully coated.
3. Place the squash strips on the prepared baking sheet in a single layer. Roast for about 20 minutes, flipping the strips halfway through.
4. Remove from the oven and serve on plates.

Nutrition

- Calories 78
- Carbohydrates 11.8 g.
- Fiber 2.1 g.

205. Roasted Asparagus and Red Peppers

Preparation Time: 5'
Cooking Time: 15'
Servings: 4

Ingredients

- 1-pound (454 g) asparagus
- 2 red bell peppers, seeded
- 1 small onion
- 2 tbsps Italian dressing

Directions

1. Ready oven to (205 °C). Wrap a baking sheet with parchment paper and set it aside.
2. Combine the asparagus with the peppers, onion, dressing in a large bowl, and toss well.
3. Arrange the vegetables on the baking sheet and roast for about 15 minutes. Flip the vegetables with a spatula once during cooking.
4. Transfer to a large platter and serve.

Nutrition

- Calories 92
- Carbohydrates 10.7 g.
- Fiber 4 g.

206. Tarragon Spring Peas

PREPARATION TIME: 10'

COOKING TIME: 12'

SERVINGS: 4

Ingredients

- 1 tbsp. unsalted butter
- 1/2 Vidalia onion
- 1 c. low-sodium vegetable broth
- 3 c. fresh shelled peas
- 1 tbsp. minced fresh tarragon

Directions

1. Cook butter in a pan at medium heat.
2. Sauté the onion in the melted butter for about 3 minutes, stirring occasionally.
3. Pour in the vegetable broth and whisk well. Add the peas and tarragon to the skillet and stir to combine.
4. Reduce the heat to low, cover, cook for about 8 minutes more, or until the peas are tender.
5. Let the peas cool for 5 minutes and serve warm.

Nutrition

- Calories 82
- Carbohydrates 12 g.
- Fiber 3.8 g.

155

207. Butter-Orange Yams

PREPARATION TIME: 7'

COOKING TIME: 45'

SERVINGS: 8

Ingredients

- 2 medium jewel yams
- 2 tbsps unsalted butter
- Juice of 1 large orange
- 1 1/2 tsps. ground cinnamon
- 1/4 tsp. ground ginger
- 3/4 teaspoon ground nutmeg
- 1/8 tsp. ground cloves

Directions

1. Set oven at 180 °C.
2. Arrange the yam dices on a rimmed baking sheet in a single layer. Set aside.
3. Add the butter, orange juice, cinnamon, ginger, nutmeg, and garlic cloves to a medium saucepan over medium-low heat. Cook for 3-5 minutes, stirring continuously.
4. Spoon the sauce over the yams and toss to coat well.
5. Bake in the prepared oven for 40 minutes.
6. Let the yams cool for 8 minutes on the baking sheet before removing and serving.

Nutrition

- Calories 129
- Carbohydrates 24.7 g.
- Fiber 5 g.

208. Roasted Tomato Brussels Sprouts

PREPARATION TIME: 15'

COOKING TIME: 20'

SERVINGS: 4

Ingredients

- 1-pound (454 g) Brussels sprouts
- 1 tbsp. extra-virgin olive oil
- 1/2 c. sun-dried tomatoes
- 2 tbsps lemon juice
- 1 tsp. lemon zest
- Salt and pepper, to taste

Directions

1. Set oven 205 °C. Prep large baking sheet with aluminum foil.
2. Toss the Brussels sprouts in olive oil in a large bowl until well coated. Sprinkle with salt and pepper.
3. Spread out the seasoned Brussels sprouts on the prepared baking sheet in a single layer.
4. Roast for 20 minutes, shaking halfway through.
5. Remove from the oven then situate in a bowl. Whisk tomatoes, lemon juice, and lemon zest, to incorporate.

Serve immediately.

Nutrition

- Calories 111
- Carbohydrates 13.7 g.
- Fiber 4.9 g.

209. Simple Saut ed Greens

PREPARATION TIME: 10'

COOKING TIME: 10'

SERVINGS: 4

Ingredients

- 2 tbsps extra-virgin olive oil
- 1 lb. (454 g.) Swiss chard
- 1-pound (454 g.) kale
- 1/2 teaspoon ground cardamom
- 1 tbsp. lemon juice
- Salt and pepper, to taste

Directions

1. Heat up olive oil in a big skillet over medium-high heat.
2. Stir in Swiss chard, kale, cardamom, lemon juice to the skillet, and stir to combine. Cook for about 10 minutes, stirring continuously, or until the greens are wilted.
3. Sprinkle with salt and pepper and stir well.
4. Serve the greens on a plate while warm.

Nutrition

- Calories 139
- Carbohydrates 15.8 g.
- Fiber 3.9 g.

210. Garlicky Mushrooms

PREPARATION TIME: **10'**

COOKING TIME: **12'**

SERVINGS: **4**

Ingredients

- 1 tbsp. butter
- 2 tsps. extra-virgin olive oil
- 2 lbs. button mushrooms
- 2 tsps. minced fresh garlic
- 1 tsp. chopped fresh thyme

Directions

1. Warm-up the butter and olive oil in a big skillet over medium-high heat.
2. Add the mushrooms and sauté for 10 minutes, stirring occasionally.
3. Stir in the garlic and thyme and cook for an additional 2 minutes.
4. Season and serve on a plate.

Nutrition

- Calories 96
- Carbohydrates 8.2 g.
- Fiber 1.7 g.

211. Green Beans in the Oven

PREPARATION TIME: **5'**

COOKING TIME: **17'**

SERVINGS: **3**

Ingredients

- 12 oz. green bean pods
- 1 tbsp. olive oil
- 1/2 tsp. onion powder
- 1/8 tsp. pepper
- 1/8 tsp. salt

Directions

1. Preheat the oven to 350 °F. Mix green beans with onion powder, salt, pepper, and oil.
2. Spread the seeds on the baking sheet.
3. Bake for 17 minutes or until you have a delicious aroma in the kitchen.

Nutrition

- Calories 37
- Protein 1.4 g.
- Carbohydrates 5.5 g.

212. Parmesan Broiled Flounder

Preparation time: 10'
Cooking time: 7'
Servings: 2

Ingredients

- 2 (4-oz.) flounder
- 1.5 tbsp. Parmesan cheese
- 1.5 tbsp. reduced-fat mayonnaise
- 1/8 tsp. soy sauce
- 1/4 tsp. chili sauce
- 1/8 tsp. salt-free lemon-pepper seasoning
- Salt and pepper, to taste

Directions

1. Preheat flounder.
2. Mix cheese, reduced-fat mayonnaise, soy sauce, chili sauce, seasoning.
3. Put fish on a baking sheet coated with cooking spray, sprinkle with salt and pepper.
4. Spread Parmesan mixture over flounder.
5. Broil 6–8 minutes or until a crust appears on the fish.

Nutrition

- Calories 200
- Fat 17 g.
- Carbohydrate 7 g.

213. Fish with Fresh Tomato Basil Sauce

Preparation time: 10'
Cooking time: 15'
Servings: 2

Ingredients

- 2 (4-oz) tilapia fillets
- 1 tbsp. fresh basil, chopped
- 1/8 tsp. salt
- 1 pinch of crushed red pepper
- 1 c. cherry tomatoes, chopped
- 2 tsp. extra-virgin olive oil

Directions

1. Preheat the oven to 400 °F.
2. Arrange rinsed and patted dry fish fillets on foil (coat a foil baking sheet with cooking spray).
3. Sprinkle tilapia fillets with salt and red pepper.
4. Bake 12–15 minutes.
5. Meanwhile, mix the leftover ingredients in a saucepan.
6. Cook over medium-high heat until tomatoes are tender.
7. Top fish fillets properly with tomato mixture.

Nutrition

- Calories 130
- Protein 30 g.
- Carbohydrates 1 g.

214. Baked Chicken

PREPARATION TIME: 15'

COOKING TIME: 25'

SERVINGS: 4

Ingredients

- 2 (6-oz) bone-in chicken breasts
- 1/8 tsp. salt
- 1/8 tsp. pepper
- 3 tsp. extra-virgin olive oil
- 1/2 tsp. dried oregano
- / pitted kalamata olives
- 1 c. cherry tomatoes
- 1/2 c. onion
- 1 (9-oz) pkg. frozen artichoke hearts
- 1 lemon

Directions

1. Preheat the oven to 400 °F.
2. Sprinkle chicken with pepper, salt, and oregano.
3. Heat oil, add chicken, and cook until it browned.
4. Place chicken in a baking dish. Arrange tomatoes, coarsely chopped olives, onion, artichokes, and lemon cut into wedges around the chicken.
5. Bake for 20 minutes or until chicken is done and vegetables are tender.

Nutrition

- Calories 160
- Fat 3 g.
- Carbohydrates 1 g.

215. Seared Chicken with Roasted Vegetables

PREPARATION TIME: 20'

COOKING TIME: 30'

SERVINGS: 1

Ingredients

- 1 (8-oz) boneless, skinless chicken breasts
- 3/4 lb. small Brussels sprouts
- 2 large carrots
- 1 large red bell pepper
- 1 small red onion
- 2 cloves garlic halved
- 2 tbsp. extra-virgin olive oil
- 1/2 tsp. dried dill
- 1/4 tsp. pepper
- 1/4 tsp. salt

Directions

1. Preheat the oven to 425 °F.
2. Match Brussels sprouts cut in half, red onion cut into wedges, sliced carrots, bell pepper cut into pieces, and halved garlic on a baking sheet.
3. Sprinkle with 1 tbsp. oil and with 1/8 tsp. salt and 1/8 tsp. pepper. Bake until well-roasted, cool slightly.
4. In the Meantime, sprinkle chicken with dill, remaining 1/8 tsp. salt, and 1/8 tsp. pepper. Cook until the chicken is done. Put roasted vegetables with drippings over chicken.

Nutrition

- Calories 170
- Fat 7 g.
- Protein 12 g.

216. Fish Simmered in Tomato-Pepper Sauce

Preparation time: 5'

Cooking time: 10'

Servings: 2

Ingredients

- 2 (4-oz) cod fillets
- 1 big tomato
- 1/3 c. red peppers (roasted)
- 3 tbsp. almonds
- 2 cloves garlic
- 2 tbsp. fresh basil leaves
- 2 tbsp. extra-virgin olive oil
- 1/4 tsp. salt
- 1/8 tsp. pepper

Directions

1. Toast sliced almonds in a pan until fragrant.
2. Grind almonds, basil, minced garlic, 1-2 tsp. oil in a food processor until finely ground.
3. Add coarsely-chopped tomato and red peppers; grind until smooth.
4. Season fish with salt and pepper.
5. Cook in hot oil in a large pan over medium-high heat until fish is browned. Pour sauce around fish. Cook 6 minutes more.

Nutrition

- Calories 90
- Fat 5 g.
- Carbohydrates 7 g.

217. Cheese and Pea Casserole

Preparation time: 10'

Cooking time: 35'

Servings: 3

Ingredients

- 1 tbsp. olive oil
- 3/4 c. green peas
- 1/2 c. red onion
- 1/4 tsp. dried rosemary
- 1/4 tsp. salt
- 1/8 tsp. pepper

Directions

1. Prepare the oven to 350 °F.
2. Cook 1 tsp of oil in a skillet. Stir in thinly sliced onions and cook. Remove from pan.
3. Situate half of the thinly sliced onions in the bottom of a skillet; top with peas, crushed dried rosemary, and 1/8 tsp. each salt and pepper.
4. Place remaining onions on top. Season with remaining 1/8 tsp. salt.
5. Bake 35 minutes, pour the remaining 2 tsp. oil, and sprinkle with cheese.

Nutrition

- Calories 80
- Protein 2 g.
- Carbohydrates 18 g.

218. Oven-Fried Tilapia

PREPARATION TIME: 7'

COOKING TIME: 15'

SERVINGS: 2

Ingredients

- 2 (4-oz) tilapia fillets
- 1/4 c. yellow cornmeal
- 2 tbsp. light ranch dressing
- 1 tbsp. canola oil
- 1 tsp. dill (dried)
- 1/8 tsp. salt

Directions

1. Preheat the oven to 425 °F. Brush both sides of the rinsed and patted the dry tilapia fish fillets with the dressing.
2. Combine cornmeal, oil, dill, and salt.
3. Sprinkle fish fillets with cornmeal mixture.
4. Put fish on a prepared baking sheet.
5. Bake 15 minutes.

Nutrition

- Calories 96
- Protein 21 g.
- Fat 2 g.

219. Chicken with Coconut Sauce

PREPARATION TIME: 15'

COOKING TIME: 20'

SERVINGS: 2

Ingredients

- 1/2 lb. chicken breasts
- 1/3 c. red onion
- 1 tbsp. paprika (smoked)
- 2 tsp. cornstarch
- 1/2 c. light coconut milk
- 1 tsp. extra-virgin olive oil
- 2 tbsp. fresh cilantro
- 1 (10-oz) can tomatoes and green chilies
- 1/4 c. water

Directions

1. Cut chicken into little cubes; sprinkle with 1.5 tsp of paprika.
2. Heat oil, add chicken, and cook for 3-5 minutes.
3. Remove from the skillet, and fry the finely-chopped onion for 5 minutes.
4. Return the chicken to the pan. Add tomato, 1.5 tsp of paprika, and water. Bring to a boil, and then simmer for 4 minutes.
5. Mix cornstarch and coconut milk; stir into chicken mixture, and cook until it has done.
6. Sprinkle with chopped cilantro.

Nutrition

- Calories 200
- Protein 13 g.
- Fat 10 g.

220. Fish with Fresh Herb Sauce

Preparation time: 10'
Cooking time: 10'
Servings: 2

Ingredients

- 2 (4-oz) cod fillets
- 1/3 c. fresh cilantro
- 1/4 tsp. cumin
- 1 tbsp. red onion
- 2 tsp. extra-virgin olive oil
- 1 tsp. red wine vinegar
- 1 small clove garlic
- 1/8 tsp. salt
- 1/8 black pepper

Directions

1. 2 (4-oz) cod fillets
2. 1/3 c. fresh cilantro
3. 1/4 tsp. cumin
4. 1 tbsp. red onion
5. 2 tsp. extra-virgin olive oil
6. 1 tsp. red wine vinegar
7. 1 small clove garlic
8. 1/8 tsp. salt
9. 1/8 black pepper

Nutrition

- Calories 90
- Fat 4 g.
- Carbohydrates 3 g.

221. Skillet Turkey Patties

Preparation time: 7'
Cooking time: 8'
Servings: 2

Ingredients

- 1/2 lb. lean ground turkey
- 1/2 c. low-sodium chicken broth
- 1/4 c. red onion
- 1/2 tsp. Worcestershire sauce
- 1 tsp. extra-virgin olive oil
- 1/4 tsp. oregano (dried)
- 1/8 tsp. pepper

Directions

1. Combine turkey, chopped onion, Worcestershire sauce, dried oregano, and pepper; make 2 patties.
2. Warm-up oil and cook patties 4 minutes per side; set aside.
3. Add broth to the skillet, bring to a boil. Boil for 2 minutes, spoon sauce over patties.

Nutrition

- Calories 180
- Fat 11 g.
- Carbohydrates 9 g.

222. Turkey Loaf

PREPARATION TIME: 10'

COOKING TIME: 50'

SERVINGS: 2

Ingredients

- 1/2 lb. 93 % lean ground turkey
- 1/3 c. panko breadcrumbs
- 1/2 c. green onion
- 1 egg
- 1/2 c. green bell pepper
- 1 tbsp. ketchup
- 1/4 c. sauce (Picante)
- 1/2 tsp. cumin, ground

Directions

1. Preheat the oven to 350 °F. Mix lean ground turkey, 3 tbsp. Picante sauce, panko breadcrumbs, egg, chopped green onion, chopped green bell pepper, and cumin in a bowl (mix well);
2. Put the mixture into a baking sheet; shape into an oval (about 1.5 in. thick). Bake for 45 minutes.
3. Mix the remaining picante sauce and the ketchup; apply over the loaf. Bake for 5 minutes longer. Let stand for 5 minutes.

Nutrition

- Calories 161
- Protein 20 g.
- Fat 8 g.

223. Mushroom Pasta

PREPARATION TIME: 7'

COOKING TIME: 10'

SERVINGS: 4

Ingredients

- 4 oz. whole-grain linguine
- 1 tsp. extra-virgin olive oil
- 1/2 c. light sauce
- 2 tbsp. green onion
- 1 (8-oz) pkg. mushrooms
- 1 clove garlic
- 1/8 tsp. salt
- 1/8 tsp. pepper

Directions

1. Cook the pasta according to the package directions; drain.
2. Fry sliced the mushrooms for 4 minutes.
3. Stir in the fettuccine, minced garlic, salt, and pepper. Cook 2 minutes.
4. Heat the sauce until heated; top the pasta mixture properly with the sauce and with finely-chopped green onion.

Nutrition

- Calories 300
- Fat 1 g.
- Carbohydrates 15 g.

224. Chicken Tikka Masala

PREPARATION TIME: 5'

COOKING TIME: 15'

SERVINGS: 2

Ingredients

- 1/2 lb. chicken breasts
- 1/4 c. onion
- 1.5 tsp. extra-virgin olive oil
- 1 (14.5-oz) can of tomatoes
- 1 tsp. ginger
- 1 tsp. fresh lemon juice
- 1/3 c. plain Greek yogurt (fat-free)
- 1 tbsp. garam masala
- 1/4 tsp. salt
- 1/4 tsp. pepper

Directions

1. Flavor the chicken cut into 1-in. cubes with 1.5 tsp. garam masala, 1/8 tsp. salt, and pepper.
2. Cook the chicken and diced onion for 4-5 minutes.
3. Add diced tomatoes, grated ginger, 1.5 tsp. garam masala, 1/8 tsp. salt. Cook for 8-10 minutes.
4. Add lemon juice and yogurt until blended.

Nutrition

- Calories 200
- Protein 26 g.
- Fat 10 g.

225. Tomato and Roasted Cod

PREPARATION TIME: 10'

COOKING TIME: 35'

SERVINGS: 2

Ingredients

- 2 (4-oz) cod fillets
- 1 c. cherry tomatoes
- 2/3 c. onion
- 2 tsp. orange rind
- 1 tbsp. extra-virgin olive oil
- 1 tsp. thyme (dried)
- 1/4 tsp. salt, divided
- 1/4 tsp. pepper, divided

Directions

1. Preheat the oven to 400 °F. Mix in half of tomatoes, sliced onion, grated orange rind, extra-virgin olive oil, dried thyme, and 1/8 salt and pepper. Fry for 25 minutes. Remove from the oven.
2. Arrange the fish on a pan, and flavor with the remaining 1/8 tsp. each salt and pepper. Put the reserved tomato mixture over the fish. Bake 10 minutes.

Nutrition

- Calories 120
- Protein 9 g.
- Fat 2 g.

226. French Broccoli Salad

Preparation Time: 10'
Cooking Time: 10'
Servings: 4

Ingredients

- 8 c. broccoli florets
- 3 strips of bacon, cooked and crumbled
- 1/4 c. sunflower kernels
- 1 bunch of green onion, sliced

What you will need from the store cupboard:
- 3 tbsps seasoned rice vinegar
- 3 tbsps canola oil
- 1/2 c. dried cranberries

Directions

1. Combine the green onion, cranberries, and broccoli in a bowl.
2. Whisk the vinegar, and oil in another bowl. Blend well.
3. Now drizzle over the broccoli mix.
4. Coat well by tossing.
5. Sprinkle bacon and sunflower kernels before serving.

Nutrition

- Calories 121
- Carbohydrates 14 g.
- Cholesterol 2 mg.
- Fiber 3 g.
- Sugar 1 g.
- Fat 7 g.
- Protein 3 g.
- Sodium 233 mg.

227. Tenderloin Grilled Salad

Preparation Time: 10'
Cooking Time: 20'
Servings: 5

Ingredients

- 1 lb. pork tenderloin
- 10 c. mixed salad greens
- 2 oranges, seedless, cut into bite-sized pieces
- 1 tbsp. orange zest, grated

For the Dressing
- 2 tbsps of cider vinegar
- 2 tbsps olive oil
- 2 tsps. Dijon mustard
- 1/2 c. juice of an orange
- 2 tsps. honey
- 1/2 tsp. ground pepper

Directions

1. Bring together all the dressing ingredients in a bowl.
2. Grill each side of the pork covered over medium heat for 9 minutes.
3. Slice after 5 minutes.
4. Slice the tenderloin thinly.
5. Keep the greens on your serving plate.
6. Top with the pork and oranges.
7. Sprinkle nuts (optional).

Nutrition

- Calories 211
- Carbohydrates 13 g.
- Cholesterol 51 mg.
- Fiber 3 g.
- Sugar 0.8 g.
- Fat 9 g.
- Protein 20 g.
- Sodium 113 mg.

228. Barley Veggie Salad

Preparation time: 10'
Cooking time: 20'
Servings: 6

Ingredients

- 1 tomato, seeded and chopped
- 2 tbsps parsley, minced
- 1 yellow pepper, chopped
- 1 tbsp. basil, minced
- 1/4 c. almonds, toasted

What you will need from the store cupboard:
- 1-1/4 c. vegetable broth
- 1 c. barley
- 1 tbsp. lemon juice
- 2 tbsps of white wine vinegar
- 3 tbsps olive oil
- 1/4 tsp. pepper
- 1/2 tsp. salt
- 1 c of water

Directions

1. Boil the broth, barley, and water in a saucepan.
2. Reduce the heat. Cover and let it simmer for 10 minutes.
3. Take out from the heat.
4. In the meantime, bring together the parsley, yellow pepper, and tomato in a bowl.
5. Stir the barley in.
6. Whisk the vinegar, oil, basil, lemon juice, water, pepper, and salt in a bowl.
7. Pour this over your barley mix. Toss to coat well.
8. Stir the almonds in before serving.

Nutrition

- Calories 211
- Carbohydrates 27 g.
- Cholesterol 0 mg.
- Fiber 7 g.
- Sugar 0 g.
- Fat 10 g.
- Protein 6 g.
- Sodium 334 mg.

229. Spinach Shrimp Salad

Preparation time: 10'
Cooking time: 10'
Servings: 4

Ingredients

- 1 lb. uncooked shrimp, peeled and deveined
- 2 tbsps parsley, minced
- 3/4 c. halved cherry tomatoes
- 1 medium lemon
- 4 c. baby spinach

What you will need from the store cupboard:
- 2 tbsps butter
- 3 minced garlic cloves
- 1/4 tsp. pepper
- 1/4 tsp. salt

Directions

1. Melt the butter over medium temperature in a nonstick skillet.
2. Add the shrimp.
3. Now cook the shrimp for 3 minutes until your shrimp becomes pink.
4. Add the parsley and garlic.
5. Cook for another minute. Take out from the heat.
6. Keep the spinach in your salad bowl.
7. Top with the shrimp mix and tomatoes.
8. Drizzle lemon juice on the salad.
9. Sprinkle pepper and salt.

Nutrition

- Calories 201
- Carbohydrates 6 g.
- Cholesterol 153 mg.
- Fiber 2 g.
- Sugar 0 g.
- Fat 10 g.
- Protein 21 g.
- Sodium 350 mg

230. Roasted Beet Salad

Preparation time: 10'
Cooking time: 10'
Servings: 4

Ingredients
- 2 beets
- 1 garlic clove, minced
- 2 tbsps walnuts, chopped and toasted
- 1 c. fennel bulb, sliced

What you will need from the store cupboard:
- 3 tbsps balsamic vinegar
- 1 tsp. Dijon mustard
- 1 tbsp. honey
- 3 tbsps olive oil
- 1/4 tsp. pepper
- 1/4 tsp. salt
- 3 tbsps water

Directions
1. Scrub the beets. Trim the tops to 1 in.
2. Wrap in foil and keep on a baking sheet.
3. Bake until tender. Take off the foil.
4. Cover. Microwave for 5 minutes. Drain off.
5. Now peel the beets. Cut into small wedges.
6. Arrange the fennel and beets on 4 salad plates.
7. Sprinkle nuts.
8. Whisk the honey, mustard, vinegar, water, garlic, pepper, and salt.
9. Whisk in oil gradually.
10. Drizzle over the salad.

Nutrition
- Calories 270
- Carbohydrates 37 g.
- Cholesterol 0 mg.
- Fiber 6 g.
- Sugar 0.3 g.
- Fat 13 g.
- Protein 5 g.
- Sodium 309 mg.

167

231. Calico Salad

Preparation time: 15'
Cooking time: 5'
Servings: 4

Ingredients
- 1-1/2 c. kernel corn, cooked
- 1/2 c. green pepper, diced
- 1/2 c. red onion, chopped
- 1 c. carrot, shredded

What you will need from the store cupboard:
- 1/2 c. olive oil
- 1/4 c. vinegar
- 1-1/2 tsps. chili powder
- 1 tsp. salt
- Dash of hot pepper sauce

Directions
1. Keep all the ingredients for the store cupboard together in a jar.
2. Close it and shake well.
3. Combine with carrot, green pepper, onion, and corn in your salad bowl.
4. Pour the dressing over.
5. Now toss lightly.

Nutrition
- Calories 146
- Carbohydrates 17 g.
- Cholesterol 0 mg.
- Fiber 0 g.
- Sugar 0 g.
- Fat 9 g.
- Protein 2 g.
- Sodium 212 mg.

232. Mango and Jicama Salad

Preparation time: 15'
Cooking time: 5'
Servings: 8

Ingredients

- 1 jicama, peeled
- 1 mango, peeled
- 1 tsp. ginger root, minced
- 1/3 c. chives, minced
- 1/2 c. cilantro, chopped

What you will need from the store cupboard:
- 1/4 c. canola oil
- 1/2 c. white wine vinegar
- 2 tbsps of lime juice
- 1/4 c. honey
- 1/8 tsp. pepper
- 1/4 tsp. salt

Directions

1. Whisk together the vinegar, honey, canola oil, gingerroot, paper, and salt.
2. Cut the mango and jicama into matchsticks.
3. Keep in a bowl.
4. Now toss with the lime juice.
5. Add the dressing and herbs. Combine well by tossing.

Nutrition

- Calories 143
- Carbohydrates 20 g.
- Cholesterol 0 mg.
- Fiber 3 g.
- Sugar 1.6 g.
- Fat 7 g.
- Protein 1 g.
- Sodium 78 mg.

168

233. Asian Crispy Chicken Salad

Preparation time: 10'
Cooking time: 10'
Servings: 2

Ingredients

- 2 chicken breasts halved, skinless
- 1/2 c. panko bread crumbs
- 4 c. spring mix salad greens
- 4 tsps of sesame seeds
- 1/2 c. mushrooms, sliced

What you will need from the store cupboard:
- 1 tsp. sesame oil
- 2 tsps of canola oil
- 2 tsps. hoisin sauce
- 1/4 c. sesame ginger salad dressing

Directions

1. Flatten the chicken breasts to half-inch thickness.
2. Mix the sesame oil, canola oil, and hoisin sauce. Brush over the chicken.
3. Combine the sesame seeds and panko in a bowl.
4. Now dip the chicken mix in it.
5. Cook each side of the chicken for 5 minutes.
6. In the meantime, divide the salad greens between two plates.
7. Top with mushroom.
8. Slice the chicken and keep it on top. Drizzle the dressing.

Nutrition

- Calories 386
- Carbohydrates 29 g.
- Cholesterol 63 mg.
- Fiber 6 g.
- Sugar 1 g.
- Fat 17 g.
- Protein 30 g.
- Sodium 620 mg.

234. Kale, Grape, and Bulgur Salad

Preparation time: 10'

Cooking time: 15'

Servings: 6

Ingredients

- 1 c. bulgur
- 1 c. pecan, toasted and chopped
- 1/4 c. scallions, sliced
- 1/2 c. parsley, chopped
- 2 c. California grapes, seedless and halved

What you will need from the store cupboard:
- 2 tbsps of extra-virgin olive oil
- 1/4 c of juice from a lemon
- Pinch of kosher salt
- Pinch of black pepper
- 2 c of water

Directions

1. Boil 2 c of water in a saucepan
2. Stir the bulgur in and 1/2 tsp of salt.
3. Take out from the heat.
4. Keep covered. Drain.
5. Stir in the other ingredients.
6. Season with pepper and salt.

Nutrition

- Calories 289
- Carbohydrates 33 g.
- Fat 17 g.
- Protein 6 g.
- Sodium 181 mg.

235. Strawberry Salsa

Preparation time: 10'

Cooking time: 5'

Servings: 4

Ingredients

- 4 tomatoes, seeded and chopped
- 1-pint strawberry, chopped
- 1 red onion, chopped
- 2 tbsps of juice from a lime
- 1 jalapeno pepper, minced

What you will need from the store cupboard:
- 1 tbsp. olive oil
- 2 garlic cloves, minced

Directions

1. Bring together the strawberries, tomatoes, jalapeno, and onion in the bowl.
2. Stir in the garlic, oil, and lime juice.
3. Refrigerate. Serve with separately cooked pork or poultry

Nutrition

- Calories 19
- Carbohydrates 3 g.
- Fiber 1 g.
- Sugar 0.2 g.
- Cholesterol 0 mg.
- Total Fat 1 g.
- Protein 0 g.

236. Garden Wraps

PREPARATION TIME: 20'

COOKING TIME: 10'

SERVINGS: 8

Ingredients

- 1 cucumber, chopped
- 1 sweet corn
- 1 cabbage, shredded
- 1 tbsp. lettuce, minced
- 1 tomato, chopped

What you will need from the store cupboard:

- 3 tbsps of rice vinegar
- 2 tsps. peanut butter
- 1/3 c. onion paste
- 1/3 c. chili sauce
- 2 tsps of low-sodium soy sauce

Directions

1. Cut corn from the cob. Keep in a bowl.
2. Add the tomato, cabbage, cucumber, and onion paste.
3. Now whisk the vinegar, peanut butter, soy sauce, and chili sauce together.
4. Pour this over the vegetable mix. Toss for coating.
5. Let this stand for 10 minutes.
6. Take your slotted spoon and place 1/2 c. salad in every lettuce leaf.
7. Fold the lettuce over your filling.

Nutrition

- Calories 64
- Carbohydrates 13 g.
- Fiber 2 g.
- Sugar 1 g.
- Cholesterol 0 mg.
- Total Fat 1 g.
- Protein 2 g.

237. Party Shrimp

PREPARATION TIME: 15'

COOKING TIME: 10'

SERVINGS: 30

Ingredients

- 16 oz. uncooked shrimp, peeled and deveined
- 1-1/2 tsps of juice from a lemon
- 1/2 tsp. basil, chopped
- 1 tsp. coriander, chopped
- 1/2 c. tomato

What you will need from the store cupboard:

- 1 tbsp of olive oil
- 1/2 tsp. Italian seasoning
- 1/2 tsp. paprika
- 1 sliced garlic clove
- 1/4 tsp. pepper

Directions

1. Bring together everything except the shrimp in a dish or bowl.
2. Add the shrimp. Coat well by tossing. Set aside.
3. Drain the shrimp. Discard the marinade.
4. Keep them on a baking sheet. It should not be greased.
5. Broil each side for 4 minutes. The shrimp should become pink.

Nutrition

- Calories 14
- Carbohydrates 0 g.
- Fiber 0 g.
- Sugar 0 g.
- Cholesterol 18 mg.
- Total Fat 0 g.
- Protein 2 g.

238. Zucchini Mini Pizzas

Preparation Time: 10'
Cooking Time: 20'
Servings: 24

Ingredients

- 1 zucchini, cut into 1/4 in. slices diagonally
- 1/2 c. pepperoni, small slices
- 1 tsp. basil, minced
- 1/2 c. onion, chopped
- 1 c. tomatoes

What you will need from the store cupboard:
- 1/8 tsp. pepper
- 1/8 tsp. salt
- 3/4 c. mozzarella cheese, shredded
- 1/3 c. pizza sauce

Directions

1. Preheat your broiler. Keep the zucchini in 1 layer on your greased baking sheet.
2. Add the onion and tomatoes. Broil each side for 1-2 minutes till they become tender and crisp.
3. Now sprinkle pepper and salt.
4. Top with cheese, pepperoni, and sauce.
5. Broil for a minute. The cheese should melt.
6. Sprinkle basil on top.

Nutrition

- Calories 29
- Carbohydrates 1 g.
- Fiber 0 g.
- Sugar 1 g.
- Cholesterol 5 mg.
- Total Fat 2 g.
- Protein 2 g.

239. Garlic-Sesame Pumpkin Seeds

Preparation Time: 10'
Cooking Time: 20'
Servings: 2

Ingredients

- 1 egg white
- 1 tsp. onion, minced
- 1/2 tsp. caraway seeds
- 2 c. pumpkin seeds
- 1 tsp. sesame seeds

What you will need from the store cupboard:
- 1 garlic clove, minced
- 1 tbsp of canola oil
- 3/4 teaspoon of kosher salt

Directions

1. Preheat your oven to 350 °F.
2. Whisk together the oil and egg white in a bowl.
3. Include pumpkin seeds. Coat well by tossing.
4. Now stir in the onion, garlic, sesame seeds, caraway seeds, and salt.
5. Spread in 1 layer in your parchment-lined baking pan.
6. Bake for 15 minutes until it turns golden brown.

Nutrition

- Calories 95
- Carbohydrates 9 g.
- Fiber 3 g.
- Sugar 0 g.
- Cholesterol 0 mg.
- Total Fat 5 g.
- Protein 4 g.

Chapter 10: Seafood Recipes

240. Lemony Salmon

Preparation time: 10'
Cooking time: 3'
Servings: 3

Ingredients

- 1 lb. salmon fillet, cut into 3 pieces
- 3 tsps. fresh dill, chopped
- 5 tbsps fresh lemon juice, divided
- Salt and ground black pepper, as required

Directions

1. Arrange a steamer trivet in the instant pot and pour 1/4 c of lemon juice.
2. Season the salmon with salt and black pepper evenly.
3. Place the salmon pieces on top of the trivet, skin side down, and drizzle with the remaining lemon juice.
4. Now, sprinkle the salmon pieces with dill evenly.
5. Close the lid and place the pressure valve in the "Seal" position.
6. Press Steam and use the default time of 3 minutes.
7. Press "Cancel" and allow a "Natural" release.
8. Open the lid and serve hot.

Nutrition

- Calories 20
- Fats 9.6 g.
- Carbohydrates 1.1 g.
- Sugar 0.5 g.
- Proteins 29.7 g.
- Sodium 74 mg.

241. Shrimp with Green Beans

Preparation time: 10'
Cooking time: 2'
Servings: 4

Ingredients

- 3/4 pound fresh green beans, trimmed
- 1-pound medium frozen shrimp, peeled and deveined
- 2 tbsps fresh lemon juice
- 2 tbsps olive oil
- Salt and ground black pepper, as required

Directions

1. Arrange a steamer trivet in the instant pot and pour a cup of water.
2. Arrange the green beans on top of the trivet in a single layer and top with the shrimp.
3. Drizzle with oil and lemon juice.
4. Sprinkle with salt and black pepper.
5. Close the lid and place the pressure valve in the "Seal" position.
6. Press Steam and just use the default time of 2 minutes.
7. Press "Cancel" and allow a "Natural" release.
8. Open the lid and serve.

Nutrition

- Calories 223
- Fats 1 g.
- Carbohydrates 7.9 g.
- Sugar 1.4 g.
- Proteins 27.4 g.
- Sodium 322 mg.

242. Crab Curry

PREPARATION TIME: **10'**

COOKING TIME: **20'**

SERVINGS: **2**

Ingredients
- 0.5 lb. chopped crab
- 1 thinly sliced red onion
- 0.5 c. chopped tomato
- 3 tbsp. curry paste
- 1 tbsp. oil or ghee

Directions
1. Set the instant pot to sauté and add the onion, oil, and curry paste.
2. When the onion is soft, add the remaining ingredients and seal.
3. Cook on Stew for 20 minutes.
4. Release the pressure naturally.

Nutrition
- Calories 2
- Carbohydrates 11 g.
- Sugar 4 g.
- Fat 10 g.
- Protein 24 g.
- GL: 9 g.

243. Mixed Chowder

PREPARATION TIME: **10'**

COOKING TIME: **35'**

SERVINGS: **2**

Ingredients
- 1 lb. fish stew mix
- 2 c. white sauce
- 3 tbsp. old bay seasoning

Directions
1. Mix all the ingredients in your instant pot.
2. Cook on Stew for 35 minutes.
3. Release the pressure naturally.

Nutrition
- Calories 320
- Carbohydrates 9 g.
- Sugar 2 g.
- Fat 16 g.
- GL: 4 g.

244. Mussels in Tomato Sauce

Preparation Time: 10'
Cooking Time: 3'
Servings: 4

Ingredients

- 2 tomatoes, seeded and chopped finely
- 2 lbs. mussels, scrubbed and de-bearded
- 1 c. low-sodium chicken broth
- 1 tbsp. fresh lemon juice
- 2 garlic cloves, minced

Directions

1. In the instant pot, place tomatoes, garlic, and broth and stir to combine.
2. Arrange the mussels on top.
3. Close the lid and place the pressure valve in "Seal" position.
4. Press "Manual" and cook under "High Pressure" for about 3 minutes.
5. Press "Cancel" and carefully allow a "Quick" release.
6. Open the lid and serve hot with a squeeze of lemon juice.

Nutrition

- Calories 213
- Fats 25.2 g.
- Carbohydrates 11 g.
- Sugar 1 g.
- Proteins 28.2 g.
- Sodium 670 mg.

245. Citrus Salmon

Preparation Time: 10'
Cooking Time: 7'
Servings: 4

Ingredients

- 4 (4-oz.) salmon fillets
- 1 c. low-sodium chicken broth
- 1 tsp. fresh ginger, minced
- 2 tsps. fresh orange zest, grated finely
- 3 tbsps fresh orange juice
- 1 tbsp. olive oil
- Ground black pepper, as required

Directions

1. In the instant pot, add all ingredients and mix.
2. Close the lid and place the pressure valve in "Seal" position.
3. Press "Manual" and cook under "High Pressure" for about 7 minutes.
4. Press "Cancel" and allow a "Natural" release.
5. Open the lid and serve the salmon fillets with the cooking sauce.

Nutrition

- Calories 190
- Fats 10.5 g.
- Carbohydrates 1.8 g.
- Sugar 1 g.
- Proteins 22 g.
- Sodium 68 mg.

246. Herbed Salmon

PREPARATION TIME: 10'

COOKING TIME: 3'

SERVINGS: 4

Ingredients

- 4 (4-oz.) salmon fillets
- 1/4 c. olive oil
- 2 tbsps fresh lemon juice
- 1 garlic clove, minced
- 1/4 tsp. dried oregano
- Salt and ground black pepper, as required
- 4 fresh rosemary sprigs
- 4 lemon slices

Directions

1. For the dressing: In a large bowl, add oil, lemon juice, garlic, oregano, salt, and black pepper and blend until well combined.
2. Arrange a steamer trivet in the instant pot and pour 1 1/2 c of water into the instant pot.
3. Place the salmon fillets on top of the trivet in a single layer and top with the dressing.
4. Arrange 1 rosemary sprig and 1 lemon slice over each fillet.
5. Close the lid and place the pressure valve in the "Seal" position.
6. Press Steam and just use the default time of 3 minutes.
7. Press "Cancel" and carefully allow a "Quick" release.
8. Open the lid and serve hot.

Nutrition

- Calories 262
- Fats 17 g.
- Carbohydrates 0.7 g.
- Sugar 0.2 g.
- Proteins 22.1 g.
- Sodium 91 mg.

247. Salmon in Green Sauce

PREPARATION TIME: 10'

COOKING TIME: 12'

SERVINGS: 4

Ingredients

- 4 (6-oz.) salmon fillets
- 1 avocado, peeled, pitted, and chopped
- 1/2 c. fresh basil, chopped
- 3 garlic cloves, chopped
- 1 tbsp. fresh lemon zest, grated finely

Directions

1. Grease a large piece of foil.
2. In a large bowl, add all ingredients except salmon and water, and with a fork, mash completely.
3. Place fillets in the center of the foil and top with the avocado mixture evenly.
4. Fold the foil around fillets to seal them.
5. Arrange a steamer trivet in the instant pot and pour 1/2 c of water.
6. Place the foil packet on top of the trivet.
7. Close the lid and place the pressure valve in "Seal" position.
8. Press "Manual" and cook under "High Pressure" for about minutes.
9. Meanwhile, preheat the oven to broiler.
10. Press "Cancel" and allow a "Natural" release.
11. Open the lid and transfer the salmon fillets onto a broiler pan.
12. Broil for about 3-4 minutes.
13. Serve warm.

Nutrition

- Calories 333
- Fats 20.3 g.
- Carbohydrates 5.5 g.
- Sugar 0.4 g.
- Proteins 34.2 g.
- Sodium 79 mg.

248. Braised Shrimp

Preparation time: 10'
Cooking time: 4'
Servings: 4

Ingredients

- 1-pound frozen large shrimp, peeled and deveined
- 2 shallots, chopped
- 3/4 c. low-sodium chicken broth
- 2 tbsps fresh lemon juice
- 2 tbsps olive oil
- 1 tbsp. garlic, crushed
- Ground black pepper, as required

Directions

1. In the instant pot, place oil and press "Sauté". Now add the shallots and cook for about 2 minutes.
2. Add the garlic and cook for about 1 minute.
3. Press "Cancel" and stir in the shrimp, broth, lemon juice, and black pepper.
4. Close the lid and place the pressure valve in "Seal" position.
5. Press "Manual" and cook under "High Pressure" for about 1 minute.
6. Press "Cancel" and carefully allow a "Quick" release.
7. Open the lid and serve hot.

Nutrition

- Calories 209
- Fats 9 g.
- Carbohydrates 4.3 g.
- Sugar 0.2 g.
- Proteins 26.6 g.
- Sodium 293 mg.

249. Shrimp Coconut Curry

Preparation time: 10'
Cooking time: 20'
Servings: 2

Ingredients

- 0.5 lb. cooked shrimp
- 1 thinly sliced onion
- 1 c. coconut yogurt
- 3 tbsp. curry paste
- 1 tbsp. oil or ghee

Directions

1. Set the instant pot to sauté and add the onion, oil, and curry paste.
2. When the onion is soft, add the remaining ingredients and seal.
3. Cook on Stew for 20 minutes.
4. Release the pressure naturally.

Nutrition

- Calories 380
- Carbohydrates 13 g.
- Sugar 4 g.
- Fat 22 g.
- Protein 40 g.
- GL: 14 g.

250. Trout Bake

PREPARATION TIME: **10'**

COOKING TIME: **35'**

SERVINGS: **2**

Ingredients

- 1 lb. trout fillets, boneless
- 1 lb. chopped winter vegetables
- 1 c. low sodium fish broth
- 1 tbsp. mixed herbs
- Sea salt as desired

Directions

1. Mix all the ingredients except the broth in a foil pouch.
2. Place the pouch in the steamer basket of your instant pot.
3. Pour the broth into the instant pot.
4. Cook on Steam for 35 minutes.
5. Release the pressure naturally.

Nutrition

- Calories 310
- Carbohydrates 14 g.
- Sugar 2 g.
- Fat 12 g.
- Protein 40 g.
- GL : 5 g.

251. Sardine Curry

PREPARATION TIME: **10'**

COOKING TIME: **35'**

SERVINGS: **2**

Ingredients

- 5 tins of sardines in tomato
- 1 lb. chopped vegetables
- 1 c. low sodium fish broth
- 3 tbsp. curry paste

Directions

1. Mix all the ingredients in your instant pot.
2. Cook on Stew for 35 minutes.
3. Release the pressure naturally.

Nutrition

- Calories 320
- Carbohydrates 8 g.
- Sugar 2 g.
- Fat 16 g.
- GL : 3 g.

252. Swordfish Steak

PREPARATION TIME: **10'**

COOKING TIME: **35'**

SERVINGS: **2**

Ingredients

- 1 lb. swordfish steak, whole
- 1 lb. chopped Mediterranean vegetables
- 1 c. low sodium fish broth
- 2 tbsp. soy sauce

Directions

1. Mix all the ingredients except the broth in a foil pouch.
2. Place the pouch in the steamer basket of your instant pot.
3. Pour the broth into the instant pot. Lower the steamer basket into the instant pot.
4. Cook on Steam for 35 minutes.
5. Release the pressure naturally.

Nutrition

- Calories 270
- Carbohydrates 5 g.
- Sugar 1 g.
- Fat 10 g.
- Protein 48 g.
- GL: 1 g.

253. Lemon Sole

PREPARATION TIME: **10'**

COOKING TIME: **5'**

SERVINGS: **2**

Ingredients

- 1 lb. sole fillets, boned and skinned
- 1 c. low sodium fish broth
- 2 shredded sweet onions
- Juice of half a lemon
- 2 tbsp. dried cilantro

Directions

1. Mix all the ingredients in your instant pot.
2. Cook on Stew for 5 minutes.
3. Release the pressure naturally.

Nutrition

- Calories 230
- Sugar 1 g.
- Fat 6 g.
- Protein 46 g.
- GL: 1 g.

254. Tuna Sweet Corn Casserole

PREPARATION TIME: 10'

COOKING TIME: 35'

SERVINGS: 2

Ingredients

- 3 small tins of tuna
- 0.5 lb. sweet corn kernels
- 1 lb. chopped vegetables
- 1 c. low sodium vegetable broth
- 2 tbsp. spicy seasoning

Directions

1. Mix all the ingredients in your instant pot.
2. Cook on Stew for 35 minutes.
3. Release the pressure naturally.

Nutrition

- Calories 300
- Carbohydrates 6 g.
- Sugar 1 g.
- Fat 9 g.
- GL : 2 g.

255. Lemon Pepper Salmon

PREPARATION TIME: 10'

COOKING TIME: 10'

SERVINGS: 4

Ingredients

- 3 tbsps ghee or avocado oil
- 1 lb. skin-on salmon filet
- 1 julienned red bell pepper
- 1 julienned green zucchini
- 1 julienned carrot
- 3/4 c. water
- A few sprigs of parsley, tarragon, dill, basil, or a combination
- 1/2 sliced lemon
- 1/2 tsp. black pepper
- 1/4 tsp. sea salt

Directions

1. Add the water and the herbs into the bottom of the instant pot and put in a wire steamer rack making sure the handles extend upwards.
2. Place the salmon filet onto the wire rack, with the skin side facing down.
3. Drizzle the salmon with ghee, season with black pepper and salt, and top with the lemon slices.
4. Close and seal the instant pot, making sure the vent is turned to "Sealing."
5. Select the Steam setting and cook for 3 minutes.
6. While the salmon cooks, julienne the vegetables and set aside.
7. Once done, quickly release the pressure, and then press the "Keep Warm/Cancel" button.
8. Uncover and wearing oven mitts, carefully remove the steamer rack with the salmon.
9. Remove the herbs and discard them.
10. Add the vegetables to the pot and put the lid back on.
11. Select the "Sauté" function and cook for 1-2 minutes.
12. Serve the vegetables with salmon and add the remaining fat to the pot.
13. Pour a little of the sauce over the fish and vegetables if desired.

Nutrition

- Calories 296
- Carbohydrates 8 g.
- Fat 15 g.
- Protein 31 g.
- Potassium 1084 mg.
- Sodium 284 mg.

256. Baked Salmon with Garlic Parmesan Topping

Preparation Time: 5'

Cooking Time: 20'

Servings: 4

Ingredients

- 1 lb. wild caught salmon filets
- 2 tbsp. margarine

What you'll need from the store cupboard:

- 1/4 c. reduced-fat parmesan cheese, grated
- 1/4 c. light mayonnaise
- 2-3 cloves garlic, diced
- 2 tbsp. parsley
- Salt and pepper

Directions

1. Heat oven to 350 °F and line a baking pan with parchment paper.
2. Place salmon on a pan and season with salt and pepper.
3. In a medium skillet, over medium heat, melt the margarine. Add garlic and cook, stirring for 1 minute.
4. Reduce the heat to low and add the remaining ingredients. Stir until everything is melted and combined.
5. Spread evenly over the salmon and bake for 15 minutes for thawed fish or 20 for frozen. Salmon is done when it flakes easily with a fork. Serve.

Nutrition

- Calories 408
- Total Carbohydrates 4 g.
- Protein 41 g.
- Fat 24 g.
- Sugar 1 g.
- Fiber 0 g.

257. Blackened Shrimp

Preparation Time: 5'

Cooking Time: 5'

Servings: 4

Ingredients

- 1 1/2 lbs. shrimp, peel and devein
- 4 lime wedges
- 4 tbsp. cilantro, chopped

What you'll need from the store cupboard:

- 4 cloves garlic, diced
- 1 tbsp. chili powder
- 1 tbsp. paprika
- 1 tbsp. olive oil
- 2 tsp. Splenda brown sugar
- 1 tsp. cumin
- 1 tsp. oregano
- 1 tsp. garlic powder
- 1 tsp. salt
- 1/2 tsp. pepper

Directions

1. In a small bowl, combine seasonings and Splenda brown sugar.
2. Heat oil in a skillet over med-high heat. Add the shrimp, in a single layer, and cook 1-2 minutes per side.
3. Add seasonings and cook, stirring for 30 seconds. Serve garnished with cilantro and a lime wedge.

Nutrition

- Calories 252
- Total Carbohydrates 7 g.
- Net Carbohydrates 6 g.
- Protein 39 g.
- Fat 7 g.
- Sugar 2 g.
- Fiber 1 g.

258. Cajun Catfish

PREPARATION TIME: 5'

COOKING TIME: 15'

SERVINGS: 4

Ingredients

- 4 (8 oz.) catfish fillets

What you'll need from the store cupboard:
- 2 tbsp. olive oil
- 2 tsp. garlic salt
- 2 tsp. thyme
- 2 tsp. paprika
- 1/2 tsp. cayenne pepper
- 1/2 tsp. red hot sauce
- 1/4 tsp. black pepper
- Nonstick cooking spray

Directions

1. Heat the oven to 450 °F. Spray a 9x13-in. baking dish with cooking spray.
2. In a small bowl, whisk together everything but the catfish. Brush both sides of the fillets, using all the spice mix.
3. Bake 10-13 minutes or until fish flakes easily with a fork. Serve.

Nutrition

- Calories 366
- Total Carbohydrates 0 g.
- Protein 35 g.
- Fat 24 g.
- Sugar 0 g.
- Fiber 0 g.

183

259. Cajun Flounder and Tomatoes

PREPARATION TIME: 10'

COOKING TIME: 15'

SERVINGS: 4

Ingredients

- 4 flounder fillets
- 2 1/2 c. tomatoes, diced
- 3/4 c. onion, diced
- 3/4 c. green bell pepper, diced

What you'll need from the store cupboard:
- 2 cloves garlic, diced fine
- 1 tbsp. Cajun seasoning
- 1 tsp. olive oil

Directions

1. Heat oil in a large skillet over med-high heat. Add the onion and garlic and cook for 2 minutes or until soft. Add tomatoes, peppers, and spices, and cook for 2-3 minutes until tomatoes soften.
2. Lay the fish over the top. Cover, reduce heat to medium and cook for 5-8 minutes, or until the fish flakes easily with a fork. Transfer the fish to serving plates and top with sauce.

Nutrition

- Calories 194
- Total Carbohydrates 8 g.
- Net Carbohydrates 6 g.
- Protein 32 g.
- Fat 3 g.
- Sugar 5 g.
- Fiber 2 g.

260. Cajun Shrimp and Roasted Vegetables

PREPARATION TIME: 5'
COOKING TIME: 15'
SERVINGS: 4

Ingredients

- 1 lb. large shrimp, peeled and deveined
- 2 zucchinis, sliced
- 2 yellow squash, sliced
- 1/2 bunch asparagus, cut into thirds
- 2 red bell pepper, cut into chunks

What you'll need from the store cupboard:
- 2 tbsp. olive oil
- 2 tbsp. Cajun Seasoning
- Salt and pepper, to taste

Directions

1. Heat the oven to 400 °F.
2. Combine the shrimp and vegetables in a large bowl. Add oil and seasoning and toss to coat.
3. Spread evenly in a large baking sheet and bake 15–20 minutes, or until vegetables are tender. Serve.

Nutrition

- Calories 251
- Total Carbohydrates 13 g.
- Net Carbohydrates 9 g.
- Protein 30 g.
- Fat 9 g.
- Sugar 6 g.
- Fiber 4 g.

261. Cilantro Lime Grilled Shrimp

PREPARATION TIME: 5'
COOKING TIME: 5'
SERVINGS: 6

Ingredients

- 1 1/2 lbs. large shrimp raw, peeled, deveined with tails on
- Juice and zest of 1 lime
- 2 tbsp. fresh cilantro chopped

What you'll need from the store cupboard:
- 1/4 c. olive oil
- 2 cloves garlic, diced fine
- 1 tsp. smoked paprika
- 1/4 tsp. cumin
- 1/2 tsp. salt
- 1/4 tsp. cayenne pepper

Directions

1. Place the shrimp in a large Ziploc bag.
2. Mix the remaining ingredients in a small bowl and pour over the shrimp. Let marinate for 20–30 minutes.
3. Heat up the grill. Skewer the shrimp and cook 2–3 minutes, per side, just until they turn pink. Be careful not to overcook them. Serve garnished with cilantro.

Nutrition

- Calories 317
- Total Carbohydrates 4 g.
- Protein 39 g.
- Fat 15 g.
- Sugar 0 g.
- Fiber 0 g.

262. Crab Frittata

PREPARATION TIME: 10'

COOKING TIME: 50'

SERVINGS: 4

Ingredients
- 4 eggs
- 2 c. lump crabmeat
- 1 c. half-n-half
- 1 c. green onions, diced

What you'll need from the store cupboard:
- 1 c. reduced-fat parmesan cheese, grated
- 1 tsp. salt
- 1 tsp. pepper
- 1 tsp. smoked paprika
- 1 tsp. Italian seasoning
- Nonstick cooking spray

Directions
1. Heat oven to 350 °F. Spray an 8-in. springform pan or pie plate with cooking spray.
2. In a large bowl, whisk together the eggs and half-n-half. Add seasonings and parmesan cheese, stir to mix.
3. Stir in the onions and crabmeat. Pour into the prepared pan and bake for 35-40 minutes, or till the eggs are set and the top is lightly browned.
4. Let cool for 10 minutes, then slice and serve warm or at room temperature.

Nutrition
- Calories 276
- Total Carbohydrates 5 g.
- Net Carbohydrates 4 g.
- Protein 25 g.
- Fat 17 g.
- Sugar 1 g.
- Fiber 1 g.

263. Crunchy Lemon Shrimp

PREPARATION TIME: 5'

COOKING TIME: 10'

SERVINGS: 4

Ingredients
- 1 lb. raw shrimp, peeled and deveined
- 2 tbsp. Italian parsley, roughly chopped
- 2 tbsp. lemon juice, divided

What you'll need from the store cupboard:
- 2/3 c. panko bread crumbs
- 2 1/2 tbsp. olive oil, divided
- Salt and pepper, to taste

Directions
1. Heat the oven to 400 °F.
2. Place the shrimp evenly in a baking dish and sprinkle with salt and pepper. Drizzle on 1 tbsp of lemon juice and 1 tbsp of olive oil. Set aside.
3. In a medium bowl, combine parsley, remaining lemon juice, bread crumbs, remaining olive oil, and 1/4 tsp. each of salt and pepper. Layer the panko mixture evenly on top of the shrimp.
4. Bake 8-10 minutes or until the shrimp are cooked through and the panko is golden brown.

Nutrition
- Calories 283
- Total Carbohydrates 15 g.
- Net Carbohydrates 14 g.
- Protein 28 g.
- Fat 12 g.
- Sugar 1 g.
- Fiber 1 g.

264. Grilled Tuna Steaks

Preparation time: 5'

Cooking time: 10'

Servings: 6

Ingredients
- 6 (6 oz.) tuna steaks
- 3 tbsp. fresh basil, diced

What you'll need from the store cupboard:
- 4 1/2 tsp. olive oil
- 3/4 tsp. salt
- 1/4 tsp. pepper
- Nonstick cooking spray

Directions
1. Heat grill to medium heat. Spray the rack with cooking spray.
2. Drizzle both sides of the tuna with oil. Sprinkle with basil, salt, and pepper.
3. Place on the grill and cook 5 minutes per side; tuna should be slightly pink in the center. Serve.

Nutrition
- Calories 343
- Total Carbohydrates 0 g.
- Protein 51 g.
- Fat 14 g.
- Sugar 0 g.
- Fiber 0 g.

265. Red Clam Sauce and Pasta

Preparation time: 10'

Cooking time: 3 hours

Servings: 4

Ingredients
- 1 onion, diced
- 1/4 c. fresh parsley, diced

What you'll need from the store cupboard:
- 2 6 1/2 oz. cans clams, chopped, undrained
- 14 1/2 oz. tomatoes, diced, undrained
- 6 oz. tomato paste
- 2 cloves garlic, diced
- 1 bay leaf
- 1 tbsp. sunflower oil
- 1 tsp. Splenda
- 1 tsp. basil
- 1/2 tsp. thyme
- 1/2 Homemade Pasta, cook and drain

Directions
1. Heat oil in a small skillet over med-high heat. Add onion and cook until tender, add garlic and cook 1 minute more. Transfer to the crock pot.
2. Add the remaining ingredients, except pasta, cover, and cook on low for 3-4 hours.
3. Discard the bay leaf and serve over the cooked pasta.

Nutrition
- Calories 223
- Total Carbohydrates 32 g.
- Net Carbohydrates 27 g.
- Protein 12 g.
- Fat 6 g.
- Sugar 15 g.
- Fiber 5 g.

266. Salmon Milano

PREPARATION TIME: **10'**

COOKING TIME: **20'**

SERVINGS: **6**

Ingredients

- 2 1/2 lb. salmon filet
- 2 tomatoes, sliced
- 1/2 c. margarine

What you'll need from the store cupboard:

- 1/2 c. basil pesto

Directions

1. Heat the oven to 400 °F. Line a 9x15-in. baking sheet with foil, making sure it covers the sides. Place another large piece of foil onto the baking sheet and place the salmon filet on top of it.
2. Place the pesto and margarine in a blender or food processor and pulse until smooth. Spread evenly over the salmon. Place the tomato slices on top.
3. Wrap the foil around the salmon, tenting around the top to prevent foil from touching the salmon as much as possible. Bake for 15–25 minutes, or salmon flakes easily with a fork. Serve.

Nutrition

- Calories 444
- Total Carbohydrates 2 g.
- Protein 55 g.
- Fat 24 g.
- Sugar 1 g.
- Fiber 0 g.

187

267. Shrimp and Artichoke Skillet

PREPARATION TIME: **5'**

COOKING TIME: **10'**

SERVINGS: **4**

Ingredients

- 1 1/2 c. shrimp, peel and devein
- 2 shallots, diced
- 1 tbsp. margarine

What you'll need from the store cupboard

- 2 12 oz. jars artichoke hearts, drain and rinse
- 2 c. white wine
- 2 cloves garlic, diced fine

Directions

1. Melt margarine in a large skillet over med-high heat. Add shallot and garlic and cook until they start to brown, stirring frequently.
2. Add artichokes and cook for 5 minutes. Reduce the heat and add wine. Cook for 3 minutes, stirring occasionally.
3. Add the shrimp and cook just until they turn pink. Serve.

Nutrition

- Calories 487
- Total Carbohydrates 26 g.
- Net Carbohydrates 17 g.
- Protein 64 g.
- Fat 5 g.
- Sugar 3 g.
- Fiber 9 g.

268. Tuna Carbonara

PREPARATION TIME: 5'

COOKING TIME: 25'

SERVINGS: 4

Ingredients

- 1/2 lb. tuna fillet, cut into pieces
- 2 eggs
- 4 tbsp. fresh parsley, diced

What you'll need from the store cupboard:

- 1/2 homemade pasta, cook and drain,
- 1/2 c. reduced-fat parmesan cheese
- 2 cloves garlic, peeled
- 2 tbsp. extra-virgin olive oil
- Salt and pepper, to taste

Directions

1. In a small bowl, beat the eggs, parmesan, and a dash of pepper.
2. Heat the oil in a large skillet over med-high heat. Add the garlic and cook until browned. Add the tuna and cook 2-3 minutes, or until the tuna is almost cooked through. Discard the garlic.
3. Add the pasta and reduce heat. Stir in the egg mixture and cook, stirring constantly for 2 minutes. If the sauce is too thick, thin with water, a little bit at a time until it has a creamy texture.
4. Salt and pepper to taste and serve garnished with parsley.

Nutrition

- Calories 409
- Total Carbohydrates 7 g.
- Net Carbohydrates 6 g.
- Protein 25 g.
- Fat 30 g.
- Sugar 3 g.
- Fiber 1 g.

269. Mediterranean Fish Fillets

PREPARATION TIME: 10'

COOKING TIME: 3'

SERVINGS: 4

Ingredients

- 4 cod fillets
- 1 lb. grape tomatoes, halved
- 1 c. olives, pitted and sliced
- 2 tbsp. capers
- 1 tsp. dried thyme
- 2 tbsp. olive oil
- 1 tsp. garlic, minced
- Pepper
- Salt

Directions

1. Pour 1 c of water into the instant pot then place the steamer rack in the pot.
2. Spray the heat-safe baking dish with cooking spray.
3. Add half-grape tomatoes into the dish and season with pepper and salt.
4. Arrange the fish fillets on top of the cherry tomatoes. Drizzle with oil and season with garlic, thyme, capers, pepper, and salt.
5. Spread the olives and the remaining grape tomatoes on top of the fish fillets.
6. Place the dish on top of the steamer rack in the pot.
7. Seal the pot with a lid and select manual and cook on high for 3 minutes.
8. Once done, release the pressure using the quick release. Remove the lid.
9. Serve and enjoy.

Nutrition

- Calories 212
- Fat 11.9 g.
- Carbohydrates 7.1 g.
- Sugar 3 g.
- Protein 21.4 g.
- Cholesterol 55 mg.

Chapter 11: Meat Recipes

270. Pork Chops with Grape Sauce

Preparation time: 15'
Cooking time: 25'
Servings: 4

Ingredients

- Cooking spray
- 4 pork chops
- 1/4 c. onion, sliced
- 1 clove garlic, minced
- 1/2 c. low-sodium chicken broth
- 3/4 c. apple juice
- 1 tbsp. cornstarch
- 1 tbsp. balsamic vinegar
- 1 tsp. honey
- 1 c. seedless red grapes, sliced in half

Directions

1. Spray oil on your pan.
2. Put it over medium heat.
3. Add the pork chops to the pan.
4. Cook for 5 minutes per side.
5. Remove and set aside.
6. Add the onion and garlic.
7. Cook for 2 minutes.
8. Pour in the broth and apple juice.
9. Bring to a boil.
10. Reduce the heat to simmer.
11. Put the pork chops back to the skillet.
12. Simmer for 4 minutes.
13. In a bowl, mix the cornstarch, vinegar, and honey.
14. Add to the pan.
15. Cook until the sauce has thickened.
16. Add the grapes.
17. Pour the sauce over the pork chops before serving.

Nutrition

- Calories 188
- Total Fat 4 g.
- Saturated Fat 1 g.
- Cholesterol 47 mg
- Sodium 117 mg
- Total Carbohydrate 18 g.
- Dietary Fiber 1 g.
- Total Sugars 13 g.
- Protein 19 g.
- Potassium 759 mg.

271. Roasted Pork and Apples

Preparation time: 15'
Cooking time: 30'
Servings: 4

Ingredients

- Salt and pepper to taste
- 1 lb. pork tenderloin
- 1 tbsp. canola oil
- 1 onion, sliced into wedges
- 3 cooking apples, sliced into wedges
- 2/3 c. apple cider
- Sprigs fresh sage

Directions

1. In a bowl, mix salt, pepper, and sage.
2. Season both sides of pork with this mixture.
3. Place a pan over medium heat.
4. Brown both sides.
5. Transfer to a roasting pan.
6. Add the onion on top and around the pork.
7. Drizzle oil on top of the pork and apples.
8. Roast in the oven at 425 °F for 10 minutes.
9. Add the apples, roast for another 15 minutes.
10. In a pan, boil the apple cider and then simmer for 10 minutes.
11. Pour the apple cider sauce over the pork before serving.

Nutrition

- Calories 239
- Total Fat 6 g.
- Saturated Fat 1 g.
- Cholesterol 74 mg
- Sodium 209 mg
- Total Carbohydrate 22 g.
- Dietary Fiber 3 g.
- Total Sugars 16 g.
- Protein 24 g.
- Potassium 655 mg.

272. Pork with Cranberry Relish

PREPARATION TIME: 30'
COOKING TIME: 30'
SERVINGS: 4

Ingredients

- 12 oz. pork tenderloin, fat trimmed and sliced crosswise
- Salt and pepper to taste
- 1/4 c. all-purpose flour
- 2 tbsps olive oil
- 1 onion, sliced thinly
- 1/4 c. dried cranberries
- 1/4 c. low-sodium chicken broth
- 1 tbsp. balsamic vinegar

Directions

1. Flatten each slice of the pork using a mallet.
2. In a dish, mix the salt, pepper, and flour.
3. Dip each pork slice into the flour mixture.
4. Add oil to a pan over medium-high heat.
5. Cook the pork for 3 minutes per side or until golden crispy.
6. Transfer to a serving plate and cover with foil.
7. Cook the onion in the pan for 4 minutes.
8. Stir in the rest of the ingredients.
9. Simmer until the sauce has thickened.

Nutrition

- Calories 211
- Total Fat 9 g.
- Saturated Fat 2 g.
- Cholesterol 53 mg
- Sodium 116 mg
- Total Carbohydrate 15 g.
- Dietary Fiber 1 g.
- Total Sugars 6 g.
- Protein 18 g.
- Potassium 378 mg.

273. Sesame Pork with Mustard Sauce

PREPARATION TIME: 25'
COOKING TIME: 25'
SERVINGS: 4

Ingredients

- 2 tbsps low-sodium teriyaki sauce
- 1/4 c. chili sauce
- 2 cloves garlic, minced
- 2 tsps. ginger, grated
- 2 pork tenderloins
- 2 tsps. sesame seeds
- 1/4 c. low-fat sour cream
- 1 tsp. Dijon mustard
- Salt to taste
- 1 scallion, chopped

Directions

1. Preheat your oven to 425 °F.
2. Mix the teriyaki sauce, chili sauce, garlic, and ginger.
3. Put the pork on a roasting pan.
4. Brush the sauce on both sides of the pork.
5. Bake in the oven for 15 minutes.
6. Brush with more sauce.
7. Top with sesame seeds.
8. Roast for 10 more minutes.
9. Mix the rest of the ingredients.
10. Serve the pork with mustard sauce.

Nutrition

- Calories 135
- Total Fat 3 g.
- Saturated Fat 1 g.
- Cholesterol 56X mg
- Sodium 302 mg
- Total Carbohydrate 7 g.
- Dietary Fiber 1 g.
- Total Sugars 15 g.
- Protein 20 g.
- Potassium 755 mg.

274. Steak with Mushroom Sauce

Preparation time: 20'
Cooking time: 5'
Servings: 4

Ingredients

- 12 oz. sirloin steak, sliced and trimmed
- 2 tsps. grilling seasoning
- 2 tsps. oil
- 6 oz. broccoli, trimmed
- 2 c. frozen peas
- 3 c. fresh mushrooms, sliced
- 1 c. beef broth (unsalted)
- 1 tbsp. mustard
- 2 tsps. cornstarch
- Salt to taste

Directions

1. Preheat your oven to 350 °F.
2. Season the meat with the grilling seasoning.
3. In a pan over medium-high heat, cook the meat and broccoli for 4 minutes.
4. Sprinkle the peas around the steak.
5. Put the pan inside the oven and bake for 8 minutes.
6. Remove both the meat and vegetables from the pan.
7. Add the mushrooms to the pan.
8. Cook for 3 minutes.
9. Mix the broth, mustard, salt and cornstarch.
10. Add to the mushrooms.
11. Cook for 1 minute.
12. Pour sauce over meat and vegetables before serving.

Nutrition

- Calories 226
- Total Fat 6 g.
- Saturated Fat 2 g.
- Cholesterol 51 mg
- Sodium 356 mg
- Total Carbohydrate 16 g.
- Dietary Fiber 5 g.
- Total Sugars 6 g.
- Protein 26 g.
- Potassium 780 mg.

192

275. Steak with Tomato and Herbs

Preparation time: 30'
Cooking time: 30'
Servings: 2

Ingredients

- 8 oz. beef loin steak, sliced in half
- Salt and pepper to taste
- Cooking spray
- 1 tsp. fresh basil, snipped
- 1/4 c. green onion, sliced
- 1/2 c. tomato, chopped

Directions

1. Season the steak with salt and pepper.
2. Spray oil on your pan.
3. Put the pan over medium-high heat.
4. Once hot, add the steaks.
5. Reduce the heat to medium.
6. Cook for 10-13 minutes for medium, turning once.
7. Add the basil and green onion.
8. Cook for 2 minutes.
9. Add the tomato.
10. Cook for 1 minute.
11. Let cool a little before slicing.

Nutrition

- Calories 170
- Total Fat 6 g.
- Saturated Fat 2 g.
- Cholesterol 66 mg
- Sodium 207 mg
- Total Carbohydrate 3 g.
- Dietary Fiber 1 g.
- Total Sugars 5 g.
- Protein 25 g.
- Potassium 477 mg.

276. Barbecue Beef Brisket

Preparation time: 25'
Cooking time: 10 hours
Servings: 10

Ingredients

- 4 lb. beef brisket (boneless), trimmed and sliced
- 1 bay leaf
- 2 onions, sliced into rings
- 1/2 tsp. dried thyme, crushed
- 1/4 c. chili sauce
- 1 garlic clove, minced
- Salt and pepper to taste
- 2 tbsps light brown sugar
- 2 tbsps cornstarch
- 2 tbsps cold water

Directions

1. Put the meat in a slow cooker.
2. Add the bay leaf and onion.
3. In a bowl, mix the thyme, chili sauce, salt, pepper, and sugar.
4. Pour the sauce over the meat.
5. Mix well.
6. Seal the pot and cook on low heat for 10 hours.
7. Discard the bay leaf.
8. Pour the cooking liquid into a pan.
9. Add the mixed water and cornstarch.
10. Simmer until the sauce has thickened.
11. Pour the sauce over the meat.

Nutrition

- Calories 182
- Total Fat 6 g.
- Saturated Fat 2 g.
- Cholesterol 57 mg.
- Sodium 217 mg
- Total Sugars 4 g.
- Protein 20 g.
- Potassium 383 mg.

277. Beef and Asparagus

Preparation time: 15'
Cooking time: 10'
Servings: 4

Ingredients

- 2 tsps. olive oil
- 1 lb. lean beef sirloin, trimmed and sliced
- 1 carrot, shredded
- Salt and pepper to taste
- 12 oz. asparagus, trimmed and sliced
- 1 tsp. dried herbes de Provence, crushed
- 1/2 c. Marsala
- 1/4 tsp. lemon zest

Directions

1. Pour oil in a pan over medium heat.
2. Add the beef and carrot.
3. Season with salt and pepper.
4. Cook for 3 minutes.
5. Add the asparagus and herbs.
6. Cook for 2 minutes.
7. Add the Marsala and lemon zest.
8. Cook for 5 minutes, stirring frequently.

Nutrition

- Calories 327
- Total Fat 7 g.
- Saturated Fat 2 g.
- Cholesterol 69 mg
- Sodium 209 mg
- Total Carbohydrate 29 g.
- Dietary Fiber 2 g.
- Total Sugars 3 g.
- Protein 28 g.
- Potassium 576 mg.

278. Italian Beef

PREPARATION TIME: 20'

COOKING TIME: 1H 20'

SERVINGS: 4

Ingredients

- Cooking spray
- 1 lb. beef round steak, trimmed and sliced
- 1 c. onion, chopped
- 2 cloves garlic, minced
- 1 c. green bell pepper, chopped
- 1/2 c. celery, chopped
- 2 c. mushrooms, sliced
- 14 1/2 oz. canned diced tomatoes
- 1/2 tsp. dried basil
- 1/4 tsp. dried oregano
- 1/8 tsp. crushed red pepper
- 2 tbsps Parmesan cheese, grated

Directions

1. Spray oil on the pan over medium heat.
2. Cook the meat until brown on both sides.
3. Transfer the meat to a plate.
4. Add the onion, garlic, bell pepper, celery, and mushroom to the pan.
5. Cook until tender.
6. Add the tomatoes, herbs, and pepper.
7. Put the meat back to the pan.
8. Simmer while covered for 1 hour and 15 minutes.
9. Stir occasionally.
10. Sprinkle Parmesan cheese on top of the dish before serving.

Nutrition

- Calories 212
- Total Fat 4 g.
- Saturated Fat 1 g.
- Cholesterol 51 mg
- Sodium 296 mg
- Total Sugars 6 g.
- Protein 30 g.
- Potassium 876 mg.

279. Lamb with Broccoli and Carrots

PREPARATION TIME: 20'

COOKING TIME: 10'

SERVINGS: 4

Ingredients

- 2 cloves garlic, minced
- 1 tbsp. fresh ginger, grated
- 1/4 tsp. red pepper, crushed
- 2 tbsps low-sodium soy sauce
- 1 tbsp. white vinegar
- 1 tbsp. cornstarch
- 12 oz. lamb meat, trimmed and sliced
- 2 tsps. cooking oil
- 1 lb. broccoli, sliced into florets
- 2 carrots, sliced into strips
- 3/4 c. low-sodium beef broth
- 4 green onions, chopped
- 2 c. cooked spaghetti squash pasta

Directions

1. Combine the garlic, ginger, red pepper, soy sauce, vinegar, and cornstarch in a bowl.
2. Add the lamb to the marinade.
3. Marinate for 10 minutes.
4. Discard the marinade.
5. In a pan over medium heat, add the oil.
6. Add the lamb and cook for 3 minutes.
7. Transfer the lamb to a plate.
8. Add the broccoli and carrots.
9. Cook for 1 minute.
10. Pour in the beef broth.
11. Cook for 5 minutes.
12. Put the meat back to the pan.
13. Sprinkle with green onion and serve on top of spaghetti squash.

Nutrition

- Calories 205
- Total Fat 6 g.
- Saturated Fat 1 g.
- Cholesterol 40 mg
- Sodium 659 mg
- Total Carbohydrate 17 g.

280. Rosemary Lamb

PREPARATION TIME: **15'**

COOKING TIME: **2 HOURS**

SERVINGS: **14**

Ingredients

- Salt and pepper to taste
- 2 tsps. fresh rosemary, snipped
- 5 lb. whole leg of lamb, trimmed and cut with slits on all sides
- 3 cloves garlic, slivered
- 1 c. water

Directions

1. Preheat your oven to 375 °F.
2. Mix salt, pepper, and rosemary in a bowl.
3. Sprinkle the mixture all over the lamb.
4. Insert slivers of garlic into the slits.
5. Put the lamb on a roasting pan.
6. Add water to the pan.
7. Roast for 2 hours.

Nutrition

- Calories 136
- Total Fat 4 g.
- Saturated Fat 1 g.
- Cholesterol 71 mg
- Sodium 218 mg
- Protein 23 g.
- Potassium 248 mg

281. Mediterranean Lamb Meatballs

PREPARATION TIME: **10'**

COOKING TIME: **20'**

SERVINGS: **8**

Ingredients

- 12 oz. roasted red peppers
- 1 1/2 c. whole wheat breadcrumbs
- 2 eggs, beaten
- 1/3 c. tomato sauce
- 1/2 c. fresh basil
- 1/4 c. parsley, snipped
- Salt and pepper to taste
- 2 lb. lean ground lamb

Directions

1. Preheat your oven to 350 °F.
2. In a bowl, mix all the ingredients and then form them into meatballs.
3. Put the meatballs on a baking pan.
4. Bake in the oven for 20 minutes.

Nutrition

- Calories 94
- Total Fat 3 g.
- Saturated Fat 1 g.
- Cholesterol 35 mg
- Sodium 170 mg
- Total Carbohydrate 2 g.
- Dietary Fiber 1 g.
- Total Sugars 0 g.

Chapter 12: Main

282. Blueberry and Chicken Salad

PREPARATION TIME: **10'**

COOKING TIME: **0'**

SERVINGS: **4**

Ingredients

- 2 c. chopped cooked chicken
- 1 c. fresh blueberries
- 1/4 c. almonds
- 1 celery stalk
- 1/4 c. red onion
- 1 tbsp. fresh basil
- 1 tbsp. fresh cilantro
- 1/2 c. plain yogurt
- 1/4 tsp. salt
- 1/4 tsp. freshly ground black pepper
- 8 c. salad greens

Directions

1. Toss the chicken, blueberries, almonds, celery, onion, basil, and cilantro.
2. Blend yogurt, salt, and pepper. Stir the chicken salad to combine.
3. Situate 2 c of salad greens on each of 4 plates and divide the chicken salad among the plates to serve.

Nutrition

- Calories 207
- Carbohydrates 11 g.
- Sugars 6 g.

283. Beef and Red Bean Chili

PREPARATION TIME: **10'**

COOKING TIME: **6 HOURS**

SERVINGS: **4**

Ingredients

- 1 c. dry red beans
- 1 tbsp. olive oil
- 2 lbs. boneless beef chuck
- 1 large onion, coarsely chopped
- 1 (14 oz.) can of beef broth
- 2 chipotle chili peppers in adobo sauce
- 2 tsps. dried oregano, crushed
- 1 tsp. ground cumin
- 1/2 teaspoon salt
- 1 (14.5 oz.) can of tomatoes with mild green chilies
- 1 (15 oz.) can tomato sauce
- 1/4 c. snipped fresh cilantro
- 1 medium red sweet pepper

Directions

1. Rinse out the beans and place them into a Dutch oven or big saucepan, then add in water enough to cover them. Allow the beans to boil then drop the heat down. Simmer the beans without a cover for 10 minutes. Take off the heat and keep covered for an hour.
2. In a big fry pan, heat up the oil upon medium-high heat, then cook the onion and half of the beef until they brown a bit over medium-high heat. Move into a 3 1/2- or 4-quart crockery cooker. Do this again with what's left of the beef. Add in tomato sauce, tomatoes (not drained), salt, cumin, oregano, adobo sauce, chipotle peppers, and broth, stirring to blend. Strain out and rinse the beans and stir in the cooker.
3. Cook while covered on a low setting for around 10-12 hours or on the high setting for 5-6 hours. Spoon the chili into bowls or mugs and top with sweet pepper and cilantro.

Nutrition

- Calories 288
- Carbohydrate 24 g.
- Sugar 5 g.

284. Berry Apple Cider

PREPARATION TIME: 15'

COOKING TIME: 3 HOURS

SERVINGS: 3

Ingredients

- 4 cinnamon sticks, cut into 1-in. pieces
- 1 1/2 tsps. whole cloves
- 4 c. apple cider
- 4 c. low-calorie cranberry-raspberry juice drink
- 1 medium apple

Directions

1. To make the spice bag, cut out a 6-in. square from double-thick, pure cotton cheesecloth. Put in the cloves and cinnamon, then bring the corners up, tie it closed using a clean kitchen string that is pure cotton.
2. In a 3 1/2–5-qt. slow cooker, combine cranberry-raspberry juice, apple cider, and the spice bag.
3. Cook while covered over the low heat setting for around 4–6 hours or on a high heat setting for 2–2 1/2 hours.
4. Throw out the spice bag. Serve right away or keep it warm while covered on warm or low-heat setting up to 2 hours, occasionally stirring. Garnish each serving with apples (thinly sliced).

Nutrition

- Calories 89
- Carbohydrate 22 g.
- Sugar 19 g.

285. Brunswick Stew

PREPARATION TIME: 10'

COOKING TIME: 45'

SERVINGS: 3

Ingredients

- 4 oz. diced salt pork
- 2 lbs. chicken parts
- 8 c. water
- 3 onions, chopped
- 1 (28 oz.) can whole peeled tomatoes
- 2 c. canned whole kernel corn
- 1 (10 oz.) package frozen lima beans
- 1 tbsp. Worcestershire sauce
- 1/2 tsp. salt
- 1/4 tsp. ground black pepper

Directions

1. Mix and boil the water, chicken, and salt pork in a big pot on high heat. Lower heat to low. Cover then simmer until the chicken is tender for 45 minutes.
2. Take out the chicken. Let cool until easily handled. Take the meat out. Throw out the bones and skin. Chop the meat into bite-sized pieces. Put back in the soup.
3. Add ground black pepper, salt, Worcestershire sauce, lima beans, corn, tomatoes, and onions. Mix well. Stir and simmer for 1 hour, uncovered.

Nutrition

- Calories 368
- Carbohydrate 25.9 g.
- Protein 27.9 g.

286. Buffalo Chicken Salads

Preparation time: 7'
Cooking time: 3 hours
Servings: 5

Ingredients

- 1 1/2 lbs. chicken breast halves
- 1/2 c. Wing Time Buffalo chicken sauce
- 4 tsps. cider vinegar
- 1 tsp. Worcestershire sauce
- 1 tsp. paprika
- 1/3 c. light mayonnaise
- 2 tbsps fat-free milk
- 2 tbsps crumbled blue cheese
- 2 romaine hearts, chopped
- 1 c. whole-grain croutons
- 1/2 c. very thinly sliced red onion

Directions

1. Place the chicken in a 2-quarts slow cooker. Mix together the Worcestershire sauce, 2 tsps of vinegar, and Buffalo sauce in a small bowl; pour over the chicken. Dust with paprika. Close and cook for 3 hours on the low-heat setting.
2. Mix the leftover 2 tsps of vinegar with milk and light mayonnaise together in a small bowl at serving time; mix in blue cheese. While the chicken is still in the slow cooker, pull the meat into bite-sized pieces using two forks.
3. Split the romaine among 6 dishes. Spoon the sauce and chicken over the lettuce. Pour with blue cheese dressing then add red onion slices and croutons on top.

Nutrition

- Calories 274
- Carbohydrate 11 g.
- Fiber 2 g.

200

287. Cacciatore Style Chicken

Preparation time: 10'
Cooking time: 4 hours
Servings: 6

Ingredients

- 2 c. sliced fresh mushrooms
- 1 c. sliced celery
- 1 c. chopped carrot
- 2 medium onions, cut into wedges
- 1 green, yellow, or red sweet peppers
- 4 cloves garlic, minced
- 12 chicken drumsticks
- 1/2 c. chicken broth
- 1/4 c. dry white wine
- 2 tbsps quick-cooking tapioca
- 2 bay leaves
- 1 tsp. dried oregano, crushed
- 1 tsp. sugar
- 1/2 teaspoon salt
- 1/4 tsp. pepper
- 1 (14.5 oz.) can diced tomatoes
- 1/3 c. tomato paste
- Hot cooked pasta or rice

Directions

1. Mix the garlic, sweet pepper, onions, carrot, celery, and mushrooms in a 5- or 6-qt. slow cooker. Cover the veggies with the chicken. Add pepper, salt, sugar, oregano, bay leaves, tapioca, wine, and broth.
2. Cover. Cook for 3-3 1/2 hours on the high-heat setting.
3. Take the chicken out; keep warm. Discard the bay leaves. Turn to the high-heat setting if using the low-heat setting. Mix the tomato paste and undrained tomatoes in. Cover. Cook on high-heat setting for 15 more minutes. Serving: Put the veggie mixture on top of the pasta and chicken.

Nutrition

- Calories 288
- Total fat 11 g.
- Saturated fat 1 g.
- Protein 10 g.
- Carbohydrates 38 g.
- Sugar 7 g.
- Fiber 10 g.
- Cholesterol 0 mg.
- Sodium 329 mg.

288. Carnitas Tacos

Preparation time: 10'
Cooking time: 5 hours
Servings: 4

Ingredients

- 3–3 1/2-lbs. bone-in pork shoulder roast
- 1/2 c. chopped onion
- 1/3 c. orange juice
- 1 tbsp. ground cumin
- 1 1/2 tsps. kosher salt
- 1 tsp. dried oregano, crushed
- 1/4 tsp. cayenne pepper
- 1 lime
- 2 (5.3 oz.) containers of plain low-fat Greek yogurt
- 1 pinch kosher salt
- 16 (6 in.) soft yellow corn tortillas, such as Mission brand
- 4 leaves green cabbage, quartered
- 1 c. very thinly sliced red onion
- 1 c. salsa (optional)

Directions

1. Take off the meat from the bone; throw away the bone. Trim the meat fat. Slice the meat into 2–3-in. pieces; put in a slow cooker of 3 1/2 or 4-quart in size. Mix in cayenne, oregano, salt, cumin, orange juice, and onion.
2. Cover and cook for 4–5 hours on high. Take out the meat from the cooker. Shred the meat with two forks. Mix in enough cooking liquid to moisten.
3. Take out 1 tsp of zest lime, then squeeze 2 tbsps lime juice. Mix a dash of salt, yogurt, and lime juice in a small bowl.
4. Serve lime crema, salsa (if wished), red onion, and cabbage with the meat in tortillas. Scatter with lime zest.

Nutrition

- Calories 301
- Carbohydrate 28 g.
- Sugar 7 g.

201

289. Chicken Chili

Preparation time: 6'
Cooking time: 1 hour
Servings: 4

Ingredients

- 3 tbsps vegetable oil
- 2 cloves garlic, minced
- 1 green bell pepper, chopped
- 1 onion, chopped
- 1 stalk celery, sliced
- 1/4-pound mushrooms, chopped
- 1-pound chicken breast
- 1 tbsp. chili powder
- 1 tsp. dried oregano
- 1 tsp. ground cumin
- 1/2 tsp. paprika
- 1/2 tsp. cocoa powder
- 1/4 tsp. salt
- 1 pinch crushed red pepper flakes
- 1 pinch ground black pepper
- 1 (14.5 oz) can tomatoes with juice
- 1 (19 oz) can kidney beans

Directions

1. Fill 2 tbsps of oil into a big skillet and heat it at moderate heat. Add mushrooms, celery, onion, bell pepper, and garlic, sautéing for 5 minutes. Set aside.
2. Insert the leftover 1 tbsp of oil into the skillet. At high heat, cook the chicken until browned and its exterior turns firm. Transfer the vegetable mixture back into the skillet.
3. Stir in ground black pepper, hot pepper flakes, salt, cocoa powder, paprika, oregano, cumin, and chili powder. Continue stirring for several minutes to avoid burning. Pour in the beans and tomatoes and lead the entire mixture to a boiling point then adjust the setting to low heat. Place a lid on the skillet and leave it simmering for 15 minutes. Uncover the skillet and leave it simmering for another 15 minutes.

Nutrition

- Calories 308
- Carbohydrate 25.9 g.
- Protein 29 g.

290. Chicken Vera Cruz

PREPARATION TIME: 7'
COOKING TIME: 10 HOURS
SERVINGS: 5

Ingredients

- 1 medium onion, cut into wedges
- 6 skinless, boneless chicken thighs
- 2 (14.5 oz.) cans of no-salt-added diced tomatoes
- 1 fresh jalapeño chili pepper
- 2 tbsps Worcestershire sauce
- 1 tbsp. chopped garlic
- 1 tsp. dried oregano, crushed
- 1/4 tsp. ground cinnamon
- 1/8 tsp. ground cloves
- 1/2 c. snipped fresh parsley
- 1/4 c. chopped pimiento-stuffed green olives

Directions

1. Put the onion in a 3 1/2- or 4-quart slow cooker. Place the chicken thighs on top. Drain and discard the juices from a can of tomatoes. Stir undrained and drained tomatoes, cloves, cinnamon, oregano, garlic, Worcestershire sauce, and jalapeño pepper together in a bowl. Pour over all in the cooker.
2. Cook with a cover for 10 hours on the low-heat setting.
3. To make the topping: Stir the chopped pimiento-stuffed green olives and snipped fresh parsley together in a small bowl. Drizzle the topping over each serving of chicken.

Nutrition

- Calories 228
- Sugar 9 g.
- Carbohydrate 25 g.

291. Chicken and Cornmeal Dumplings

PREPARATION TIME: 8'
COOKING TIME: 8 HOURS
SERVINGS: 4

Ingredients

For the Chicken and Vegetable Filling
- 2 medium carrots, thinly sliced
- 1 stalk celery, thinly sliced
- 1/3 c. corn kernels
- 1/2 of a medium onion, thinly sliced
- 2 cloves garlic, minced
- 1 tsp. snipped fresh rosemary
- 1/4 tsp. ground black pepper
- 2 chicken thighs, skinned
- 1 c. low-sodium chicken broth
- 1/2 c. fat-free milk
- 1 tbsp. all-purpose flour

For the Cornmeal Dumplings
- 1/4 c. flour
- 1/4 c. cornmeal
- 1/2 teaspoon baking powder
- 1 egg white
- 1 tbsp. fat-free milk
- 1 tbsp. canola oil

Directions

1. Mix 1/4 tsp. the pepper, carrots, garlic, celery, rosemary, corn, and onion in a 1 1/2 or 2-quart slow cooker. Place the chicken on top. Pour the broth atop the mixture into the cooker.
2. Close and cook on low-heat for 7-8 hours.
3. If cooking with the low-heat setting, switch to the high-heat setting (or if the heat setting is not available, continue to cook). Place the chicken onto a cutting board and let cool slightly. Once cool enough to handle, chop off the chicken from the bones and get rid of the bones. Chop the chicken and place it back into the mixture in the cooker. Mix flour and milk in a small bowl until smooth. Stir into the mixture in the cooker.
4. Mix together 1/2 tsp. baking powder, 1/4 c. flour, a dash of salt, and 1/4 c. cornmeal in a medium bowl. Mix 1 tbsp. canola oil, 1 egg white, and 1 tbsp. fat-free milk in a small bowl. Pour the egg mixture into the flour mixture. Mix just until moistened.
5. Drop the Cornmeal Dumplings dough into 4 mounds atop the hot chicken mixture using two spoons. Cover and cook for 20-25 minutes more or until a toothpick comes out clean when inserted into a dumpling. (Avoid lifting the lid when cooking.) Sprinkle each of the serving with coarse pepper if desired.

Nutrition

- Calories 369
- Sugar 9 g.
- Carbohydrate 47 g.

292. Chicken and Pepperoni

Preparation time: 4'
Cooking time: 4 hours
Servings: 5

Ingredients

- 3 1/2–4 lbs. meaty chicken pieces
- 1/8 tsp. salt
- 1/8 tsp. black pepper
- 2 oz. sliced turkey pepperoni
- 1/4 c. sliced pitted ripe olives
- 1/2 c. reduced-sodium chicken broth
- 1 tbsp. tomato paste
- 1 tsp. dried Italian seasoning, crushed
- 1/2 c. shredded part-skim mozzarella cheese (2 oz.)

Directions

1. Put the chicken into a 3 1/2–5-qt. slow cooker. Sprinkle pepper and salt on the chicken. Slice pepperoni slices in half. Put olives and pepperoni into the slow cooker. In a small bowl, blend Italian seasoning, tomato paste, and chicken broth together. Transfer the mixture into the slow cooker.
2. Cook with a cover for 3–3 1/2 hours on high.
3. Transfer the olives, pepperoni, and chicken onto a serving platter with a slotted spoon. Discard the cooking liquid. Sprinkle cheese over the chicken. Use foil to loosely cover and allow to sit for 5 minutes to melt the cheese.

Nutrition

- Calories 243
- Carbohydrate 1 g.
- Protein 41 g.

293. Chicken and Sausage Gumbo

Preparation time: 6'
Cooking time: 4 hours
Servings: 4

Ingredients

- 1/3 c. all-purpose flour
- 1 (14 oz.) can reduced-sodium chicken broth
- 2 c. chicken breast
- 8 oz. smoked turkey sausage links
- 2 c. sliced fresh okra
- 1 c. water
- 1 c. coarsely chopped onion
- 1 c. sweet pepper
- 1/2 c. sliced celery
- 4 cloves garlic, minced
- 1 tsp. dried thyme
- 1/2 teaspoon ground black pepper
- 1/4 tsp. cayenne pepper
- 3 c. hot cooked brown rice

Directions

1. To make the roux: Cook the flour upon medium heat in a heavy medium-sized saucepan, stirring periodically, for roughly 6 minutes or until the flour browns. Take off the heat and slightly cool, then slowly stir in the broth. Cook the roux until it bubbles and thickens up.
2. Pour the roux in a 3 1/2- or 4-quart slow cooker, then add in cayenne pepper, black pepper, thyme, garlic, celery, sweet pepper, onion, water, okra, sausage, and chicken.
3. Cook the soup covered on a high setting for 3 - 3 1/2 hours. Take the fat off the top and serve atop hot cooked brown rice.

Nutrition

- Calories 230
- Sugar 3 g.
- Protein 19 g.

294. Chicken, Barley, and Leek Stew

Preparation time: 10'
Cooking time: 3 hours
Servings: 2

Ingredients

- 1-pound chicken thighs
- 1 tbsp. olive oil
- 1 (49 oz.) can reduced-sodium chicken broth
- 1 c. regular barley (not quick-cooking)
- 2 medium leeks, halved lengthwise and sliced
- 2 medium carrots, thinly sliced
- 1 1/2 tsps. dried basil or Italian seasoning, crushed
- 1/4 tsp. cracked black pepper

Directions

1. In the big skillet, cook the chicken in hot oil till becoming brown on all sides. In the 4-5-qt. slow cooker, whisk the pepper, dried basil, carrots, leeks, barley, chicken broth, and chicken.
2. Keep covered and cooked over the high heat setting for 2-2.5 hours or till the barley softens. As you wish, drizzle with the parsley or fresh basil prior to serving.

Nutrition

- Calories 248
- Fiber 6 g.
- Carbohydrate 27 g.

295. Cider Pork Stew

Preparation time: 9'
Cooking time: 12 hours
Servings: 3

Ingredients

- 2 lbs. pork shoulder roast
- 3 medium carrots
- 2 medium onions, sliced
- 1 c. coarsely chopped apple
- 1/2 c. coarsely chopped celery
- 3 tbsps quick-cooking tapioca
- 2 c. apple juice
- 1 tsp. salt
- 1 tsp. caraway seeds
- 1/4 tsp. black pepper

Directions

1. Chop the meat into 1-in. cubes. In the 3.5-5.5 qt. slow cooker, mix the tapioca, celery, apple, onions, carrots, and meat. Whisk in pepper, caraway seeds, salt, and apple juice.
2. Keep covered and cook over the low heat setting for 10-12 hours. If you want, use the celery leaves to decorate each of the servings.

Nutrition

- Calories 244
- Fiber 5 g.
- Carbohydrate 33 g.

296. Creamy Chicken Noodle Soup

PREPARATION TIME: 7'

COOKING TIME: 8 HOURS

SERVINGS: 4

Ingredients

- 1 (32 fl. oz.) container reduced-sodium chicken broth
- 3 c. water
- 2 1/2 c. chopped cooked chicken
- 3 medium carrots, sliced
- 3 stalks celery
- 1 1/2 c. sliced fresh mushrooms
- 1/4 c. chopped onion
- 1 1/2 tsps. dried thyme, crushed
- 3/4 teaspoon garlic-pepper seasoning
- 3 oz. reduced-fat cream cheese (Neufchâtel), cut up
- 2 c. dried egg noodles

Directions

1. Mix together the garlic-pepper seasoning, thyme, onion, mushrooms, celery, carrots, chicken, water, and broth in a 5–6-quart slow cooker.
2. Put the lid and let it cook for 6–8 hours in the low-heat setting.
3. Increase to the high-heat setting if you are using the low-heat setting. Mix in the cream cheese until blended. Mix in the uncooked noodles. Put the cover and let it cook for an additional 20–30 minutes or just until the noodles become tender.

Nutrition

- Calories 170
- Sugar 3 g.
- Fiber 2 g.

297. Cuban Pulled Pork Sandwich

205

PREPARATION TIME: 6'

COOKING TIME: 5 HOURS

SERVINGS: 5

Ingredients

- 1 tsp. dried oregano, crushed
- 3/4 teaspoon ground cumin
- 1/2 teaspoon ground coriander
- 1/4 tsp. salt
- 1/4 tsp. black pepper
- 1/4 tsp. ground allspice
- 1 2-2 1/2-pound boneless pork shoulder roast
- 1 tbsp. olive oil
- Nonstick cooking spray
- 2 c. sliced onions
- 2 green sweet peppers, cut into bite-size strips
- 1/2 to 1 fresh jalapeño pepper
- 4 cloves garlic, minced
- 1/4 c. orange juice
- 1/4 c. lime juice
- 6 heart-healthy wheat hamburger buns, toasted
- 2 tbsps jalapeño mustard

Directions

1. Mix allspice, oregano, black pepper, cumin, salt, and coriander together in a small bowl. Press each side of the roast into the spice mixture. On medium-high heat, heat oil in a big non-stick pan; put in the roast. Cook for 5 minutes or until both sides of the roast are light brown; turn the roast one time.
2. Using a cooking spray, grease a 3 1/2–4 qt. slow cooker; arrange the garlic, onions, jalapeno, and green peppers in a layer. Pour in lime juice and orange juice. Slice the roast if needed to fit inside the cooker; put on top of the vegetables covered or 4 1/2–5 hrs. on high heat setting.
3. Move the roast to a cutting board using a slotted spoon. Drain the cooking liquid and keep the jalapeno, green peppers, and onions. Shred the roast with 2 forks then place it back in the cooker. Remove the fat from the liquid. Mix half cup of the cooking liquid and reserved vegetables into the cooker. Pour in more cooking liquid if desired. Discard the remaining cooking liquid.
4. Slather mustard on rolls. Split the meat between the bottom roll halves. Add avocado on top if desired. Place the roll tops on sandwiches.

Nutrition

- Calories 379
- Carbohydrate 32 g.
- Fiber 4 g.

298. Gazpacho

PREPARATION TIME: **15'**

COOKING TIME: **0'**

SERVINGS: **4**

Ingredients

- 3 lbs. ripe tomatoes
- 1 c. low-sodium tomato juice
- 1/2 red onion, chopped
- 1 cucumber
- 1 red bell pepper
- 2 celery stalks
- 2 tbsps parsley
- 2 garlic cloves
- 2 tbsps extra-virgin olive oil
- 2 tbsps red wine vinegar
- 1 tsp. honey
- 1/2 teaspoon salt
- 1/4 tsp. freshly ground black pepper

Directions

1. In a blender jar, combine the tomatoes, tomato juice, onion, cucumber, bell pepper, celery, parsley, garlic, olive oil, vinegar, honey, salt, and pepper. Pulse until blended but still slightly chunky.
2. Adjust the seasonings as needed and serve.

Nutrition

- Calories 170
- Carbohydrates 24 g.
- Sugars 16 g.

206

299. Tomato and Kale Soup

PREPARATION TIME: **10'**

COOKING TIME: **15'**

SERVINGS: **4**

Ingredients

- 1 tbsp. extra-virgin olive oil
- 1 medium onion
- 2 carrots
- 3 garlic cloves
- 4 c. low-sodium vegetable broth
- 1 (28-oz.) can crushed tomatoes
- 1/2 teaspoon dried oregano
- 1/4 tsp. dried basil
- 4 c. chopped baby kale leaves
- 1/4 tsp. salt

Directions

1. In a big pot, heat up oil over medium heat. Sauté the onion and carrots for 3-5 minutes. Add the garlic and sauté for 30 seconds more, until fragrant.
2. Add the vegetable broth, tomatoes, oregano, and basil to the pot and boil. Decrease the heat to low and simmer for 5 minutes.
3. Using an immersion blender, purée the soup.
4. Add the kale and simmer for 3 more minutes. Season with salt. Serve immediately.

Nutrition

- Calories 170
- Carbohydrates 31 g.
- Sugars 13 g.

300. Comforting Summer Squash Soup with Crispy Chickpeas

Preparation time: 10'

Cooking time: 20'

Servings: 4

Ingredients

- 1 (15-oz.) can low-sodium chickpeas
- 1 tsp. extra-virgin olive oil
- 1/4 tsp. smoked paprika
- Pinch salt, plus 1/2 teaspoon
- 3 medium zucchinis
- 3 c. low-sodium vegetable broth
- 1/2 onion
- 3 garlic cloves
- 2 tbsps plain low-fat Greek yogurt
- Freshly ground black pepper

Directions

1. Preheat the oven to 425 °F. Line a baking sheet with parchment paper.
2. In a medium mixing bowl, toss the chickpeas with 1 tsp of olive oil, the smoked paprika, and a pinch of salt. Transfer to the prepared baking sheet and roast until crispy, about 20 minutes, stirring once. Set aside.
3. Meanwhile, in a medium pot, heat the remaining 1 tbsp of oil over medium heat.
4. Add the zucchini, broth, onion, and garlic to the pot, and boil. Simmer, and cook for 20 minutes.
5. In a blender jar, purée the soup. Return to the pot.
6. Add the yogurt, remaining 1/2 teaspoon of salt, and pepper, and stir well. Serve topped with roasted chickpeas.

Nutrition

- Calories 188
- Carbohydrates 24 g.
- Sugars 7 g.

301. Curried Carrot Soup

Preparation time: 10'

Cooking time: 5'

Servings: 6

Ingredients

- 1 tbsp. extra-virgin olive oil
- 1 small onion
- 2 celery stalks
- 1 1/2 tsps. curry powder
- 1 tsp. ground cumin
- 1 tsp. minced fresh ginger
- 6 medium carrots
- 4 c. low-sodium vegetable broth
- 1/4 tsp. salt
- 1 c. canned coconut milk
- 1/4 tsp. freshly ground black pepper
- 1 tbsp. chopped fresh cilantro

Directions

1. Heat an instant pot to high and add the olive oil.
2. Sauté the onion and celery for 2-3 minutes. Add the curry powder, cumin, and ginger to the pot and cook until fragrant, about 30 seconds.
3. Add the carrots, vegetable broth, and salt to the pot. Close and seal, and set for 5 minutes on high. Allow the pressure to release naturally.
4. In a blender jar, carefully purée the soup in batches and transfer it back to the pot.
5. Stir in the coconut milk and pepper, and heat through. Top with cilantro and serve.

Nutrition

- Calories 145
- Carbohydrates 13 g.
- Sugars 4 g.

302. Thai Peanut, Carrot, and Shrimp Soup

Preparation time: 10'

Cooking time: 10'

Servings: 4

Ingredients

- 1 tbsp. coconut oil
- 1 tbsp. Thai red curry paste
- 1/2 onion
- 3 garlic cloves
- 2 c. chopped carrots
- 1/2 c. whole unsalted peanuts
- 4 c. low-sodium vegetable broth
- 1/2 c. unsweetened plain almond milk
- 1/2 lb. shrimp
- Minced fresh cilantro, for garnish

Directions

1. In a big pan, heat up oil over medium-high heat until shimmering.
2. Cook curry paste, stirring continuously, for 1 minute. Add the onion, garlic, carrots, and peanuts to the pan, and continue to cook for 2-3 minutes.
3. Boil the broth. Reduce the heat to low and simmer for 5-6 minutes.
4. Purée the soup until smooth and return it to the pot. Over low heat, pour almond milk and stir to combine. Cook shrimp in the pot for 2-3 minutes.
5. Garnish with cilantro and serve.

Nutrition

- Calories 237
- Carbohydrates 17 g.
- Sugars 6 g.

208

303. Chicken Tortilla Soup

Preparation time: 10'

Cooking time: 35'

Servings: 4

Ingredients

- 1 tbsp. extra-virgin olive oil
- 1 onion, thinly sliced
- 1 garlic clove, minced
- 1 jalapeño pepper, diced
- 2 boneless, skinless chicken breasts
- 4 c. low-sodium chicken broth
- 1 Roma tomato, diced
- 1/2 teaspoon salt
- 2 (6-in.) corn tortillas
- Juice of 1 lime
- Minced fresh cilantro, for garnish
- 1/4 c. shredded cheddar cheese, for garnish

Directions

1. In a medium pot, cook oil over medium-high heat. Add the onion and cook for 3-5 minutes until it begins to soften. Add the garlic and jalapeño, and cook until fragrant, about 1 minute more.
2. Add the chicken, chicken broth, tomato, and salt to the pot and boil. Lower heat to medium and simmer mildly for 20-25 minutes. Remove the chicken from the pot and set it aside.
3. Preheat a broiler to high.
4. Spray the tortilla strips with nonstick cooking spray and toss to coat. Spread in a single layer on a baking sheet and broil for 3-5 minutes, flipping once, until crisp.
5. Once the chicken is cooked, shred it with two forks and return to the pot.
6. Season the soup with lime juice. Serve hot, garnished with cilantro, cheese, and tortilla strips.

Nutrition

- Calories 191
- Carbohydrates 13 g.
- Sugars 2 g.

304. Beef and Mushroom Barley Soup

Preparation time: 10'
Cooking time: 80'
Servings: 6

Ingredients

- 1-pound beef stew meat, cubed
- 1/4 tsp. salt
- 1/4 tsp. freshly ground black pepper
- 1 tbsp. extra-virgin olive oil
- 8 oz. sliced mushrooms
- 1 onion, chopped
- 2 carrots, chopped
- 3 celery stalks, chopped
- 6 garlic cloves, minced
- 1/2 teaspoon dried thyme
- 4 c. low-sodium beef broth
- 1 c. water
- 1/2 c. pearl barley

Directions

1. Season the meat well.
2. In an instant pot, heat the oil over high heat. Cook the meat on all sides. Remove from the pot and set aside.
3. Add the mushrooms to the pot and cook for 1–2 minutes. Remove the mushrooms and set them aside with the meat.
4. Sauté the onion, carrots, and celery for 3–4 minutes. Add the garlic and continue to cook until fragrant, for about 30 seconds.
5. Return the meat and mushrooms to the pot, then add the thyme, beef broth, and water. Adjust the pressure on high and cook for 15 minutes. Let the pressure release naturally.
6. Open the instant pot and add the barley. Use the slow cooker function on the instant pot, affix the lid (vent open), and continue to cook for 1 hour. Serve.

Nutrition

- Calories 245
- Carbohydrates 19 g.
- Sugars 3 g.

209

305. Cucumber, Tomato, and Avocado Salad

Preparation time: 10'
Cooking time: 0'
Servings: 4

Ingredients

- 1 c. cherry tomatoes
- 1 large cucumber
- 1 small red onion
- 1 avocado
- 2 tbsps chopped fresh dill
- 2 tbsps extra-virgin olive oil
- Juice of 1 lemon
- 1/4 tsp. salt
- 1/4 tsp. freshly ground black pepper

Directions

1. In a big mixing bowl, mix the tomatoes, cucumber, onion, avocado, and dill.
2. In a small bowl, combine the oil, lemon juice, salt, and pepper, and mix well.
3. Drizzle the dressing over the vegetables and toss to combine. Serve.

Nutrition

- In a big mixing bowl, mix the tomatoes, cucumber, onion, avocado, and dill.
- In a small bowl, combine the oil, lemon juice, salt, and pepper, and mix well.
- Drizzle the dressing over the vegetables and toss to combine. Serve.

306. Cabbage Slaw Salad

PREPARATION TIME: **15'**

COOKING TIME: **0'**

SERVINGS: **4**

Ingredients

- 2 c. green cabbage
- 2 c. red cabbage
- 2 c. grated carrots
- 3 scallions
- 2 tbsps extra-virgin olive oil
- 2 tbsps rice vinegar
- 1 tsp. honey
- 1 garlic clove
- 1/4 tsp. salt

Directions

1. Throw together the green and red cabbage, carrots, and scallions.
2. In a small bowl, whisk together the oil, vinegar, honey, garlic, and salt.
3. Pour the dressing over the veggies and mix to combine thoroughly.
4. Serve immediately, or cover and chill for several hours before serving.

Nutrition

- Calories 80
- Carbohydrates 10 g.
- Sugars 6 g.

307. Green Salad with Blackberries and Goat Cheese

PREPARATION TIME: **15'**

COOKING TIME: **20'**

SERVINGS: **4**

Ingredients

For the Vinaigrette
- 1-pint blackberries
- 2 tbsps red wine vinegar
- 1 tbsp. honey
- 3 tbsps extra-virgin olive oil
- 1/4 tsp. salt
- Freshly ground black pepper

For the Salad
- 1 tsp. extra-virgin olive oil
- 8 c. salad greens (baby spinach, spicy greens, romaine)
- 1/2 red onion, sliced
- 1/4 c. crumbled goat cheese

Directions

1. To make the vinaigrette: In a blender jar, combine the blackberries, vinegar, honey, oil, salt, and pepper, and process until smooth. Set aside.
2. To make the salad: Preheat the oven to 425 °F. Line a baking sheet with parchment paper.
3. In a large bowl, toss the greens with the red onion, and drizzle with the vinaigrette. Serve topped with 1 tbsp of goat cheese per serving.

Nutrition

- Calories 196
- Carbohydrates 21 g.
- Sugars 10 g.

308. Three Bean and Basil Salad

PREPARATION TIME: 10'
COOKING TIME: 0'
SERVINGS: 8

Ingredients

- 1 (15-oz.) can of low-sodium chickpeas
- 1 (15-oz.) can of low-sodium kidney beans
- 1 (15-oz.) can of low-sodium white beans
- 1 red bell pepper
- 1/4 c. chopped scallions
- 1/4 c. finely chopped fresh basil
- 3 garlic cloves, minced
- 2 tbsps extra-virgin olive oil
- 1 tbsp. red wine vinegar
- 1 tsp. Dijon mustard
- 1/4 tsp. freshly ground black pepper

Directions

1. Toss chickpeas, kidney beans, white beans, bell pepper, scallions, basil, and garlic gently.
2. Blend together olive oil, vinegar, mustard, and pepper. Toss with the salad.
3. Wrap and chill for 1 hour.

Nutrition

- Calories 193
- Carbohydrates 29 g.
- Sugars 3 g.

309. Rainbow Black Bean Salad

PREPARATION TIME: 15'
COOKING TIME: 0'
SERVINGS: 5

Ingredients

- 1 (15-oz.) can of low-sodium black beans
- 1 avocado, diced
- 1 c. cherry tomatoes, halved
- 1 c. chopped baby spinach
- 1/2 c. red bell pepper
- 1/4 c. jicama
- 1/2 c. scallions
- 1/4 c. fresh cilantro
- 2 tbsps lime juice
- 1 tbsp. extra-virgin olive oil
- 2 garlic cloves, minced
- 1 tsp. honey
- 1/4 tsp. salt
- 1/4 tsp. freshly ground black pepper

Directions

1. Mix black beans, avocado, tomatoes, spinach, bell pepper, jicama, scallions, and cilantro.
2. Blend lime juice, oil, garlic, honey, salt, and pepper. Add to the salad and toss.
3. Chill for 1 hour before serving.

Nutrition

- Calories 169
- Carbohydrates 22 g.
- Sugars 3 g.

310. Warm Barley and Squash Salad

Preparation time: 20'

Cooking time: 40'

Servings: 8

Ingredients

- 1 small butternut squash
- 3 tbsps extra-virgin olive oil
- 2 c. broccoli florets
- 1 c. pearl barley
- 1 c. toasted chopped walnuts
- 2 c. baby kale
- 1/2 red onion, sliced
- 2 tbsps balsamic vinegar
- 2 garlic cloves, minced
- 1/2 teaspoon salt
- 1/4 tsp. black pepper

Directions

1. Preheat the oven to 400 °F. Line a baking sheet with parchment paper.
2. Peel off the squash, and slice into dice. In a large bowl, toss the squash with 2 tsps of olive oil. Transfer to the prepared baking sheet and roast for 20 minutes.
3. While the squash is roasting, toss the broccoli in the same bowl with 1 tsp of olive oil. After 20 minutes, flip the squash and push it to one side of the baking sheet. Add the broccoli to the other side and continue to roast for 20 more minutes until tender.
4. While the veggies are roasting, in a medium pot, cover the barley with several inches of water. Boil, then adjust heat, cover, and simmer for 30 minutes until tender. Drain and rinse.
5. Transfer the barley to a large bowl, and toss with the cooked squash and broccoli, walnuts, kale, and onion.
6. In a small bowl, mix the remaining 2 tbsps of olive oil, balsamic vinegar, garlic, salt, and pepper. Drizzle dressing over the salad and toss.

Nutrition

- Calories 274
- Carbohydrates 32 g.
- Sugars 3 g.

311. Winter Chicken and Citrus Salad

Preparation time: 10'

Cooking time: 0'

Servings: 4

Ingredients

- 4 c. baby spinach
- 2 tbsps extra-virgin olive oil
- 1 tbsp. lemon juice
- 1/8 tsp. salt
- 1/8 tsp. pepper
- 2 c. chopped cooked chicken
- 2 mandarin oranges
- 1/2 peeled grapefruit, sectioned
- 1/4 c. sliced almonds

Directions

1. Toss the spinach with olive oil, lemon juice, salt, and pepper.
2. Add the chicken, oranges, grapefruit, and almonds to the bowl. Toss gently.
3. Arrange on 4 plates and serve.

Nutrition

- Calories 249
- Carbohydrates 11 g.
- Sugars 7 g.

Chapter 13: Side

312. Brussels Sprouts

PREPARATION TIME: **5'**

COOKING TIME: **3'**

SERVINGS: **5**

Ingredients
- 1 tsp. extra-virgin olive oil
- 1 lb. halved Brussels sprouts
- 3 tbsps apple cider vinegar
- 3 tbsps gluten-free tamari soy sauce
- 3 tbsps chopped sun-dried tomatoes

Directions
1. Select the "Sauté" function on your instant pot, add oil, and allow the pot to get hot.
2. Cancel the "Sauté" function and add the Brussels sprouts.
3. Stir well and allow the sprouts to cook in the residual heat for 2-3 minutes.
4. Add the tamari soy sauce and vinegar and then stir.
5. Cover the instant pot, sealing the pressure valve by pointing it to "Sealing."
6. Select the "Manual, High Pressure" setting and cook for 3 minutes.
7. Once the cook cycle is done, do a quick pressure release, and then stir in the chopped sun-dried tomatoes.
8. Serve immediately.

Nutrition
- Calories 62
- Carbohydrates 10 g.
- Fat 1 g.

313. Garlic and Herb Carrots

PREPARATION TIME: **2'**

COOKING TIME: **18'**

SERVINGS: **3**

Ingredients
- 2 tbsps butter
- 1 lb. baby carrots
- 1 c. water
- 1 tsp. fresh thyme or oregano
- 1 tsp. minced garlic
- Black pepper
- Coarse sea salt

Directions
1. Fill water into the inner pot of the instant pot and then put it in a steamer basket.
2. Layer the carrots into the steamer basket.
3. Close and seal the lid, with the pressure vent in the "Sealing" position.
4. Select the Steam setting and cook for 2 minutes on high pressure.
5. Quick release the pressure and then carefully remove the steamer basket with the steamed carrots, discarding the water.
6. Add butter to the inner pot of the instant pot and allow it to melt on the "Sauté" function.
7. Add garlic and sauté for 30 seconds, and then add the carrots. Mix well.
8. Stir in the fresh herbs and cook for 2-3 minutes.
9. Season with salt and black pepper, and transfer to a serving bowl.
10. Serve warm and enjoy!

Nutrition
- Calories 122
- Carbohydrates 12 g.
- Fat 7 g.

314. Cilantro Lime Drumsticks

Preparation time: 5'
Cooking time: 15'
Servings: 6

Ingredients

- 1 tbsp. olive oil
- 6 chicken drumsticks
- 4 minced garlic cloves
- 1/2 c. low-sodium chicken broth
- 1 tsp. cayenne pepper
- 1 tsp. crushed red peppers
- 2 tbsp. fresh cilantro
- 1 tsp. fine sea salt
- Juice of 1 lime
- To Serve
- 2 tbsp. chopped cilantro
- Extra lime zest

Directions

1. Pour olive oil into the instant pot and set it on the "Sauté" function.
2. Once the oil is hot, add the chicken drumsticks and garlic, and season them well.
3. Using tongs, stir the drumsticks and brown the drumsticks for 2 minutes per side.
4. Add the lime juice, salt, pepper, cilantro, and chicken broth to the pot.
5. Lock and seal the lid, turning the pressure valve to "Sealing."
6. Cook the drumsticks on the "Manual, High Pressure" setting for 9 minutes.
7. Once done, let the pressure release naturally.
8. Carefully transfer the drumsticks to an aluminum-foiled baking sheet and broil them in the oven for 3–5 minutes until golden brown.
9. Serve warm, garnished with more cilantro and lime zest.

Nutrition

- Calories 480
- Carbohydrates 3.3 g.
- Fat 29 g.

315. Eggplant Spread

Preparation time: 5'
Cooking time: 18'
Servings: 5

Ingredients

- 4 tbsps extra-virgin olive oil
- 2 lbs. eggplant
- 4 skin-on garlic cloves
- 1/2 c. water
- 1/4 c. pitted black olives
- 3 sprigs fresh thyme
- Juice of 1 lemon
- 1 tbsp. tahini
- 1 tsp. sea salt
- Fresh extra-virgin olive oil

Directions

1. Peel the eggplant in alternating stripes, leaving some areas with skin and some with no skin.
2. Slice into big chunks and layer at the bottom of your instant pot.
3. Add olive oil to the pot, and on the "Sauté" function, fry and caramelize the eggplant on one side, about 5 minutes.
4. Add in the garlic cloves with the skin on.
5. Flip over the eggplant and then add in the remaining uncooked eggplant chunks, salt, and water.
6. Close the lid, ensure the pressure release valve is set to "Sealing."
7. Cook for 5 minutes on the "Manual, High Pressure" setting.
8. Once done, carefully open the pot by quickly releasing the pressure through the steam valve.
9. Discard most of the brown cooking liquid.
10. Remove the garlic cloves and peel them.
11. Add the lemon juice, tahini, cooked and fresh garlic cloves, and pitted black olives to the pot.
12. Using a hand-held immersion blender, process all the ingredients until smooth.
13. Pour out the spread into a serving dish and season with fresh thyme, whole black olives, and some extra-virgin olive oil, prior to serving.

Nutrition

- Calories 155
- Carbohydrates 16.8 g.
- Fat 11.7 g.

316. Carrot Hummus

Preparation time: 15'
Cooking time: 10'
Servings: 2

Ingredients

- 1 chopped carrot
- 2 oz. cooked chickpeas
- 1 tsp. lemon juice
- 1 tsp. tahini
- 1 tsp. fresh parsley
- 1 c. water

Directions

1. Place the carrot and chickpeas in your instant pot.
2. Add a cup of water, seal, and cook for 10 minutes on Stew.
3. Depressurize naturally. Blend with the remaining ingredients.

Nutrition

- Calories 58
- Carbohydrates 8 g.
- Fat 2 g.

317. Vegetable Rice Pilaf

Preparation time: 5'
Cooking time: 25'
Servings: 6

Ingredients

- 1 tbsp. olive oil
- 1/2 medium yellow onion, diced
- 1 c. uncooked long-grain brown rice
- 2 cloves minced garlic
- 1/2 teaspoon dried basil
- Salt and pepper
- 2 c. fat-free chicken broth
- 1 c. frozen mixed veggies

Directions

1. Cook oil in a large skillet over medium heat.
2. Add the onion and sauté for 3 minutes until translucent.
3. Stir in the rice and cook until lightly toasted.
4. Add the garlic, basil, salt, and pepper then stir to combine.
5. Stir in the chicken broth then bring to a boil.
6. Decrease heat and simmer, covered, for 10 minutes.
7. Stir in the frozen veggies then cover and cook for another 10 minutes until heated through. Serve hot.

Nutrition

- Calories 90
- Carbohydrates 12.6 g.
- Fiber 2.2 g.

318. Curry Roasted Cauliflower Florets

Preparation time: 5'
Cooking time: 25'
Servings: 6

Ingredients

- 8 c. cauliflower florets
- 2 tbsps olive oil
- 1 tsp. curry powder
- 1/2 teaspoon garlic powder
- Salt and pepper

Directions

1. Prep the oven to 425 °F and line a baking sheet with foil.
2. Toss the cauliflower with olive oil and spread on the baking sheet.
3. Sprinkle with curry powder, garlic powder, salt, and pepper.
4. Roast for 25 minutes or until just tender. Serve hot.

Nutrition

- Calories 75
- Carbohydrates 7.4 g.
- Fiber 3.5 g.

319. Mushroom Barley Risotto

Preparation time: 5'
Cooking time: 25'
Servings: 8

Ingredients

- 4 c. fat-free beef broth
- 2 tbsps olive oil
- 1 small onion, diced well
- 2 cloves minced garlic
- 8 oz. thinly sliced mushrooms
- 1/4 tsp. dried thyme
- Salt and pepper
- 1 c. pearled barley
- 1/2 c. dry white wine

Directions

1. Heat the beef broth in a medium saucepan and keep it warm.
2. Heat the oil in a large, deep skillet over medium heat.
3. Add the onions and garlic and sauté for 2 minutes then stir in the mushrooms and thyme.
4. Season with salt and pepper and sauté for 2 minutes more.
5. Add the barley and sauté for 1 minute then pour in the wine.
6. Ladle about 1/2 c of the beef broth into the skillet and stir well to combine.
7. Cook until most of the broth has been absorbed then add another ladle.
8. Repeat until you have used all of the broth and the barley is cooked to al dente.
9. Season and serve hot.

Nutrition

- Calories 155
- Carbohydrates 21.9 g.
- Fiber 4.4 g.

320. Braised Summer Squash

PREPARATION TIME: **10'**

COOKING TIME: **20'**

SERVINGS: **6**

Ingredients

- 3 tbsps olive oil
- 3 cloves minced garlic
- 1/4 tsp. crushed red pepper flakes
- 1-pound summer squash, sliced
- 1-pound zucchini, sliced
- 1 tsp. dried oregano
- Salt and pepper

Directions

1. Cook oil in a large skillet over medium heat.
2. Add the garlic and crushed red pepper and cook for 2 minutes.
3. Add the summer squash and zucchini and cook for 15 minutes, stirring often, until just tender.
4. Stir in the oregano then season with salt and pepper to taste. Serve hot.

Nutrition

- Calories 90
- Carbohydrates 6.2 g.
- Fiber 1.8 g.

321. Lemon Garlic Green Beans

PREPARATION TIME: **5'**

COOKING TIME: **10'**

SERVINGS: **6**

Ingredients

- 1 1/2 lbs. green beans, trimmed
- 2 tbsps olive oil
- 1 tbsp. fresh lemon juice
- 2 cloves minced garlic
- Salt and pepper

Directions

1. Fill a large bowl with ice water and set aside.
2. Bring a pot of salted water to boil then add the green beans.
3. Cook for 3 minutes then drain and immediately place in the ice water.
4. Cool the beans completely then drain them well.
5. Heat the oil in a large skillet over medium-high heat.
6. Add the green beans, tossing to coat, then add the lemon juice, garlic, salt, and pepper.
7. Sauté for 3 minutes until the beans are tender-crisp then serve hot.

Nutrition

- Calories 75
- Total Fat 4.8 g.
- Saturated Fat 0.7 g.
- Total Carbohydrates 8.5 g.
- Net Carbohydrates 4.6 g.
- Protein 2.1 g.
- Sugar 1.7 g.
- Fiber 3.9 g.
- Sodium 7 mg.

322. Brown Rice and Lentil Salad

Preparation time: 10'
Cooking time: 10'
Servings: 4

Ingredients

- 1 c. water
- 1/2 c. instant brown rice
- 2 tbsps olive oil
- 2 tbsps red wine vinegar
- 1 tbsp. Dijon mustard
- 1 tbsp. minced onion
- 1/2 tsp. paprika
- Salt and pepper
- 1 (15-oz.) can brown lentils, rinsed and drained
- 1 medium carrot, shredded
- 2 tbsps fresh chopped parsley

Directions

1. Stir together the water and instant brown rice in a medium saucepan.
2. Bring to a boil then simmer for 10 minutes, covered.
3. Remove from heat and set aside while you prepare the salad.
4. Whisk together the olive oil, vinegar, Dijon mustard, onion, paprika, salt, and pepper in a medium bowl.
5. Toss in the cooked rice, lentils, carrots, and parsley.
6. Adjust seasoning to taste then stir well and serve warm

Nutrition

- Calories 145
- Total Fat 7.7 g.
- Saturated Fat 1 g.
- Total Carbohydrates 13.1 g.
- Net Carbohydrates 10.9 g.
- Protein 6 g.
- Sugar 1 g.
- Fiber 2.2 g.
- Sodium 57 mg.

323. Mashed Butternut Squash

Preparation time: 5'
Cooking time: 25'
Servings: 6

Ingredients

- 3 lbs. whole butternut squash (about 2 medium)
- 2 tbsps olive oil
- Salt and pepper

Directions

1. Preheat the oven to 400 °F and line a baking sheet with parchment.
2. Cut the squash in half and remove the seeds.
3. Cut the squash into cubes and toss with oil then spread on the baking sheet.
4. Roast for 25 minutes until tender then places in a food processor.
5. Blend smooth then season with salt and pepper to taste.

Nutrition

- Calories 90
- Total Fat 4.8 g.
- Saturated Fat 0.7 g.
- Total Carbohydrates 12.3 g.
- Net Carbohydrates 10.2 g.
- Protein 1.1 g.
- Sugar 2.3 g.
- Fiber 2.1 g.
- Sodium 4 mg.

324. Cilantro Lime Quinoa

Preparation time: 5'
Cooking time: 25'
Servings: 6

Ingredients

- 1 c. uncooked quinoa
- 1 tbsp. olive oil
- 1 medium yellow onion, diced
- 2 cloves minced garlic
- 1 (4-oz.) can diced green chilies, drained
- 1 1/2 c. fat-free chicken broth
- 3/4 c. fresh chopped cilantro
- 1/2 c. sliced green onion
- 2 tbsps lime juice
- Salt and pepper

Directions

1. Rinse the quinoa thoroughly in cool water using a fine-mesh sieve.
2. Heat the oil in a large saucepan over medium heat.
3. Add the onion and sauté for 2 minutes then stir in the chili and garlic.
4. Cook for 1 minute then stir in the quinoa and chicken broth.
5. Bring to a boil then reduce heat and simmer, covered, until the quinoa absorbs the liquid – for about 20-25 minutes.
6. Remove from the heat then stir in the cilantro, green onions, and lime juice.
7. Season with salt and pepper to taste and serve hot.

Nutrition

- Calories 150
- Total Fat 4.1 g.
- Saturated Fat 0.5 g.
- Total Carbohydrates 22.5 g.
- Net Carbohydrates 19.8 g.
- Protein 6 g.
- Sugar 1.7 g.
- Fiber 2.7 g.
- Sodium 179 mg.

325. Oven-Roasted Veggies

Preparation time: 5'
Cooking time: 25'
Servings: 6

Ingredients

- 1 lb. cauliflower florets
- 1/2-pound broccoli florets
- 1 large yellow onion, cut into chunks
- 1 large red pepper, cored and chopped
- 2 medium carrots, peeled and sliced
- 2 tbsps olive oil
- 2 tbsps apple cider vinegar
- Salt and pepper

Directions

1. Preheat the oven to 425 °F and line a large rimmed baking sheet with parchment.
2. Spread the veggies on the baking sheet and drizzle with oil and vinegar.
3. Toss well and season with salt and pepper.
4. Spread the veggies in a single layer then roast for 20-25 minutes, stirring every 10 minutes, until tender.
5. Adjust seasoning to taste and serve hot.

Nutrition

- Calories 100
- Total Fat 5 g.
- Saturated Fat 0.7 g.
- Total Carbohydrates 12.4 g.
- Net Carbohydrates 8.2 g.
- Protein 3.2 g.
- Sugar 5.5 g.
- Fiber 4.2 g.
- Sodium 51 mg.

326. Parsley Tabbouleh

PREPARATION TIME: 5'

COOKING TIME: 25'

SERVINGS: 6

Ingredients

- 1 c. water
- 1/2 c. bulgur
- 1/4 c. fresh lemon juice
- 2 tbsps olive oil
- 2 cloves minced garlic
- Salt and pepper
- 2 c. fresh chopped parsley
- 2 medium tomatoes, died
- 1 small cucumber, diced
- 1/4 c. fresh chopped mint

Directions

1. Bring the water and bulgur to a boil in a small saucepan then remove from heat.
2. Cover and let stand until the water is fully absorbed, about 25 minutes.
3. Meanwhile, whisk together the lemon juice, olive oil, garlic, salt, and pepper in a medium bowl.
4. Toss in the cooked bulgur along with the parsley, tomatoes, cucumber, and mint.
5. Season with salt and pepper to taste and serve.

Nutrition

- Calories 110
- Total Fat 5.3 g.
- Saturated Fat 0.9 g.
- Total Carbohydrates 14.4 g.
- Net Carbohydrates 10.5 g.
- Protein 3 g.
- Sugar 2.4 g.
- Fiber 3.9 g.
- Sodium 21 mg.

327. Garlic Saut ed Spinach

PREPARATION TIME: 5'

COOKING TIME: 10'

SERVINGS: 4

Ingredients

- 1 1/2 tbsps olive oil
- 4 cloves minced garlic
- 6 c. fresh baby spinach
- Salt and pepper

Directions

1. Heat the oil in a large skillet over medium-high heat.
2. Add the garlic and cook for 1 minute.
3. Stir in the spinach and season with salt and pepper.
4. Sauté for 1-2 minutes until just wilted. Serve hot.

Nutrition

- Calories 60
- Total Fat 5.5 g.
- Saturated Fat 0.8 g.
- Total Carbohydrates 2.6 g.
- Net Carbohydrates 1.5 g.
- Protein 1.5 g.
- Sugar 0.2 g.
- Fiber 1.1 g.
- Sodium 36 mg.

328. French Lentils

PREPARATION TIME: 5'

COOKING TIME: 25'

SERVINGS: 10

Ingredients

- 2 tbsps olive oil
- 1 medium onion, diced
- 1 medium carrot, peeled and diced
- 2 cloves minced garlic
- 5 1/2 c. water
- 2 1/4 c. French lentils, rinsed and drained
- 1 tsp. dried thyme
- 2 small bay leaves
- Salt and pepper

Directions

1. Heat the oil in a large saucepan over medium heat.
2. Add the onions, carrot, and garlic and sauté for 3 minutes.
3. Stir in the water, lentils, thyme, and bay leaves season with salt and pepper.
4. Bring to a boil then reduce to a simmer and cook until tender, about 20 minutes.
5. Drain any excess water and adjust seasoning to taste. Serve hot.

Nutrition

- Calories 185
- Total Fat 3.3 g.
- Saturated Fat 0.5 g.
- Total Carbohydrates 27.9 g.
- Net Carbohydrates 14.2 g.
- Protein 11.4 g.
- Sugar 1.7 g.
- Fiber 13.7 g.
- Sodium 11 mg.

329. Grain-Free Berry Cobbler

PREPARATION TIME: 5'

COOKING TIME: 25'

SERVINGS: 10

Ingredients

- 4 c. fresh mixed berries
- 1/2 c. ground flaxseed
- 1/4 c. almond meal
- 1/4 c. unsweetened shredded coconut
- 1/2 tbsp. baking powder
- 1 tsp. ground cinnamon
- 1/4 tsp. salt
- Powdered stevia, to taste
- 6 tbsps coconut oil

Directions

1. Preheat the oven to 375 °F and lightly grease a 10-in. cast-iron skillet.
2. Spread the berries on the bottom of the skillet.
3. Whisk together the dry ingredients in a mixing bowl.
4. Cut in the coconut oil using a fork to create a crumbled mixture.
5. Spread the crumble over the berries and bake for 25 minutes until hot and bubbling.
6. Cool the cobbler for 5-10 minutes before serving.

Nutrition

- Calories 215
- Total Fat 16.8 g.
- Saturated Fat 10.4 g.
- Total Carbohydrates 13.1 g.
- Net Carbohydrates 6.7 g.
- Protein 3.7 g.
- Sugar 5.3 g.
- Fiber 6.4 g.
- Sodium 61 mg.

330. Coffee-Steamed Carrots

Preparation time: 10'
Cooking time: 3'
Servings: 4

Ingredients

- 1 c. brewed coffee
- 1 tsp. light brown sugar
- 1/2 teaspoon kosher salt
- Freshly ground black pepper
- 1-pound baby carrots
- Chopped fresh parsley
- 1 tsp. grated lemon zest

Directions

1. Pour the coffee into the electric pressure cooker. Stir in the brown sugar, salt, and pepper. Add the carrots.
2. Close the pressure cooker. Set to sealing.
3. Cook on high pressure for minutes.
4. Once complete, click Cancel and quickly release the pressure.
5. Once the pin drops, open and remove the lid.
6. Using a slotted spoon, portion carrots to a serving bowl. Topped with the parsley and lemon zest, and serve.

Nutrition

- Calories 51
- Carbohydrates 12 g.
- Fiber 4 g.

331. Dandelion Strawberry Salad

Preparation time: 15'
Cooking time: 10'
Servings: 2

Ingredients

- 2 tbsp. grapeseed oil
- 1 medium red onion, sliced
- 10 ripe strawberries, sliced
- 2 tbsp. key lime juice
- 4 c. dandelion greens
- Sea salt to taste

Directions

1. First of all, warm grapeseed oil in a 12-in. non-stick frying pan over medium heat. Add some sliced onions and a small pinch of sea salt. Cook until the onions are soft, lightly brown, and reduced to about 1/3 of raw volume, stirring frequently.
2. Then toss the strawberry slices in a tiny bowl with 1 tsp of key lime juice. Rinse the dandelion greens and, if you prefer, slice them into chunks of bite-size.
3. When it's about to be cooked, put the remaining key lime juice into the saucepan and keep on cooking until it has thickened to coat the onions for 1–2 minutes. Remove the onions from the heat.
4. Combine the vegetables, onions, and strawberries with all their juices in a salad bowl. Sprinkle with sea salt.

Nutrition

- Calories 151
- Carbohydrates 2 g.
- Fat 13 g.
- Protein 7 g.

332. Corn on the Cob

PREPARATION TIME: **10'**

COOKING TIME: **5'**

SERVINGS: **12**

Ingredients
- 6 ears corn
- 1 c of water

Directions

1. Take off husks and silk from the corn. Cut or break each ear in half.
2. Pour 1 c of water into the bottom of the electric pressure cooker. Insert a wire rack or trivet.
3. Place the corn upright on the rack, cut-side down. Seal the lid of the pressure cooker.
4. Cook on high pressure for 5 minutes.
5. When it's complete, select Cancel and quickly release the pressure.
6. When the pin drops, unlock and take off the lid.
7. Pull out the corn from the pot. Season as desired and serve immediately.

Nutrition
- Calories 62
- Carbohydrates 14 g.
- Fiber 1 g.

333. Chili Lime Salmon

PREPARATION TIME: **6'**

COOKING TIME: **10'**

SERVINGS: **2**

Ingredients

For the Sauce
- 1 jalapeno pepper
- 1 tbsp. chopped parsley
- 1 tsp. minced garlic
- 1/2 tsp. cumin
- 1/2 tsp. paprika
- 1/2 tsp. lime zest
- 1 tbsp. honey
- 1 tbsp. lime juice
- 1 tbsp. olive oil
- 1 tbsp. water

For the Fish
- 2 salmon fillets, each about 5 oz.
- 1 c. water
- 1/2 tsp. salt
- 1/8 tsp. ground black pepper

Directions

1. Season the salmon with salt and black pepper until evenly coated.
2. Plugin the instant pot, insert the inner pot, pour in water, then place steamer basket and place the seasoned salmon on it.
3. Seal the instant pot with its lid, press the steam button, then press the timer to set the cooking time to 5 minutes and cook on high pressure, for 5 minutes.
4. Transfer all the ingredients for the sauce to a bowl, whisk until combined, and set aside until required.
5. When the timer beeps, press the cancel button and do a quick pressure release until the pressure nob drops down.
6. Open the instant pot, then transfer the salmon to a serving plate and drizzle generously with the prepared sauce.
7. Serve straight away.

Nutrition
- Calories 305
- Carbohydrates 29 g.
- Fiber 6 g.

334. Collard Greens

Preparation time: 5'
Cooking time: 6 hours
Servings: 12

Ingredients

- 2 lbs. chopped collard greens
- 3/4 c. chopped white onion
- 1 tsp. onion powder
- 1 tsp. garlic powder
- 1 tsp. salt
- 2 tsps. brown sugar
- 1/2 teaspoon ground black pepper
- 1/2 teaspoon red chili powder
- 1/4 tsp. crushed red pepper flakes
- 3 tbsps apple cider vinegar
- 2 tbsps olive oil
- 14.5-oz. vegetable broth
- 1/2 c. water

Directions

1. Plugin the instant pot, insert the inner pot, add the onion and collard, and then pour in the vegetable broth and water.
2. Close the instant pot with its lid, seal, press the 'slow cook' button, then press the timer to set the cooking time to 6 hours at the high heat setting.
3. When the timer beeps, press cancel button and do natural pressure release until pressure nob drops down.
4. Open the instant pot, add the remaining ingredients and stir until mixed.
5. Then press the sauté/simmer button and cook for 3 minutes or more until collards reach to desired texture.
6. Serve straight away.

Nutrition

- Calories 49
- Carbohydrates 2.3 g.
- Fiber 0.5 g.

335. Mashed Pumpkin

Preparation time: 9'
Cooking time: 15'
Servings: 2

Ingredients

- 2 c. chopped pumpkin
- 0.5 c. water
- 2 tbsp. powdered sugar-free sweetener of choice
- 1 tbsp. cinnamon

Directions

1. Place the pumpkin and water in your instant pot.
2. Seal and cook on Stew for 15 minutes.
3. Remove and mash with the sweetener and cinnamon.

Nutrition

- Calories 12
- Carbohydrates 3 g.
- Sugar 1 g.

336. Parmesan-Topped Acorn Squash

Preparation time: 8'
Cooking time: 20'
Servings: 4

Ingredients

- 1 acorn squash (about 1 lb.)
- 1 tbsp. extra-virgin olive oil
- 1 tsp. dried sage leaves, crumbled
- 1/4 tsp. freshly grated nutmeg
- 1/8 tsp. kosher salt
- 1/8 tsp. freshly ground black pepper
- 2 tbsps freshly grated Parmesan cheese

Directions

1. Chop the acorn squash in half lengthwise and remove the seeds. Cut each half in half for a total of 4 wedges. Snap off the stem if it's easy to do.
2. In a small bowl, combine the olive oil, sage, nutmeg, salt, and pepper. Brush the cut sides of the squash with the olive oil mixture.
3. Fill 1 c of water into the electric pressure cooker and insert a wire rack or trivet.
4. Place the squash on the trivet in a single layer, skin-side down.
5. Set the lid of the pressure cooker on sealing.
6. Cook on high pressure for 20 minutes.
7. Once done, press Cancel and quickly release the pressure.
8. Once the pin drops, open it.
9. Carefully remove the squash from the pot, sprinkle with the Parmesan, and serve.

Nutrition

- Calories 85
- Carbohydrates 12 g.
- Fiber 2 g.

337. Quinoa Tabbouleh

Preparation time: 8'
Cooking time: 16'
Servings: 6

Ingredients

- 1 c. quinoa, rinsed
- 1 large English cucumber
- 2 scallions, sliced
- 2 c. cherry tomatoes, halved
- 2/3 c. chopped parsley
- 1/2 c. chopped mint
- 1/2 teaspoon minced garlic
- 1/2 tsp. salt
- 1/2 teaspoon ground black pepper
- 2 tbsp. lemon juice
- 1/2 c. olive oil

Directions

1. Plugin the instant pot, insert the inner pot, add quinoa, then pour in water and stir until mixed.
2. Close the instant pot with its lid and turn the pressure knob to seal the pot.
3. Select the manual button, then set the timer to 1 minute and cook in high pressure, it may take 7 minutes.
4. Once the timer stops, select the cancel button and do natural pressure release for 10 minutes, and then do a quick pressure release until pressure nob drops down.
5. Open the instant pot, fluff quinoa with a fork, then spoon it on a rimmed baking sheet, spread quinoa evenly and let cool.
6. Meanwhile, place lime juice in a small bowl, add garlic and stir until just mixed.
7. Then add salt, black pepper, and olive oil and whisk until combined.
8. Transfer cooled quinoa to a large bowl, add the remaining ingredients, then drizzle generously with the prepared lime juice mixture and toss until evenly coated.
9. Taste quinoa to adjust seasoning and then serve.

Nutrition

- Calories 283
- Carbohydrates 30.6 g.
- Fiber 3.4 g.

338. Wild Rice Salad with Cranberries and Almonds

Preparation Time: 6'
Cooking Time: 25'
Servings: 18

Ingredients

For the Rice
- 2 c. wild rice blend, rinsed
- 1 tsp. kosher salt
- 2 1/2 c. vegetable broth

For the Dressing
- 1/4 c. extra-virgin olive oil
- 1/4 c. white wine vinegar
- 1 1/2 tsps. grated orange zest
- Juice of 1 medium orange (about 1/4 c.)
- 1 tsp. honey or pure maple syrup

For the Salad
- 3/4 c. unsweetened dried cranberries
- 1/2 c. sliced almonds, toasted
- Freshly ground black pepper

Directions

1. To make the rice: In the electric pressure cooker, combine the rice, salt, and broth.
2. Close and lock the lid. Set the valve to sealing.
3. Cook on high pressure for 25 minutes.
4. When the cooking is complete, hit Cancel and allow the pressure to release naturally for 1 minute, then quickly release any remaining pressure.
5. Once the pin drops, unlock and remove the lid.
6. Let the rice cool briefly, then fluff it with a fork.
7. To make the dressing: While the rice cooks, make the dressing: In a small jar with a screw-top lid, combine the olive oil, vinegar, zest, juice, and honey. (If you don't have a jar, whisk the ingredients together in a small bowl.) Shake to combine.
8. To make the salad: Mix rice, cranberries, and almonds. Add the dressing and season with pepper.
9. Serve warm or refrigerate.

Nutrition

- Calories 126
- Carbohydrates 18 g.
- Fiber 2 g.

339. Basil Avocado Pasta Salad

Preparation Time: 5'
Cooking Time: 0'
Servings: 1

Ingredients

- 1 avocado, chopped
- 1 c. fresh basil, chopped
- 1-pint cherry tomatoes halved
- 1 tbsp. key lime juice
- 1 tsp. agave syrup
- 1/4 c. olive oil
- 4 c. cooked spelt-pasta
- Sea salt, to taste

Directions

1. Place the cooked pasta in a big bowl. Add the avocado, basil, and tomatoes and mix until thoroughly blended.
2. Whisk the oil, lime juice, agave syrup, and sea salt in a deep mixing pot. Toss over the pasta, then stir to blend.

Nutrition

- Calories 491
- Carbohydrates 50 g.
- Fat 26 g.
- Protein 15 g.

340. Roasted Parsnips

PREPARATION TIME: **9'**

COOKING TIME: **25'**

SERVINGS: **2**

Ingredients

- 1 lb. parsnips
- 1 c. vegetable stock
- 2 tbsp. herbs
- 2 tbsp. olive oil

Directions

1. Put the parsnips in the steamer basket and add the stock into the instant pot.
2. Steam the parsnips in your instant pot for 15 minutes.
3. Depressurize and pour away the remaining stock.
4. Set to sauté and add the oil, herbs, and parsnips.
5. Cook until golden and crisp.

Nutrition

- Calories 130
- Carbohydrates 14 g.
- Protein 4 g.

341. Lower Carb Hummus

PREPARATION TIME: **9'**

COOKING TIME: **60'**

SERVINGS: **2**

Ingredients

- 0.5 c. dry chickpeas
- 1 c. vegetable stock
- 1 c. pumpkin puree
- 2 tbsp. smoked paprika
- Salt and pepper to taste

Directions

1. Soak the chickpeas overnight.
2. Place the chickpeas and stock in the instant pot.
3. Cook on Beans for 60 minutes.
4. Depressurize naturally.
5. Blend the chickpeas with the remaining ingredients.

Nutrition

- Calories 135
- Carbohydrates 18 g.
- Fat 3 g.

342. Sweet and Sour Red Cabbage

PREPARATION TIME: **7'**

COOKING TIME: **10'**

SERVINGS: **8**

Ingredients

- 2 c. Spiced Pear Applesauce
- 1 small onion, chopped
- 1/2 c. apple cider vinegar
- 1/2 teaspoon kosher salt
- 1 head red cabbage

Directions

1. In the electric pressure cooker, combine the applesauce, onion, vinegar, salt, and a cup of water. Stir in the cabbage.
2. Seal the lid of the pressure cooker.
3. Cook on high pressure for 10 minutes.
4. When the cooking is complete, hit Cancel and quickly release the pressure.
5. Once the pin drops, unlock and remove the lid.
6. Spoon into a bowl or platter and serve.

Nutrition

- Calories 91
- Carbohydrates 18 g.
- Fiber 4 g.

343. Pinto Beans

PREPARATION TIME: **6'**

COOKING TIME: **55'**

SERVINGS: **10**

Ingredients

- 2 c. pinto beans, dried
- 1 medium white onion
- 1 1/2 teaspoon minced garlic
- 3/4 teaspoon salt
- 1/4 tsp. ground black pepper
- 1 tsp. red chili powder
- 1/4 tsp. cumin
- 1 tbsp. olive oil
- 1 tsp. chopped cilantro
- 5 1/2 c. vegetable stock

Directions

1. Plugin the instant pot, insert the inner pot, press sauté/simmer button, add oil and when hot, add onion and garlic and cook for 3 minutes or until onions begin to soften.
2. Add the remaining ingredients, stir well, then press the cancel button, shut the instant pot with its lid, and seal the pot.
3. Click the manual button, then press the timer to set the cooking time to 45 minutes and cook at high pressure.
4. Once done, click the cancel button and do natural pressure release for 10 minutes until pressure nob drops down.
5. Open the instant pot, spoon beans into the plates, and serve.

Nutrition

- Calories 107
- Carbohydrates 11.7 g.
- Fiber 4 g.

344. Parmesan Cauliflower Mash

PREPARATION TIME: 19'

COOKING TIME: 5'

SERVINGS: 4

Ingredients

- 1 head cauliflower
- 1/2 teaspoon kosher salt
- 1/2 teaspoon garlic pepper
- 2 tbsps plain Greek yogurt
- 3/4 c. freshly grated Parmesan cheese
- 1 tbsp. unsalted butter or ghee (optional)
- Chopped fresh chives

Directions

1. Pour a cup of water into the electric pressure cooker and insert a steamer basket or wire rack.
2. Place the cauliflower in the basket.
3. Cover the lid of the pressure cooker to seal.
4. Cook on high pressure for 5 minutes.
5. Once complete, hit Cancel and quickly release the pressure.
6. When the pin drops, remove the lid.
7. Remove the cauliflower from the pot and pour out the water. Return the cauliflower to the pot and add the salt, garlic pepper, yogurt, and cheese. Use an immersion blender to purée or mash the cauliflower in the pot.
8. Spoon into a serving bowl and garnish with butter (if using) and chives.

Nutrition

- Calories 141
- Carbohydrates 12 g.
- Fiber 4 g.

345. Steamed Asparagus

PREPARATION TIME: 3'

COOKING TIME: 2'

SERVINGS: 4

Ingredients

- 1 lb. fresh asparagus, rinsed and tough ends trimmed
- 1 c. water

Directions

1. Place the asparagus into a wire steamer rack and set it inside your instant pot.
2. Add water to the pot. Close and seal the lid, turning the steam release valve to the "Sealing" position.
3. Select the Steam function to cook on high pressure for 2 minutes.
4. Once done, do a quick pressure release of the steam.
5. Lift the wire steamer basket out of the pot and place the asparagus onto a serving plate.
6. Season as desired and serve.

Nutrition

- Calories 22
- Carbohydrates 4 g.
- Protein 2 g.

346. Squash Medley

Preparation time: 10'

Cooking time: 20'

Servings: 2

Ingredients

- 2 lbs. mixed squash
- 1/2 c. mixed veg
- 1 c. vegetable stock
- 2 tbsps olive oil
- 2 tbsps mixed herbs

Directions

1. Put the squash in the steamer basket and add the stock into the instant pot.
2. Steam the squash in your instant pot for 10 minutes.
3. Depressurize and pour away the remaining stock.
4. Set to sauté and add the oil and remaining ingredients.
5. Cook until a light crust forms.

Nutrition

- Calories 100
- Carbohydrates 10 g.
- Fat 6 g.

347. Eggplant Curry

Preparation time: 15'

Cooking time: 20'

Servings: 2

Ingredients

- 3 c. chopped eggplant
- 1 thinly sliced onion
- 1 c. coconut milk
- 3 tbsps curry paste
- 1 tbsp. oil or ghee

Directions

1. Select the instant pot to sauté and put the onion, oil, and curry paste.
2. Once the onion is soft, stir in the remaining ingredients and seal.
3. Cook on Stew for 20 minutes. Release the pressure naturally.

Nutrition

- Calories 350
- Carbohydrates 15 g.
- Fat 25 g.

348. Lentil and Eggplant Stew

Preparation time: 15'

Cooking time: 35'

Servings: 2

Ingredients

- 1 lb. eggplant
- 1 lb. dry lentils
- 1 c. chopped vegetables
- 1 c. low sodium vegetable broth

Directions

1. Incorporate all the ingredients in your instant pot, cook on Stew for 35 minutes.
2. Release the pressure naturally and serve.

Nutrition

- Calories 310
- Carbohydrates 22 g.
- Fat 10 g.

349. Tofu Curry

Preparation time: 15'

Cooking time: 20'

Servings: 2

Ingredients

- 2 c. cubed extra firm tofu
- 2 c. mixed stir fry vegetables
- 1/2 c. soy yogurt
- 3 tbsps curry paste
- 1 tbsp. oil or ghee

Directions

1. Set the instant pot to sauté and add the oil and curry paste.
2. Once soft, place the remaining ingredients except for the yogurt and seal.
3. Cook on Stew for 20 minutes.
4. Release the pressure naturally and serve with a scoop of soy yogurt.

Nutrition

- Calories 300
- Carbohydrates 9 g.
- Fat 14 g.

350. Lentil and Chickpea Curry

Preparation time: 15'

Cooking time: 20'

Servings: 2

Ingredients

- 2 c. dry lentils and chickpeas
- 1 thinly sliced onion
- 1 c. chopped tomato
- 3 tbsps curry paste
- 1 tbsp. oil or ghee

Directions

1. Press the instant pot to sauté and mix onion, oil, and curry paste.
2. Once the onion is cooked, stir the remaining ingredients and seal.
3. Cook on Stew for 20 minutes.
4. Release the pressure naturally and serve.

Nutrition

- Calories 360
- Carbohydrates 26 g.
- Fat 19 g.

351. Split Pea Stew

Preparation time: 5'

Cooking time: 35'

Servings: 2

Ingredients

- 1 c. dry split peas
- 1 lb. chopped vegetables
- 1 c. mushroom soup
- 2 tbsps old bay seasoning

Directions

1. Incorporate all the ingredients in the instant pot, cook for 33 minutes.
2. Release the pressure naturally.

Nutrition

- Calories 300
- Carbohydrates 7 g.
- Fat 2 g.

352. Fried Tofu Hotpot

PREPARATION TIME: **15'**

COOKING TIME: **15'**

SERVINGS: **2**

Ingredients

- 1/2 lb. fried tofu
- 1 lb. chopped Chinese vegetable mix
- 1 c. low sodium vegetable broth
- 2 tbsps 5 spice seasoning
- 1 tbsp. smoked paprika

Directions

1. Combine all the ingredients in your instant pot; set on Stew for 15 minutes.
2. Release the pressure naturally and serve.

Nutrition

- Calories 320
- Carbohydrates 11 g.
- Fat 23 g.

353. Chili sin Carne

PREPARATION TIME: **15'**

COOKING TIME: **35'**

SERVINGS: **2**

Ingredients

- 3 c. mixed cooked beans
- 2 c. chopped tomatoes
- 1 tbsp. yeast extract
- 2 squares very dark chocolate
- 1 tbsp. red chili flakes

Directions

1. Combine all the ingredients in your instant pot, cook for 35 minutes.
2. Release the pressure naturally and serve.

Nutrition

- Calories 240
- Carbohydrates 20 g.
- Fat 3 g.

Chapter 14: Snacks and Bread

354. Chick Pea and Kale Dish

PREPARATION TIME: 15'

COOKING TIME: 25-30'

SERVINGS: 4

Ingredients

- 2 c. chickpea flour
- 1/2 c. green bell pepper, diced
- 1/2 c. onions, minced
- 1 tbsp. oregano
- 1 tbsp. salt
- 1 tsp. cayenne
- 4 c. spring water
- 2 tbsps grape seed oil

Directions

1. Boil spring water in a large pot.
2. Lower heat into medium and whisk in chickpea flour.
3. Add some minced onions, diced green bell pepper, and seasoning to the pot, and cook for 10 minutes.
4. Cover the dish using a baking sheet, grease with oil.
5. Pour the batter into the sheet and spread with a spatula.
6. Cover with another sheet.
7. Transfer to a fridge and chill for 20 minutes.
8. Remove from the freezer and cut the batter into fry shapes.
9. Preheat the air fryer, to 385 °F.
10. Transfer the fries into the cooking basket, lightly greased, and cover with parchment
11. Bake for about 15 minutes; flip and bake for 10 minutes more until golden brown
12. Serve and enjoy!

Nutrition

- Calories 271
- Carbohydrates 28 g.
- Fat 15 g.
- Protein 9 g.

355. Zucchini Chips

PREPARATION TIME: 10'

COOKING TIME: 12-15'

SERVINGS: 4

Ingredients

- Salt as needed
- Grapeseed oil as needed
- 6 zucchinis

Directions

1. Preheat the air fryer at 330 °F.
2. Wash zucchini and slice it into thin strips.
3. Put slices in a bowl and add oil, salt, and toss.
4. Spread over the cooking basket, fry for 12-15 minutes.
5. Serve and enjoy!

Nutrition

- Calories 92
- Carbohydrates 6 g.
- Fat 7 g.
- Protein 2 g.

356. Classic Blueberry Spelt Muffins

Preparation time: 10'
Cooking time: 12-15'
Servings: 4

Ingredients

- 1/4 sea salt
- 1/3 c. maple syrup
- 1 tsp. baking powder
- 1/2 c. sea moss
- 3/4 c. spelt flour
- 3/4 c. Kamut flour
- 1 c. hemp milk
- 1 c. blueberries

Directions

1. Preheat the air fryer at 380 °F.
2. Take your muffin tins and gently grease them.
3. Take a bowl and add flour, syrup, salt, baking powder, sea moss and mix well.
4. Add milk and mix well.
5. Fold in blueberries.
6. Pour into muffin tins.
7. Transfer to the cooking basket and bake for 20-25 minutes until nicely baked.
8. Serve and enjoy!

Nutrition

- Calories 217
- Carbohydrates 32 g.
- Fat 9 g.
- Protein 4 g.

357. Genuine Healthy Crackers

Preparation time: 10'
Cooking time: 12-15'
Servings: 4

Ingredients

- 1/2 c. Rye flour
- 1 c. spelt flour
- 2 tsps. sesame seed
- 1 tsp. agave syrup
- 1 tsp. salt
- 2 tbsps grapeseed oil
- 3/4 c. spring water

Directions

1. Preheat the air fryer at 330 °F.
2. Take a medium bowl and add all the ingredients; mix well.
3. Make a dough ball.
4. Prepare a place for rolling out the dough, cover with a piece of parchment.
5. Lightly grease a paper with grape seed oil and place the dough.
6. Roll out the dough with a rolling pin; add more flour if needed.
7. Take a shape cutter and cut the dough into squares.
8. Place the squares in the air fryer cooking basket.
9. Brush with more oil.
10. Sprinkle salt.
11. Bake for 10-15 minutes until golden.
12. Let it cool, serve, and enjoy!

Nutrition

- Calories 226
- Carbohydrates 41 g.
- Fat 3 g.
- Protein 11 g.

358. Tortilla Chips

PREPARATION TIME: **10'**

COOKING TIME: **8-12'**

SERVINGS: **4**

Ingredients

- 2 c of spelt flour
- 1 tsp of salt
- 1/2 c of spring water
- 1/3 c of grapeseed oil

Directions

1. Preheat your air fryer to 320 °F.
2. Take the food processor then add salt, flour, and process well for 15 seconds.
3. Gradually add grapeseed oil until mixed.
4. Keep mixing until you have a nice dough.
5. Prepare a work surface and cover with a piece of parchment; sprinkle flour.
6. Knead the dough for 1-2 minutes.
7. Grease a cooking basket with oil.
8. Transfer the dough to the cooking basket, brush oil and sprinkle salt.
9. Cut the dough into 8 triangles.
10. Bake for about 8-12 minutes until golden brown.
11. Serve and enjoy once done!

Nutrition

- Calories 288
- Carbohydrates 18 g.
- Fat 17 g.
- Protein 16 g.

359. Pumpkin Spice Crackers

PREPARATION TIME: **10'**

COOKING TIME: **60'**

SERVINGS: **6**

Ingredients

- 1/3 c. coconut flour
- 2 tbsps pumpkin pie spice
- 3/4 c. sunflower seeds
- 3/4 c. flaxseed
- 1/3 c. sesame seeds
- 1 tbsp. ground psyllium husk powder
- 1 tsp. sea salt
- 3 tbsps coconut oil, melted
- 1 1/3 c. alkaline water

Directions

1. Set your oven to 300 °F.
2. Combine all the dry ingredients in a bowl.
3. Add water and oil to the mixture and mix well.
4. Let the dough stay for 2-3 minutes.
5. Spread the dough evenly on a cookie sheet lined with parchment paper.
6. Bake for 30 minutes.
7. Reduce the oven heat to low and bake for another 30 minutes.
8. Crack the bread into bite-size pieces.
9. Serve.

Nutrition

- Calories 248
- Total Fat 15.7 g.
- Saturated Fat 2.7 g.
- Cholesterol 75 mg.
- Sodium 94 mg.
- Total Carbohydrates 0.4 g.
- Fiber 0 g.
- Sugar 0 g.
- Protein 24.9 g.

360. Spicy Roasted Nuts

Preparation time: 10'
Cooking time: 15'
Servings: 4

Ingredients
- 8 oz. pecans or almonds or walnuts
- 1 tsp. sea salt
- 1 tbsp. olive oil or coconut oil
- 1 tsp. ground cumin
- 1 tsp. paprika powder or chili powder

Directions
1. Add all the ingredients to a skillet.
2. Roast the nuts until golden brown.
3. Serve and enjoy.

Nutrition
- Calories 287
- Total Fat 29.5 g.
- Saturated Fat 3 g.
- Cholesterol 0 mg.
- Total Carbohydrates 5.9 g.
- Sugar 1.4 g.
- Fiber 4.3 g.
- Sodium 388 mg.
- Protein 4.2 g.

361. Wheat Crackers

Preparation time: 10'
Cooking time: 20'
Servings: 4

Ingredients
- 1 3/4 c. almond flour
- 1 1/2 c. coconut flour
- 3/4 tsp. sea salt
- 1/3 c. vegetable oil
- 1 c. alkaline water
- Sea salt for sprinkling

Directions
1. Set your oven to 350 °F.
2. Mix the coconut flour, almond flour, and salt in a bowl.
3. Stir in vegetable oil and water. Mix well until smooth.
4. Spread this dough on a floured surface into a thin sheet.
5. Cut small squares out of this sheet.
6. Arrange the dough squares on a baking sheet lined with parchment paper.
7. For about 20 minutes, bake until light golden in color.
8. Serve.

Nutrition
- Calories 64
- Total Fat 9.2 g.
- Saturated Fat 2.4 g.
- Cholesterol 110 mg
- Sodium 276 mg
- Total Carbohydrates 9.2 g.
- Fiber 0.9 g.
- Sugar 1.4 g.
- Protein 1.5 g.

362. Veggie Fritters

PREPARATION TIME: 5'

COOKING TIME: 10'

SERVINGS: 2

Ingredients

- 1 bell pepper
- 2 onions
- 2 c. mushrooms
- 1 tsp of sea salt
- 1 tbsp. onion powder
- 1 tsp. oregano
- 1 tbsp. basil
- A pinch cayenne
- 1 c. chickpea flour
- 1 tbsp. grapeseed oil

Directions

1. Clean and chop the vegetables into small chunks. Not too small. Transfer the vegetables into a bowl and add all the seasonings.
2. Stir everything and let sit for about 5 minutes. Stir in chickpea flour, then add 1/2 c of water.
3. Stir while adding more flour until the desired consistency. Make sure everything holds nicely.
4. Heat a pan, then add oil but not too much. Spoon the fritter mix into the pan, creating little mounds.
5. Now cook for about 2-3 minutes until brown underneath and crispy. Flip and slightly press down to flatter them. Cook for about 2 minutes. Serve and Enjoy.

Nutrition

- Calories 522
- Protein 24 g.
- Fiber 22.5 g.
- Fat 11 g.
- Carbohydrates 82.1 g.

363. Zucchini Pepper Chips

PREPARATION TIME: 10'

COOKING TIME: 15'

SERVINGS: 4

Ingredients

- 1 2/3 c. vegetable oil
- 1 tsp. garlic powder
- 1 tsp. onion powder
- 1/2 tsp. black pepper
- 3 tbsps crushed red pepper flakes
- 2 zucchinis, thinly sliced

Directions

1. Mix oil with all the spices in a bowl.
2. Add zucchini slices and mix well.
3. Transfer the mixture to a Ziploc bag and seal it.
4. Refrigerate for 10 minutes.
5. Spread the zucchini slices on a greased baking sheet.
6. Bake for 15 minutes
7. Serve.

Nutrition

- Calories 172
- Total Fat 11.1 g.
- Saturated Fat 5.8 g.
- Cholesterol 610 mg.
- Sodium 749 mg.
- Total Carbohydrates 19.9 g.
- Fiber 0.2 g.
- Sugar 0.2 g.
- Protein 13.5 g.

364. Apple Chips

Preparation time: 5'
Cooking time: 45'
Servings: 4

Ingredients

- 2 Golden Delicious apples, cored and thinly sliced
- 1 1/2 tsps. white sugar
- 1/2 tsp. ground cinnamon

Directions

1. Set your oven to 225 °F.
2. Place the apple slices on a baking sheet.
3. Sprinkle sugar and cinnamon over the apple slices.
4. Bake for 45 minutes.
5. Serve.

Nutrition

- Calories 127
- Total Fat 3.5 g.
- Saturated Fat 0.5 g.
- Cholesterol 162 mg
- Sodium 142 mg
- Total Carbohydrates 33.6 g.
- Fiber 0.4 g.
- Sugar 0.5 g.
- Protein 4.5 g.

365. Kale Crisps

Preparation time: 10'
Cooking time: 10'
Servings: 4

Ingredients

- 1 bunch kale, remove the stems, leaves torn into even pieces
- 1 tbsp. olive oil
- 1 tsp. sea salt

Directions

1. Set your oven to 350 °F. Layer a baking sheet with parchment paper.
2. Spread the kale leaves on a paper towel to absorb all the moisture.
3. Toss the leaves with sea salt, and olive oil.
4. Kindly spread them, on the baking sheet and bake for 10 minutes.
5. Serve.

Nutrition

- Calories 113
- Total Fat 7.5 g.
- Saturated Fat 1.1 g.
- Cholesterol 20 mg
- Sodium 97 mg
- Total Carbohydrates 1.4 g.
- Fiber 0 g.
- Sugar 0 g.
- Protein 1.1 g.

366. Carrot Chips

PREPARATION TIME: 5'

COOKING TIME: 12'

SERVINGS: 4

Ingredients

- 4 carrots, washed, peeled and sliced
- 2 tsps. extra-virgin olive oil
- 1/4 tsp. sea salt

Directions

1. Set your oven to 350 °F.
2. Toss carrots with salt and olive oil.
3. Spread the slices into two baking sheets in a single layer.
4. Bake for 6 minutes on upper and lower rack of the oven.
5. Switch the baking racks and bake for another 6 minutes.
6. Serve.

Nutrition

- Calories 153
- Total Fat 7.5 g.
- Saturated Fat 1.1 g.
- Cholesterol 20 mg.
- Sodium 97 mg.
- Total Carbohydrates 20.4 g.
- Fiber 0 g.
- Sugar 0 g.
- Protein 3.1 g.

367. Pita Chips

PREPARATION TIME: 5'

COOKING TIME: 12'

SERVINGS: 4

Ingredients

- 12 pita bread pockets, sliced into triangles
- 1/2 c. olive oil
- 1/2 tsp. ground black pepper
- 1 tsp. garlic salt
- 1/2 tsp. dried basil
- 1 tsp. dried chervil

Directions

1. Set your oven to 400 °F.
2. Toss pita with all the remaining ingredients in a bowl.
3. Spread the seasoned triangles on a baking sheet.
4. Bake for 7 minutes until golden brown.
5. Serve with your favorite hummus.

Nutrition

- Calories 201
- Total Fat 5.5 g.
- Saturated Fat 2.1 g.
- Cholesterol 10 mg
- Sodium 597 mg
- Total Carbohydrates 2.4 g.
- Fiber 0 g.
- Sugar 0 g.
- Protein 3.1 g.

368. Awesome Lemon Bell Peppers

PREPARATION TIME: 10'

COOKING TIME: 5'

SERVINGS: 4

Ingredients

- 4 bell peppers
- 1 tsp. olive oil
- 1 tbsp. lemon juice
- 1/4 tsp. garlic, minced
- 1 tsp. parsley, chopped
- 1 pinch sea salt
- Pinch of pepper

Directions

1. Warm your air fryer at 390 F in the "AIR FRY" mode. Add bell pepper to the Air fryer.
2. Drizzle it with the olive oil and air fry for 5 minutes. Take a serving plate and transfer it.
3. Take a small bowl and add garlic, parsley, lemon juice, salt, and pepper. Mix it well and drizzle the mixture over the peppers. Serve and Enjoy!

Nutrition

- Calories 59
- Protein 2 g.
- Fiber 0.9 g.
- Fat 4 g.
- Carbohydrates 6 g.

369. Spinach and Sesame Crackers

PREPARATION TIME: 5'

COOKING TIME: 15'

SERVINGS: 4

Ingredients

- 2 tbsps white sesame seeds
- 1 c. fresh spinach, washed
- 1 2/3 c. all-purpose flour
- 1/2 c. water
- 1/2 tsp. baking powder
- 1 tsp. olive oil
- 1 tsp. salt

Directions

1. Transfer the spinach to a blender with a half cup of water and blend until smooth.
2. Add 2 tbsps white sesame seeds, 1/2 teaspoon baking powder, 1 2/3 c. all-purpose flour, and 1 tsp. salt to a bowl and stir well until combined. Add in 1 tsp. olive oil and spinach water. Mix again and knead by using your hands until you obtain a smooth dough.
3. If the made dough is too gluey, then add more flour.
4. Using your parchment paper lightly roll out the dough as thin as possible. Cut into squares with a pizza cutter.
5. Bake into a preheated oven at 400°, for about 15-20 minutes. Once done, let cool and then serve.

Nutrition

- Calories 223
- Fat 3 g.
- Total carbohydrates 41 g.
- Protein 6 g.

370. Mini Nacho Pizzas

PREPARATION TIME: 5'

COOKING TIME: 10'

SERVINGS: 4

Ingredients

- 1/4 c. refried beans, vegan
- 2 tbsps tomato, diced
- 2 English muffins, split in half
- 1/4 c. onion, sliced
- 1/3 c. vegan cheese, shredded
- 1 small jalapeno, sliced
- 1/3 c. roasted tomato salsa
- 1/2 avocado, diced and tossed in lemon juice

Directions

1. Add the refried beans/salsa onto the muffin bread. Sprinkle with shredded vegan cheese followed by the veggie toppings.
2. Transfer to a baking sheet and place in a preheated oven at 350-400 F on a top rack.
3. Put into the oven for 10 minutes and then broil for 2 minutes, so that the top becomes bubbly.
4. Take out from the oven and let them cool at room temperature.
5. Top with avocado. Enjoy!

Nutrition

- Calories 133
- Fat 4.2 g.
- Total carbohydrates 19 g.
- Protein 6 g.

371. Pizza Sticks

PREPARATION TIME: 10'

COOKING TIME: 30'

SERVINGS: 16 STICKS

Ingredients

- 5 tbsps tomato sauce
- Few pinches of dried basil
- 1 block extra firm tofu
- 2 tbsp. + 2 tsp. nutritional yeast

Directions

1. Cape the tofu in a paper tissue and put a cutting board on top, place something heavy on top and drain for about 10-15 minutes.
2. In the meantime, line your baking sheet with parchment paper. Cut the tofu into 16 equal pieces and place them on a baking sheet.
3. Spread each pizza stick with a teaspoon of the tomato sauce.
4. Sprinkle each stick with half teaspoon of yeast, followed by basil on top.
5. Bake into a preheated oven at 425 F for about 28-30 minutes. Serve and enjoy!

Nutrition

- Calories 33
- Fat 1.7 g.
- Total carbs 2 g.
- Protein 3 g.

372. Raw Broccoli Poppers

PREPARATION TIME: 2'
COOKING TIME: 8'
SERVINGS: 4

Ingredients

- 1/8 c. water
- 1/8 tsp. fine sea salt
- 4 c. broccoli florets, washed and cut into 1-in. pieces
- 1/4 tsp. turmeric powder
- 1 c. unsalted cashews, soaked overnight or at least 3-4 hours and drained
- 1/4 tsp. onion powder
- 1 red bell pepper, seeded
- 2 heaping tablespoons nutritional yeast
- 2 tbsps lemon juice

Directions

1. Transfer the drained cashews to a high-speed blender and pulse for about 30 seconds. Add in the chopped pepper and pulse again for 30 seconds.
2. Add 2 tbsps lemon juice, 1/8 c. water, 2 tbsps of nutritional yeast, 1/4 tsp. onion powder, 1/8 tsp. fine sea salt, and 1/4 tsp. turmeric powder. Pulse for about 45 seconds until smooth.
3. Handover the broccoli into a bowl and add in chopped cheesy cashew mixture. Toss well until coated.
4. Transfer the pieces of broccoli to the trays of a yeast dehydrator.
5. Follow the dehydrator's instructions and dehydrate for about 8 minutes at 125 °F or until crunchy.

Nutrition

- Calories 408
- Fat 32 g.
- Total carbohydrates 22 g.
- Protein 15 g.

373. Blueberry Cauliflower

PREPARATION TIME: 2'
COOKING TIME: 5'
SERVINGS: 1

Ingredients

- 1/4 c. frozen strawberries
- 2 tsps. maple syrup
- 3/4 c. unsweetened cashew milk
- 1 tsp. vanilla extract
- 1/2 c. plain cashew yogurt
- 5 tbsps powdered peanut butter
- 3/4 c. frozen wild blueberries
- 1/2 c. cauliflower florets, coarsely chopped

Directions

1. Add all the smoothie ingredients to a high-speed blender.
2. Blitz to combine until smooth.
3. Pour into a chilled glass and serve.

Nutrition

- Calories 340
- Fat 11 g.
- Total carbohydrates 48 g.
- Protein 16 g.

374. Candied Ginger

Preparation time: 10'
Cooking time: 40'
Servings: 3-5

Ingredients

- 2 1/2 c. salted pistachios, shelled
- 1 1/4 tsps. powdered ginger
- 3 tbsps pure maple syrup

Directions

1. Add 1 1/4 tsps. powdered ginger to a bowl with pistachios. Stir well until combined. There should be no lumps.
2. Drizzle with 3 tbsps of maple syrup and stir well.
3. Transfer to a baking sheet lined with parchment paper and spread evenly.
4. Cook into a preheated oven at 275 F for about 20 minutes.
5. Take out from the oven, stir, and cook for further 10-15 minutes.
6. Let it cool for a few minutes until crispy. Enjoy!

Nutrition

- Calories 378
- Fat 27.6 g.
- Total carbohydrates 26 g.
- Protein 13 g.

375. Chia Crackers

Preparation time: 20'
Cooking time: 1 hour
Servings: 24-26 crackers

Ingredients

- 1/2 c. pecans, chopped
- 1/2 c. chia seeds
- 1/2 tsp. cayenne pepper
- 1 c. water
- 1/4 c. nutritional yeast
- 1/2 c. pumpkin seeds
- 1/4 c. ground flax
- Salt and pepper, to taste

Directions

1. Mix around 1/2 c. chia seeds and 1 c. water. Keep it aside.
2. Take another bowl and combine all the remaining ingredients. Combine well and stir in the chia water mixture until a dough is formed.
3. Transfer the dough onto a baking sheet and rollout (1/4-in. thick).
4. Transfer into a preheated oven at 325 °F and bake for about half an hour.
5. Take out from the oven, flip over the dough, and cut it into the desired cracker shape/squares.
6. Spread and back again for a further half an hour, or until crispy and browned.
7. Once done, take them out from the oven and let them cool at room temperature. Enjoy!

Nutrition

- Calories 41
- Fat 3.1 g.
- Total carbohydrates 2 g.
- Protein 2 g.

376. Orange-Spiced Pumpkin Hummus

Preparation Time: 2'
Cooking Time: 5'
Servings: 4 c.

Ingredients

- 1 tbsp. maple syrup
- 1/2 tsp. salt
- 1 can (16 oz.) garbanzo beans
- 1/8 tsp. ginger or nutmeg
- 1 c. canned pumpkin blend
- 1/8 tsp. cinnamon
- 1/4 c. tahini
- 1 tbsp. fresh orange juice
- Pinch of orange zest, for garnish
- 1 tbsp. apple cider vinegar

Directions

1. Mix all the ingredients into a food processor blender and blend until slightly chunky.
2. Serve right away and enjoy!

Nutrition

- Calories 291
- Fat 22.9 g.
- Total carbohydrates 15 g.
- Protein 12 g.

377. Crazy Mac and Cheese

Preparation Time: 10'
Cooking Time: 20-25'
Servings: 4

Ingredients

- 12 oz. alkaline pasta
- 1/4 c. chickpea flour
- 1 c. raw brazil nuts
- 1/2 tsp. onion powder
- 1 tsp. salt
- 2 tsps. grapeseed oil
- 1 c. hemp seed milk
- 1 c of water
- 1/2 key lime, juiced

Directions

1. Take a bowl and add the nuts; soak overnight. Cook the pasta according to the package instructions.
2. Preheat your air fryer to 325 °F.
3. Transfer the cooked pasta to a baking dish and drizzle oil; add the remaining ingredients to a blender and blend until smooth. Pour the mix over the mac and blend.
4. Transfer to the air fryer and bake for 25 minutes. Serve and Enjoy!

Nutrition

- Calories 255
- Protein 12 g.
- Fiber 7.7 g.
- Fat 23 g.
- Carbohydrates 1 g.

378. Cheesy Kale Chips

PREPARATION TIME: 3'

COOKING TIME: 12'

SERVINGS: 4

Ingredients

- 3 tbsps nutritional yeast
- 1 head curly kale, washed, ribs
- 3/4 tsp. garlic powder
- 1 tbsp. olive oil
- 1 tsp. onion powder
- Salt, to taste

Directions

1. Line a cookie sheet with parchment paper.
2. Drain the kale leaves and spread them on a paper towel.
3. Then, kindly transfer the leaves to a bowl and torn the leaves into chip-sized pieces.
4. Add in 1 tsp. onion powder, 3 tbsps nutritional yeast, 1 tbsp. olive oil, and 3/4 teaspoon garlic powder. Mix with your hands.
5. Spread the kale onto the prepared cookie sheets. They shouldn't touch each other.
6. Bake into a preheated oven for about 350 F for about 10 to 12 minutes.
7. Once crisp, take out from the oven, and sprinkle with a bit of salt. Serve and enjoy!

Nutrition

- Calories 71
- Fat 4 g.
- Total carbohydrates 5 g.
- Protein 4 g.

379. Lemon Roasted Bell Pepper

PREPARATION TIME: 10'

COOKING TIME: 5'

SERVINGS: 4

Ingredients

- 4 bell peppers
- 1 tsp. olive oil
- 1 tbsp. mango juice
- 1/4 tsp. garlic, minced
- 1 tsps. oregano
- 1 pinch salt
- 1 pinch pepper

Directions

1. Start heating the air fryer to 390 °F
2. Place some bell pepper in the Air fryer
3. Drizzle it with the olive oil and air fry for 5 minutes
4. Take a serving plate and transfer it
5. Take a small bowl and add garlic, oregano, mango juice, salt, and pepper
6. Mix them well and drizzle the mixture over the peppers
7. Serve and enjoy!

Nutrition

- Calories 59
- Carbohydrates 6 g.
- Fat 5 g.
- Protein 4 g.

380. Subtle Roasted Mushrooms

Preparation Time: 10'
Cooking Time: 5'
Servings: 4

Ingredients
- 2 tsps. mixed Sebi-friendly herbs
- 1 tbsp. olive oil
- 1/2 tsp. garlic powder
- 2 lbs. mushrooms
- 2 tbsps date sugar

Directions
1. Wash the mushrooms and turn dry in a plate of mixed greens spinner.
2. Quarter them and put in a safe spot.
3. Put garlic, oil, and herbs in the dish of your oar type air fryer.
4. Warmth for 2 minutes.
5. Stir it.
6. Add some mushrooms and cook for 25 minutes
7. Serve and enjoy!

Nutrition
- Calories 94
- Carbohydrates 3 g.
- Fat 8 g.
- Protein 2 g.

249

381. Fancy Spelt Bread

Preparation Time: 10'
Cooking Time: 5'
Servings: 4

Ingredients
- 1 c. spring water
- 1/2 c of coconut milk
- 3 tbsps avocado oil
- 1 tsp. baking soda
- 1 tbsp. agave nectar
- 4 and 1/2 c. spelt flour
- 1 and 1/2 tsp. salt

Directions
1. Preheat your air fryer to 355 °F.
2. Take a big bowl and add baking soda, salt, and flour; whisk well.
3. Add 3/4 c of water, coconut milk, agave, oil and mix well.
4. Sprinkle your working surface with flour, add the dough to the flour.
5. Roll well.
6. Knead for about three minutes, adding small amounts of flour until the dough is a nice ball.
7. Place parchment paper in your cooking basket.
8. Lightly grease your pan and put the dough inside.
9. Transfer into the air fryer and bake for 30–45 minutes until done.
10. Remove then insert a stick to check for doneness.
11. If done already serve and enjoy, if not, let it cook for a few minutes more.

Nutrition
- Calories 203
- Carbohydrates 37 g.
- Fat 4 g.
- Protein 7 g.

382. Crispy Crunchy Hummus

PREPARATION TIME: 10'

COOKING TIME: 10-15'

SERVINGS: 4

Ingredients

- 1/2 a red onion
- 2 tbsps fresh coriander
- 1/4 c. cherry tomatoes
- 1/2 a red bell pepper
- 1 tbsp. dulse flakes
- Juice of lime
- Salt to taste
- 3 tbsps olive oil
- 2 tbsps tahini
- 1 c. warm chickpeas

Directions

1. Prepare your air fryer cooking basket
2. Add the chickpeas to your cooking container and cook for 10-15 minutes, making a point to continue blending them every once in a while, until they are altogether warmed
3. Add warmed chickpeas to a bowl and include tahini, salt, lime
4. Utilize a fork to pound the chickpeas and fixings in a glue until smooth
5. Include the hacked onion, coriander, cherry tomatoes, pepper, dulse flakes, and olive oil
6. Blend well until consolidated
7. Serve the hummus with a couple of cuts of spelt bread

Nutrition

- Calories 95
- Carbohydrates 5 g.
- Fat 5 g.
- Protein 5 g.

Chapter 15: Dessert

383. Peanut Butter c.

PREPARATION TIME: **5'**

COOKING TIME: **10'**

SERVINGS: **4**

Ingredients
- 1 packet plain gelatin
- 1/4 c. sugar substitute
- 2 c. nonfat cream
- 1/2 teaspoon vanilla
- 1/4 c. low-fat peanut butter
- 2 tbsps unsalted peanuts, chopped

Directions
1. Mix gelatin, sugar substitute, and cream in a pan.
2. Let sit for 5 minutes.
3. Place over medium heat and cook until gelatin has been dissolved.
4. Stir in vanilla and peanut butter.
5. Pour into custard cups. Chill for 3 hours.
6. Top with the peanuts and serve.

Nutrition
- Calories 1/1
- Carbohydrate 21 g.
- Protein 6.8 g.

384. Fruit Pizza

PREPARATION TIME: **5'**

COOKING TIME: **10'**

SERVINGS: **4**

Ingredients
- 1 tsp. maple syrup
- 1/4 tsp. vanilla extract
- 1/2 c. coconut milk yogurt
- 2 round slices watermelon
- 1/2 c. blackberries, sliced
- 1/2 c. strawberries, sliced
- 2 tbsps coconut flakes, unsweetened

Directions
1. Mix maple syrup, vanilla, and yogurt in a bowl.
2. Spread the mixture on top of the watermelon slice.
3. Top with the berries and coconut flakes.

Nutrition
- Calories 70
- Carbohydrate 14.6 g.
- Protein 1.2 g.

385. Choco Peppermint Cake

PREPARATION TIME: 5'

COOKING TIME: 10'

SERVINGS: 4

Ingredients

- Cooking spray
- 1/3 c. oil
- 15 oz. package chocolate cake mix
- 3 eggs, beaten
- 1 c. water
- 1/4 tsp. peppermint extract

Directions

1. Spray a slow cooker with oil.
2. Mix all the ingredients in a bowl.
3. Use an electric mixer on medium speed setting to mix ingredients for 2 minutes.
4. Pour mixture into the slow cooker.
5. Cover the pot and cook on low for 3 hours.
6. Let cool before slicing and serving.

Nutrition

- Calories 185
- Carbohydrate 27 g.
- Protein 3.8 g.

386. Roasted Mango

PREPARATION TIME: 5'

COOKING TIME: 10'

SERVINGS: 4

Ingredients

- 2 mangoes, sliced
- 2 tsps. crystallized ginger, chopped
- 2 tsps. orange zest
- 2 tbsps coconut flakes, unsweetened

Directions

1. Preheat your oven to 350 °F.
2. Add mango slices in custard cups.
3. Top with the ginger, orange zest, and coconut flakes.
4. Bake in the oven for 10 minutes.

Nutrition

- Calories 89
- Carbohydrate 20 g.
- Protein 0.8 g.

387. Roasted Plums

PREPARATION TIME: 5'

COOKING TIME: 10'

SERVINGS: 4

Ingredients

- Cooking spray
- 6 plums, sliced
- 1/2 c. pineapple juice, unsweetened
- 1 tbsp. brown sugar
- 1/4 tsp. ground cardamom
- 1/2 teaspoon ground cinnamon
- 1/8 tsp. ground cumin

Directions

1. Combine all the ingredients in a baking pan.
2. Roast in the oven at 450 °F for 20 minutes.

Nutrition

- Calories 102
- Carbohydrate 18.7 g.
- Protein 2 g.

388. Figs with Honey and Yogurt

PREPARATION TIME: 5'

COOKING TIME: 10'

SERVINGS: 4

Ingredients

- 1/2 teaspoon vanilla
- 8 oz. nonfat yogurt
- 2 figs, sliced
- 1 tbsp. walnuts, chopped and toasted
- 2 tsps. honey

Directions

1. Stir vanilla into yogurt.
2. Mix well.
3. Top with the figs and sprinkle with walnuts.
4. Drizzle with honey and serve.

Nutrition

- Calories 157
- Carbohydrate 24 g.
- Protein 7 g.

389. Lava Cake

PREPARATION TIME: 10'

COOKING TIME: 10'

SERVINGS: 2

Ingredients

- 2 oz of dark chocolate; you should at least use chocolate of 85 % cocoa solids
- 1 tbsp of super-fine almond flour
- 2 oz of unsalted almond butter
- 2 big eggs
- Pomegranate seeds

Directions

1. Heat your oven to a temperature of about 350 °F.
2. Grease 2 heat proof ramekins with almond butter.
3. Now, melt the chocolate and the almond butter and stir very well.
4. Beat the eggs very well with a mixer.
5. Add the eggs to the chocolate and the butter mixture and mix very well with almond flour; then stir.
6. Pour the dough into 2 ramekins.
7. Bake for about 9-10 minutes.
8. Turn the cakes over plates and serve with pomegranate seeds!

Nutrition

- Calories 459
- Carbohydrates 3 5 g.
- Fiber 0.8 g.

390. Cheese Cake

PREPARATION TIME: 15'

COOKING TIME: 50'

SERVINGS: 6

Ingredients

For the Almond Flour Cheesecake Crust
- 2 c of blanched almond flour
- 1/3 c of almond butter
- 3 tbsps of erythritol (powdered or granular)
- 1 tsp of vanilla extract

For the Keto Cheesecake Filling
- 32 oz of softened cream cheese
- 1 1/4 c of powdered erythritol
- 3 large eggs
- 1 tbsp of lemon juice
- 1 tsp of vanilla extract

Directions

1. Preheat your oven to a temperature of about 350 °F.
2. Grease a spring form pan of 9 in. with cooking spray or just line its bottom with a parchment paper.
3. In order to make the cheesecake rust, stir in the melted butter, the almond flour, the vanilla extract, and the erythritol in a large bowl.
4. The dough will be a bit crumbly; so, press it into the bottom of your prepared tray.
5. Bake for about 12 minutes; then let cool for about 10 minutes.
6. In the meantime, beat the softened cream cheese and the powdered sweetener at a low speed until it becomes smooth.
7. Crack in the eggs and beat them in at a low to medium speed until it becomes fluffy. Make sure to add one a time.
8. Add in the lemon juice and the vanilla extract and mix at a low to medium speed with a mixer.
9. Pour your filling into your pan right on top of the crust. You can use a spatula to smooth the top of the cake.
10. Bake for about 45-50 minutes.
11. Remove the baked cheesecake from your oven and run a knife around its edge.
12. Let the cake cool for about 4 hours in the refrigerator.
13. Serve and enjoy your delicious cheese cake!

Nutrition

- Calories 325
- Carbohydrates 6 g.
- Fiber 1 g.

391. Madeleine

Preparation time: 10'
Cooking time: 15'
Servings: 12

Ingredients

- 2 large pastured eggs
- 3/4 c of almond flour
- 1 1/2 tbsps of swerve
- 1/4 c of cooled, melted coconut oil
- 1 tsp of vanilla extract
- 1 tsp of almond extract
- 1 tsp of lemon zest
- 1/4 tsp of salt

Directions

1. Preheat your oven to a temperature of about 350 °F.
2. Combine the eggs with the salt and whisk on a high speed for about 5 minutes.
3. Slowly add in the swerve and keep mixing on high for 2 additional minutes.
4. Stir in the almond flour until it is very well-incorporated; then add in the vanilla and the almond extracts.
5. Add in the melted coconut oil and stir all your ingredients together.
6. Pour the obtained batter into equal parts in a greased madeleine tray.
7. Bake your Ketogenic Madeleine for about 13 minutes or until the edges start to have a brown color.
8. Flip the madeleines out of the baking tray.

Nutrition

- Calories 87
- Carbohydrates 3 g.
- Fiber 3 g.

392. Waffles

Preparation time: 20'
Cooking time: 30'
Servings: 3

Ingredients

- 1 c. steel-cut oats
- 2 c. almond milk
- 3/4 c. water
- 1 tsp. ground cinnamon
- 1/4 tsp. salt
- 2 c. chopped fresh fruit, such as blueberries, strawberries, raspberries, or peaches
- 1/2 c. chopped walnuts
- 1/4 c. chia seeds

Directions

1. To make the waffles: Make sure all your ingredients are exactly at room temperature.
2. Place all your ingredients for the waffles from cream cheese to pastured eggs, coconut flour, Xanthan gum, salt, vanilla extract, the Swerve, and the baking soda, except for the almond milk, with the help of a processor.
3. Blend your ingredients until it becomes smooth and creamy; then transfer the batter to a bowl.
4. Add the almond milk and mix your ingredients with a spatula.
5. Heat a waffle maker to a temperature of high.
6. Spray your waffle maker with coconut oil and add about 1/4 of the batter in it evenly with a spatula into your waffle iron.
7. Close your waffle and cook until you get the color you want.
8. Carefully remove the waffles to a platter.
9. For the ketogenic maple syrup: Place 1 1/4 c of water, the swerve, and the maple in a small pan and bring to a boil over a low heat; then let simmer for about 10 minutes.
10. Add the almond butter.
11. Sprinkle the Xanthan gum over the top of the waffle and use an immersion blender to blend smoothly.
12. Serve and enjoy your delicious waffles!

Nutrition

- Calories 316
- Carbohydrates 7 g.
- Fiber 3 g.

393. Pretzels

Preparation time: 10'
Cooking time: 20'
Servings: 8

Ingredients

- 1 1/2 c of pre-shredded mozzarella
- 2 tbsps of full fat cream cheese
- 1 large egg
- 3/4 c of almond flour + 2 tbsps of ground almonds or almond meal
- 1/2 tsp of baking powder
- 1 pinch of coarse sea salt

Directions

1. Heat your oven to a temperature of about 180 °C/356 °F.
2. Melt the cream cheese and the mozzarella cheese and stir over a low heat until the cheeses are perfectly melted.
3. If you choose to microwave the cheese, just do that for about 1 minute, no more; and if you want to do it on the stove, turn off the heat as soon as the cheese is completely melted.
4. Add the large egg to the prepared warm dough; then stir until your ingredients are very well combined. If the egg is cold; you will need to heat it gently.
5. Add in the ground almonds or the almond flour and the baking powder and stir until your ingredients are very well combined.
6. Take one pinch of the dough of cheese and roll it or stretch it in your hands until it is about 18–20 cm of length; if your dough is sticky, you can oil your hands to avoid that.
7. Now, form pretzels from the cheese dough and nicely shape it; then place it over a baking sheet.
8. Sprinkle with a little bit of salt and bake for about 17 minutes.

Nutrition

- Calories 113
- Carbohydrates 2.5 g.
- Fiber 0.8 g.

394. Cheesy Taco Bites

Preparation time: 5'
Cooking time: 10'
Servings: 12

Ingredients

- 2 c of packaged shredded cheddar cheese
- 2 tbsp of chili powder
- 2 tbsps of cumin
- 1 tsp of salt
- 8 tsps of coconut cream for garnishing
- Use Pico de Gallo for garnishing as well

Directions

1. Preheat your oven to a temperature of about 350 °F.
2. Over a baking sheet lined with a parchment paper, place 1 tbsp. piles of cheese and make sure to a space of 2 in. between each.
3. Place the baking sheet in your oven and bake for about 5 minutes.
4. Remove from the oven and let the cheese cool down for about 1 minute; then carefully lift up and press each into the cups of a mini muffin tin.
5. Make sure to press the edges of the cheese to form the shape of mini muffins.
6. Let the cheese cool completely; then remove it.
7. Fill the cheese cups with the coconut cream, then top with Pico de Gallo.

Nutrition

- Calories 73
- Carbohydrates 3 g.
- Protein 4 g.

395. Nut Squares

PREPARATION TIME: **30'**

COOKING TIME: **10'**

SERVINGS: **10**

Ingredients

- 2 c of almonds, pumpkin seeds, sunflower seeds, and walnuts
- 1/2 c of desiccated coconut
- 1 tbsp of chia seeds
- 1/4 tsp of salt
- 2 tbsps of coconut oil
- 1 tsp of vanilla extract
- 3 tbsps of almond or peanut butter
- 1/3 c of Sukrin Gold Fiber Syrup

Directions

1. Line a square baking tin with a baking paper; then lightly grease it with cooking spray.
2. Chop all the nuts roughly; then slightly grease it; you can also leave them as whole.
3. Mix the nuts in a large bowl; then combine them with the coconut, the chia seeds, and the salt.
4. In a microwave-proof bowl; add the coconut oil; then add the vanilla, the almond butter, and the fiber syrup and microwave the mixture for about 30 seconds.
5. Stir your ingredients together very well; then pour the melted mixture right on top of the nuts.
6. Press the mixture into your prepared baking tin with the help of the back of a measuring cup and push very well.
7. Freeze your treat for about 1 hour before cutting it.
8. Cut your frozen nut batter into small cubes or squares of the same size.

Nutrition

- Calories 268
- Carbohydrates 14 g.
- Fiber 1 g.

396. Pumpkin and Banana Ice Cream

PREPARATION TIME: **5'**

COOKING TIME: **10'**

SERVINGS: **4**

Ingredients

- 15 oz. pumpkin puree
- 4 bananas, sliced and frozen
- 1 tsp. pumpkin pie spice
- Chopped pecans

Directions

1. Add pumpkin puree, bananas, and pumpkin pie spice in a food processor.
2. Pulse until smooth.
3. Chill in the refrigerator.
4. Garnish with pecans.

Nutrition

- Calories 71
- Carbohydrate 18 g.
- Protein 1.2 g.

397. Brulee Oranges

Preparation time: 5'

Cooking time: 10'

Servings: 4

Ingredients

- 4 oranges, sliced into segments
- 1 tsp. ground cardamom
- 6 tsps. brown sugar
- 1 c. nonfat Greek yogurt

Directions

1. Preheat your broiler.
2. Arrange the orange slices in a baking pan.
3. In a bowl, mix the cardamom and sugar.
4. Sprinkle mixture on top of the oranges. Broil for 5 minutes.
5. Serve the oranges with yogurt.

Nutrition

- Calories 168
- Carbohydrate 26.9 g.
- Protein 6.8 g.

398. Frozen Lemon and Blueberry

Preparation time: 5'

Cooking time: 10'

Servings: 4

Ingredients

- 6 c. fresh blueberries
- 8 sprigs fresh thyme
- 3/4 c. light brown sugar
- 1 tsp. lemon zest
- 1/4 c. lemon juice
- 2 c. water

Directions

1. Add blueberries, thyme, and sugar in a pan over medium heat.
2. Cook for 6-8 minutes.
3. Transfer the mixture to a blender.
4. Remove thyme sprigs.
5. Stir in the remaining ingredients.
6. Pulse until smooth.
7. Strain the mixture and freeze for 1 hour.

Nutrition

- Calories 78
- Carbohydrate 20 g.
- Protein 3 g.

399. Peanut Butter Choco Chip Cookies

PREPARATION TIME: 5'

COOKING TIME: 10'

SERVINGS: 4

Ingredients

- 1 egg
- 1/2 c. light brown sugar
- 1 c. natural unsweetened peanut butter
- Pinch salt
- 1/4 c. dark chocolate chips

Directions

1. Preheat your oven to 375 °F.
2. Mix egg, sugar, peanut butter, salt, and chocolate chips in a bowl.
3. Form into cookies and place them in a baking pan.
4. Bake the cookie for 10 minutes.
5. Let cool before serving.

Nutrition

- Calories 159
- Carbohydrate 12 g.
- Protein 4.3 g.

400. Watermelon Sherbet

PREPARATION TIME: 5'

COOKING TIME: 3'

SERVINGS: 4

Ingredients

- 6 c. watermelon, sliced into cubes
- 14 oz. almond milk
- 1 tbsp. honey
- 1/4 c. lime juice
- Salt to taste

Directions

1. Freeze the watermelon for 4 hours.
2. Add the frozen watermelon and the other ingredients in a blender.
3. Blend until smooth.
4. Transfer to a container with seal.
5. Seal and freeze for 4 hours.

Nutrition

- Calories 132
- Carbohydrate 24.5 g.
- Protein 3.1 g.

401. Strawberry and Mango Ice Cream

PREPARATION TIME: 5'

COOKING TIME: 10'

SERVINGS: 4

Ingredients

- 8 oz. strawberries, sliced
- 12 oz. mango, sliced into cubes
- 1 tbsp. lime juice

Directions

1. Add all the ingredients in a food processor.
2. Pulse for 2 minutes.
3. Chill before serving.

Nutrition

- Calories 70
- Carbohydrate 17.4 g.
- Protein 1.1 g.

402. Sparkling Fruit Drink

PREPARATION TIME: 5'

COOKING TIME: 10'

SERVINGS: 4

Ingredients

- 8 oz. unsweetened grape juice
- 8 oz. unsweetened apple juice
- 8 oz. unsweetened orange juice
- 1 qt. homemade ginger ale
- Ice

Directions

1. Mix first the 4 ingredients together in a pitcher. Stir in ice cubes and 9 oz of the beverage to each glass. Serve immediately.

Nutrition

- Calories 60
- Protein 1.1 g.

403. Tiramisu Shots

PREPARATION TIME: 5'

COOKING TIME: 10'

SERVINGS: 4

Ingredients

- 1 pack silken tofu
- 1 oz. dark chocolate, finely chopped
- 1/4 c. sugar substitute
- 1 tsp. lemon juice
- 1/4 c. brewed espresso
- Pinch salt
- 24 slices angel food cake
- Cocoa powder, unsweetened

Directions

1. Add tofu, chocolate, sugar substitute, lemon juice, espresso, and salt in a food processor.
2. Pulse until smooth.
3. Add the angel food cake pieces into shot glasses.
4. Drizzle with the cocoa powder.
5. Pour the tofu mixture on top.
6. Top with the remaining angel food cake pieces.
7. Chill for 30 minutes and serve.

Nutrition

- Calories 75
- Carbohydrate 12 g.
- Protein 2.9 g.

404. Ice Cream Brownie Cake

PREPARATION TIME: 5'

COOKING TIME: 10'

SERVINGS: 4

Ingredients

- Cooking spray
- 12 oz. no-sugar brownie mix
- 1/4 c. oil
- 2 egg whites
- 3 tbsps water
- 2 c. sugar-free ice cream

Directions

1. Preheat your oven to 325 °F.
2. Spray your baking pan with oil.
3. Mix the brownie mix, oil, egg whites, and water in a bowl.
4. Pour into the baking pan.
5. Bake for 25 minutes.
6. Let cool.
7. Freeze the brownie for 2 hours.
8. Spread ice cream over the brownie.
9. Freeze for 8 hours.

Nutrition

- Calories 198
- Carbohydrate 33 g.
- Protein 3 g.

405. Berry Sorbet

Preparation time: 10'
Cooking time: 20'
Servings: 6

Ingredients

- 2 c. water
- 2 c. blend strawberries
- 1.5 tsp. spelt flour
- .5 c. date sugar

Directions

1. Add the water into a large pot and let the water begin to warm. Add the flour and date sugar and stir until dissolved. Allow this mixture to start boiling and continue to cook for around ten minutes. It should have started to thicken. Take off the heat and set to the side to cool.
2. Once the syrup has cooled off, add in the strawberries, and stir well to combine.
3. Pour into a container that is freezer safe and put it into the freezer until frozen.
4. Take sorbet out of the freezer, cut into chunks, and put it either into a blender or a food processor. Hit the pulse button until the mixture is creamy.
5. Pour this into the same freezer-safe container and put it back into the freezer for 4 hours.

Nutrition

- Calories 99
- Carbohydrates 8 g.

406. Quinoa Porridge

Preparation time: 5'
Cooking time: 15'
Servings: 4

Ingredients

- Zest of 1 lime
- .5 c. coconut milk
- 5 tsp. cloves
- 1.5 tsp. ground ginger
- 2 c. spring water
- 1 c. quinoa
- 1 grated apple
- Nuts and seeds

Directions

1. Cook the quinoa. Follow the instructions on the package. When the quinoa has been cooked, drain well. Place it back into the pot and stir in the spices.
2. Add coconut milk and stir well to combine.
3. Grate the apple and stir well.
4. Divide equally into bowls and add the lime zest on top. Sprinkle with nuts and seeds of choice.

Nutrition

- Calories 180
- Fat 3 g.
- Carbohydrates 40 g.
- Protein 10 g.

407. Apple Quinoa

PREPARATION TIME: **15'**

COOKING TIME: **30'**

SERVINGS: **4**

Ingredients

- 1 tbsp. coconut oil
- Ginger
- .5 key lime
- 1 apple
- .5 c quinoa
- Optional Toppings
- Seeds
- Nuts
- Berries

Directions

1. Cook the quinoa according to the instructions on the package. When you are getting close to the end of the cooking time, grate in the apple and cook for 30 seconds.
2. Zest the lime into the quinoa and squeeze the juice in. Stir in the coconut oil.
3. Divide evenly into bowls and sprinkle with some ginger.
4. You can add in some berries, nuts, and seeds right before you eat.

Nutrition

- Calories 146
- Fiber 2.3 g.
- Fat 8.3 g.

408. Kamut Porridge

PREPARATION TIME: **10'**

COOKING TIME: **25'**

SERVINGS: **4**

Ingredients

- 4 tbsp. agave syrup
- 1 tbsp. coconut oil
- 5 tsp. sea salt
- 3.75 c. coconut milk
- 1 c. kamut berries
- Optional Toppings
- Berries
- Coconut chips
- Ground nutmeg
- Ground cloves

Directions

1. You need to "crack" the Kamut berries. You can try this by placing the berries into a food processor and pulsing until you have 1.25 c of Kamut.
2. Place the cracked Kamut in a pot with salt and coconut milk. Give it a good stir in order to combine everything. Allow this mixture to come to a full rolling boil and then turn the heat down until the mixture is simmering. Stir every now and then until the Kamut has thickened to your likeness. This normally takes about 10 minutes.
3. Take off the heat, stir in agave syrup and coconut oil.
4. Garnish with the toppings of choice and enjoy.

Nutrition

- Calories 114
- Protein 5 g.
- Carbohydrates 24 g.
- Fiber 4 g.

409. Hot Kamut with Peaches, Walnuts, and Coconut

PREPARATION TIME: 10'

COOKING TIME: 35'

SERVINGS: 4

Ingredients

- 4 tbsp. toasted coconut
- .5 c. toasted and chopped walnuts
- 8 chopped dried peaches
- 3 c. coconut milk
- 1 c. kamut cereal
- Berries

Directions

1. Mix the coconut milk into a saucepan and allow it to warm up. When it begins simmering, add in the Kamut. Let this cook for about 15 minutes, while stirring every now and then.
2. When done, divide evenly into bowls and top with the toasted coconut, walnuts, and peaches.
3. You could even go one more and add some fresh berries.

Nutrition

- Calories 156
- Protein 5.8 g.
- Carbohydrates 25 g.
- Fiber 6 g.

410. Overnight "Oats"

PREPARATION TIME: 5'

COOKING TIME: 0'

SERVINGS: 4

Ingredients

- .5 c. berry of choice
- .5 tbsp. walnut butter
- .5 burro banana
- .5 tsp. ginger
- .5 c. coconut milk
- .5 c. hemp seeds
- Salt, to taste

Directions

1. Put the hemp seeds, salt, and coconut milk into a glass jar. Mix well.
2. Place the lid on the jar then put in the refrigerator to sit overnight.
3. The next morning, add the ginger, berries, and banana. Stir well and enjoy.

Nutrition

- Calories 139
- Fat 4.1 g.
- Protein 9 g.
- Sugar 7 g.

411. Blueberry Cupcakes

PREPARATION TIME: 15'

COOKING TIME: 40'

SERVINGS: 4

Ingredients

- Grapeseed oil
- .5 tsp. sea salt
- .25 c. sea moss gel
- .3 c. agave
- .5 c. blueberries
- .75 c. teff flour
- .75 c. spelt flour
- 1 c. coconut milk

Directions

1. Warm your oven to 365 °F. Place paper liners into a muffin tin.
2. Place oil, sea moss gel, sea salt, agave, flour, and milk in large bowl. Mix well to combine. Gently fold in blueberries.
3. Gently pour batter into paper liners. Place in the oven and bake for 30 minutes.
4. They are done if they have turned a nice golden color, and they spring back when you touch them.

Nutrition

- Calories 85
- Fat 0.7 g.
- Carbohydrates 12 g.
- Protein 1.4 g.
- Fiber 5 g.

266

412. Brazil Nut Cheese

PREPARATION TIME: 2'

COOKING TIME: 0'

SERVINGS: 4

Ingredients

- 2 tsp. Grapeseed oil
- 1.5 c. Water
- 1.5 c. Hemp milk
- .5 tsp. Cayenne
- 1 tsp. Onion powder
- Juice of .5 lime
- 2 tsp. Sea salt
- 1 lb. Brazil nuts
- 1 tsp. Onion powder

Directions

1. Soak the Brazil nuts in some water. Put the nuts into a bowl and make sure the water covers them. Soak no less than 2 hours or overnight. Overnight would be best.
2. Put everything except water into a food processor or blender.
3. Add just .5 c of water and blend for 2 minutes.
4. Continue adding .5 c of water and blending until you have the consistency you want.
5. Scrape into an airtight container and enjoy.

Nutrition

- Calories 187
- Protein 4.1 g.
- Fat 19 g.
- Carbohydrates 3.3 g.
- Fiber 2.1 g.

413. Slow Cooker Peaches

Preparation time: 10'
Cooking time: 4H 20'
Servings: 4-6

Ingredients

- 4 c. peaches, sliced
- 2/3 c. rolled oats
- 1/3 c. bisque
- 1/4 tsp. cinnamon
- 1/2 c. brown sugar
- 1/2 c. granulated sugar

Directions

1. Spray the slow cooker pot with a cooking spray.
2. Mix oats, bisque, cinnamon, and all the sugars in the pot.
3. Add the peaches and stir well to combine. Cook on low for 4-6 hours.

Nutrition

- Calories 617
- Fat 3.6 g.
- Total Carbs 13 g.
- Protein 9 g.

414. Pumpkin Custard

Preparation time: 10'
Cooking time: 2H 30'
Servings: 6

Ingredients

- 1/2 c. almond flour
- 4 eggs
- 1 c. pumpkin puree
- 1/2 c. stevia/erythritol blend, granulated
- 1/8 tsp. sea salt
- 1 tsp. vanilla extract or maple flavoring
- 4 tbsps butter, ghee, or coconut oil melted
- 1 tsp. pumpkin pie spice

Directions

1. Grease or spray a slow cooker with butter or coconut oil spray.
2. In a medium mixing bowl, beat the eggs until smooth. Then add in the sweetener.
3. To the egg mixture, add in the pumpkin puree along with vanilla or maple extract.
4. Then add almond flour to the mixture along with the pumpkin pie spice and salt. Add melted butter, coconut oil or ghee.
5. Transfer the mixture into a slow cooker. Close the lid. Cook for 2-2 3/4 hours on low.
6. When through, serve with whipped cream, and then sprinkle with little nutmeg if need be. Enjoy!

Nutrition

- Calories 147
- Fat 12 g.
- Total carbs 4 g.
- Protein 5 g.

415. Blueberry Lemon Custard Cake

PREPARATION TIME: 10'

COOKING TIME: 3 HOURS

SERVINGS: 12

Ingredients

- 6 eggs, separated
- 2 c. light cream
- 1/2 c. coconut flour
- 1/2 tsp. salt
- 2 tsp. lemon zest
- 1/2 c. granulated sugar substitute
- 1/3 c. lemon juice
- 1/2 c. blueberries fresh
- 1 tsp. lemon liquid stevia
- Sugar-free whipped cream

Directions

1. Into a stand mixer, add the egg whites and whip them well until stiff peaks have formed; set aside.
2. Whisk the yolks together with the remaining ingredients except blueberries, to form the batter.
3. When done, fold the egg whites into the formed batter a little at a time until slightly combined.
4. Grease the crock pot and then pour in the mixture. Then sprinkle the batter with the blueberries.
5. Close the lid then cook for 3 hours on low. When the cooking time is over, open the lid and let cool for an hour, and then let chill in the refrigerator for at least 2 hours or overnight.
6. Serve cold with little sugar-free whipped cream and enjoy!

Nutrition

- Calories 165
- Fat 10 g.
- Total carbs 14 g.
- Protein 4 g.

416. Sugar Free Carrot Cake

PREPARATION TIME: 20'

COOKING TIME: 4 HOURS

SERVINGS: 8

Ingredients

For the Carrot Cake
- 2 eggs
- 1 1/2 almond flour
- 1/2 c. butter, melted
- 1/4 c. heavy cream
- 1 tsp. baking powder
- 1 tsp. vanilla extract or almond extract, optional
- 1 c. sugar substitute
- 1 c. carrots, finely shredded
- 1 tsp. cinnamon
- 1/4 tsp. nutmeg
- 1/8 tsp. allspice
- 1 tsp. ginger
- 1/2 tsp. baking soda

For Cream Cheese Frosting
- 1 c. confectioner's sugar substitute
- 1/4 c. butter, softened
- 1 tsp. almond extract
- 4 oz. cream cheese, softened

Directions

1. Grease a loaf pan well and then set it aside.
2. Using a mixer, combine butter together with eggs, vanilla, sugar substitute, and heavy cream in a mixing bowl until well blended.
3. Combine almond flour together with baking powder, spices, and the baking soda in another bowl until well blended.
4. When done, combine the wet ingredients together with the dry ingredients until well blended, and then stir in the carrots.
5. Pour the mixer into the prepared loaf pan, and then place the pan into a slow cooker on a trivet. Add 1 c of water inside.
6. Cook for about 4-5 hours on low. Be aware that the cake will be very moist.
7. When the cooking time is over, let the cake cool completely.
8. To prepare the cream cheese frosting: Blend the cream cheese together with extract, butter, and powdered sugar substitute until frosting is formed.
9. Top the cake with the frosting.

Nutrition

- Calories 299
- Fat 25.4 g.
- Total carbs 15 g.
- Protein 4 g.

417. Sugar Free Chocolate Molten Lava Cake

Preparation time: 10'
Cooking time: 3 hours
Servings: 12

Ingredients

- 3 egg yolks
- 1 1/2 c. Swerve sweetener, divided
- 1 tsp. baking powder
- 1/2 c. flour, gluten free
- 3 whole eggs
- 5 tbsps cocoa powder, unsweetened, divided
- 4 oz. chocolate chips, sugar-free
- 1/2 tsp. salt
- 1/2 tsp. vanilla liquid stevia
- 1/2 c. butter, melted, cooled
- 2 c. hot water
- 1 tsp. vanilla extract

Directions

1. Grease the crockpot well with cooking spray.
2. Whisk 1 1/4 c of swerve together with flour, salt, baking powder, and 3 tbsps cocoa powder in a bowl.
3. Stir the cooled melted butter together with eggs, yolks, liquid stevia, and the vanilla extract in a separate bowl.
4. When done, add the wet ingredients to the dry ingredient until nicely combined, and then pour the mixture into the prepared crock pot.
5. Then top the mixture in the crockpot with chocolate chips.
6. Whisk the rest of the swerve sweetener and the remaining cocoa powder with the hot water, and then pour this mixture over the chocolate chips top.
7. Close the lid and cook for 3 hours on low. When the cooking time is over, let cool a bit and then serve. Enjoy!

Nutrition

- Calories 157
- Fat 13 g.
- Total carbs 10.5 g.
- Protein 3.9 g.

418. Chocolate Quinoa Brownies

Preparation time: 10'
Cooking time: 2 hours
Servings: 16

Ingredients

- 2 eggs
- 3 c. quinoa, cooked
- 1 tsp. vanilla liquid stevia
- 1 1/4 chocolate chips, sugar-free
- 1 tsp. vanilla extract
- 1/3 c. flaxseed ground
- 1/4 tsp. salt
- 1/3 c. cocoa powder, unsweetened
- 1/2 tsp. baking powder
- 1 tsp. pure stevia extract
- 1/2 c. applesauce, unsweetened

For the Sugar-Frees Frosting
- 1/4 c. heavy cream
- 1 tsp. chocolate liquid stevia
- 1/4 c. cocoa powder, unsweetened
- 1/2 tsp. vanilla extract

Directions

1. Add all the ingredients to a food processor. Then process until well incorporated.
2. Line a crock pot with a parchment paper, and then spread the batter into the lined pot.
3. Close the lid and cook for 4 hours on low or 2 hours on high. Let cool.
4. Prepare the frosting. Whisk all the ingredients together and then microwave for 20 seconds. Taste and adjust on sweetener if desired.
5. When the frosting is ready, stir it well again and then pour it over the sliced brownies.
6. Serve and enjoy!

Nutrition

- Calories 133
- Fat 7.9 g.
- Total carbs 18.4 g.
- Protein 4.3 g.

419. Blueberry Crisp

Preparation time: 10'

Cooking time: 3-4 hours

Servings: 10

Ingredients

- 1/4 c. butter, melted
- 24 oz. blueberries, frozen
- 3/4 tsp. salt
- 1 1/2 c. rolled oats, coarsely ground
- 3/4 c. almond flour, blanched
- 1/4 c. coconut oil, melted
- 6 tbsps sweetener
- 1 c. pecans or walnuts, coarsely chopped

Directions

1. Using a non-stick cooking spray, spray the slow cooker pot well.
2. Into a bowl, add ground oats and chopped nuts along with salt, blanched almond flour, and then stir in the coconut/butter mixture. Stir well to combine.
3. When done, spread crisp topping over blueberries. Cook for 3-4 hours, until the mixture has become bubbling hot and you can smell the blueberries.
4. Serve while still hot with the whipped cream or the ice cream if desired. Enjoy!

Nutrition

- Calories 261
- Fat 16.6 g.
- Total carbs 32 g.
- Protein 4 g.

420. Maple Custard

Preparation time: 10'

Cooking time: 2 hours

Servings: 6

Ingredients

- 1 tsp. maple extract
- 2 egg yolks
- 1 c. heavy cream
- 2 eggs
- 1/2 c. whole milk
- 1/4 tsp. salt
- 1/4 c. Sukrin Gold or any sugar-free brown sugar substitute
- 1/2 tsp. cinnamon

Directions

1. Combine all ingredients together in a blender, process well.
2. Grease 6 ramekins and then pour the batter evenly into each ramekin.
3. To the bottom of the slow cooker, add 4 ramekins and then arrange the remaining 2 against the side of a slow cooker, and not at the top of the bottom ramekins.
4. Close the lid and cook on high for 2 hours, until the center is cooked through but the middle is still jiggly.
5. Let cool at a room temperature for an hour after removing from the slow cooker, and then chill in the fridge for at least 2 hours.
6. Serve and enjoy with a sprinkle of cinnamon and little sugar-free whipped cream.

Nutrition

- Calories 190
- Fat 18 g.
- Total carbs 2 g.
- Protein 4 g.

421. Raspberry Cream Cheese Coffee Cake

Preparation time: 10'
Cooking time: 4 hours
Servings: 12

Ingredients

- 1 1/4 almond flour
- 2/3 c. water
- 1/2 c. Swerve
- 3 eggs
- 1/4 c. coconut flour
- 1/4 c. protein powder
- 1/4 tsp. salt
- 1 1/2 tsp. baking powder
- 6 tbsps butter, melted

For the Filling
- 1 1/2 c. fresh raspberries
- 8 oz. cream cheese
- 1/2 tsp. vanilla extract
- 1 large egg
- 1/3 c. powdered Swerve
- 2 tbsp. whipping cream

Directions

1. Grease the slow cooker pot. Prepare the cake batter. In a bowl, combine almond flour together with coconut flour, sweetener, baking powder, protein powder, and salt, and then stir in the melted butter along with eggs and water until well combined. Set aside.
2. Prepare the filling. Beat cream cheese thoroughly with the sweetener until have smoothened, and then beat in whipping cream along with the egg and vanilla extract until well combined.
3. Assemble the cake. Spread around 2/3 of batter in the slow cooker as you smoothen the top using a spatula or knife.
4. Pour the cream cheese mixture over the batter in the pan, evenly spread it, and then sprinkle with raspberries. Add the rest of batter over the filling.
5. Cook for 3-4 hours on low. Let cool completely.
6. Serve and enjoy!

Nutrition

- Calories 239
- Fat 19.18 g.
- Total carbs 6.9 g.
- Protein 7.5 g.

422. Pumpkin Pie Bars

Preparation time: 10'
Cooking time: 3 hours
Servings: 2

Ingredients

For the Crust
- 3/4 c. coconut, shredded
- 4 tbsps butter, unsalted, softened
- 1/4 c. cocoa powder, unsweetened
- 1/4 tsp. salt
- 1/2 c. raw sunflower seeds or sunflower seed flour
- 1/4 c. confectioners Swerve

For the Filling
- 2 tsps. cinnamon liquid stevia
- 1 c. heavy cream
- 1 can pumpkin puree
- 6 eggs
- 1 tbsp. pumpkin pie spice
- 1/2 tsp. salt
- 1 tbsp. vanilla extract
- 1/2 c. sugar-free chocolate chips, optional

Directions

1. Add all the crust ingredients to a food processor. Then process until fine crumbs are formed.
2. Grease the slow cooker pan well. When done, press the crust mixture onto the greased bottom.
3. In a stand mixer, combine all the ingredients for the filling, and then blend well until combined.
4. Top the filling with chocolate chips if using, and then pour the mixture onto the prepared crust.
5. Close the lid and cook for 3 hours on low. Open the lid and let cool for at least 30 minutes, and then place the slow cooker into the refrigerator for at least 3 hours.
6. Slice the pumpkin pie bar and serve it with sugar-free whipped cream. Enjoy!

Nutrition

- Calories 169
- Fat 15 g.
- Total carbs 6 g.
- Protein 4 g.

423. Dark Chocolate Cake

PREPARATION TIME: 10'

COOKING TIME: 3 HOURS

SERVINGS: 10

Ingredients

- 1 c. almond flour
- 3 eggs
- 1/4 tsp. salt
- 1/2 c. Swerve Granular
- 3/4 tsp. vanilla extract
- 2/3 c. almond milk, unsweetened
- 1/2 c. cocoa powder
- 6 tbsps butter, melted
- 1 1/2 tsp. baking powder
- 3 tbsps unflavored whey protein powder or egg white protein powder
- 1/3 c. sugar-free chocolate chips, optional

Directions

1. Grease the slow cooker well.
2. Whisk the almond flour together with cocoa powder, sweetener, whey protein powder, salt, and baking powder in a bowl. Then stir in butter along with almond milk, eggs, and the vanilla extract until well combined, and then stir in the chocolate chips if desired.
3. When done, pour into the slow cooker. Allow to cook for 2–2 1/2 hours on low.
4. When through, turn off the slow cooker and let the cake cool for about 20–30 minutes.
5. When cooled, cut the cake into pieces and serve warm with lightly sweetened whipped cream. Enjoy!

Nutrition

- Calories 205
- Fat 17 g.
- Total carbs 8.4 g.
- Protein 12 g.

424. Lemon Custard

PREPARATION TIME: 10'

COOKING TIME: 3 HOURS

SERVINGS: 4

Ingredients

- 2 c. whipping cream or coconut cream
- 5 egg yolks
- 1 tbsp. lemon zest
- 1 tsp. vanilla extract
- 1/4 c. fresh lemon juice, squeezed
- 1/2 tsp. liquid stevia

Directions

1. Whisk egg yolks together with lemon zest, liquid stevia, and vanilla in a bowl, and then whisk in the cream.
2. Divide the mixture among 4 small jars or ramekins.
3. To the bottom of a slow cooker, add a rack, and then add the ramekins on top of the rack and enough water to cover half of the ramekins.
4. Close the lid and cook for 3 hours on low. Remove the ramekins.
5. Let cool to room temperature, and then place into the refrigerator to cool completely for about 3 hours.
6. When through, top with the whipped cream and serve. Enjoy!

Nutrition

- Calories 319
- Fat 30 g.
- Total carbs 3 g.
- Protein 7 g.

425. Baked Stuffed Pears

PREPARATION TIME: **15'**

COOKING TIME: **35'**

SERVINGS: **4**

Ingredients

- 4 tbsp. agave syrup
- .25 tsp. cloves
- 4 tbsp. chopped walnuts
- 1 c. currants
- 4 pears

Directions

1. Make sure your oven has been warmed to 375 °F.
2. Slice the pears in two lengthwise and remove the core. To get the pear to lay flat, you can slice a small piece off the back side.
3. Place the agave syrup, currants, walnuts, and cloves in a small bowl and mix well. Set this to the side to be used later.
4. Put the pears on a cookie sheet that has parchment paper on it. Make sure the cored sides are facing up. Sprinkle each pear half with about .5 tbsp of the chopped walnut mixture.
5. Place into the oven and cook for 25–30 minutes. Pears should be tender.

Nutrition

- Calories 103.9
- Fiber 3.1 g.
- Carbohydrates 22 g.

426. Butternut Squash Pie

PREPARATION TIME: **25'**

COOKING TIME: **35'**

SERVINGS: **4**

Ingredients

For the Crust
- Cold water
- Agave, splash
- A pinch of sea salt
- .5 c grapeseed oil
- .5 c. coconut flour
- 1 c. spelt flour

For the Filling
- Butternut squash, peeled, chopped
- Water
- Allspice, to taste
- Agave syrup, to taste
- 1 c. hemp milk
- 4 tbsp. sea moss

Directions

1. You will need to warm your oven to 350 °F.
2. For the Crust
3. Place the grapeseed oil and water into the refrigerator to get it cold. This will take about 1 hour.
4. Place all the ingredients into a large bowl. Now you need to add in the cold water a little bit in small amounts until a dough is form. Place this onto a surface that has been sprinkled with some coconut flour. Knead for a few minutes and roll the dough as thin as you can get it. Carefully, pick it up and place it inside a pie plate.
5. Place the butternut squash into a Dutch oven and pour in enough water to cover. Bring this to a full rolling boil. Let this cook until the squash has become soft.
6. Completely drain and place into bowl. Using a masher, mash the squash. Add in some allspice and agave to taste. Add in the sea moss and hemp milk. Using a hand mixer, blend well. Pour into the pie crust.
7. Place into an oven and bake for about 1 hour.

Nutrition

- Calories 245
- Carbohydrates 50 g.
- Fat 10 g.

427. Coconut Chia Cream Pot

Preparation time: 5'
Cooking time: 5
Servings: 4

Ingredients

- 1 date
- 1 c. coconut milk (organic)
- 1 c. coconut yogurt
- 1/2 teaspoon vanilla extract
- 1/4 c. chia seeds
- 1 teaspoon sesame seeds
- 1 tbsp. flaxseed, ground, or flax meal

For the Toppings
- 1 fig
- 1 handful of blueberries
- Mixed nuts (Brazil nuts, almonds, pistachios, macadamia, etc.)
- 1 tsp. cinnamon, ground

Directions

1. First, blend the date with coconut milk (the idea is to sweeten the coconut milk).
2. Get a mixing bowl and add the coconut milk with the vanilla, sesame seeds, chia seeds, and flax meal.
3. Refrigerate for between 20-30 minutes or wait till the chia expands.
4. To serve, pour a layer of coconut yogurt in a small glass, then add the chia mix, followed by pouring another layer of the coconut yogurt.
5. It's alkaline, creamy, and delicious.

Nutrition

- Calories 310
- Carbohydrates 39 g.
- Protein 4 g.
- Fiber 8.1 g.

428. Chocolate Avocado Mousse

Preparation time: 10'
Cooking time: 5'
Servings: 4

Ingredients

- 2/3 c. coconut water
- 1/2 hass avocado
- 2 tsps. raw cacao
- 1 tsp. vanilla
- 3 dates
- 1 tsp. sea salt
- Dark chocolate shavings

Directions

1. Blend all the ingredients.
2. Blast until it becomes thick and smooth, as you wish.
3. Put in a fridge and allow it to get firm.

Nutrition

- Calories 181.8
- Fat 151 g.
- Protein 12 g.

429. Chia Vanilla Coconut Pudding

Preparation Time: 5'
Cooking Time: 5'
Servings: 2

Ingredients

- 2 tbsps coconut oil
- 1/2 c. raw cashew
- 1/2 c. coconut water
- 1 tsp. cinnamon
- 3 dates (pitted)
- 2 tsps. vanilla
- 1 tsp. coconut flakes, unsweetened
- Salt (Himalayan or Celtic Grey)
- 6 tbsps chia seeds
- Cinnamon or pomegranate seeds for garnish (optional)

Directions

1. Get a blender, add all the ingredients (minus the pomegranate and chia seeds), and blend for about 40–60 seconds.
2. Reduce the blender speed to the lowest and add the chia seeds.
3. Pour the content into an airtight container and put in a refrigerator for 5–6 hours.
4. To serve, you can garnish with the cinnamon powder of pomegranate seeds.

Nutrition

- Calories 201
- Fat 10 g.
- Sodium 32.8 mg.

430. Sweet Tahini Dip with Ginger Cinnamon Fruit

Preparation Time: 10'
Cooking Time: 5'
Servings: 2

Ingredients

- 1 tsp. cinnamon
- 1 green apple
- 1 pear
- 2–3 fresh ginger
- 1 tsp. Celtic sea salt

For the Sweet Tahini
- 3 tsps. almond butter (raw)
- 3 tsps. tahini (one big scoop)
- 2 tsps. coconut oil
- 1/4 tsp. cayenne (optional)
- 2 tsps. wheat-free tamari
- 1 tsp. liquid coconut nectar

Directions

1. Get a clean mixing bowl.
2. Grate the ginger, add cinnamon, sea salt, and mix together in the bowl.
3. Dice the apple and pear into little cubes, turn into the bowl and mix.
4. Get a mixing bowl and mix all the ingredients.
5. Then add the Sweet Tahini dip all over the Ginger Cinnamon Fruit.
6. Serve.

Nutrition

- Calories 109
- Fat 10.8 g.
- Sodium 258 mg.

431. Coconut Butter and Chopped Berries with Mint

PREPARATION TIME: 5'

COOKING TIME: 5'

SERVINGS: 4

Ingredients
- 1 tbsp. chopped mint
- 2 tbsps coconut butter, melted
- Mixed berries (strawberries, blueberries, and raspberries)

Directions
1. Get a small bowl and add the berries.
2. Drizzle the melted coconut butter and sprinkle the mint.
3. Serve.

Nutrition
- Calories 159
- Fat 12 g.
- Carbohydrates 18 g.

432. Alkaline Raw Pumpkin Pie

PREPARATION TIME: 5'

COOKING TIME: 5'

SERVINGS: 4

Ingredients
For the Pie Crust
- 1 tbsp. cinnamon
- 1 c. dates/Turkish apricots
- 1 c. raw almonds
- 1 c. coconut flakes, unsweetened

For the Pie Filling
- 6 dates
- 1/2 tsp. cinnamon
- 1/2 tsp. nutmeg
- 1 c. pecans, soaked overnight
- 1 1/4 c. (12 oz.) organic pumpkin blends
- 1/2 tsp. nutmeg
- 1/4 tsp. sea salt (Himalayan or Celtic sea salt)
- 1 tsp. vanilla
- Gluten-free tamari

Directions
1. To make the pie crust: Get a food processor and blend all the pie crust ingredients at the same time. Make sure the mixture turns oily and sticky before you stop mixing. Put the mixture in a pie pan and mold against the sides and the floor, to make it stick properly.
2. For the pie filling: Mix the ingredients together in a blender. Add the mixture to fill in the pie crust. Pour some cinnamon on top. Refrigerate till it's cold. Then mold.

Nutrition
- Calories 135
- Calories from Fat 41.4
- Total Fat 4.6 g.
- Cholesterol 11.3 mg

433. Strawberry Sorbet

Preparation time: 5'
Cooking time: 4 hours
Servings: 4

Ingredients

- 2 c of strawberries*
- 1 1/2 tsps of spelt flour
- 1/2 c of date sugar
- 2 c of spring water

Directions

1. Add date sugar, spring water, and spelt flour to a medium pot and boil on low heat for about 10 minutes. The mixture should thicken, like syrup.
2. Remove the pot from the heat and allow it to cool.
3. After cooling, add the strawberry blend and mix gently.
4. Put the mixture in a container and freeze.
5. Cut it into pieces, put the sorbet into a processor and blend until smooth.
6. Put everything back in the container and leave in the refrigerator for at least 4 hours.
7. Serve and enjoy your Strawberry Sorbet!

Nutrition

- Calories 198
- Carbohydrates 28 g.

434. Blueberry Muffins

Preparation time: 5'
Cooking time: 1 hour
Servings: 3

Ingredients

- 1/2 c of blueberries
- 3/4 c of teff flour
- 3/4 c of spelt flour
- 1/3 c of agave syrup
- 1/2 tsp of pure sea salt
- 1 c of coconut milk
- 1/4 c of sea moss gel (optional)
- Grape seed oil

Directions

1. Preheat your oven to 365 °F.
2. Grease or line 6 standard muffin cups.
3. Add teff, spelt flour, pure sea salt, coconut milk, sea moss gel, and agave syrup to a large bowl. Mix them together.
4. Add Blueberries to the mixture and mix well.
5. Divide the muffin batter among the 6 muffin cups.
6. Bake for 30 minutes until golden brown.
7. Serve and enjoy your Blueberry Muffins!

Nutrition

- Calories 65
- Fat 0.7 g.
- Carbohydrates 12 g.
- Protein 1.4 g.
- Fiber 5 g.

435. Banana Strawberry Ice Cream

PREPARATION TIME: **5'**

COOKING TIME: **4 HOURS**

SERVINGS: **5**

Ingredients

- 1 c of strawberry*
- 5 quartered baby bananas*
- 1/2 avocado, chopped
- 1 tbsp of agave syrup
- 1/4 c of homemade walnut milk

Directions

1. Mix the ingredients into the blender and blend them well.
2. Taste. If it is too thick, add extra milk or agave syrup if you want it sweeter.
3. Put in a container with a lid and allow to freeze for at least 5-6 hours.
4. Serve it and enjoy your Banana Strawberry Ice Cream!

Nutrition

- Calories 200
- Fat 0.5 g.
- Carbohydrates 44 g.

436. Homemade Whipped Cream

PREPARATION TIME: **5'**

COOKING TIME: **10'**

SERVINGS: **1 CUP**

Ingredients

- 1 c of aquafaba
- 1/4 c of agave syrup

Directions

1. Add agave syrup and aquafaba into a bowl.
2. Mix at high speed around 5 minutes with a stand mixer or 10-15 minutes with a hand mixer.
3. Serve and enjoy your Homemade Whipped Cream!

Nutrition

- Calories 21
- Fat 0 g.
- Sodium 0.3 g.
- Carbohydrates 5.3 g.
- Fiber 0 g.
- Sugars 4.7 g.
- Protein 0 g.

437. Chocolate Crunch Bars

PREPARATION TIME: 5'

COOKING TIME: 5'

SERVINGS: 4

Ingredients

- 1 1/2 c. sugar-free chocolate chips
- 1 c. almond butter
- Stevia to taste
- 1/4 c. coconut oil
- 3 c. pecans, chopped

Directions

1. Layer an 8-in. baking pan with parchment paper.
2. Mix the chocolate chips with butter, coconut oil, and sweetener in a bowl.
3. Melt it by heating in a microwave for 2-3 minutes until well mixed.
4. Stir in nuts and seeds. Mix gently.
5. Pour this batter carefully into the baking pan and spread evenly.
6. Refrigerate for 2-3 hours.
7. Slice and serve.

Nutrition

- Calories 316
- Total fat 30.9 g.
- Saturated fat 8.1 g.
- Cholesterol 0 mg.
- Total carbohydrates 8.3 g.
- Sugar 1.8 g.
- Fiber 3.8 g.
- Sodium 8 mg.
- Protein 6.4 g.

438. Homemade Protein Bar

PREPARATION TIME: 5'

COOKING TIME: 10'

SERVINGS: 4

Ingredients

- 1 c. nut butter
- 4 tbsps coconut oil
- 2 scoops vanilla protein
- Stevia, to taste
- 1/2 teaspoon sea salt

Optional Ingredients:
- 1 tsp. cinnamon

Directions

1. Mix coconut oil with butter, protein, stevia, and salt in a dish.
2. Stir in cinnamon and chocolate chip.
3. Press the mixture firmly and freeze until firm.
4. Cut the crust into small bars.
5. Serve and enjoy.

Nutrition

- Calories 179
- Total fat 15.7 g.
- Saturated fat 8 g.
- Cholesterol 0 mg.
- Total carbohydrates 4.8 g.
- Sugar 3.6 g.
- Fiber 0.8 g.
- Sodium 43 mg.
- Protein 5.6 g.

439. Shortbread Cookies

PREPARATION TIME: **10'**

COOKING TIME: **70'**

SERVINGS: **6**

Ingredients

- 2 1/2 c. almond flour
- 6 tbsps nut butter
- 1/2 c. erythritol
- 1 tsp. vanilla essence

Directions

1. Preheat your oven to 350 °F.
2. Layer a cookie sheet with parchment paper.
3. Beat butter with erythritol until fluffy.
4. Stir in the vanilla essence and almond flour. Mix well until becomes crumbly.
5. Spoon out a tablespoon of cookie dough onto the cookie sheet.
6. Add more dough to make as many cookies.
7. Bake for 15 minutes until brown.
8. Serve.

Nutrition

- Calories 288
- Total Fat 25.3 g.
- Saturated Fat 6.7 g.
- Cholesterol 23 mg.
- Total Carbohydrates 9.6 g.
- Sugar 0.1 g.
- Fiber 3.8 g.
- Sodium 74 mg.
- Potassium 3 mg.
- Protein 7.6 g.

280

440. Coconut Chip Cookies

PREPARATION TIME: **10'**

COOKING TIME: **15'**

SERVINGS: **4**

Ingredients

- 1 c. almond flour
- 1/2 c. cacao nibs
- 1/2 c. coconut flakes, unsweetened
- 1/3 c. erythritol
- 1/2 c. almond butter
- 1/4 c. nut butter, melted
- 1/4 c. almond milk
- Stevia, to taste
- 1/4 tsp. sea salt

Directions

1. Preheat your oven to 350 °F.
2. Layer a cookie sheet with parchment paper.
3. Add and then combine all the dry ingredients in a glass bowl.
4. Whisk in butter, almond milk, stevia, and almond butter.
5. Beat well then stir in the dry mixture. Mix well.
6. Spoon out a tablespoon of cookie dough on the cookie sheet.
7. Add more dough to make as many as 16 cookies.
8. Flatten each cookie using your fingers.
9. Bake for 25 minutes until golden brown.
10. Let them sit for 15 minutes.
11. Serve.

Nutrition

- Calories 192
- Total Fat 17.44 g.
- Saturated Fat 11.5 g.
- Cholesterol 125 mg
- Total Carbohydrates 2.2 g.
- Sugar 1.4 g.
- Fiber 2.1 g.
- Sodium 135 mg
- Protein 4.7 g.

441. Peanut Butter Bars

Preparation time: 10'
Cooking time: 10'
Servings: 6

Ingredients

- 3/4 c. almond flour
- 2 oz. almond butter
- 1/4 c. Swerve
- 1/2 c. peanut butter
- 1/2 tsp. vanilla

Directions

1. Combine all the ingredients for bars.
2. Transfer this mixture to 6-in. small pan. Press it firmly.
3. Refrigerate for 30 minutes.
4. Slice and serve.

Nutrition

- Calories 214
- Total Fat 19 g.
- Saturated Fat 5.8 g.
- Cholesterol 15 mg
- Total Carbohydrates 6.5 g.
- Sugar 1.9 g.
- Fiber 2.1 g.
- Sodium 123 mg
- Protein 6.5 g.

442. Zucchini Bread Pancakes

Preparation time: 15'
Cooking time: 35'
Servings: 3

Ingredients

- 1 tbsp. grapeseed oil
- .5 c. chopped walnuts
- 2 c. walnut milk
- 1 c. shredded zucchini
- .25 c. mashed burro banana
- 2 tbsp. date sugar
- 2 c. kamut flour or spelt

Directions

1. Place the date sugar and flour into a bowl. Whisk together.
2. Add in the mashed banana and walnut milk. Stir until combined. Remember to scrape the bowl to get all the dry mixture. Add in walnuts and zucchini. Stir well until combined.
3. Place the grapeseed oil onto a griddle and warm.
4. Pour .25 c. batter on the hot griddle. Leave it along until bubbles begin forming on to surface. Carefully turn over the pancake and cook for another 4 minutes until cooked through.
5. Place the pancakes onto a serving plate and enjoy with some agave syrup.

Nutrition

- Calories 246
- Carbohydrates 49.2 g.
- Fiber 4.6 g.
- Protein 7.8.

443. Flourless Chocolate Cake

Preparation time: 10'

Cooking time: 45'

Servings: 6

Ingredients
- 1/2 c of stevia
- 12 oz of unsweetened baking chocolate
- 2/3 c of ghee
- 1/3 c of warm water
- 1/4 tsp of salt
- 4 large pastured eggs
- 2 c of boiling water

Directions
1. Line the bottom of a 9-in. pan of a spring form with a parchment paper.
2. Heat the water in a small pot; then add the salt and the stevia over the water until the mixture becomes completely dissolved.
3. Melt the baking chocolate into a double boiler or simply microwave it for about 30 seconds.
4. Mix the melted chocolate and the butter in a large bowl with an electric mixer.
5. Beat in your hot mixture; then crack in the egg and whisk after adding each of the eggs.
6. Pour the obtained mixture into your prepared spring-form tray.
7. Wrap the spring-form tray with a foil paper.
8. Place the spring-form tray in a large cake tray and add boiling water right to the outside; make sure the depth doesn't exceed 1 in.
9. Bake the cake into the water bath for about 45 minutes at a temperature of about 350 °F.
10. Remove the tray from the boiling water and transfer to a wire to cool.
11. Let the cake chill for an overnight in the refrigerator.
12. Serve and enjoy your delicious cake!

Nutrition
- Calories 295
- Fat 26 g.
- Carbohydrates 6 g.
- Fiber 4 g.
- Protein 8 g.

444. Raspberry Cake with White Chocolate Sauce

Preparation time: 15'

Cooking time: 60'

Servings: 6

Ingredients

- 5 oz of melted cacao butter
- 2 oz of grass-fed ghee
- 1/2 c of coconut cream
- 1 c of green banana flour
- 3 tsps of pure vanilla
- 4 large eggs
- 1/2 c of Lakanto Monk Fruit
- 1 tsp of baking powder
- 2 tsps of apple cider vinegar
- 2 c of raspberries

For the White Chocolate Sauce
- 3 1/2 oz of cacao butter
- 1/2 c of coconut cream
- 2 tsps of pure vanilla extract
- 1 pinch of salt

Directions

1. Preheat your oven to a temperature of about 280 °Fahrenheit.
2. Combine the green banana flour with the pure vanilla extract, the baking powder, the coconut cream, the eggs, the cider vinegar, and the monk fruit and mix very well.
3. Leave the raspberries aside and line a cake loaf tin with a baking paper.
4. Pour in the batter into the baking tray and scatter the raspberries over the top of the cake.
5. Place the tray in your oven and bake it for about 60 minutes; in the meantime, prepare the sauce.
6. To make the sauce: Combine the coconut cream, the vanilla extract, the cacao butter, and the salt in a saucepan over a low heat.
7. Mix all your ingredients with a fork to make sure the cacao butter mixes very well with the cream.
8. Remove from the heat and set aside to cool a little bit; but don't let it harden.
9. Drizzle with the chocolate sauce.
10. Scatter the cake with more raspberries.
11. Slice your cake; then serve and enjoy it!

Nutrition

- Calories 323
- Fat 31.5 g.
- Carbohydrates 9.9 g.
- Fiber 4 g.
- Protein 5 g.

445. Ketogenic Lava Cake

Preparation time: 10'
Cooking time: 10'
Servings: 2

Ingredients

- 2 oz of dark chocolate; you should, at least, use chocolate of 85 % cocoa solids
- 1 tbsp of super-fine almond flour
- 2 oz of unsalted almond butter
- 2 large eggs
- Pomegranate seeds

Directions

1. Heat your oven to a temperature of about 350 °F.
2. Grease 2 heat proof ramekins with almond butter.
3. Now, melt the chocolate and the almond butter and stir very well.
4. Beat the eggs very well with a mixer.
5. Add the eggs to the chocolate and the butter mixture and mix very well with almond flour and the swerve; then stir.
6. Pour the dough into 2 ramekins.
7. Bake for about 9-10 minutes.
8. Turn the cakes over plates and serve with pomegranate seeds!

Nutrition

- Calories 459
- Fat 39 g.
- Carbohydrates 3.5 g.
- Fiber 0.8 g.
- Protein 11.7 g.

446. Ketogenic Cheese Cake

284
Preparation time: 15'
Cooking time: 50'
Servings: 6

Ingredients

For the Almond Flour Cheesecake Crust
- 2 c of blanched almond flour
- 1/3 c of almond butter
- 3 tbsps of erythritol (powdered or granular)
- 1 tsp of vanilla extract

For the Keto Cheesecake Filling
- 32 oz of softened cream cheese
- 1 1/4 c of powdered erythritol
- 3 large eggs
- 1 tbsp of lemon juice
- 1 tsp of vanilla extract

Directions

1. Preheat your oven to a temperature of about 350 °F.
2. Grease a spring form pan of 9 in. with cooking spray or just line its bottom with a parchment paper.
3. In order to make the cheesecake rust, stir in the melted butter, the almond flour, the vanilla extract, and the erythritol in a large bowl.
4. The dough will be a bit crumbly; so, press it into the bottom of your prepared tray.
5. Bake for about 12 minutes; then let cool for about 10 minutes.
6. In the meantime, beat the softened cream cheese and the powdered sweetener at a low speed until it becomes smooth.
7. Crack in the eggs and beat them in at a low to medium speed until it becomes fluffy. Make sure to add one a time.
8. Add in the lemon juice and the vanilla extract and mix at a low to medium speed with a mixer.
9. Pour your filling into your pan right on top of the crust. You can use a spatula to smooth the top of the cake.
10. Bake for about 45-50 minutes.
11. Remove the baked cheesecake from your oven and run a knife around its edge.
12. Let the cake cool for about 4 hours in the refrigerator.
13. Serve and enjoy your delicious cheese cake!

Nutrition

- Calories 325
- Fat 29 g.
- Carbohydrates 6 g.
- Fiber 1 g.
- Protein 7 g.

447. Cake with Whipped Cream Icing

PREPARATION TIME: 20'

COOKING TIME: 25'

SERVINGS: 7

Ingredients

- 3/4 c. coconut flour
- 3/4 c of swerve sweetener
- 1/2 c of cocoa powder
- 2 tsps of baking powder
- 6 large eggs
- 2/3 c of heavy whipping cream
- 1/2 c of melted almond butter
- For the Whipped Cream Icing
- 1 c of heavy whipping cream
- 1/4 c of swerve sweetener
- 1 tsp of vanilla extract
- 1/3 c of sifted cocoa powder

Directions

1. Pre-heat your oven to a temperature of about 350 °F.
2. Grease an 8x8 cake tray with cooking spray.
3. Add the coconut flour, the Swerve sweetener; the cocoa powder, the baking powder, the eggs, the melted butter; and combine very well with an electric or a hand mixer.
4. Pour your batter into the cake tray and bake for about 25 minutes.
5. Remove the cake tray from the oven and let cool for about 5 minutes.
6. For the icing: Whip the cream until it becomes fluffy; then add in the Swerve, the vanilla, and the cocoa powder.
7. Add the Swerve, the vanilla and the cocoa powder; then continue mixing until your ingredients are very well combined.
8. Frost your baked cake with the icing; then slice it; serve, and enjoy your delicious cake!

Nutrition

- Calories 357
- Fat 33 g.
- Carbohydrates 11 g.
- Fiber 2 g.
- Protein 8 g.

448. Walnut-Fruit Cake

PREPARATION TIME: **15'**

COOKING TIME: **20'**

SERVINGS: **6**

Ingredients

- 1/2 c of almond butter, softened
- 1/4 c of granulated erythritol
- 1 tbsp of ground cinnamon
- 1/2 tsp of ground nutmeg
- 1/4 tsp of ground cloves
- 4 large pastured eggs
- 1 tsp of vanilla extract
- 1/2 tsp of almond extract
- 2 c of almond flour
- 1/2 c of chopped walnuts
- 1/4 c of dried of unsweetened cranberries
- 1/4 c of seedless raisins

Directions

1. Preheat your oven to a temperature of about 350 °F and grease an 8-in. baking tin of round shape with almond butter.
2. Beat the granulated erythritol on a high speed until it becomes fluffy.
3. Add the cinnamon, the nutmeg, and the cloves; then blend your ingredients until they become smooth.
4. Crack in the eggs and beat very well by adding one at a time, plus the almond extract and the vanilla.
5. Whisk in the almond flour until it forms a smooth batter then fold in the nuts and the fruit.
6. Spread your mixture into your prepared baking pan and bake it for about 20 minutes.
7. Remove the cake from the oven and let cool for about 5 minutes.
8. Dust the cake with the powdered erythritol.
9. Serve and enjoy your cake!

Nutrition

- Calories 192
- Total Fat 17.44 g.
- Saturated Fat 11.5 g.
- Cholesterol 125 mg
- Total Carbohydrates 2.2 g.
- Sugar 1.4 g.
- Fiber 2.1 g.
- Sodium 135 mg
- Protein 4.7 g.

449. Ginger Cake

Preparation time: 15'
Cooking time: 20'
Servings: 9

Ingredients

- 1/2 tbsp of unsalted almond butter to grease the pan
- 4 Large eggs
- 1/4 c. coconut milk
- 2 tbsps of unsalted almond butter
- 1 and 1/2 tsps of stevia
- 1 tbsp of ground cinnamon
- 1 tbsp of natural and unsweetened cocoa powder
- 1 tbsp of fresh ground ginger
- 1/2 tsp of kosher salt
- 1 1/2 c of blanched almond flour
- 1/2 tsp of baking soda

Directions

1. 1/2 tbsp of unsalted almond butter to grease the pan
2. 4 Large eggs
3. 1/4 c. coconut milk
4. 2 tbsps of unsalted almond butter
5. 1 and 1/2 tsps of stevia
6. 1 tbsp of ground cinnamon
7. 1 tbsp of natural and unsweetened cocoa powder
8. 1 tbsp of fresh ground ginger
9. 1/2 tsp of kosher salt
10. 1 1/2 c of blanched almond flour
11. 1/2 tsp of baking soda

Nutrition

- Calories 175
- Fat 15 g.
- Carbohydrates 5 g.
- Fiber 1.9 g.
- Protein 5 g.

450. Ketogenic Orange Cake

Preparation time: 10'
Cooking time: 50'
Servings: 8

Ingredients

- 2 1/2 c of almond flour
- 2 washed oranges
- 5 large eggs, separated
- 1 tsp of baking powder
- 2 tsps of orange extract
- 1 tsp of vanilla bean powder
- 6 seeds of cardamom pods crushed
- 16 drops of liquid stevia; about 3 tsps.
- 1 handful of flaked almonds to decorate

Directions

1. Preheat your oven to a temperature of about 350 °F.
2. Line a rectangular bread baking tray with a parchment paper.
3. Place the oranges into a pan filled with cold water and cover it with a lid.
4. Bring the saucepan to a boil, then let simmer for about 1 hour and make sure the oranges are totally submerged.
5. Make sure the oranges are always submerged to remove any taste of bitterness.
6. Cut the oranges into halves; then remove any seeds; and drain the water and set the oranges aside to cool down.
7. Cut the oranges in half, then puree it with a blender or a food processor.
8. Separate the eggs; then whisk the egg whites until you see stiff peaks forming.
9. Add all your ingredients except for the egg whites to the orange mixture. Next, add in the egg whites; then mix.
10. Pour the batter into the cake tin and sprinkle with the flaked almonds right on top.
11. Bake your cake for about 50 minutes.
12. Remove the cake from the oven and set aside to cool for 5 minutes.
13. Slice your cake; then serve and enjoy its incredible taste!

Nutrition

- Calories 164
- Fat 12 g.
- Carbohydrates 7.1
- Fiber 2.7 g.
- Protein 10.9 g.

451. Lemon Cake

PREPARATION TIME: **20'**

COOKING TIME: **20'**

SERVINGS: **6**

Ingredients

- 2 medium lemons
- 4 large eggs
- 2 tbsps of almond butter
- 2 tbsps of avocado oil
- 1/3 c of coconut flour
- 4-5 tbsps of honey (or another sweetener of your choice)
- 1/2 tbsp of baking soda

Directions

1. Preheat your oven to a temperature of about 350 °F.
2. Crack the eggs in a large bowl and set 2 egg whites aside.
3. Whisk the 2 eggs whites with the egg yolks, the honey, the oil, the almond butter, the lemon zest, and the juice and whisk very well together.
4. Combine the baking soda with the coconut flour and gradually add this dry mixture to the wet ingredients and keep whisking for a couple of minutes.
5. Beat the 2 eggs with a hand mixer and beat the egg into foam.
6. Add the white egg foam gradually to the mixture with a silicone spatula.
7. Transfer your obtained batter to the tray covered with a baking paper.
8. Bake your cake for about 20-22 minutes.
9. Let the cake cool for 5 minutes; then slice your cake.
10. Serve and enjoy your delicious cake!

Nutrition

- Calories 164
- Fat 12 g.
- Carbohydrates 7.1
- Fiber 2.7 g.
- Protein 10.9 g.

452. Cinnamon Cake

Preparation time: 15'
Cooking time: 35'
Servings: 4

Ingredients

For the Cinnamon Filling
- 3 tbsps of Swerve Sweetener
- 2 tsps of ground cinnamon

For the Cake
- 3 c of almond flour
- 3/4 c of Swerve Sweetener
- 1/4 c of unflavored whey protein powder
- 2 tsp of baking powder
- 1/2 tsp of salt
- 3 large pastured eggs
- 1/2 c. + 1 tbsp of melted coconut oil
- 1/2 tsp of vanilla extract
- 1/2 c of almond milk

For the Cream Cheese Frosting
- 3 tbsps of softened cream cheese
- 2 tbsps of powdered erythritol sweetener
- 1 tbsp of coconut heavy whipping cream
- 1/2 tsp of vanilla extract

Directions

1. Preheat your oven to a temperature of about 325 F and grease a baking tray of 8x8 in.
2. For the filling, mix the Swerve and the cinnamon in a mixing bowl and mix very well; then set it aside.
3. For the preparation of the cake; whisk all together the almond flour, the sweetener, the protein powder, the baking powder, and the salt in a mixing bowl.
4. Add in the eggs, the melted coconut oil and the vanilla extract and mix very well.
5. Add in the almond milk and keep stirring until your ingredients are very well combined.
6. Spread about half of the batter in the prepared pan; then sprinkle with about two thirds of the filling mixture.
7. Spread the remaining mixture of the batter over the filling and smooth it with a spatula.
8. Bake for about 35 minutes in the oven.
9. Brush with the melted coconut oil and sprinkle with the remaining cinnamon filling.
10. Prepare the frosting by beating the cream cheese, the powdered erythritol, the cream and the vanilla extract in a mixing bowl until it becomes smooth.
11. Drizzle the frost over the cooled cake.
12. Slice the cake; then serve and enjoy!

Nutrition

- Calories 222
- Fat 19.2 g.
- Carbohydrates 5.4 g.
- Fiber 1.5 g.
- Protein 7.3 g.

453. Banana Nut Muffins

PREPARATION TIME: 5'

COOKING TIME: 1 HOUR

SERVINGS: 6

Ingredients

Dry Ingredients:
- 1 1/2 c of spell or teff flour
- 1/2 tsp of pure sea salt
- 3/4 c of date syrup

Wet Ingredients:
- 2 medium blend burro bananas
- 1/4 c of grape seed oil
- 3/4 c of homemade walnut milk
- 1 tbsp of key lime juice

Filling Ingredients:
- 1/2 c of chopped walnuts (plus extra for decorating)
- 1 chopped burro banana

Directions

1. Preheat your oven to 400 °F.
2. Take a muffin tray and grease 12 c. or line with cupcake liners.
3. Put all the dry ingredients in a large bowl and mix them thoroughly.
4. Add all the wet ingredients to a separate, smaller bowl and mix well with the bananas.
5. Mix the ingredients from the two bowls in one large container. Be careful not to over mix.
6. Add the filling ingredients and fold in gently.
7. Pour the muffin batter into the 12 prepared muffin cups and garnish with walnuts.
8. Bake it for 22-26 minutes until golden brown.
9. Allow to cool for 10 minutes.
10. Serve and enjoy your Banana Nut Muffins!

Nutrition

- Calories 150
- Fat 10 g.
- Carbohydrates 30 g.
- Protein 2.4 g.
- Fiber 2 g.

454. Mango Nut Cheesecake

PREPARATION TIME: 20'

COOKING TIME: 4H 30'

SERVINGS: 8

Ingredients

For the Filling:
- 2 c of Brazil nuts
- 5-6 dates
- 1 tbsp of sea moss gel
- 1/4 c of agave syrup
- 1/4 tsp of pure sea salt
- 2 tbsps of lime juice
- 1 1/2 c of homemade walnut milk

For the Crust:
- 1 1/2 c of quartered dates
- 1/4 c of agave syrup
- 1 1/2 c of coconut flakes
- 1/4 tsp of pure sea salt

For the Topping
- Sliced mango
- Sliced strawberries

Directions

1. Put all the crust ingredients, in a food processor and blend for 30 seconds.
2. With parchment paper, cover a baking tray and spread out the blended crust ingredients.
3. Put the sliced mango across the crust and freeze for 10 minutes.
4. Mix all the filling ingredients, using a blender until it becomes smooth
5. Pour the filling above the crust, cover with foil or parchment paper and let it stand for about 3-4 hours in the refrigerator.
6. Take out from the baking form and garnish with the toppings.
7. Serve and enjoy your Mango Nut Cheesecake!

Nutrition

- Calories 53
- Fat 0.7 g.
- Carbohydrates 15 g.

455. Blackberry Jam

PREPARATION TIME: 5'

COOKING TIME: 4H 30'

SERVINGS: 1 c.

Ingredients

- 3/4 c of blackberries
- 1 tbsp of key lime juice
- 3 tbsps of agave syrup
- 1/4 c of sea moss gel + extra 2 tbsps

Directions

1. Put the rinsed blackberries into a medium pot and cook on medium heat.
2. Stir the blackberries until the liquid appears.
3. Once the berries soften, use your immersion blender to chop up any large pieces. If you don't have a blender put the mixture in a food processor, mix it well, and then return to the pot.
4. Add sea moss gel, key lime juice, and agave syrup to the blended mixture. Boil on medium heat and stir well until it becomes thick.
5. Remove from the heat and leave it to cool for 10 minutes.
6. Serve it with bread pieces or flatbread.
7. Enjoy your Blackberry Jam!

Nutrition

- Calories 43
- Fat 0.5 g.
- Carbohydrates 13 g.

456. Blackberry Bars

PREPARATION TIME: 5'

COOKING TIME: 1H 20'

SERVINGS: 4

Ingredients

- 3 burro bananas or 4 baby bananas
- 1 c of spelt flour
- 2 c of quinoa flakes
- 1/4 c of agave syrup
- 1/4 tsp of pure sea salt
- 1/2 c of grape seed oil
- 1 c of prepared blackberry jam

Directions

1. Preheat your oven to 350 °F.
2. Remove the skin of bananas and mash with a fork in a large bowl.
3. Combine agave syrup, salt, and grape seed oil with the blend and mix well.
4. Add spelt flour and quinoa flakes. Knead the dough until it becomes sticky to your fingers.
5. Cover a 9x9-in. Baking pan with parchment paper.
6. Take 2/3 of the dough and smooth it out over the parchment pan with your fingers.
7. Spread blackberry jam over the dough.
8. Crumble the remainder dough and sprinkle on the top.
9. Bake for 20 minutes.
10. Remove from the oven and let it cool for at 10-15 minutes.
11. Cut into small pieces.
12. Serve and enjoy your Blackberry Bars!

Nutrition

- Calories 43
- Fat 0.5 g.
- Carbohydrates 10 g.
- Protein 1.4 g.
- Fiber 5 g.

457. Detox Berry Smoothie

PREPARATION TIME: **15'**

COOKING TIME: **0'**

SERVINGS: **1**

Ingredients

- Spring water
- 1/4 avocado, pitted
- 1 medium burro banana
- 1 Seville orange
- 2 c of fresh lettuce
- 1 tbsp of hemp seeds
- 1 c of berries (blueberries or an aggregate of blueberries, strawberries, and raspberries)

Directions

1. Add the spring water to your blender.
2. Put the fruits and vegies right inside the blender.
3. Blend all the ingredients till smooth.

Nutrition

- Calories 202.4
- Fat 4.5 g.
- Carbohydrates 32.9 g.
- Protein 13.3 g.

Chapter 16: Smoothies and Juice

458. Dandelion Avocado Smoothie

PREPARATION TIME: **15'**

COOKING TIME: **0'**

SERVINGS: **1**

Ingredients

- 1 c of dandelion
- 1 orange, juiced
- Coconut water
- 1 avocado
- 1 key lime, juiced

Directions

1. In a high-speed blender until smooth, blend the ingredients.

Nutrition

- Calories 160
- Fat 15 g.
- Carbohydrates 9 g.
- Protein 2 g.

459. Amaranth Greens and Avocado Smoothie

PREPARATION TIME: **15'**

COOKING TIME: **0'**

SERVINGS: **1**

Ingredients

- 1 key lime, juice
- 2 sliced apples, seeded
- 1/2 avocado
- 2 cupsful of amaranth greens
- 2 cupsful of watercress
- 1 cupful of water

Directions

1. Add the whole recipes together and transfer them into the blender. Blend thoroughly until smooth.

Nutrition

- Calories 160
- Fat 15 g.
- Carbohydrates 9 g.
- Protein 2 g

460. Lettuce, Orange, and Banana Smoothie

PREPARATION TIME: 15'
COOKING TIME: 0'
SERVINGS: 1

Ingredients

- 1 and a half cupsful of fresh lettuce
- 1 large banana
- 1 cup of mixed berries of your choice
- 1 juiced orange

Directions

1. First, add the orange juice to your blender.
2. Add the remaining ingredients and blend thoroughly.
3. Enjoy!

Nutrition

- Calories 252.1
- Protein 4.1 g.

461. Delicious Elderberry Smoothie

PREPARATION TIME: 15'
COOKING TIME: 0'
SERVINGS: 1

Ingredients

- 1 cupful of Elderberry
- 1 cupful of Cucumber
- 1 large apple
- 1/4 cupful of water

Directions

1. Add the whole ingredients together into a blender. Grind very well until they are uniformly smooth and enjoy.

Nutrition

- Calories 106
- Carbohydrates 26.68 g.

462. Peaches Zucchini Smoothie

PREPARATION TIME: **15'**

COOKING TIME: **0'**

SERVINGS: **1**

Ingredients

- 1/2 cupful of squash.
- 1/2 cupful of peaches
- 1/4 cupful of coconut water
- 1/2 cupful of zucchini

Directions

1. Add the whole ingredients together into a blender and blend until smooth and serve.

Nutrition

- Calories 55
- Fat 0 g.
- Protein 2 g.
- Sodium 10 mg.
- Carbohydrate 14 g.
- Fiber 2 g.

463. Ginger Orange and Strawberry Smoothie

PREPARATION TIME: **15'**

COOKING TIME: **0'**

SERVINGS: **1**

Ingredients

- 1 c of strawberry
- 1 large orange, juice
- 1 large banana
- 1/4 small sized ginger, peeled and sliced
- Water

Directions

1. Transfer the orange juice to a clean blender.
2. Add the remaining ingredients and blend thoroughly until smooth.
3. Enjoy!

Nutrition

- Calories 32
- Fat 0.3 g.
- Protein 2 g.
- Sodium 10 mg.
- Carbohydrate 14 g.
- Fiber 2 g.

464. Kale Parsley and Chia Seeds Detox Smoothie

Preparation time: 15
Cooking time: 0'
Servings: 1

Ingredients

- 3 tbsp. chia seeds, grounded
- 1 cupful of water
- 1 sliced banana
- 1 pear, chopped
- 1 cupful of organic kale
- 1 cupful of parsley
- Two tbsp of lemon juice.
- A dash of cinnamon.

Directions

1. Add the whole ingredients together into a blender and pour the water before blending. Blend at high speed until smooth and enjoy. You may or may not place it in the refrigerator depending on how hot or cold the weather appears.

Nutrition

- Calories 75
- Fat 1 g.
- Protein 5 g.
- Fiber 10 g.

465. Watermelon Lemonade

Preparation time: 5'
Cooking time: 0'
Servings: 6

Ingredients

- 4 c. diced watermelon
- 4 c. cold water
- 2 tbsps freshly squeezed lemon juice
- 1 tbsp. freshly squeezed lime juice

Directions

1. In a blender, combine the watermelon, water, lemon juice, and lime juice, and blend for 1 minute.
2. Strain the contents through a fine-mesh sieve or nut-milk bag. Serve chilled. Store in the refrigerator for up to 3 days.
3. Serving tip: Slice up a few lemon or lime wedges to serve with your Watermelon Lemonade, or top it with a few fresh mint leaves to give it an extra-crisp, minty flavor.

Nutrition

- Calories 60

466. Bubbly Orange Soda

PREPARATION TIME: 5'

COOKING TIME: 0'

SERVINGS: 4

Ingredients

- 4 c. carbonated water
- 2 c. pulp-free orange juice (4 oranges, freshly squeezed and strained)

Directions

1. For each serving, pour 2 parts carbonated water and 1-part orange juice over ice right before serving.
2. Stir and enjoy.
3. Serving tip: This recipe is best made right before drinking. The amount of fizz in the carbonated water will decrease the longer it's open, so if you're going to make it ahead of time, make sure it's stored in an airtight, refrigerator-safe container.

Nutrition

- Calories 56

467. Creamy Cashew Milk

PREPARATION TIME: 5'

COOKING TIME: 0'

SERVINGS: 8

Ingredients

- 4 c. water
- 1/4 c. raw cashews, soaked overnight

Directions

1. In a blender, blend the water and cashews on high speed for 2 minutes.
2. Strain with a nut-milk bag or cheesecloth, then store in the refrigerator for up to 5 days.
3. Variation tip: This recipe makes unsweetened cashew milk that can be used in savory and sweet dishes. For a creamier version to put in your coffee, cut the amount of water in half. For a sweeter version, add 1-2 tbsps maple syrup and 1 tsp. vanilla extract before blending.

Nutrition

- Calories 18

468. Homemade Oat Milk

Preparation time: 5'

Cooking time: 0'

Servings: 8

Ingredients

- 1 c. rolled oats
- 4 c. water

Directions

1. Put the oats in a medium bowl, and cover with cold water. Soak for 15 minutes, then drain and rinse the oats.
2. Pour the cold water and the soaked oats into a blender. Blend for 60-90 seconds, or just until the mixture is a creamy white color throughout. (Blending any further may over blend the oats, resulting in a gummy milk.)
3. Strain through a nut-milk bag or colander, then store in the refrigerator for up to 5 days.
4. Variation tip: This recipe can easily be made into chocolate oat milk. Once you've strained the oat milk, return it to a blender with 3 tbsps cocoa powder, 2 tbsps maple syrup, and 1 tsp. vanilla extract, then blend for 30 seconds.

Nutrition

- Calories 39

469. Lucky Mint Smoothie

Preparation time: 5'

Cooking time: 0'

Servings: 2

Ingredients

- 2 c. plant-based milk
- 2 frozen bananas, halved
- 1 tbsp. fresh mint leaves or 1/4 tsp. peppermint extract
- 1 tsp. vanilla extract

Directions

1. In a blender, combine the milk, bananas, mint, and vanilla. Blend on high for 1-2 minutes, or until the contents reach a smooth and creamy consistency, and serve.
2. Variation tip: If you like to sneak greens into smoothies, add a cup or two of spinach to boost the health benefits of this smoothie and give it an even greener appearance.

Nutrition

- Calories 152

470. Paradise Island Smoothie

PREPARATION TIME: 5'

COOKING TIME: 0'

SERVINGS: 2

Ingredients

- 2 c. plant-based milk
- 1 frozen banana
- 1/2 c. frozen mango chunks
- 1/2 c. frozen pineapple chunks
- 1 tsp. vanilla extract

Directions

1. In a blender, combine the milk, banana, mango, pineapple, and vanilla. Blend on high for 1-2 minutes, or until the contents reach a smooth and creamy consistency, and serve.
2. Leftover tip: If you have any leftover smoothie, you can put it in a jar with some rolled oats and allow the mixture to soak in the refrigerator overnight to create a tropical version of overnight oats.

Nutrition

- Calories 176

471. Apple Pie Smoothie

PREPARATION TIME: 5'

COOKING TIME: 0'

SERVINGS: 2

Ingredients

This smoothie is great for a quick breakfast or a cool dessert. Its combination of sweet apples and warming cinnamon is sure to win over children and adults alike. If the holidays find you in a warm area, this smoothie may just be the cool treat you've been looking for to take the place of pie at dessert time.

- 2 sweet crisp apples, cut into 1-in. cubes
- 2 c. plant-based milk
- 1 c. ice
- 1 tbsp. maple syrup
- 1 tsp. ground cinnamon
- 1 tsp. vanilla extract

Directions

1. In a blender, combine the apples, milk, ice, maple syrup, cinnamon, and vanilla. Blend on high for 1-2 minutes, or until the contents reach a smooth and creamy consistency, and serve.
2. Variation tip: You can also use this recipe for making overnight oatmeal. Blend your smoothie, mix it with 2 c. rolled oats, and refrigerate overnight for a premade breakfast for two.

Nutrition

- Calories 198

472. Choco-Nut Milkshake

Preparation time: 10'

Cooking time: 0'

Servings: 2

Ingredients

- 2 c. unsweetened coconut, almond
- 1 banana, sliced and frozen
- 1/4 c. unsweetened coconut flakes
- 1 c. ice cubes
- 1/4 c. macadamia nuts, chopped
- 3 tbsps sugar-free sweetener
- 2 tbsps raw unsweetened cocoa powder
- Whipped coconut cream

Directions

1. Place all ingredients into a blender and blend on high until smooth and creamy.
2. Divide evenly between 4 "mocktail" glasses and top with whipped coconut cream, if desired.
3. Add a cocktail umbrella and toasted coconut for added flair.
4. Enjoy your delicious Choco-Nut Smoothie!

Nutrition

- Carbohydrates 12 g.
- Protein 3 g.
- Calories 199

473. Pineapple and Strawberry Smoothie

Preparation time: 7'

Cooking time: 0'

Servings: 2

Ingredients

- 1 c. strawberries
- 1 c. pineapple, chopped
- 3/4 c. almond milk
- 1 tbsp. almond butter

Directions

1. Add all ingredients to a blender.
2. Blend until smooth.
3. Add more almond milk until it reaches your desired consistency.
4. Chill before serving.

Nutrition

- Calories 255
- Carbohydrate 39 g.
- Protein 5.6 g.

474. Cantaloupe Smoothie

PREPARATION TIME: **11'**

COOKING TIME: **0'**

SERVINGS: **2**

Ingredients

- 3/4 c. carrot juice
- 4 c. cantaloupe, sliced into cubes
- Pinch of salt
- Frozen melon balls
- Fresh basil

Directions

1. Add the carrot juice and cantaloupe cubes to a blender. Sprinkle with salt.
2. Process until smooth.
3. Transfer to a bowl.
4. Chill in the refrigerator for at least 30 minutes.
5. Top with the frozen melon balls and basil before serving.

Nutrition

- Calories 135
- Carbohydrate 31 g.
- Protein 3.4 g.

475. Berry Smoothie with Mint

PREPARATION TIME: **7'**

COOKING TIME: **0'**

SERVINGS: **2**

Ingredients

- 1/4 c. orange juice
- 1/2 c. blueberries
- 1/2 c. blackberries
- 1 c. reduced-fat plain kefir
- 1 tbsp. honey
- 2 tbsps fresh mint leaves

Directions

1. Add all the ingredients to a blender.
2. Blend until smooth.

Nutrition

- Calories 137
- Carbohydrate 27 g.
- Protein 6 g.

476. Green Smoothie

Preparation time: 12'
Cooking time: 0'
Servings: 2

Ingredients

- 1 c. vanilla almond milk, unsweetened
- 1/4 ripe avocado, chopped
- 1 c. kale, chopped
- 1 banana
- 2 tsps. honey
- 1 tbsp. chia seeds
- 1 c. ice cubes

Directions

1. Combine all the ingredients in a blender.
2. Process until creamy.

Nutrition

- Calories 343
- Carbohydrate 14.7 g.
- Protein 5.9 g.

477. Banana, Cauliflower, and Berry Smoothie

Preparation time: 9'
Cooking time: 0'
Servings: 2

Ingredients

- 2 c. almond milk, unsweetened
- 1 c. banana, sliced
- 1/2 c. blueberries
- 1/2 c. blackberries
- 1 c. cauliflower rice
- 2 tsps. maple syrup

Directions

1. Pour almond milk into a blender.
2. Stir in the rest of the ingredients.
3. Process until smooth.
4. Chill before serving.

Nutrition

- Calories 149
- Carbohydrate 29 g.
- Protein 3 g.

478. Berry and Spinach Smoothie

PREPARATION TIME: **11'**

COOKING TIME: **0'**

SERVINGS: **2**

Ingredients

- 2 c. strawberries
- 1 c. raspberries
- 1 c. blueberries
- 1 c. fresh baby spinach leaves
- 1 c. pomegranate juice
- 3 tbsps milk powder, unsweetened

Directions

1. Mix all the ingredients in a blender.
2. Blend until smooth.
3. Chill before serving.

Nutrition

- Calories 118
- Carbohydrate 25.7 g.
- Protein 4.6 g.

479. Peanut Butter Smoothie with Blueberries

PREPARATION TIME: **12'**

COOKING TIME: **0'**

SERVINGS: **2**

Ingredients

- 2 tbsps creamy peanut butter
- 1 c. vanilla almond milk, unsweetened
- 6 oz. soft silken tofu
- 1/2 c. grape juice
- 1 c. blueberries
- Crushed ice

Directions

1. Mix all the ingredients in a blender.
2. Process until smooth.

Nutrition

- Calories 247
- Carbohydrate 30 g.
- Protein 10.7 g.

480. Peach and Apricot Smoothie

Preparation time: 11'
Cooking time: 0'
Servings: 2

Ingredients

- 1 c. almond milk, unsweetened
- 1 tsp. honey
- 1/2 c. apricots, sliced
- 1/2 c. peaches, sliced
- 1/2 c. carrot, chopped
- 1 tsp. vanilla extract

Directions

1. Mix milk and honey.
2. Pour into a blender.
3. Add the apricots, peaches, and carrots.
4. Stir in the vanilla.
5. Blend until smooth.

Nutrition

- Calories 153
- Carbohydrate 30 g.
- Protein 32.6 g.

481. Tropical Smoothie

Preparation time: 8'
Cooking time: 0'
Servings: 2

Ingredients

- 1 banana, sliced
- 1 c. mango, sliced
- 1 c. pineapple, sliced
- 1 c. peaches, sliced
- 6 oz. nonfat coconut yogurt
- Pineapple wedges

Directions

1. Freeze the fruit slices for 1 hour.
2. Transfer to a blender.
3. Stir in the rest of the ingredients except pineapple wedges.
4. Process until smooth.
5. Garnish with pineapple wedges.

Nutrition

- Calories 102
- Carbohydrate 22.6 g.
- Protein 2.5 g.

482. Banana and Strawberry Smoothie

PREPARATION TIME: **7'**

COOKING TIME: **0'**

SERVINGS: **2**

Ingredients

- 1 banana, sliced
- 4 c. fresh strawberries, sliced
- 1 c. ice cubes
- 6 oz. yogurt
- 1 kiwi fruit, sliced

Directions

1. Add banana, strawberries, ice cubes, and yogurt in a blender.
2. Blend until smooth.
3. Garnish with kiwi fruit slices and serve.

Nutrition

- Add banana, strawberries, ice cubes, and yogurt in a blender.
- Blend until smooth.
- Garnish with kiwi fruit slices and serve.

483. Cantaloupe and Papaya Smoothie

PREPARATION TIME: **9'**

COOKING TIME: **0'**

SERVINGS: **2**

Ingredients

- 3/4 c. low-fat milk
- 1/2 c. papaya, chopped
- 1/2 c. cantaloupe, chopped
- 1/2 c. mango, cubed
- 4 ice cubes
- Lime zest

Directions

1. Pour milk into a blender.
2. Add the chopped fruits and ice cubes.
3. Blend until smooth.
4. Garnish with lime zest and serve.

Nutrition

- Calories 207
- Carbohydrate 18.4 g.
- Protein 7.7 g.

484. Watermelon and Cantaloupe Smoothie

Preparation time: 10'

Cooking time: 0'

Servings: 2

Ingredients

- 2 c. watermelon, sliced
- 1 c. cantaloupe, sliced
- 1/2 c. nonfat yogurt
- 1/4 c. orange juice

Directions

1. Add all the ingredients to a blender.
2. Blend until creamy and smooth.
3. Chill before serving.

Nutrition

- Calories 114
- Carbohydrate 13 g.
- Protein 4.8 g.

485. Raspberry and Peanut Butter Smoothie

Preparation time: 10'

Cooking time: 0'

Servings: 2

Ingredients

- 2 tbsp. peanut butter, smooth and natural
- 2 tbsp. skim milk
- 1 or 1 1/2 c. raspberries, fresh
- 1 c. ice cubes
- 2 tsp. stevia

Directions

1. Situate all the ingredients in your blender. Set the mixer to puree. Serve.

Nutrition

- Calories 170
- Fat 8.6 g.
- Carbohydrate 20 g.

486. Strawberry, Kale, and Ginger Smoothie

PREPARATION TIME: 13'

COOKING TIME: 0'

SERVINGS: 2

Ingredients

- 6 pcs. curly kale leaves, fresh and large with stems removed
- 2 tsp. grated ginger, raw and peeled
- 1/2 c. water, cold
- 3 tbsp. lime juice
- 2 tsp. honey
- 1 or 1 1/2 c. strawberries, fresh and trimmed
- 1 c. ice cubes

Directions

1. Position all the ingredients in your blender. Set to puree. Serve.

Nutrition

- Calories 205
- Fat 2.9 g.
- Carbohydrates 42.4 g.

487. Berry Mint Smoothie

PREPARATION TIME: 5'

COOKING TIME: 5'

SERVINGS: 2

Ingredients

- 1 tbsp. low-carb sweetener of your choice
- 1 c. kefir or low fat-yoghurt
- 2 tbsp. mint
- 1/4 c. orange
- 1 c. mixed berries

Directions

1. Place all of the ingredients in a high-speed blender and then blend it until smooth.
2. Transfer the smoothie to a serving glass and enjoy it.

Nutrition

- Calories 137
- Carbohydrates 11 g.
- Proteins 6 g.
- Fat 1 g.
- Sodium 64 mg.

488. Greenie Smoothie

Preparation time: 5'
Cooking time: 5'
Servings: 2

Ingredients

- 1 1/2 c. water
- 1 tsp. stevia
- 1 green apple, ripe
- 1 tsp. stevia
- 1 green pear, chopped into chunks
- 1 lime
- 2 c. kale, fresh
- 3/4 tsp. cinnamon
- 12 ice cubes
- 20 green grapes
- 1/2 c. mint, fresh

Directions

1. Pour water, kale, and pear in a high-speed blender and blend them for 2-3 minutes until mixed.
2. Stir in all the remaining ingredients into it and blend until it becomes smooth.
3. Transfer the smoothie to serving glass.

Nutrition

- Calories 123
- Carbohydrates 27 g.
- Proteins 2 g.
- Fat 2 g.
- Sodium 30 mg.

489. Coconut Spinach Smoothie

Preparation time: 5'
Cooking time: 5'
Servings: 2

Ingredients

- 1 1/4 c. coconut milk
- A bunch of spinach
- 2 ice cubes
- 2 tbsp. chia seeds
- 1 scoop of protein powder, preferably vanilla
- 1 c. spin

Directions

1. Pour coconut milk along with spinach, chia seeds, protein powder, and ice cubes in a high-speed blender.
2. Blend for 2 minutes to get a smooth and luscious smoothie.
3. Serve in a glass and enjoy it.

Nutrition

- Calories 251
- Carbohydrates 10.9 g.
- Proteins 20.3 g.
- Fat 15.1 g.
- Sodium 102 mg.

490. Oats Coffee Smoothie

PREPARATION TIME: 5'

COOKING TIME: 5'

SERVINGS: 2

Ingredients

- 1 c. oats, uncooked and grounded
- 2 tbsp. instant coffee
- 3 c. milk, skimmed
- 2 bananas, frozen and sliced into chunks
- 2 tbsp. flax seeds, grounded

Directions

1. Place all of the ingredients in a high-speed blender and blend for 2 minutes or until smooth and luscious.
2. Serve and enjoy.

Nutrition

- Place all of the ingredients in a high-speed blender and blend for 2 minutes or until smooth and luscious.
- Serve and enjoy.

491. Veggie Smoothie

PREPARATION TIME: 5'

COOKING TIME: 5'

SERVINGS: 1

Ingredients

- 1/4 of 1 red bell pepper, sliced
- 1/2 tbsp. coconut oil
- 1 c. almond milk, unsweetened
- 1/4 tsp. turmeric
- 4 strawberries, chopped
- A pinch of cinnamon
- 1/2 of 1 banana, preferably frozen

Directions

1. Combine all the ingredients required to make the smoothie in a high-speed blender.
2. Blend for 3 minutes to get a smooth and silky mixture.
3. Serve and enjoy.

Nutrition

- Calories 169
- Carbohydrates 17 g.
- Proteins 2.3 g.
- Fat 9.8 g.
- Sodium 162 mg.

492. Avocado Smoothie

Preparation time: 10'
Cooking time: 0'
Servings: 2

Ingredients

- 1 avocado, ripe and pit removed
- 2 c. baby spinach
- 2 c. water
- 1 c. baby kale
- 1 tbsp. lemon juice
- 2 sprigs of mint
- 1/2 c. ice cubes

Directions

1. Place all the ingredients needed to make the smoothie in a high-speed blender then blend until smooth.
2. Transfer to a serving glass and enjoy it.

Nutrition

- Calories 214
- Carbohydrates 15 g.
- Proteins 2 g.
- Fat 17 g.
- Sodium 25 mg.

493. Orange Carrot Smoothie

Preparation time: 5'
Cooking time: 0'
Servings: 1

Ingredients

- 1 1/2 c. almond milk
- 1/4 c. cauliflower, blanched and frozen
- 1 orange
- 1 tbsp. flax seed
- 1/3 c. carrot, grated
- 1 tsp. vanilla extract

Directions

1. Mix all the ingredients in a high-speed blender and blend for 2 minutes or until you get the desired consistency.
2. Transfer to a serving glass and enjoy it.

Nutrition

- Calories 216
- Carbohydrates 10 g.
- Proteins 15 g.
- Fat 7 g.
- Sodium 25 mg.

494. Blackberry Smoothie

Preparation time: 5'
Cooking time: 0'
Servings: 1

Ingredients

- 1 1/2 c. almond milk
- 1/4 c. cauliflower, blanched and frozen
- 1 orange
- 1 tbsp. flax seed
- 1/3 c. carrot, grated
- 1 tsp. vanilla extract

Directions

1. Place all the ingredients needed to make the blackberry smoothie in a high-speed blender and blend for 2 minutes until you get a smooth mixture.
2. Transfer to a serving glass and enjoy it.

Nutrition

- Calories 275
- Carbohydrates 9 g.
- Proteins 11 g.
- Fat 17 g.
- Sodium 73 mg.

495. Key Lime Pie Smoothie

Preparation time: 5'
Cooking time: 0'
Servings: 1

Ingredients

- 1/2 c. cottage cheese
- 1 tbsp. sweetener of your choice
- 1/2 c. water
- 1/2 c. spinach
- 1 tbsp. lime juice
- 1 c. ice cubes

Directions

1. Spoon in the ingredients to a high-speed blender and blend until silky smooth.
2. Transfer to a serving glass and enjoy it.

Nutrition

- Calories 180
- Carbohydrates 7 g.
- Proteins 36 g.
- Fat 1 g.
- Sodium 35 mg.

496. Cinnamon Roll Smoothie

Preparation time: 5'
Cooking time: 0'
Servings: 1

Ingredients

- 1 tsp. flax meal or oats, if preferred
- 1 c. almond milk
- 1/2 tsp. cinnamon
- 2 tbsp. protein powder
- 1 c. ice
- 1/4 tsp. vanilla extract
- 4 tsp. sweetener of your choice

Directions

1. Pour the milk into the blender, followed by the protein powder, sweetener, flax meal, cinnamon, vanilla extract, and ice.
2. Blend for 40 seconds or until smooth.
3. Serve and enjoy.

Nutrition

- Calories 145
- Carbohydrates 1.6 g.
- Proteins 26.5 g.
- Fat 3.25 g.
- Sodium 30 mg.

497. Strawberry Cheesecake Smoothie

Preparation time: 5'
Cooking time: 0'
Servings: 1

Ingredients

- 1/4 c. soy milk, unsweetened
- 1/2 c. cottage cheese, low-fat
- 1/2 tsp. vanilla extract
- 2 oz. cream cheese
- 1 c. ice cubes
- 1/2 c. strawberries
- 4 tbsp. low-carb sweetener of your choice

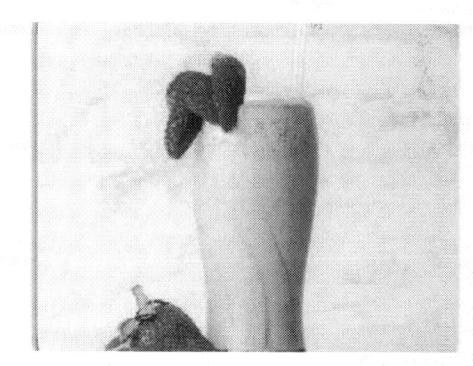

Directions

1. Add all the ingredients for making the strawberry cheesecake smoothie to a high-speed blender until you get the desired smooth consistency.
2. Serve and enjoy.

Nutrition

- Calories 347
- Carbohydrates 10.05 g.
- Proteins 17.5 g.
- Fat 24 g.
- Sodium 45 mg.

498. Peanut Butter Banana Smoothie

Preparation time: 5'
Cooking time: 2'
Servings: 1

Ingredients

- 1/4 c. Greek yoghurt, plain
- 1/2 tbsp. chia seeds
- 1/2 c. ice cubes
- 1/2 of 1 banana
- 1/2 c. water
- 1 tbsp. peanut butter

Directions

1. Place all the ingredients needed to make the smoothie in a high-speed blender and blend to get a smooth mixture.
2. Transfer the smoothie to a serving glass and enjoy it.

Nutrition

- Calories 202
- Carbohydrates 14 g.
- Proteins 10 g.
- Fat 9 g.
- Sodium 30 mg.

499. Avocado Turmeric Smoothie

Preparation time: 5'
Cooking time: 2'
Servings: 1

Ingredients

- 1/2 of 1 avocado
- 1 c. ice, crushed
- 3/4 c. coconut milk, full-fat
- 1 tsp. lemon juice
- 1/4 c. almond milk
- 1/2 tsp. turmeric
- 1 tsp. ginger, freshly grated

Directions

1. Place all the ingredients excluding the crushed ice in a high-speed blender and blend for 2-3 minutes or until smooth.
2. Transfer to a serving glass and enjoy it.

Nutrition

- Calories 232
- Carbohydrates 4.1 g.
- Proteins 1.7 g.
- Fat 22.4 g.
- Sodium 25 mg.

500. Lemon Blueberry Smoothie

PREPARATION TIME: 5'
COOKING TIME: 2'
SERVINGS: 2

Ingredients
- 1 tbsp. lemon juice
- 1 3/4 c. coconut milk, full-fat
- 1/2 tsp. vanilla extract
- 3 oz. blueberries, frozen

Directions
1. Combine coconut milk, blueberries, lemon juice, and vanilla extract in a high-speed blender.
2. Blend for 2 minutes for a smooth and luscious smoothie.
3. Serve and enjoy.

Nutrition
- Combine coconut milk, blueberries, lemon juice, and vanilla extract in a high-speed blender.
- Blend for 2 minutes for a smooth and luscious smoothie.
- Serve and enjoy.

501. Matcha Green Smoothie

PREPARATION TIME: 5'
COOKING TIME: 2'
SERVINGS: 2

Ingredients
- 1/4 c. heavy whipping cream
- 1/2 tsp. vanilla extract
- 1 tsp. matcha green tea powder
- 2 tbsp. protein powder
- 1 tbsp. hot water
- 1 1/4 c. almond milk, unsweetened
- 1/2 of 1 avocado, medium

Directions
1. Place all the ingredients in the high-blender for 1-2 minutes.
2. Serve and enjoy.

Nutrition
- Calories 229
- Carbohydrates 1.5 g.
- Proteins 14.1 g.
- Fat 43 g.
- Sodium 35 mg.

502. Blueberry Smoothie

PREPARATION TIME: **10'**

COOKING TIME: **0'**

SERVINGS: **2**

Ingredients

- 2 c. frozen blueberries
- 1 small banana
- 1 1/2 c. unsweetened almond milk
- 1/4 c. ice cubes

Directions

1. Place all the ingredients in a high-speed blender and pulse until creamy.
2. Pour the smoothie into two glasses and serve immediately.

Nutrition

- Calories 158
- Total Fat 3.3 g.
- Saturated Fat 0.3 g.
- Cholesterol 0 mg
- Sodium 137 mg
- Total Carbohydrates 34 g.
- Fiber 5.6 g.
- Sugar 20.6 g.
- Protein 2.4 g.

503. Beet and Strawberry Smoothie

PREPARATION TIME: **10'**

COOKING TIME: **0'**

SERVINGS: **2**

Ingredients

- 2 c. frozen strawberries, pitted and chopped
- 2/3 c. roasted and frozen beet, chopped
- 1 tsp. fresh ginger, peeled and grated
- 1 tsp. fresh turmeric, peeled and grated
- 1/2 c. fresh orange juice
- 1 c. unsweetened almond milk

Directions

1. Place all the ingredients in a high-speed blender and pulse until creamy.
2. Pour the smoothie into two glasses and serve immediately.

Nutrition

- Calories 258
- Total Fat 1.5 g.
- Saturated Fat 0.1 g.
- Cholesterol 0 mg
- Sodium 134 mg
- Total Carbohydrates 26.7 g.
- Fiber 4.9 g.
- Sugar 18.7 g.
- Protein 2.9 g.

504. Kiwi Smoothie

PREPARATION TIME: 10'

COOKING TIME: 0'

SERVINGS: 2

Ingredients

- 4 kiwis
- 2 small bananas, peeled
- 1 1/2 c. unsweetened almond milk
- 1-2 drops liquid stevia
- 1/4 c. ice cubes

Directions

1. Place all the ingredients in a high-speed blender and pulse until creamy.
2. Pour the smoothie into two glasses and serve immediately.

Nutrition

- Calories 228
- Total Fat 3.8 g.
- Saturated Fat 0.4 g.
- Cholesterol 0 mg
- Sodium 141 mg
- Total Carbohydrates 50.7 g.
- Fiber 8.4 g.
- Sugar 28.1 g.
- Protein 3.8 g.

505. Pineapple and Carrot Smoothie

PREPARATION TIME: 10'

COOKING TIME: 0'

SERVINGS: 2

Ingredients

- 1 c. frozen pineapple
- 1 large ripe banana, peeled and sliced
- 1/2 tbsp. fresh ginger, peeled and chopped
- 1/4 tsp. ground turmeric
- 1 c. unsweetened almond milk
- 1/2 c. fresh carrot juice
- 1 tbsp. fresh lemon juice

Directions

1. Place all the ingredients in a high-speed blender and pulse until creamy.
2. Pour the smoothie into two glasses and serve immediately.

Nutrition

- Calories 132
- Total Fat 2.2 g.
- Saturated Fat 0.3 g.
- Cholesterol 0 mg.
- Sodium 113 mg.
- Total Carbohydrates 629.3 g.
- Fiber 4.1 g.
- Sugar 16.9 g.
- Protein 2 g.

506. Oats and Orange Smoothie

Preparation Time: 10'

Cooking Time: 0'

Servings: 4

Ingredients

- 2/3 c. rolled oats
- 2 oranges, peeled, seeded, and sectioned
- 2 large bananas, peeled and sliced
- 2 c. unsweetened almond milk
- 1 c. ice cubes, crushed

Directions

1. Place all the ingredients in a high-speed blender and pulse until creamy.
2. Pour the smoothie into four glasses and serve immediately.

Nutrition

- Calories 175
- Total Fat 3 g.
- Saturated Fat 0.4 g.
- Cholesterol 0 mg.
- Sodium 93 mg.
- Total Carbohydrates 36.6 g.
- Fiber 5.9 g.
- Sugar 17.1 g.
- Protein 3.9 g.

507. Pumpkin Smoothie

Preparation Time: 10'

Cooking Time: 0'

Servings: 2

Ingredients

- 1 c. homemade pumpkin puree
- 1 medium banana, peeled and sliced
- 1 tbsp. maple syrup
- 1 tsp. ground flaxseeds
- 1/2 teaspoon ground cinnamon
- 1/4 tsp. ground ginger
- 1 1/2 c. unsweetened almond milk
- 1/4 c. ice cubes

Directions

1. Place all the ingredients in a high-speed blender and pulse until creamy.
2. Pour the smoothie into two glasses and serve immediately.

Nutrition

- Calories 159
- Total Fat 3.6 g.
- Saturated Fat 0.5 g.
- Cholesterol 0 mg
- Sodium 143 mg
- Total Carbohydrates 32.6 g.
- Fiber 6.5 g.
- Sugar 17.3 g.
- Protein 3 g.

508. Red Veggie and Fruit Smoothie

Preparation time: 10'
Cooking time: 0'
Servings: 2

Ingredients

- 1/2 c. fresh raspberries
- 1/2 c. fresh strawberries
- 1/2 red bell pepper, seeded and chopped
- 1/2 c. red cabbage, chopped
- 1 small tomato
- 1 c. water
- 1/2 c. ice cubes

Directions

1. Place all the ingredients in a high-speed blender and pulse until creamy.
2. Pour the smoothie into two glasses and serve immediately.

Nutrition

- Calories 39
- Cholesterol 0 mg.
- Saturated Fat 0 g.
- Sodium 10 mg.
- Total Carbohydrates 8.9 g.
- Fiber 3.5 g.
- Sugar 4.8 g.
- Protein 1.3 g.
- Total Fat 0.4 g.

509. Kale Smoothie

Preparation time: 10'
Cooking time: 0'
Servings: 2

Ingredients

- 3 stalks fresh kale, trimmed and chopped
- 1-2 celery stalks, chopped
- 1/2 avocado, peeled, pitted, and chopped
- 1/2-inch piece ginger root, chopped
- 1/2-inch piece turmeric root, chopped
- 2 c. coconut milk

Directions

1. Place all the ingredients in a high-speed blender and pulse until creamy.
2. Pour the smoothie into two glasses and serve immediately.

Nutrition

- Calories 248
- Total Fat 21.8 g.
- Saturated Fat 12 g.
- Cholesterol 0 mg.
- Sodium 59 mg.
- Total Carbohydrates 11.3 g.
- Fiber 4.2 g.
- Sugar 0.5 g.
- Protein 3.5 g.

510. Green Tofu Smoothie

Preparation time: 10'
Cooking time: 0'
Servings: 2

Ingredients

- 1 1/2 c. cucumber, peeled and chopped roughly
- 3 c. fresh baby spinach
- 2 c. frozen broccoli
- 1/2 c. silken tofu, drained and pressed
- 1 tbsp. fresh lime juice
- 4-5 drops liquid stevia
- 1 c. unsweetened almond milk
- 1/2 c. ice, crushed

Directions

1. Place all the ingredients in a high-speed blender and pulse until creamy.
2. Pour the smoothie into two glasses and serve immediately.

Nutrition

- Calories 118
- Total Fat 15 g.
- Saturated Fat 0.8 g.
- Cholesterol 0 mg.
- Sodium 165 mg.
- Total Carbohydrates 12.6 g.
- Fiber 4.8 g.
- Sugar 3.4 g.
- Protein 10 g.

511. Grape and Swiss Chard Smoothie

Preparation time: 10'
Cooking time: 0'
Servings: 2

Ingredients

- 2 c. seedless green grapes
- 2 c. fresh Swiss chard, trimmed and chopped
- 2 tbsps maple syrup
- 1 tsp. fresh lemon juice
- 1 1/2 c. water
- 4 ice cubes

Directions

1. Place all the ingredients in a high-speed blender and pulse until creamy.
2. Pour the smoothie into two glasses and serve immediately.

Nutrition

- Calories 176
- Total Fat 0.2 g.
- Saturated Fat 0 g.
- Cholesterol 0 mg.
- Sodium 83 mg.
- Total Carbohydrates 44.9 g.
- Fiber 1.7 g.
- Sugar 37.9 g.
- Protein 0.7 g.

512. Matcha Smoothie

PREPARATION TIME: 10'

COOKING TIME: 0'

SERVINGS: 2

Ingredients

- 2 tbsps chia seeds
- 2 tsps. matcha green tea powder
- 1/2 teaspoon fresh lemon juice
- 1/2 teaspoon xanthan gum
- 8–10 drops liquid stevia
- 4 tbsps coconut cream
- 1 1/2 c. unsweetened almond milk
- 1/4 c. ice cubes

Directions

1. Place all the ingredients in a high-speed blender and pulse until creamy.
2. Pour the smoothie into two glasses and serve immediately.

Nutrition

- Calories 132
- Total Fat 12.3 g.
- Saturated Fat 6.8 g.
- Cholesterol 0 mg.
- Sodium 15 mg.
- Total Carbohydrates 7 g.
- Fiber 4.8 g.
- Sugar 1 g.
- Protein 3 g.

513. Banana Smoothie

PREPARATION TIME: 10'

COOKING TIME: 0'

SERVINGS: 2

Ingredients

- 2 c. chilled unsweetened almond milk
- 1 large frozen banana, peeled and sliced
- 1 tbsp. almonds, chopped
- 1 tsp. organic vanilla extract

Directions

1. Place all the ingredients in a high-speed blender and pulse until creamy.
2. Pour the smoothie into two glasses and serve immediately.

Nutrition

- Calories 124
- Total Fat 5.2 g.
- Saturated Fat 0.5 g.
- Cholesterol 0 mg.
- Sodium 181 mg.
- Total Carbohydrates 18.4 g.
- Fiber 3.1 g.
- Sugar 8.7 g.
- Protein 2.4 g.

514. Strawberry Smoothie

PREPARATION TIME: **10'**

COOKING TIME: **0'**

SERVINGS: **2**

Ingredients

- 2 c. chilled unsweetened almond milk
- 1 1/2 c. frozen strawberries
- 1 banana, peeled and sliced
- 1/4 tsp. organic vanilla extract

Directions

1. Add all the ingredients in a high-speed blender and pulse until smooth.
2. Pour the smoothie into two glasses and serve immediately.

Nutrition

- Calories 131
- Total Fat 3.7 g.
- Saturated Fat 0.4 g.
- Cholesterol 0 mg.
- Sodium 181 mg.
- Total Carbohydrates 25.3 g.
- Fiber 4.8 g.
- Sugar 14 g.
- Protein 1.6 g.

515. Raspberry and Tofu Smoothie

PREPARATION TIME: **15'**

COOKING TIME: **0'**

SERVINGS: **2**

Ingredients

- 1 1/2 c. fresh raspberries
- 6 oz. firm silken tofu, drained
- 1/8 tsp. coconut extract
- 1 tsp. powdered stevia
- 1 1/2 c. unsweetened almond milk
- 1/4 c. ice cubes, crushed

Directions

1. Add all the ingredients in a high-speed blender and pulse until smooth.
2. Pour the smoothie into two glasses and serve immediately.

Nutrition

- Calories 131
- Total Fat 5.5 g.
- Saturated Fat 0.6 g.
- Cholesterol 0 mg.
- Sodium 167 mg.
- Total Carbohydrates 14.6 g.
- Fiber 6.8 g.
- Sugar 5.2 g.
- Protein 7.7 g.

516. Mango Smoothie

Preparation time: 10'
Cooking time: 0'
Servings: 2

Ingredients

- 2 c. frozen mango, peeled, pitted and chopped
- 1/4 c. almond butter
- Pinch of ground turmeric
- 2 tbsps fresh lemon juice
- 1 1/4 c. unsweetened almond milk
- 1/4 c. ice cubes

Directions

1. Add all the ingredients in a high-speed blender and pulse until smooth.
2. Pour the smoothie into two glasses and serve immediately.

Nutrition

- Calories 140
- Total Fat 4.1 g.
- Saturated Fat 0.6 g.
- Cholesterol 0 mg.
- Sodium 118 mg.
- Total Carbohydrates 26.8 g.
- Fiber 3.6 g.
- Sugar 23 g.
- Protein 2.5 g.

517. Pineapple Smoothie

Preparation time: 10'
Cooking time: 0'
Servings: 2

Ingredients

- 2 c. pineapple, chopped
- 1/2 teaspoon fresh ginger, peeled and chopped
- 1/2 teaspoon ground turmeric
- 1 tsp. natural immune support supplement
- 1 tsp. chia seeds
- 1 1/2 c. cold green tea
- 1/2 c. ice, crushed

Directions

1. Add all the ingredients in a high-speed blender and pulse until smooth.
2. Pour the smoothie into two glasses and serve immediately.

Nutrition

- Calories 152
- Total Fat 1 g.
- Saturated Fat 0 g.
- Cholesterol 0 mg.
- Sodium 9 mg.
- Total Carbohydrates 30 g.
- Fiber 3.5 g.
- Sugar 29.8 g.
- Protein 1.5 g.

518. Kale and Pineapple Smoothie

PREPARATION TIME: **15'**

COOKING TIME: **0'**

SERVINGS: **2**

Ingredients

- 1 1/2 c. fresh kale, trimmed and chopped
- 1 frozen banana, peeled and chopped
- 1/2 c. fresh pineapple chunks
- 1 c. unsweetened coconut milk
- 1/2 c. fresh orange juice
- 1/2 c. ice

Directions

1. Add all the ingredients in a high-speed blender and pulse until smooth.
2. Pour the smoothie into two glasses and serve immediately.

Nutrition

- Calories 148
- Total Fat 2.4 g.
- Saturated Fat 2.1 g.
- Cholesterol 0 mg.
- Sodium 23 mg.
- Total Carbohydrates 31.6 g.
- Fiber 3.5 g.
- Sugar 16.5 g.
- Protein 2.8 g.

519. Green Veggies Smoothie

PREPARATION TIME: **15'**

COOKING TIME: **0'**

SERVINGS: **2**

Ingredients

- 1 medium avocado, peeled, pitted, and chopped
- 1 large cucumber, peeled and chopped
- 2 fresh tomatoes, chopped
- 1 small green bell pepper, seeded and chopped
- 1 c. fresh spinach, torn
- 2 tbsps fresh lime juice
- 2 tbsps homemade vegetable broth
- 1 c. alkaline water

Directions

1. Add all the ingredients in a high-speed blender and pulse until smooth.
2. Pour the smoothie into glasses and serve immediately.

Nutrition

- Calories 275
- Total Fat 20.3 g.
- Saturated Fat 4.2 g.
- Cholesterol 0 mg.
- Sodium 76 mg
- Total Carbohydrates 24.1 g.
- Fiber 10.1 g.
- Sugar 9.3 g.
- Protein 5.3 g.

520. Avocado and Spinach Smoothie

Preparation time: 10'
Cooking time: 0'
Servings: 2

Ingredients

- 2 c. fresh baby spinach
- 1/2 avocado, peeled, pitted, and chopped
- 4–6 drops liquid stevia
- 1/2 teaspoon ground cinnamon
- 1 tbsp. hemp seeds
- 2 c. chilled alkaline water

Directions

1. Add all the ingredients in a high-speed blender and pulse until smooth.
2. Pour the smoothie into two glasses and serve immediately.

Nutrition

- Calories 132
- Total Fat 11.7 g.
- Saturated Fat 2.2 g.
- Cholesterol 0 mg.
- Sodium 27 mg.
- Total Carbohydrates 6.1 g.
- Fiber 4.5 g.
- Sugar 0.4 g.
- Protein 3.1 g.

521. Raisins-Plume Smoothie (RPS)

Preparation time: 10'
Cooking time: 0'
Servings: 1

Ingredients

- 1 tsp. raisins
- 2 sweet cherry
- 1 skinned black plume
- 1 c. Dr. Sebi's Stomach Calming Herbal Tea Powder/powdered Cuachalalate
- 1/4 coconut water

Directions

1. Flash 1 tsp of raisin in warm water for 5 seconds and drain the water completely.
2. Rinse, cube sweet cherry and skinned black plum.
3. Get 1 c of water boiled; put 3/4 Dr. Sebi's Stomach Calming Herbal Tea for 10–15 minutes.
4. If you are unable to get Dr. Sebi's Stomach Calming Herbal tea, you can alternatively, cook 1 tsp of powdered Cuachalate with 1 c of water for 5–10 minutes, remove the extract and allow it to cool.
5. Pour all the ingredients inside a blender and blend till you achieve a homogenous smoothie.
6. Enjoy!

Nutrition

- Calories 150
- Fat 1.2 g.
- Carbohydrates 79 g.
- Protein 3.1 g.

522. Nori Clove Smoothies (NCS)

Preparation Time: 10'

Cooking Time: 0'

Servings: 1

Ingredients

- 1/4 c. fresh nori
- 1 c. cubed banana
- 1 tsp. diced onion or 1/4 tsp. powdered onion
- 1/2 tsp. clove
- 1 c. Dr. Sebi Energy Booster
- 1 tbsp. agave syrup

Directions

1. Rinse the ingredients with clean water.
2. Finely chop the onion to take 1 tsp. and cut the fresh Nori.
3. Boil 1 1/2 teaspoon with 2 c of water, remove the particles, allow to cool, measure 1 c of the tea extract.
4. Pour all the ingredients inside a blender with the tea extract and blend to achieve a homogenous smoothie.
5. Transfer into a clean cup and have a nice time with a lovely body detox and energizer.

Nutrition

- Calories 78
- Fat 2.3 g.
- Carbohydrates 5 g.
- Protein 6 g.

523. Brazil Lettuce Smoothies (BLS)

Preparation Time: 10'

Cooking Time: 0'

Servings: 1

Ingredients

- 1 c. raspberries
- 1/2 handful romaine lettuce
- 1/2 c. homemade walnut milk
- 2 Brazil nuts
- 1/2 large grape with seed
- 1 c. soft jelly coconut water
- Date sugar to taste

Directions

1. In a clean bowl rinse the vegetable with clean water.
2. Chop the Romaine lettuce, cubed raspberries, and add the ingredients into the blender and blend to achieve homogenous smoothies.
3. Serve your delicious medicinal detox.

Nutrition

- Calories 168
- Fat 4.5 g.
- Carbohydrates 31.3 g.
- Sugar 19.2 g.
- Protein 3.6 g.

524. Apple-Banana Smoothie (ABS)

Preparation Time: 10'
Cooking Time: 0'
Servings: 1

Ingredients

- 1 c. cubed apple
- 1/2 burro banana
- 1/2 c. cubed mango
- 1/2 c. cubed watermelon
- 1/2 tsp. powdered onion
- 3 tbsp. key lime juice
- Date sugar to taste (if you like)

Directions

1. In a clean bowl rinse the vegetable with clean water.
2. Cubed banana, apple, mango, watermelon, and add the ingredients into the blender and blend to achieve a homogenous smoothie.
3. Serve your delicious medicinal detox.
4. Alternatively, you can add 1 tbsp of finely dices raw red onion if powdered onion is not available.

Nutrition

- Calories 99
- Fat 0.3 g.
- Carbohydrates 23 g.
- Protein 1.1 g.

525. Ginger-Pear Smoothie (GPS)

Preparation Time: 10'
Cooking Time: 0'
Servings: 2

Ingredients

- 1 big pear with seed and cured
- 1/2 avocado
- 1/4 handful watercress
- 1/2 sour orange
- 1/2 c. ginger tea
- 1/2 c. coconut water
- 1/4 c. spring water
- 2 tbsp. agave syrup
- Date sugar to taste

Directions

1. Firstly, boil 1 c of ginger tea, cover the cup, and allow it to cool to room temperature.
2. Pour all the ingredients into your clean blender and homogenize them to a smooth liquid.
3. You have just prepared yourself a wonderful Detox Romaine Smoothie.

Nutrition

- Calories 101
- Protein 1 g.
- Carbohydrates 27 g.
- Fiber 6 g.

526. Cantaloupe-Amaranth Smoothie (CAS)

Preparation time: 10'
Cooking time: 0'
Servings: 1

Ingredients

- 1/2 c. cubed cantaloupe
- 1/4 handful green amaranth
- 1/2 c. homemade hemp milk
- 1/4 tsp. Dr. Sebi's Bromide Plus Powder
- 1 c. coconut water
- 1 tsp. agave syrup

Directions

1. You will have to rinse all the ingredients with clean water.
2. Chop green amaranth, cubed cantaloupe, transfer all into a blender and blend to achieve a homogenous smoothie.
3. Pour into a clean cup; add agave syrup and homemade hemp milk.
4. Stir them together and drink.

Nutrition

- Calories 55
- Fiber 1.5 g.
- Carbohydrates 8 mg.

527. Garbanzo Squash Smoothie (GSS)

Preparation time: 10'
Cooking time: 0'
Servings: 1

Ingredients

- 1 large cubed apple
- 1 fresh tomatoes
- 1 tbsp. finely chopped fresh onion or 1/4 tsp. powdered onion
- 1/4 c. boiled garbanzo bean
- 1/2 c. coconut milk
- 1/4 cubed Mexican squash chayote
- 1 c. energy booster tea

Directions

1. You will need to rinse the ingredients with clean water.
2. Boil 1 1/2 Dr. Sebi's Energy Booster Tea with 2 c of clean water. Filter the extract, measure 1 c. and allow it to cool.
3. Cook garbanzo bean, drain the water, and allow it to cool.
4. Pour all the ingredients into a high-speed blender and blend to achieve a homogenous smoothie.
5. You may add date sugar.
6. Serve your amazing smoothie and drink.

Nutrition

- Calories 82
- Carbohydrates 22 g.
- Protein 2 g.
- Fiber 7 g.

528. Strawberry-Orange Smoothies (SOS)

Preparation time: 10'
Cooking time: 0'
Servings: 1

Ingredients

- 1 c. diced strawberries
- 1 removed back of Seville orange
- 1/4 c. cubed cucumber
- 1/4 c. Romaine lettuce
- 1/2 kelp
- 1/2 burro banana
- 1 c. soft jelly coconut water
- 1/2 c. water
- Date sugar

Directions

1. Use clean water to rinse all the vegetable the ingredients into a clean bowl.
2. Chop Romaine lettuce; dice strawberry, cucumber, and banana; remove the back of Seville orange and divide into 4.
3. Transfer all the ingredients inside a clean blender and blend to achieve a homogenous smoothie.
4. Pour into a clean big cup and fortify your body with a palatable detox.

Nutrition

- Calories 298
- Calories from Fat 9.
- Fat 1 g.
- Cholesterol 2 mg.
- Sodium 73 mg.
- Potassium 998 mg.
- Carbohydrates 68 g.
- Fiber 7 g.
- Sugar 50 g.

529. Tamarind-Pear Smoothie (TPS)

Preparation time: 10'
Cooking time: 0'
Servings: 1

Ingredients

- 1/2 burro banana
- 1/2 c. watermelon
- 1 raspberries
- 1 prickly pear
- 1 grape with seed
- 3 tamarind
- 1/2 medium cucumber
- 1 c. coconut water
- 1/2 c. distilled water

Directions

1. Use clean water to rinse all the ingredients.
2. Remove the pod of tamarind and collect the edible part around the seed into a container.
3. If you must use the seeds, then you have to boil the seed for 15 minutes and add to the tamarind edible part in the container.
4. Cubed all the other vegetable fruits and transfer all the items into a high-speed blender and blend to achieve a homogenous smoothie.

Nutrition

- Calories 199
- Carbohydrates 47 g.
- Fat 1 g.
- Protein 6 g.

530. Currant Elderberry Smoothie (CES)

Preparation time: 10'

Cooking time: 0'

Servings: 1

Ingredients

- 1/4 c. cubed elderberry
- 1 sour cherry
- 2 currant
- 1 cubed burro banana
- 1 fig
- 1c. 4 bay leaves tea
- 1 c. energy booster tea
- Date sugar to taste

Directions

1. Use clean water to rinse all the ingredients.
2. Initially boil 3/4 tsp of energy booster tea with 2 c of water on a heat source and allow boiling for 10 minutes.
3. Add 4 bay leaves and boil together for another 4 minutes.
4. Drain the tea extract into a clean big cup and allow it to cool.
5. Transfer all the ingredients into a high-speed blender and blend till you achieve a homogenous smoothie.
6. Pour the palatable medicinal smoothie into a clean cup and drink.

Nutrition

- Calories 63
- Fat 0.22 g.
- Sodium 1.1 mg.
- Carbohydrates 15.5 g.
- Fiber 4.8 g.
- Sugars 8.25 g.
- Protein 1.6 g.

531. Sweet Dream Strawberry Smoothie

Preparation time: 15'

Cooking time: 0'

Servings: 1

Ingredients

- 5 strawberries
- 3 dates, pits eliminated
- 2 burro bananas or baby bananas
- Spring water for 32 fl. oz of smoothie

Directions

1. Strip off the skin of the bananas.
2. Wash the dates and strawberries.
3. Include bananas, dates, and strawberries to a blender container.
4. Include a couple of water and blend.
5. Keep on including adequate water to persuade up to be 32 oz of smoothie.

Nutrition

- Calories 282
- Fat 11 g.
- Carbohydrates 4 g.
- Protein 7 g.

532. Alkaline Green Ginger, and Banana Cleansing Smoothie

Preparation Time: 15'
Cooking Time: 0'
Servings: 1

Ingredients

- 1 handful of kale
- 1 banana, frozen
- 2 c of hemp seed milk
- 1 in of ginger, finely minced
- 1/2 c of chopped strawberries, frozen
- 1 tbsp of agave or your preferred sweetener

Directions

1. Mix all the ingredients in a blender and mix on high speed.
2. Allow it to blend evenly.
3. Pour into a pitcher with a few decorative straws and enjoy!

Nutrition

- Calories 350
- Fat 4 g.
- Carbohydrates 52 g.
- Protein 16 g.

533. Orange Mixed Detox Smoothie

Preparation Time: 15'
Cooking Time: 0'
Servings: 1

Ingredients

- 1 c of vegies (amaranth, dandelion, lettuce or watercress)
- 1/2 avocado
- 1 c of tender-jelly coconut water
- 1 Seville orange
- Juice of 1 key lime
- 1 tbsp of bromide plus powder

Directions

1. Peel and cut the Seville orange in chunks.
2. Mix all the ingredients collectively in a high-speed blender until done.

Nutrition

- Calories 71
- Fat 1 g.
- Carbohydrates 12 g.
- Protein 2 g.

534. Cucumber Toxin Flush Smoothie

PREPARATION TIME: 15'

COOKING TIME: 0'

SERVINGS: 1

Ingredients

- 1 cucumber
- 1 key lime
- 1 c of watermelon (seeded), cubed

Directions

1. Mix all the above the ingredients in a high-speed blender.
2. Considering that watermelon and cucumbers are largely water, you may not want to add any extra, however you can so if you want.
3. Juice the key lime and add into your smoothie.
4. Enjoy!

Nutrition

- Calories 219
- Fat 4 g.
- Carbohydrates 48 g.
- Protein 5 g.

535. Apple Blueberry Smoothie

PREPARATION TIME: 15'

COOKING TIME: 0'

SERVINGS: 1

Ingredients

- 1/2 apple
- 1 Date
- 1/2 c of blueberries
- 1/2 c of sparkling callaloo
- 1 tbsp of hemp seeds
- 1 tbsp of sesame seeds
- 2 c of sparkling soft-jelly coconut water
- 1/2 tbsp of bromide plus powder

Directions

1. Mix all of the ingredients in a high-speed blender and enjoy!

Nutrition

- Calories 167.4
- Fat 6.4 g.
- Carbohydrates 22.5 g.
- Protein 6.7 g.

Chapter 17: Herbal Tea Recipes

536. Lemon Rooibos Iced Tea

PREPARATION TIME: **10'**

COOKING TIME: **0'**

SERVINGS: **4**

Ingredients

- 4 bags natural, unflavored rooibos tea
- 4 c. boiling water
- 3 tbsps freshly squeezed lemon juice
- 30-40 drops liquid stevia

Directions

1. Put the tea bags into the tea pot and pour the boiling water over the bags.
2. Set aside to room temperature, then refrigerate the tea until it is ice-cold.
3. Remove the tea bags. Squeeze them gently.
4. Add the lemon juice and liquid stevia to taste and stir until well mixed.
5. Serve immediately, preferably with ice cubes and some nice garnishes, like lemon wedges.

Nutrition

- Calories 70
- Carbohydrates 16 g.
- Protein 1 g.

537. Lemon Lavender Iced Tea

PREPARATION TIME: **15'**

COOKING TIME: **0'**

SERVINGS: **4**

Ingredients

- 2 bags natural, unflavored rooibos tea
- 2 oz lemon chunks without peel and pith, seeds removed
- 1 tsp. dried lavender blossoms placed in a tea ball
- 4 c. water, at room temperature
- 20-40 drops liquid stevia

Directions

1. Place the tea bags, lemon chunks, and the tightly-closed tea ball with the lavender blossoms in a 1.5 qt. (1.5 l.) pitcher.
2. Pour in the water.
3. Refrigerate overnight.
4. Remove the tea bags, lemon chunks, and the tea ball with the lavender on the next day. Squeeze the tea bags gently to save as much liquid as possible.
5. Add the liquid stevia to taste and stir until well mixed.
6. Serve immediately with ice cubes and lemon wedges.

Nutrition

- Calories 81
- Carbohydrates 12 g.
- Protein 3 g.

538. Cherry Vanilla Iced Tea

PREPARATION TIME: 12'

COOKING TIME: 0'

SERVINGS: 4

Ingredients

- 4 bags natural, unflavored rooibos tea
- 4 c. boiling water
- 2 tbsps freshly squeezed lime juice
- 1-2 tbsps cherry flavoring
- 30-40 drops (or to taste) liquid vanilla stevia

Directions

1. Place the tea bags into the tea pot and pour the boiling water over the bags.
2. Put aside the tea cool down first, then refrigerate the tea until it is ice-cold.
3. Remove the tea bags. Squeeze them lightly.
4. Add the lime juice, cherry flavoring, and the vanilla stevia and stir until well mixed.
5. Serve immediately, preferably with ice cubes and some nice garnishes like lime wedges and fresh cherries.

Nutrition

- Calories 89
- Carbohydrates 14 g.
- Protein 2 g.

539. Elegant Blueberry Rose Water Iced Tea

PREPARATION TIME: 12'

COOKING TIME: 0'

SERVINGS: 4

Ingredients

- 2 bags herbal blueberry tea
- 4 c. boiling water
- 20 drops liquid stevia
- 1 tbsp. rose water

Directions

1. Position the tea bags into the tea pot and pour the boiling water over the bags.
2. Allow the tea cool down first, then refrigerate the tea until it is ice-cold.
3. Remove the tea bags. Press them gently.
4. Add the liquid stevia and the rose water and stir until well mixed.
5. Serve immediately, preferably with ice cubes and some nice garnishes, like fresh blueberries or natural rose petals

Nutrition

- Calories 75
- Carbohydrates 10 g.
- Protein 2 g.

540. Melba Iced Tea

Preparation time: 10'

Cooking time: 0'

Servings: 4

Ingredients

- 1 bag herbal raspberry tea
- 1 bag herbal peach tea
- 4 c. boiling water
- 10 drops liquid peach stevia
- 20-40 drops (or to taste) liquid vanilla stevia

Directions

1. Pour the boiling water over the tea bags.
2. Leave the tea cool down on room temperature, then refrigerate the tea until it is ice-cold.
3. Remove the tea bags. Press lightly.
4. Add the peach stevia and stir until well mixed.
5. Add the vanilla stevia to taste and stir until well mixed.
6. Serve immediately, preferably with ice cubes and some nice garnishes, like vanilla bean, fresh raspberries, or peach slices.

Nutrition

- Calories 81
- Carbohydrates 14 g.
- Protein 4 g.

541. Merry Raspberry Cherry Iced Tea

Preparation time: 11'

Cooking time: 0

Servings: 4

Ingredients

- 2 bags herbal raspberry tea
- 4 c. boiling water
- 1 tsp. stevia-sweetened cherry-flavored drink mix
- 1 tsp. freshly squeezed lime juice
- 10-20 drops (or to taste) liquid stevia

Directions

1. Put the tea bags into the tea pot and fill in boiling water over the bags.
2. Let the tea cool down first to room temperature, then chill until it is ice-cold.
3. Discard the tea bags. Squeeze them.
4. Add the cherry-flavored drink mix and the lime juice and stir until the drink mix is dissolved.
5. Add the liquid stevia to taste and stir until well mixed.
6. Serve immediately, preferably with ice cubes or crushed ice and some nice garnishes, like fresh raspberries and cherries.

Nutrition

- Calories 82
- Carbohydrates 11 g.
- Protein 4 g.

542. Vanilla Kissed Peach Iced Tea

PREPARATION TIME: 30'

COOKING TIME: 0'

SERVINGS: 4

Ingredients

- 2 bags herbal peach tea
- 4 c. boiling water
- 1 tsp. vanilla extract
- 1 tsp. freshly squeezed lemon juice
- 30–40 drops (or to taste) liquid stevia

Directions

1. Soak the tea bags over boiling water.
2. Allow to cool down on room temperature, then refrigerate the tea until it is ice-cold.
3. Remove and press the tea bags.
4. Add the vanilla extract and the lemon juice and stir until well mixed.
5. Add the liquid stevia to taste and stir until well mixed.
6. Serve immediately, preferably with ice cubes and some nice garnishes, like peach slices.

Nutrition

- Calories 88
- Carbohydrates 14 g.
- Protein 3 g.

543. Xtreme Berried Iced Tea

PREPARATION TIME: 10'

COOKING TIME: 0'

SERVINGS: 4

Ingredients

- 2 bags herbal Wild Berry Tea
- 4 c. (950 ml.) boiling water
- 2 tsps. freshly squeezed lime juice
- 40 drops berry-flavored liquid stevia
- 10 drops (or to taste) liquid stevia

Directions

1. Submerge the tea bags into boiling water.
2. Set aside to cool down, then refrigerate the tea until it is ice-cold.
3. Pull out the tea bags. Squeeze.
4. Add the lime juice and the berry stevia and stir until well mixed.
5. Add the liquid stevia to taste and stir until well mixed.
6. Serve immediately.

Nutrition

- Calories 76
- Carbohydrates 14 g.
- Protein 4 g.

544. Refreshingly Peppermint Iced Tea

PREPARATION TIME: 15'

COOKING TIME: 0'

SERVINGS: 5

Ingredients

- 4 bags peppermint tea
- 4 c. (950 ml.) boiling water
- 2 tsps. stevia-sweetened lime-flavored drink mix
- 1 c. (240 ml.) ice-cold sparkling water

Directions

1. Immerse the tea bags on boiling water.
2. Set aside before cooling until it is ice-cold.
3. Take out the tea bags then press.
4. Add the lime-flavored drink mix and stir until it is properly dissolved.
5. Add the sparkling water and stir very gently.
6. Serve immediately, preferably with ice cubes, mint leaves, and lime wedges.

Nutrition

- Calories 78
- Carbohydrates 17 g.
- Protein 4 g.

545. Lemongrass Mint Iced Tea

PREPARATION TIME: 12'

COOKING TIME: 0'

SERVINGS: 4

Ingredients

- 1 stalk lemongrass, chopped in 1-in.
- 1/2 c. chopped, loosely packed mint sprigs
- 4 c. boiling water
- Vanilla stevia to taste

Directions

1. Put the lemongrass and the mint into the tea pot and pour the boiling water over them.
2. Let cool down first to room temperature, then refrigerate until the tea is ice-cold.
3. Filter out the lemongrass and the mint.
4. Add the liquid vanilla stevia to taste if you prefer some sweetness and stir until well mixed.
5. Serve immediately, preferably with ice cubes and some nice garnishes, like mint sprigs and lemongrass stalks.

Nutrition

- Calories 89
- Carbohydrates 17 g.
- Protein 5 g.

546. Spiced Tea

Preparation Time: 8'
Cooking Time: 0'
Servings: 4

Ingredients

- 2 bags Bengal spice tea
- 2 tsps. freshly squeezed lemon juice
- 1 pkt. zero-carb vanilla stevia
- 1 pkt. zero-carb stevia
- 4 c. boiling water

Directions

1. Put the tea bags, lemon juice, and stevia into the tea pot.
2. Pour in the boiling water.
3. Put aside to cool over room temperature, then refrigerate.
4. Pull away the tea bags then squeeze them.
5. Stir gently.
6. Serve immediately, preferably with ice cubes or crushed ice and some lemon wedges or slices.

Nutrition

- Calories 91
- Carbohydrates 16 g.
- Protein 1 g.

547. Infused Pumpkin Spice Latte

Preparation Time: 11'
Cooking Time: 0'
Servings: 2

Ingredients

- 2 c. almond milk
- 1/4 c. coconut cream
- 2 tsps. cannabis coconut oil
- 1/4 c. pure pumpkin, canned
- 1/2 tsp. vanilla extract
- 1 1/2 tsp. pumpkin spice
- 1/2 c. coconut whipped cream
- 1 pinch of salt

Directions

1. Place all the ingredients except the coconut whipped cream in a pan over a medium low heat stove.
2. Whisk well and allow to simmer but don't boil!
3. Simmer for about 5 minutes.
4. Pour into mugs and serve.

Nutrition

- Calories 94
- Carbohydrates 17 g.
- Protein 3 g.

548. Infused Turmeric-Ginger Tea

PREPARATION TIME: **9'**

COOKING TIME: **0'**

SERVINGS: **1**

Ingredients

- 1 c. water
- 1/2 c. coconut milk
- 1 tsp. cannabis oil
- 1/2 teaspoon ground turmeric
- 1/4 c. fresh ginger root, sliced
- 1 pinch of stevia or maple syrup, to taste

Directions

1. Combine all the ingredients in a small saucepan over medium heat.
2. Heat until simmer and turn heat low.
3. Take the pan off the heat after 2 minutes
4. Let it cool, strain the mixture into a cup or mug.

Nutrition

- Calories 98
- Carbohydrates 14 g.
- Protein 2 g.

549. Infused London Fog

PREPARATION TIME: **17'**

COOKING TIME: **0'**

SERVINGS: **2**

Ingredients

- 1 c. hot water
- 1 Earl Grey teabag
- 1 tsp. cannabis coconut oil
- 1/4 c. almond milk
- 1/4 tsp. vanilla extract
- 1 pinch of stevia or sugar, to taste

Directions

1. Fill up half a mug with boiling water.
2. Add the teabag; if you prefer your tea strong, add two.
3. Add cannabis oil and stir well.
4. Add almond milk to fill your mug and stir through with the vanilla extract
5. Use stevia or sugar to sweeten your Earl Grey to taste.

Nutrition

- Calories 76
- Carbohydrates 14 g.
- Protein 2 g.

550. Infused Cranberry-Apple Snug

Preparation Time: 10'
Cooking Time: 0'
Servings: 1

Ingredients

- 1/2 c. fresh cranberry juice
- 1/2 c. fresh apple juice, cloudy
- 1/2 stick cinnamon
- 2 whole cloves
- 1/4 lemon, sliced
- 1 pinch of stevia or sugar, to taste
- Cranberries for garnish (optional)

Directions

1. Combine all the ingredients in a small saucepan over medium heat.
2. Heat until simmer and turn the heat low.
3. Let it cool, strain the mixture into a mug.
4. Serve with cinnamon stick and cranberries in a mug.

Nutrition

- Calories 88
- Carbohydrates 15 g.
- Protein 3 g.

551. Stomach Soother

Preparation Time: 5'
Cooking Time: 3'
Servings: 1

Ingredients

- 1 tbsp. agave syrup
- .5 c. ginger tea
- Dr. Sebi's Stomach Relief Herbal Tea
- 1 burro banana

Directions

1. Cook the herbal tea according to the directions on the package. Set it aside to cool.
2. Once the tea is cool, place it along with all the other ingredients into a blender. Switch on the blender and let it run until it is creamy.

Nutrition

- Calories 25
- Sugar 3 g.
- Protein 0.3 g.
- Fat 0.5

552. Sarsaparilla Syrup

Preparation time: 15'
Cooking time: 4 hours
Servings: 4

Ingredients

- 1 c. date sugar
- 1 tbsp. sassafras root
- 1 c. sarsaparilla root
- 2 c. water

Directions

1. Firstly, add all of the ingredients to a mason jar. Screw on the lid, tightly, and shake everything together. Heat a water bath up to 160 °C. Sit the mason jar into the water bath and allow it to infuse for about 2-4 hours.
2. When the infusion time is almost up, set up an ice bath. Add half and half water and ice to a bowl. Carefully take the mason jar out of the water bath and place it into the ice bath. Allow it to sit in the ice bath for 15-20 minutes.
3. Strain the infusion out and into another clean jar.

Nutrition

- Calories 37
- Sugar 2 g.
- Protein 0.4 g.
- Fat 0.3 g.

553. Dandelion "Coffee"

Preparation time: 15'
Cooking time: 0'
Servings: 4

Ingredients

- A pinch of nettle leaf
- 1 tbsp. roasted dandelion root
- 24 oz. water

Directions

1. To start, we will roast the dandelion root to help bring out its flavors. Feel free to use raw dandelion root if you want to, but roasted root brings out an earthy and complex flavor, which is perfect for cool mornings.
2. Simply add the dandelion root to a pre-warmed cast iron skillet. Allow the pieces to roast on medium heat until they start to darken in color, and you start to smell their rich aroma. Make sure that you don't let them burn because this will ruin your teas taste.
3. As the root is roasting, have the water in a pot and allow it to come up to a full, rapid boil. Once your dandelion is roasted, add it to the boiling water with the nettle leaf. Steep this for 10 minutes.
4. Strain. You can flavor your tea with some agave if you want to. Enjoy.

Nutrition

- Calories 43
- Sugar 1 g.
- Protein 0.2 g.
- Fat 0.3 g.

554. Chamomile Delight

PREPARATION TIME: 5'
COOKING TIME: 10'
SERVINGS: 3

Ingredients

- 1 tbsp. date sugar
- .5 c walnut milk
- .25 c Dr. Sebi's Nerve/Stress Relief Herbal Tea
- 1 burro banana

Directions

1. Prepare the tea according to the package directions. Set to the side and allow to cool.
2. Once the tea is cooled, add it along with the above ingredients to a blender and process until creamy and smooth.

Nutrition

- Calories 21
- Sugar 0.8 g.
- Protein 1.0 g.
- Fat 0.2 g.

555. Mucus Cleanse Tea

PREPARATION TIME: 10'
COOKING TIME: 5'
SERVINGS: 2

Ingredients

- Blue vervain
- Bladder wrack
- Irish sea moss

Directions

1. Add the sea moss to your blender. This would be best as a gel. Just make sure that it is totally dry.
2. Place equal parts of the bladder wrack to the blender. Again, this would be best as a gel. Just make sure that it is totally dry. To get the best results you need to chop these by hand.
3. Add equal parts of the blue vervain to the blender. You can use the roots to increase your iron intake and nutritional healing values.
4. Process the herbs until they form a powder. This can take up to 3 minutes.
5. Place the powder into a non-metal pot and put it on the stove. Fill the pot half full of water. Make sure the herbs are totally immersed in water. Turn on the heat and let the liquid boil. Don't let it boil more than 5 minutes.
6. Carefully strain out the herbs. You can save these for later use in other recipes.
7. You can add in some agave nectar, date sugar, or key lime juice for added flavor.

Nutrition

- Calories 36
- Sugar 6 g.
- Protein 0.7 g.
- Fat 0.3 g.

556. Immune Tea

Preparation time: 10'

Cooking time: 20'

Servings: 1

Ingredients

- 1 part of echinacea
- 1 part of astragalus
- 1 part of rosehip
- 1 part of chamomile
- 1 part of elderflowers
- 1 part of elderberries

Directions

1. Mix the herbs together and place them inside an airtight container.
2. When you are ready to make a cup of tea, place one teaspoon into a tea ball or bag, and put it in 8 oz of boiling water. Let this sit for 20 minutes.

Nutrition

- Calories 39
- Sugar 1 g.
- Protein 2 g.
- Fat 0.6 g.

557. Ginger Turmeric Tea

Preparation time: 5'

Cooking time: 15'

Servings: 3

Ingredients

- Juice of 1 key lime
- 2 slices turmeric finger
- 2 slices ginger root
- 3 c. water

Directions

1. Pour the water into a pot and let it boil. Remove from the heat and put the turmeric and ginger in. Stir well. Place the lid on the pot and let it sit for 15 minutes.
2. While you are waiting on your tea to finish steeping, juice one key lime and divide between 2 mugs.
3. Once the tea is ready, remove the turmeric and ginger and pour the tea into mugs and enjoy. If you want your tea a bit sweet, add some agave syrup or date sugar.

Nutrition

- Calories 27
- Sugar 5 g.
- Protein 3 g.
- Fat 1.0 g.

558. Tranquil Tea

PREPARATION TIME: 5'

COOKING TIME: 10'

SERVINGS: 2

Ingredients

- 2 parts of rose petals
- 2 parts of lemongrass
- 4 parts of chamomile

Directions

1. Pour all the herbs into a glass jar and shake well to mix.
2. When you are ready to make a cup of tea, add 1 tsp of the mixture for every serving to a tea strainer, ball, or bag. Cover with water that has boiled and let it sit for 10 minutes.
3. If you like a little sweetness in your tea, you can add some agave syrup or date sugar.

Nutrition

- Calories 35
- Sugar 3.4 g.
- Protein 2.3 g.
- Fat 1.5 g.

559. Energizing Lemon Tea

PREPARATION TIME: 5'

COOKING TIME: 15'

SERVINGS: 3

Ingredients

- .5 tsp. dried lemongrass
- .5 tsp. dried lemon thyme
- 1 tsp. dried lemon verbena

Directions

1. Place the dried herbs into a tea strainer, bag, or ball and place it in 1 c of water that has boiled. Let this sit for 15 minutes. Carefully strain out the tea. You can add agave syrup or date sugar, if needed.

Nutrition

- Calories 40
- Sugar 6 g.
- Protein 2.2 g.
- Fat 0.3 g.

560. Respiratory Support Tea

Preparation time: 5'
Cooking time: 18'
Servings: 4

Ingredients

- 2 parts of rosehip
- 1 part of lemon balm
- 1 part of coltsfoot leaves
- 1 part of mullein
- 1 part of osha root
- 1 part of marshmallow root

Directions

1. Place 3 c of water into a pot. Place the Osha root and marshmallow root into the pot. Allow to boil. Let this simmer for 10 minutes
2. Now put the remaining ingredients into the pot and let this sleep another 8 minutes. Strain.
3. Drink 4 c of this tea each day.
4. It's almost that time of year again when everyone is suffering from the dreaded cold. Then that cold turns into a nasty lingering cough. Having these ingredients on hand will help you be able to get ahead of this year's cold season. When you buy your ingredient, they need to be stored in glass jars. The roots and leaves need to be put into separate jars. You can drink this tea at any time, but it is great for when you need some extra respiratory support.

Nutrition

- Calories 35
- Sugar 3.4 g.
- Protein 2.3 g.
- Fat 1.5 g.

561. Thyme and Lemon Tea

Preparation time: 5'
Cooking time: 10'
Servings: 2

Ingredients

- 2 tsp. key lime juice
- 2 fresh thyme sprigs

Directions

1. Place the thyme into a canning jar. Boil enough water to cover the thyme sprigs. Cover the jar with a lid and leave it alone for 10 minutes. Add the key lime juice. Carefully strain into a mug and add some agave nectar if desired.

Nutrition

- Calories 22
- Sugar 1.4 g.
- Protein 5.3 g.
- Fat 0.6 g.

562. Sore Throat Tea

PREPARATION TIME: **8'**

COOKING TIME: **15'**

SERVINGS: **4**

INGREDIENTS

- 8-10 leaves of sage leaves

Directions

1. Place the sage leaves into a quart canning jar and add water that has boiled until it covers the leaves. Pour the lid on the jar and let sit for 15 minutes.
2. You can use this tea as a gargle to help ease a sore or scratchy throat. Usually, the pain will ease up before you even finish your first cup. This can also be used for inflammations of the throat, tonsils, and mouth since the mucous membranes get soothed by the sage oil. A normal dose would be between 3-4 c. each day. Every time you take a sip, roll it around in your mouth before swallowing it.

Nutrition

- Calories 26
- Sugar 2.0 g.
- Protein 7.6 g.
- Fat 3.2 g.

563. Autumn Tonic Tea

PREPARATION TIME: **10'**

COOKING TIME: **15'**

SERVINGS: **2**

INGREDIENTS

- 1 part of dried ginger root
- 1 part of rosehip
- 2 parts of red clover
- 2 parts of dandelion root and leaf
- 2 parts of mullein leaf
- 3 parts of lemon balm
- 4 parts of nettle leaf

Directions

1. Place all of these ingredients into a bowl. Stir everything together to mix well. Put into a glass jar with a lid and keep it in a dry place that stays cool.
2. When you want a cup of tea, place four cups of water into a pot. Let this come to a full rolling boil. Place the desired amount of tea blend into a tea strainer, ball, or bag and cover with boiling water. Let sit for 15 minutes. Strain out the herbs and drink it either cold or hot. If you like your tea sweet, add some agave syrup or date sugar.

Nutrition

- Calories 43
- Sugar 3.8 g.
- Protein 6.5 g.
- Fat 3.9 g.

564. Adrenal and Stress Health

PREPARATION TIME: 12'

COOKING TIME: 20'

SERVINGS: 2

Ingredients

- .5 c. bladder wrack
- 1 c. tulsi holy basil
- 1 c. shatavari root
- 1 c. ashwagandha root

Directions

1. Place these ingredients into a bowl. Stir well to combine.
2. Place the mixture in a glass jar with a lid and store in a dry place that stays cool.
3. When you want a cup of tea, place 2 tbsps of the tea mixture into a medium pot. Pour in 2 c of water. Let this come to a full rolling boil. Turn down heat. Let this simmer 20 minutes. Strain well. If you prefer your tea sweet, you can add some agave syrup or date sugar.

Nutrition

- Calories 43
- Sugar 2.2 g.
- Protein 4.1 g.
- Fat 2.3 g.

565. Lavender Tea

PREPARATION TIME: 5'

COOKING TIME: 15'

SERVINGS: 2

Ingredients

- Agave syrup, to taste
- 2 tbsp. dried lavender flowers
- A handful of fresh lemon balm
- 3 c water

Directions

1. Pour the water in a pot and allow to boil.
2. Pour over the lavender and lemon balm. Cover and let sit for 5 minutes.
3. Strain well. If you prefer your tea sweet, add some agave syrup.

Nutrition

- Calories 59
- Sugar 6.8 g.
- Protein 3.3 g.
- Fat 1.6 g.

Chapter 18: Other Diabetic Recipes

566. Chili Chicken Wings

PREPARATION TIME: 10'

COOKING TIME: 1H 10'

SERVINGS: 4

Ingredients

- 2 lbs. chicken wings
- 1/8 tsp. paprika
- 1/2 c. coconut flour
- 1/4 tsp. garlic powder
- 1/4 tsp. chili powder

Directions

1. Preheat the oven to 400 °F/200 °C.
2. In a mixing bowl, add all the ingredients except the chicken wings and mix well.
3. Add the chicken wings to the bowl mixture and coat well and place on a baking tray.
4. Bake in preheated oven for 55-60 minutes.
5. Serve and enjoy.

Nutrition

- Calories 440
- Fat 17.1 g.
- Carbohydrates 1.3 g.
- Sugar 0.2 g.
- Protein 65.9 g.
- Cholesterol 202 mg.

567. Garlic Chicken Wings

PREPARATION TIME: 10'

COOKING TIME: 55'

SERVINGS: 6

Ingredients

- 12 chicken wings
- 2 garlic cloves, minced
- 3 tbsp. ghee
- 1/2 tsp. turmeric
- 2 tsp. cumin seeds
- Salt and pepper to taste

Directions

1. Preheat the oven to 425 F/ 215 C.
2. In a large bowl, mix together 1 tsp. cumin, 1 tbsp. ghee, turmeric, pepper, and salt.
3. Add the chicken wings to the bowl and toss well.
4. Spread the chicken wings on a baking tray and bake in the preheated oven for 30 minutes.
5. Turn the chicken wings to another side and bake for 8 more minutes.
6. Meanwhile, heat the remaining ghee in a pan over medium heat.
7. Add the garlic and cumin to the pan and cook for a minute.
8. Remove the pan from the heat and set aside.
9. Remove chicken wings from the oven and drizzle with ghee mixture.
10. Bake the chicken wings 5 minutes more.
11. Serve and enjoy.

Nutrition

- Calories 378
- Fat 27.9 g.
- Carbohydrates 11.4 g.
- Sugar 0 g.
- Protein 19.7 g.
- Cholesterol 94 mg.

568. Spinach Cheese Pie

Preparation time: 10'
Cooking time: 40'
Servings: 8

Ingredients

- 6 eggs, lightly beaten
- 2 boxes frozen spinach, chopped
- 2 c. cheddar cheese, shredded
- 15 oz. cottage cheese
- 1 tsp. salt
- 1 tsp. pepper

Directions

1. Preheat the oven to 375 F/ 190 C.
2. Spray an 8x8-in. baking dish with cooking spray and set aside.
3. In a mixing bowl, combine together spinach, eggs, cheddar cheese, cottage cheese, pepper, and salt.
4. Pour the spinach mixture into the prepared baking dish and bake in the preheated oven for 10 minutes.
5. Serve and enjoy.

Nutrition

- Calories 229
- Fat 14 g.
- Carbohydrates 5.4 g.
- Sugar 0.9 g.
- Protein 21 g.
- Cholesterol 157 mg.

569. Tasty Harissa Chicken

Preparation time: 10'
Cooking time: 4H 10'
Servings: 4

Ingredients

- 1 lb. chicken breasts, skinless and boneless
- 1/2 tsp. ground cumin
- 1 c. harissa sauce
- 1/4 tsp. garlic powder
- 1/2 tsp. kosher salt

Directions

1. Season the chicken with garlic powder, cumin, and salt.
2. Place the chicken to the slow cooker.
3. Pour the harissa sauce over the chicken.
4. Cover the slow cooker with a lid and cook on low for 4 hours.
5. Remove the chicken from a slow cooker and shred using a fork.
6. Return the shredded chicken to the slow cooker and stir well.
7. Serve and enjoy.

Nutrition

- Calories 232
- Fat 9.7 g.
- Carbohydrates 1.3 g.
- Sugar 0.1 g.
- Protein 32.9 g.
- Cholesterol 101 mg.

570. Roasted Balsamic Mushrooms

PREPARATION TIME: **10'**

COOKING TIME: **50'**

SERVINGS: **4**

Ingredients

- 8 oz. mushrooms, sliced
- 1/2 tsp. thyme
- 2 tbsp. balsamic vinegar
- 2 tbsp. extra-virgin olive oil
- 2 onions, sliced
- Salt and pepper to taste

Directions

1. Preheat the oven to 375 F / 190 C.
2. Line a baking tray with aluminum foil and spray with cooking spray and set aside.
3. In a mixing bowl, add all the ingredients and mix well.
4. Spread the mushroom mixture onto a prepared baking tray.
5. Roast in the preheated oven for 45 minutes.
6. Season with pepper, and salt.
7. Serve and enjoy.

Nutrition

- Calories 96
- Fat 7.2 g.
- Carbohydrates 7.2 g.
- Sugar 3.3 g.
- Protein 2.4 g.
- Cholesterol 0 mg.

571. Roasted Cumin Carrots

PREPARATION TIME: **10'**

COOKING TIME: **45'**

SERVINGS: **4**

Ingredients

- 8 carrots, peeled and cut into 1/2-in.-thick slices
- 1 tsp. cumin seeds
- 1 tbsp. olive oil
- 1/2 tsp. kosher salt

Directions

1. Preheat the oven to 400 F / 200 C.
2. Line a baking tray with parchment paper.
3. Add carrots, cumin seeds, olive oil, and salt in a large bowl and toss well to coat.
4. Spread the carrots on a prepared baking tray and roast in the preheated oven for 20 minutes.
5. Turn the carrots to another side and roast for 20 more minutes.
6. Serve and enjoy.

Nutrition

- Calories 82
- Fat 3.6 g.
- Carbohydrates 12.2 g.
- Sugar 6 g.
- Protein 1.1 g.
- Cholesterol 0 mg.

572. Tasty and Tender Brussels Sprouts

Preparation Time: 10'

Cooking Time: 35'

Servings: 4

Ingredients

- 1 lb. Brussels sprouts, trimmed cut in half
- 1/4 c. balsamic vinegar
- 1 onion, sliced
- 1 tbsp. olive oil

Directions

1. Add water in a saucepan and bring to boil.
2. Add Brussels sprouts and cook over medium heat for 20 minutes. Drain well.
3. Heat oil in a pan over medium heat.
4. Add the onion and cook until softened. Add the sprouts and vinegar and stir well and cook for 1-2 minutes.
5. Serve and enjoy.

Nutrition

- Calories 93
- Fat 3.9 g.
- Carbohydrates 13 g.
- Sugar 3.7 g.
- Protein 4.2 g.
- Cholesterol 0 mg.

573. Sauteed Veggies

Preparation Time: 10'

Cooking Time: 15'

Servings: 4

Ingredients

- 1/2 c. mushrooms, sliced
- 1 zucchini, diced
- 1 squash, diced
- 2 1/2 tsp. southwest seasoning
- 3 tbsp. olive oil
- Salt and pepper to taste

Directions

1. In a medium bowl, whisk together southwest seasoning, pepper, olive oil, and salt.
2. Add the vegetables to a bowl and mix well to coat.
3. Heat the pan over medium-high heat.
4. Add vegetables in the pan and sauté for 5-7 minutes.
5. Serve and enjoy.

Nutrition

- Calories 107
- Fat 10.7 g.
- Carbohydrates 3.6 g.
- Sugar 1.5 g.
- Protein 1.2 g.
- Cholesterol 0 mg.

574. Mustard Green Beans

PREPARATION TIME: **10'**

COOKING TIME: **20'**

SERVINGS: **4**

Ingredients

- 1 lb. green beans, washed and trimmed
- 1 tsp. whole grain mustard
- 1 tbsp. olive oil
- 2 tbsp. apple cider vinegar
- 1/4 c. onion, chopped
- Salt and pepper to taste

Directions

1. Steam the green beans in the microwave until tender.
2. Meanwhile, in a pan, heat olive oil over medium heat.
3. Add the onion and sauté until softened.
4. Add water, apple cider vinegar, and mustard in the pan and stir well.
5. Add the green beans and stir to coat and heat through.
6. Season the green beans with pepper and salt.
7. Serve and enjoy.

Nutrition

- Calories 71
- Fat 3.7 g.
- Carbohydrates 8.9 g.
- Sugar 1.9 g.
- Protein 2.1 g.
- Cholesterol 0 mg.

575. Zucchini Fries

PREPARATION TIME: **10'**

COOKING TIME: **40'**

SERVINGS: **4**

Ingredients

- 1 egg
- 2 medium zucchinis, cut into fry's shape
- 1 tsp. Italian herbs
- 1 tsp. garlic powder
- 1 c. parmesan cheese, grated

Directions

1. Preheat the oven to 425 F/ 218 C.
2. Spray a baking tray with cooking spray and set aside.
3. In a small bowl, add the egg and lightly whisk it.
4. In a separate bowl, mix together the spices and parmesan cheese.
5. Dip the zucchini fries in the egg then coat with parmesan cheese mixture and place on a baking tray.
6. Bake in the preheated oven for 25-30 minutes. Turn halfway through.
7. Serve and enjoy.

Nutrition

- Calories 184
- Fat 10.3 g.
- Carbohydrates 3.9 g.
- Sugar 2 g.
- Protein 14.7 g.
- Cholesterol 71 mg.

576. Broccoli Nuggets

Preparation time: 10'

Cooking time: 25'

Servings: 4

Ingredients

- 2 c. broccoli florets
- 1/4 c. almond flour
- 2 egg whites
- 1 c. cheddar cheese, shredded
- 1/8 tsp. salt

Directions

1. Preheat the oven to 350 F/ 180 C.
2. Spray a baking tray with cooking spray and set aside.
3. Using a masher, breaks the broccoli florets into small pieces.
4. Add the remaining ingredients to the broccoli and mix well.
5. Drop 20 scoops onto a baking tray and press lightly into a nugget shape.
6. Bake in the preheated oven for 20 minutes.
7. Serve and enjoy.

Nutrition

- Calories 148
- Fat 10.4 g.
- Carbohydrates 3.9 g.
- Sugar 1.1 g.
- Protein 10.5 g.
- Cholesterol 30 mg.

577. Zucchini Cauliflower Fritters

Preparation time: 10'

Cooking time: 15'

Servings: 4

Ingredients

- 2 medium zucchinis, grated and squeezed
- 3 c. cauliflower florets
- 1 tbsp. coconut oil
- 1/4 c. coconut flour
- 1/2 tsp. sea salt

Directions

1. Steam cauliflower florets for 5 minutes.
2. Add the cauliflower into the food processor and process until it looks like rice.
3. Add all the ingredients except coconut oil to the large bowl and mix until well combined.
4. Make small round patties from the mixture and set aside.
5. Heat coconut oil in a pan over medium heat.
6. Place patties in a pan and cook for 3-4 minutes on each side.
7. Serve and enjoy.

Nutrition

- Calories 68
- Fat 3.8 g.
- Carbohydrates 7.8 g.
- Sugar 3.6 g.
- Protein 2.8 g.
- Cholesterol 0 mg.

578. Roasted Chickpeas

Preparation time: 10'

Cooking time: 30'

Servings: 4

Ingredients

- 15 oz. can chickpeas, drained, rinsed and pat dry
- 1/2 tsp. paprika
- 1 tbsp. olive oil
- 1/2 tsp. pepper
- 1/2 tsp. salt

Directions

1. Preheat the oven to 450 °F/232 °C.
2. Spray a baking tray with cooking spray and set aside.
3. In a large bowl, toss chickpeas with olive oil, paprika, pepper, and salt.
4. Spread chickpeas on a prepared baking tray and roast in preheated oven for 25 minutes. Stir every 10 minutes.
5. Serve and enjoy.

Nutrition

- Calories 158
- Fat 4.8 g.
- Carbohydrates 24.4 g.
- Sugar 0 g.
- Protein 5.3 g.
- Cholesterol 0 mg.

579. Peanut Butter Mousse

Preparation time: 10'

Cooking time: 10'

Servings: 2

Ingredients

- 1 tbsp. peanut butter
- 1 tsp. vanilla extract
- 1 tsp. stevia
- 1/2 c. heavy cream

Directions

1. Add all the ingredients into the bowl and whisk until soft peak forms.
2. Spoon into the serving bowls and enjoy.

Nutrition

- Calories 157
- Fat 15.1 g.
- Carbohydrates 5.2 g.
- Sugar 3.6 g.
- Protein 2.6 g.
- Cholesterol 41 mg.

580. Coffee Mousse

Preparation time: 10'
Cooking time: 20'
Servings: 8

Ingredients

- 4 tbsp. brewed coffee
- 16 oz. cream cheese, softened
- 1/2 c. unsweetened almond milk
- 1 c. whipping cream
- 2 tsp. liquid stevia

Directions

1. Add the coffee and cream cheese in a blender and blend until smooth.
2. Add the stevia, whipping cream, and milk and blend again until smooth.
3. Add cream and blend until thickened.
4. Pour into the serving glasses and place in the refrigerator.
5. Serve chilled and enjoy.

Nutrition

- Calories 244
- Fat 24.6 g.
- Carbohydrates 2.1 g.
- Sugar 0.1 g.
- Protein 4.7 g.
- Cholesterol 79 mg.

581. Wild Rice and Black Lentils Bowl

Preparation time: 10'
Cooking time: 50'
Servings: 4

Ingredients

For the Wild Rice
- 2 c. wild rice, uncooked
- 4 c. spring water
- 1/2 teaspoon salt
- 2 bay leaves

For the Black Lentils
- 2 c. black lentils, cooked
- 1 3/4 cups coconut milk, unsweetened
- 2 c. vegetable stock
- 1 tsp. dried thyme
- 1 tsp. dried paprika
- 1/2 of medium purple onion; peeled, sliced
- 1 tbsp. minced garlic
- 2 tsps. creole seasoning
- 1 tbsp. coconut oil

For the Plantains
- 3 large plantains, chopped into 1/4-in.-thick pieces
- 3 tbsps coconut oil

For the Brussels Sprouts
- 10 large Brussels sprouts, quartered
- 2 tbsps spring water
- 1 tsp. sea salt
- 1/2 teaspoon ground black pepper

Directions

1. Prepare the rice: Take a medium pot, place it over medium-high heat, pour in water, and add bay leaves and salt.
2. Bring the water to a boil, then switch heat to medium, add the rice, and then cook for 30–45 minutes or more until tender.
3. When done, discard the bay leaves from the rice, drain if any water remains in the pot, remove it from heat, and fluff by using a fork. Set aside until needed.
4. While the rice boils, prepare the lentils: Take a large pot, place it over medium-high heat and when hot, add the onion and cook for 5 minutes or until translucent.
5. Stir the garlic into the onion, cook for 2 minutes until fragrant and golden, then add the remaining ingredients for the lentils and stir until mixed.
6. Bring the lentils to a boil, then switch the heat to medium and simmer the lentils for 20 minutes until tender, covering the pot with a lid.
7. When done, remove the pot from the heat and set aside until needed.
8. While the rice and lentils simmer, prepare the plantains: Chop them into 1/4-in.-thick pieces.
9. Take a large skillet pan, place it over medium heat, add coconut oil and when it melts, add half of the plantain pieces and cook for 7–10 minutes per side or more until golden-brown.
10. When done, transfer the browned plantains to a plate lined with paper towels and repeat with the remaining plantain pieces; set aside until needed.
11. Prepare the sprouts: Return the skillet pan over medium heat, add more oil if needed, and then add the Brussels sprouts.
12. Toss the sprouts until coated with oil, and then let them cook for 3–4 minutes per side until brown.
13. Drizzle water over sprouts, cover the pan with the lid, and then cook for 3–5 minutes until steamed.
14. Season the sprouts with salt and black pepper, toss until mixed, and transfer the sprouts to a plate.
15. Assemble the bowl: Divide the rice evenly among 4 bowls and then top with lentils, plantain pieces, and sprouts.
16. Serve immediately.

Nutrition

- Calories 333
- Carbohydrates 49.2 g.
- Fat 10.7 g.
- Protein 6.2 g.

582. Alkaline Spaghetti Squash Recipe

Preparation time: 10'

Cooking time: 30'

Servings: 4

Ingredients

- 1 spaghetti squash
- Grapeseed oil
- Sea salt
- Cayenne powder (optional)
- Onion powder (optional)

Directions

1. Preheat your oven to 375°F
2. Carefully chop off the ends of the squash and cut it in half.
3. Scoop out the seeds into a bowl.
4. Coat the squash with oil.
5. Season the squash and flip it over for the other side to get baked. When properly baked, the outside of the squash will be tender.
6. Allow the squash to cool off, then, use a fork to scrape the inside into a bowl.
7. Add seasoning to taste.
8. Dish your alkaline spaghetti squash!

Nutrition

- Calories 672
- Carbohydrates 65 g.
- Fat 47 g.
- Protein 12 g.

583. Dairy-Free Fruit Tarts

Preparation time: 15'

Cooking time: 15'

Servings: 2

Ingredients

- 1 c. coconut whipped cream
- 1/2 easy shortbread crust (dairy-free option)
- Fresh mint sprigs
- 1/2 c. mixed fresh berries

Directions

1. Grease two 4-in. pans with detachable bottoms. Pour the shortbread mixture into pans and firmly press into the edges and bottom of each pan. Refrigerate for 15 minutes.
2. Loosen the crust carefully to remove from the pan.
3. Distribute the whipped cream between the tarts and evenly spread to the sides. Refrigerate for 1-2 hours to make it firm.
4. Use the berries and sprig of mint to garnish each of the tarts

Nutrition

- Fat 28.9 g.
- Carbohydrates 8.3 g.
- Protein 5.8 g.
- Calories 306

584. Spaghetti Squash with Peanut Sauce

Preparation Time: 15'
Cooking Time: 15'
Servings: 4

Ingredients
- 1 c. cooked shelled edamame; frozen, thawed
- 3-lbs. spaghetti squash
- 1/2 c. red bell pepper, sliced
- 1/4 c. scallions, sliced
- 1 medium carrot, shredded
- 1 tsp. minced garlic
- 1/2 teaspoon crushed red pepper
- 1 tbsp. rice vinegar
- 1/4 c. coconut aminos
- 1 tbsp. maple syrup
- 1/2 c. peanut butter
- 1/4 c. unsalted roasted peanuts, chopped
- 1/4 c. + 2 tbsps spring water, divided
- 1/4 c. fresh cilantro, chopped
- 4 lime wedges

Directions
1. Prepare the squash: Cut each squash in half lengthwise and then remove the seeds.
2. Take a microwave-proof dish, place the squash halves in it cut-side-up, drizzle with 2 tbsps water, and then microwave at high heat setting for 10-15 minutes until tender.
3. Let the squash cool for 15 minutes until able to handle. Use a fork to scrape its flesh lengthwise to make noodles, and then let the noodles cool for 10 minutes.
4. While the squash microwaves, prepare the sauce: Take a medium bowl, add butter in it along with red pepper and garlic, pour in vinegar, coconut aminos, maple syrup, and water, and then whisk until smooth.
5. When the squash noodles have cooled, distribute them evenly among four bowls, top with scallions, carrots, bell pepper, and edamame beans, and then drizzle with the prepared sauce.
6. Sprinkle cilantro and peanuts and serve each bowl with a lime wedge.

Nutrition
- Calories 419
- Carbohydrates 32.8 g.
- Fat 24 g.
- Protein 17.6 g.

585. Cauliflower Alfredo Pasta

Preparation Time: 10'
Cooking Time: 30'
Servings: 4

Ingredients
For the Alfredo Sauce
- 4 c. cauliflower florets, fresh
- 1 tbsp. minced garlic
- 1/4 c. nutritional yeast
- 1/2 teaspoon garlic powder
- 3/4 teaspoon sea salt
- 1/2 teaspoon onion powder
- 1/2 teaspoon ground black pepper
- 1/2 tbsp. olive oil
- 1 tbsp. lemon juice, and more as needed for serving
- 1/2 c. almond milk, unsweetened

For the Pasta
- 1 tbsp. minced parsley
- 1 lemon, juiced
- 1/2 teaspoon sea salt
- 1/4 tsp. ground black pepper
- 12 oz. spelt pasta; cooked, warmed

Directions
1. Take a large pot half full with water, place it over medium-high heat, and then bring it to a boil.
2. Add the cauliflower florets, cook for 10-15 minutes until tender, drain them well, and then return the florets to the pot.
3. Take a medium skillet pan, place it over low heat, add oil and when hot, add garlic and cook for 4-5 minutes until fragrant and golden-brown.
4. Spoon garlic into a food processor, add the remaining ingredients for the sauce in it, along with the cauliflower florets, and then pulse for 2-3 minutes until smooth.
5. Tip the sauce into the pot, stir it well, place it over medium-low heat, and then cook for 5 minutes until hot.
6. Add the pasta into the pot, toss well until coated, taste to adjust seasoning, and then cook for 2 minutes until the pasta gets hot.
7. Divide the pasta and the sauce among four plates, season with salt and black pepper, drizzle with lemon juice, and then top with minced parsley.
8. Serve straight away.

Nutrition
- Calories 360
- Carbohydrates 59 g.
- Fat 9 g.
- Protein 13 g.

586. Sloppy Joe

PREPARATION TIME: 8'

COOKING TIME: 12'

SERVINGS: 4

Ingredients

- 2 c. kaput or spelt wheat, cooked
- 1/2 c. white onion, diced
- 1 Roma tomato, diced
- 1 c. chickpeas, cooked
- 1/2 c. green bell peppers, diced
- 1 tsp. sea salt
- 1/8 tsp. cayenne pepper
- 1 tsp. onion powder
- 1 tbsp. grapeseed oil
- 1 1/2 c. barbecue sauce, alkaline

Directions

1. Plug in a high-power food processor, add chickpeas and spelt, cover with the lid, and then pulse for 15 seconds.
2. Take a large skillet pan, place it over medium-high heat, add oil and when hot, add onion and bell pepper, season with salt, cayenne pepper, and onion powder, and then stir until well combined.
3. Cook the vegetables for 3-5 minutes until tender. Add tomatoes, add the pulsed mixture, pour in the barbecue sauce, and then stir until well mixed.
4. Simmer for 5 minutes, then remove the pan from the heat and serve the sloppy joe with alkaline flatbread.

Nutrition

- Calories 333
- Carbohydrates 65 g.
- Fat 5 g.
- Protein 14 g.

587. Amaretti

PREPARATION TIME: 15'

COOKING TIME: 22'

SERVINGS: 2

Ingredients

- 1/2 c of granulated erythritol-based Sweetener
- 165 g. (2 c.) sliced almonds
- 1/4 c of powdered of erythritol-based sweetener
- 4 large egg whites
- Pinch of salt
- 1/2 tsp. almond extract

Directions

1. Heat the oven to 300° F and use parchment paper to line 2 baking sheets. Grease the parchment slightly.
2. Process the powdered sweetener, granulated sweetener, and sliced almonds in a food processor until it appears like coarse crumbs.
3. Beat the egg whites plus the salt and almond extracts using an electric mixer in a large bowl until they hold soft peaks. Fold in the almond mixture so that it becomes well combined.
4. Drop spoonful of the dough onto the prepared baking sheet and allow for a space of 1 in. between them. Press a sliced almond into the top of each cookie.
5. Bake in the oven for 22 minutes until the sides becomes brown. They will appear jellylike when they are taken out from the oven but will begin to be firms as it cools down.

Nutrition

- Fat 8.8 g.
- Carbohydrates 4.1 g.
- Protein 5.3 g.
- Calories 117

588. Green Fruit Juice

PREPARATION TIME: 10'

COOKING TIME: 0'

SERVINGS: 2

Ingredients

- 3 large kiwis, peeled and chopped
- 3 large green apples, cored and sliced
- 2 c. seedless green grapes
- 2 tsps. fresh lime juice

Directions

1. Add all the ingredients into a juicer and extract the juice according to the manufacturer's method.
2. Pour into 2 glasses and serve immediately.

Nutrition

- Calories 304
- Total Fat 2.2 g.
- Saturated Fat 0 g.
- Protein 6.2 g.

589. Kale Chickpea Mash

PREPARATION TIME: 15'

COOKING TIME: 12'

SERVINGS: 1

Ingredients

- 1 shallot
- 3 tbsp. garlic
- A bunch of kale
- 1/2 c. boiled chickpea
- 2 tbsp. coconut oil
- Sea salt

Directions

1. Add some garlic in olive oil
2. Chop the shallot and fry it with oil in a nonstick skillet.
3. Cook until the shallot turns golden brown.
4. Add the kale and garlic in the skillet and stir well.
5. Add the chickpeas and cook for 6 minutes. Add the rest of the ingredients and give a good stir.
6. Serve and enjoy

Nutrition

- Calories 149
- Total fat 8 g.
- Saturated fat 1 g.
- Net carbohydrates 13 g.
- Protein 4 g.
- Sugars 6 g.
- Fiber 3 g.
- Sodium 226 mg.
- Potassium 205 mg.

590. Quinoa and Apple

PREPARATION TIME: **15'**

COOKING TIME: **12'**

SERVINGS: **1**

The combination of quinoa and apple yields a delicious and filling lunch dish that can be carried to work in your lunch box.

Ingredients

- 1/2 c. quinoa
- 1 apple
- 1/2 lemon
- Cinnamon to taste

Directions

1. Cook the quinoa according to the packet directions.
2. Grate the apple and add to the cooked quinoa. Cook for 30 seconds.
3. Serve in a bowl then sprinkle lime and cinnamon. Enjoy.

Nutrition

- Calories 229
- Total fat 3.2 g.
- Net carbs 32.3 g.
- Protein 6.1 g.
- Sugars 4.2 g.
- Fiber 3.3 g.
- Sodium 35.5 mg.
- Potassium 211.8 mg.

591. Warm Avo and Quinoa Salad

PREPARATION TIME: **5'**

COOKING TIME: **12'**

SERVINGS: **4**

This is an amazing alkaline quinoa dish that will blow your mind away. It's an easy dish that will be ready in less than 20 minutes.

Ingredients

- 4 ripe avocados, quartered
- 1 c. quinoa
- 0.9 lb. chickpeas, drained
- 1 oz. flat leaf parsley
- Salt and pepper to taste

Directions

1. Add the quinoa in a pot with 2 c of water. Bring to boil then simmer for 12 minutes or until all the water has evaporated. The grains should be glassy and swollen.
2. Toss the quinoa with all the other ingredients and season with salt and pepper to taste.
3. Serve with olive oil and lemon wedges. Enjoy.

Nutrition

- Calories 354
- Total fat 16 g.
- Saturated fat 2 g.
- Net carbs 31 g.
- Protein 15 g.
- Sugars 6 g.
- Fiber 15 g.
- Sodium 226 mg.
- Potassium 205 mg.

592. Tuna Salad

Preparation time: 15'
Cooking time: 30'
Servings: 2

Ingredients

- 2 (5-oz.) cans of water packed tuna, drained
- 2 tbsps fat-free plain Greek yogurt
- Salt and ground black pepper, as required
- 2 medium carrots, peeled and shredded
- 2 apples, cored and chopped
- 2 c. fresh spinach, torn

Directions

1. In a large bowl, add the tuna, yogurt, salt, and black pepper and gently, stir to combine.
2. Add the carrots, spinach, and apples and stir to combine.
3. Serve immediately.

Nutrition

- Calories 306
- Total Fat 1.8 g.
- Saturated Fat 0 g.
- Cholesterol 63 mg
- Total Carbohydrates 38 g.
- Sugar 26 g.
- Fiber 7.6 g.
- Sodium 324 mg.
- Potassium 602 mg.
- Protein 35.8 g.

363

593. Herring and Veggies Soup

Preparation time: 15'
Cooking time: 25'
Servings: 35

Ingredients

- 2 tbsps olive oil
- 1 shallot, chopped
- 2 small garlic cloves, minced
- 1 jalapeño pepper, chopped
- 1 head cabbage, chopped
- 1 small red bell pepper, seeded and chopped finely
- 1 small yellow bell pepper, seeded and chopped finely
- 5 c. low-sodium chicken broth
- 2 (4-oz.) boneless herring fillets, cubed
- 1/4 c. fresh cilantro, minced
- 2 tbsps fresh lemon juice
- Ground black pepper and salt, as required
- 2 scallions, chopped

Directions

1. In a large soup pan, heat the oil over medium heat and sauté the shallot and garlic for 2–3 minutes.
2. Add the cabbage and peppers and sauté for about 3–4 minutes.
3. Add the broth and bring to a boil over high heat.
4. Now, reduce the heat to medium-low and simmer for about 10 minutes.
5. Add the herring cubes and cook for about 5–6 minutes.
6. Stir in the cilantro, lemon juice, salt, and black pepper and cook for about 1–2 minutes.
7. Serve hot with the topping of scallion.

Nutrition

- Calories 215
- Total Fat 11.2 g.
- Saturated Fat 2.1 g.
- Cholesterol 35 mg.
- Total Carbohydrates 14.7 g.
- Sugar 7 g.
- Fiber 4.5 g.
- Sodium 152 mg.
- Potassium 574 mg.
- Protein 15.1 g.

594. Salmon Soup

Preparation time: 15'

Cooking time: 20'

Servings: 4

Ingredients

- 1 tbsp. olive oil
- 1 yellow onion, chopped
- 1 garlic clove, minced
- 4 c. low-sodium chicken broth
- 1-pound boneless salmon, cubed
- 2 tbsp. fresh cilantro, chopped
- Ground black pepper, as required
- 1 tbsp. fresh lime juice

Directions

1. In a large pan, heat the oil over medium heat and sauté the onion for about 5 minutes.
2. Add the garlic and sauté for about 1 minute.
3. Stir in the broth and bring to a boil over high heat.
4. Now, reduce the heat to low and simmer for about 10 minutes.
5. Add the salmon and cook for about 3-4 minutes.
6. Stir in black pepper, lime juice, and cilantro and serve hot.

Nutrition

- Calories 208
- Total Fat 10.5 g.
- Saturated Fat 1.5 g.
- Cholesterol 50 mg
- Total Carbohydrates 3.9 g.
- Sugar 1.2 g.
- Fiber 0.6 g.
- Sodium 121 mg.
- Potassium 331 mg.
- Protein 24.4 g.

595. Salmon and Shrimp Stew

Preparation time: 20'

Cooking time: 21'

Servings: 6

Ingredients

- 2 tbsps olive oil
- 1/2 c. onion, chopped finely
- 2 garlic cloves, minced
- 1 Serrano pepper, chopped
- 1 tsp. smoked paprika
- 4 c. fresh tomatoes, chopped
- 4 c. low-sodium chicken broth
- 1 lb. salmon fillets, cubed
- 1 lb. shrimp, peeled and deveined
- 2 tbsps fresh lime juice
- 1/4 c. fresh basil, chopped
- 1/4 c. fresh parsley, chopped
- Ground black pepper and sea salt, as required
- 2 scallions, chopped

Directions

1. In a large soup pan, melt oil over medium-high heat and sauté the onion for about 5-6 minutes.
2. Add the garlic, Serrano pepper, and smoked paprika and sauté for about 1 minute.
3. Add the tomatoes and broth and bring to a gentle simmer over medium heat.
4. Simmer for about 5 minutes.
5. Add the salmon and simmer for about 3-4 minutes.
6. Stir in the remaining seafood and cook for about 4-5 minutes.
7. Stir in the lemon juice, basil, parsley, sea salt, and black pepper and remove from heat.
8. Serve hot with the garnishing of scallion.

Nutrition

- Calories 271
- Total Fat 11 g.
- Saturated Fat 1.8 g.
- Cholesterol 193 mg
- Total Carbohydrates 8.6 g.
- Sugar 3.8 g.
- Fiber 2.1 g.
- Sodium 273 mg.
- Potassium 763 mg.
- Protein 34.7 g.

596. Salmon Curry

Preparation time: 15'
Cooking time: 30'
Servings: 6

Ingredients

- 6 (4-oz.) salmon fillets
- 1 tsp. ground turmeric, divided
- Salt, as required
- 3 tbsp. olive oil, divided
- 1 yellow onion, chopped finely
- 1 tsp. garlic paste
- 1 tsp. fresh ginger paste
- 3–4 green chilies, halved
- 1 tsp. red chili powder
- 1/2 tsp. ground cumin
- 1/2 tsp. ground cinnamon
- 3/4 c. fat-free plain Greek yogurt, whipped
- 3/4 c. filtered water
- 3 tbsp. fresh cilantro, chopped

Directions

1. Season each salmon fillet with 1/2 tsp of the turmeric and salt.
2. In a large skillet, melt 1 tbsp of the oil over medium heat and cook the salmon fillets for about 2 minutes per side.
3. Transfer the salmon onto a plate.
4. In the same skillet, melt the remaining butter over medium heat and sauté the onion for about 4–5 minutes.
5. Add the garlic paste, ginger paste, green chilies, the remaining turmeric, and spices and sauté for about 1 minute.
6. Now, reduce the heat to medium-low.
7. Slowly, add the yogurt and water, stirring continuously until smooth.
8. Cover the skillet and simmer for about 10–15 minutes or until desired doneness of the sauce.
9. Carefully, add the salmon fillets and simmer for about 5 minutes.
10. Serve hot with the garnishing of cilantro.

Nutrition

- Calories 242
- Total Fat 14.3 g.
- Saturated Fat 2 g.
- Cholesterol 51 mg.
- Total Carbohydrates 4.1 g.
- Sugar 2 g.
- Fiber 0.8 g.
- Sodium 98 mg.
- Potassium 493 mg.
- Protein 25.4 g.

597. Salmon with Bell Peppers

Preparation time: 15'
Cooking time: 20'
Servings: 6

Ingredients

- 6 (3-oz.) salmon fillets
- Pinch of salt
- Ground black pepper, as required
- 1 yellow bell pepper, seeded and cubed
- 1 red bell pepper, seeded and cubed
- 4 plum tomatoes, cubed
- 1 small onion, sliced thinly
- 1/2 c. fresh parsley, chopped
- 1/4 c. olive oil
- 2 tbsps fresh lemon juice

Directions

1. Preheat the oven to 400 °F.
2. Season each salmon fillet with salt and black pepper lightly.
3. In a bowl, mix together the bell peppers, tomato, and onion.
4. Arrange 6 foil pieces onto a smooth surface.
5. Place 1 salmon fillet over each foil paper and sprinkle with salt and black pepper.
6. Place the veggie mixture over each fillet evenly and top with parsley and capers evenly.
7. Drizzle with oil and lemon juice.
8. Fold each foil around the salmon mixture to seal it.
9. Arrange the foil packets onto a large baking sheet in a single layer.
10. Bake for about 20 minutes.
11. Serve hot.

Nutrition

- Calories 220
- Total Fat 14 g.
- Saturated Fat 2 g.
- Cholesterol 38 mg.
- Total Carbohydrates 7.7 g.
- Sugar 4.8 g.
- Fiber 2 g.
- Sodium 74 mg.
- Potassium 647 mg.
- Protein 17.9 g.

598. Shrimp Salad

PREPARATION TIME: 20'
COOKING TIME: 0'
SERVINGS: 4

Ingredients

For the Salad
- 1 lb. shrimp, peeled and deveined
- Salt and ground black pepper, as required
- 1 tsp. olive oil
- 1 1/2 c. carrots, peeled and julienned
- 1 1/2 c. red cabbage, shredded
- 1 1/2 c. cucumber, julienned
- 5 c. fresh baby arugula
- 1/4 c. fresh basil, chopped
- 1/4 c. fresh cilantro, chopped
- 4 c. lettuce, torn
- 1/4 c. almonds, chopped

For the Dressing
- 2 tbsps natural almond butter
- 1 garlic clove, crushed
- 1 tbsp. fresh cilantro, chopped
- 1 tbsp. fresh lime juice
- 1 tbsp. unsweetened applesauce
- 2 tsps. balsamic vinegar
- 1/2 tsp. cayenne pepper
- Salt, as required
- 1 tbsp. water
- 1/3 c. olive oil

Directions

1. To make the salad: In a bowl, add shrimp, salt, black pepper, and oil and toss to coat well.
2. Heat a skillet over medium-high heat and cook the shrimp for about 2 minutes per side.
3. Remove from the heat and set aside to cool.
4. In a large bowl, add the shrimp, vegetables, and mix well.
5. To make the dressing: In a bowl, add all the ingredients except oil and beat until well combined.
6. Slowly, add the oil, beating continuously until smooth.
7. Place the dressing over the shrimp mixture and toss to coat well.
8. Serve immediately.

Nutrition

- Calories 274
- Total Fat 17.7 g.
- Saturated Fat 2.4 g.
- Cholesterol 159 mg.
- Total Carbohydrates 10 g.
- Sugar 3.8 g.
- Fiber 2.9 g.
- Sodium 242 mg.
- Potassium 481 mg.
- Protein 20.5 g.

599. Shrimp and Veggies Curry

PREPARATION TIME: 20'
COOKING TIME: 20'
SERVINGS: 6

Ingredients

- 2 tsps. olive oil
- 1 1/2 medium white onions, sliced
- 2 medium green bell peppers, seeded and sliced
- 3 medium carrots, peeled and sliced thinly
- 3 garlic cloves, chopped finely
- 1 tbsp. fresh ginger, chopped finely
- 2 1/2 tsps. curry powder
- 1 1/2 lbs. shrimp, peeled and deveined
- 1 c. filtered water
- 2 tbsps fresh lime juice
- Salt and ground black pepper, as required
- 2 tbsps fresh cilantro, chopped

Directions

1. In a large skillet, heat oil over medium-high heat and sauté the onion for about 4-5 minutes.
2. Add the bell peppers and carrots and sauté for about 3-4 minutes.
3. Add the garlic, ginger, and curry powder, salt, and pepper and sauté for about 1 minute.
4. Add the shrimp and sauté for about 1 minute.
5. Stir in the water and cook for about 4-6 minutes, stirring occasionally.
6. Stir in lime juice and remove from the heat.
7. Serve hot with the garnishing of cilantro.

Nutrition

- Calories 193
- Total Fat 3.8 g.
- Saturated Fat 0.9 g.
- Cholesterol 239 mg.
- Total Carbohydrates 12 g.
- Sugar 4.7 g.
- Fiber 2.3 g.
- Sodium 328 mg.
- Potassium 437 mg.
- Protein 27.1 g.

600. Shrimp with Zucchini

Preparation Time: 20'
Cooking Time: 0'
Servings: 4

Ingredients

- 3 tbsps olive oil
- 1-pound medium shrimp, peeled and deveined
- 1 shallot, minced
- 4 garlic cloves, minced
- 1/4 tsp. red pepper flakes, crushed
- Salt and ground black pepper, as required
- 1/4 c. low-sodium chicken broth
- 2 tbsps fresh lemon juice
- 1 tsp. fresh lemon zest, grated finely
- 1/2-pound zucchini, spiralized with Blade C

Directions

1. In a large skillet, heat the oil over medium-high heat and cook the shrimp, shallot, garlic, red pepper flakes, salt, and black pepper for about 2 minutes, stirring occasionally.
2. Stir in the broth, lemon juice, and lemon zest and bring to a gentle boil.
3. Stir in the zucchini noodles and cook for about 1-2 minutes.
4. Serve hot.

Nutrition

- Calories 245
- Total Fat 12.6 g.
- Saturated Fat 2.2 g.
- Cholesterol 239 mg.
- Total Carbohydrates 5.8 g.
- Sugar 1.2 g.
- Fiber 08 g.
- Sodium 289 mg.
- Potassium 381 mg.
- Protein 27 g.

601. Shrimp with Broccoli

Preparation Time: 15'
Cooking Time: 12'
Servings: 6

Ingredients

- 2 tbsps olive oil, divided
- 4 c. broccoli, chopped
- 2-3 tbsps filtered water
- 1 1/2 lbs. large shrimp, peeled and deveined
- 2 garlic cloves, minced
- 1 (1-in.) piece fresh ginger, minced
- Salt and ground black pepper, as required

Directions

1. In a large skillet, heat 1 tbsp of oil over medium-high heat and cook the broccoli for about 1-2 minutes stirring continuously.
2. Stir in the water and cook, covered for about 3-4 minutes, stirring occasionally.
3. With a spoon, push the broccoli to the side of the pan.
4. Add the remaining oil and let it heat.
5. Add the shrimp and cook for about 1-2 minutes, tossing occasionally.
6. Add the remaining ingredients and sauté for about 2-3 minutes.
7. Serve hot.

Nutrition

- Calories 197
- Total Fat 6.8 g.
- Saturated Fat 1.3 g.
- Cholesterol 239 mg.
- Total Carbohydrates 6.1 g.
- Sugar 1.1 g.
- Fiber 1.6 g.
- Sodium 324 mg.
- Potassium 389 mg.
- Protein 27.6 g.

Conclusion

Diabetes is a serious condition caused by a deficiency of insulin. Insulin is a hormone that is necessary for the proper functioning of the body. When a person develops diabetes, the cells in the body do not respond to insulin properly. The result is that the cells do not get the energy and nutrients they need, and then they start to die.

Being diagnosed with diabetes will bring some major changes in your lifestyle. From the time you are diagnosed with it, it would always be a constant battle with the food. You need to become a lot more careful with your food choices and the quantity that you ate. Every meal will feel like a major effort. You will be planning every day for the whole week, well in advance. Depending upon the type of food you ate, you have to keep checking your blood sugar levels. You may get used to taking long breaks between meals and staying away from snacks between dinner and breakfast.

Food would be treated as a bomb like it can go off at any time. According to an old saying, "When the body gets too hot, then your body heads straight to the kitchen."

Managing diabetes can be a very, very stressful ordeal. There will be many times that you will mark your glucose levels down on a piece of paper like you are plotting graph lines or something. You will mix your insulin shots up and then stress about whether or not you are giving yourself the right dosage. You will always be over-cautious because it involves a lot of math and a really fine margin of error. But now, those days are gone!

With the help of technology and books, you can stock your kitchen with the right foods, like meal plans, diabetic friendly dishes, etc. You can also get an app that will even do the work for you. You can also people-watch on the internet and find the know-how to cook and eat right; you will always be a few meals away from certain disasters, like a plummeting blood sugar level. Always carry some sugar in your pocket. You won't have to experience the pangs of hunger but if you are unlucky, you will have to ration your food and bring along some simple low-calorie snacks with you.

This is the future of diabetes.

As you've reached the end of this book, you have gained complete control of your diabetes and this is just the beginning of your journey towards a better, healthier life. I hope I was able to inculcate some knowledge into you and make this adventure a little bit less of a struggle.

I would like to remind you that you're not alone in having to manage this disease and that nearly 85 % of the new cases are 20 years old or younger.

Regardless of the length or seriousness of your diabetes, it can be managed! Take the information presented here and start with it!

Preparation is key to having a healthier and happier life.

It's helpful to remember that every tool at your disposal can help in some way.

Printed in Great Britain
by Amazon